vice

Your One Wild and Precious Life

Your One Wild and Precious Life

An Inspiring Guide to Becoming

Your Best Self at Any Age

DR MAUREEN GAFFNEY

PENGUIN LIFE

AN IMPRINT OF

PENGUIN BOOKS

PENGUIN LIFE

UK | USA | Canada | Ireland | Australia
India | New Zealand | South Africa

Penguin Life is part of the Penguin Random House group of companies whose
addresses can be found at global.penguinrandomhouse.com.

First published 2021
001

Set in 12/14.75pt Bembo Book MT Pro
Typeset by Jouve (UK), Milton Keynes
Printed and bound in Great Britain by Clays Ltd, Elcograf S.p.A.

The authorized representative in the EEA is Penguin Random House Ireland,
Morrison Chambers, 32 Nassau Street, Dublin D02 YH68

A CIP catalogue record for this book is available from the British Library

ISBN: 978-0-241-43772-8

www.greenpenguin.co.uk

To my husband John Harris and children
Elly and Jack Harris

We shall not cease from exploration
And the end of all our exploring
Will be to arrive where we started
And know the place for the first time.

T. S. Eliot, *Four Quartets*

Contents

Introduction: Living your one wild and precious life

How often do you think about your life and yourself? If you're like most people, you do it a *lot*. In fact, there is a special part of your brain devoted to doing just that.[1] Most of the time, however, your brain is busy making plans, getting things done, thinking about what's just happened and, most of all, imagining yourself in the future – so much so that psychologist Daniel Gilbert of Harvard University describes us as part-time residents of the future.[2] But whenever the external demands of your life let up, and your brain goes into a resting state, it primes you to start thinking about yourself and how you are living your life.

You think about what kind of person you are, and how you are the same as or different from other people. You reflect on what motivates you, what makes you happy or miserable, and if you are living the way you want to live. You think about how you have changed, or will change, as you go through the different stages of your life – and what has stayed the same. This kind of self-reflection is usually brief, squeezed into whatever undisturbed time you can carve out for yourself, or maybe when you are on holiday.

But at certain times, and in certain circumstances, your interest in understanding your own psychology quickens and becomes more urgent. When your life has taken an unexpected turn. When you face an unexpected challenge or are trying to recover from a setback, like the break-up of an important relationship. When you reach a 'Big O' birthday. When you reach midlife and naturally perform a stocktake of your life to date with a view to choosing how you want to live your life's second half. And most especially when you enter, or imagine entering, a new stage of your life.

These times are potential crucial turning points, opening up a new opportunity to review, reassess and renew who you are and how you are living your life. They can motivate you to rethink your life, to make a new plan, or to change a situation that is holding you back from your full potential for happiness. And when you do that well, it will imbue your life with a new purpose and meaning.

This book will trace the arc of your psychological development as you proceed through the different life stages and describe the three basic and interconnected psychological drives that account for most of what you do in life – the drive for closeness, the drive for autonomy and the drive for competence. It will describe how, from the moment of birth, you are wired to seek close personal relationships; how your desire for autonomy finds expression in your attempts to be your true self, and to control the direction and organization of your life; and how your drive for competence is played out in your efforts to manage your life effectively, and on your own terms.

Over the past fifty years, there has been a revolution in our understanding of human motivation, and how autonomy, closeness and competence play out in every stage of human development and determine our happiness and success in life. We now have a deeper understanding of how these three innate needs are intricately linked, and a clearer view of the central role autonomy plays in all this. The nature and importance of psychological autonomy is rarely discussed, because autonomy is often misrepresented as cool self-sufficiency. In fact, autonomy is the innate, driving human need to govern yourself, to be an active agent of your life, and to shape your destiny as best you can.

Do you ever long to break free in some area of your life? Buck at someone trying to manipulate and control what you think and do? Feel too fearful to match what you say and do with what is actually going on inside you? Do you ever feel that you have paid too high a price for love, acceptance, security or even peace in a relationship? When you feel like that, that's autonomy calling.

How often do you experience the surge of high energy, lift, forward movement that comes from knowing that you have taken your life in your hands? Or have that solid sense of being securely anchored in yourself when you face down fear and do what you know is hard but right? That's autonomy in action. And who among us doesn't want to experience that kind of autonomy more often in our personal, work or public life – especially if we know that we struggle more in one particular area of our life than others.

But if you don't identify those experiences as coming from losing or exercising autonomy, then you can't grasp their inner dynamics, and may not look in the right place for solutions. You won't be able to clearly identify what is carrying you forward in your life and development, or what is holding you back and blocking your momentum. In a completely new way, therefore, autonomy has become a premium competency.

At its most basic, the experience of autonomy is volition – knowing that what you are doing is initiated *inside* you, not forced on you by external circumstances. Your actions are *endorsed* by your whole self – heartfelt, fully owned by you, and you take responsibility for them. They come from the core of self, and you possess the inner freedom that allows you to act in a way that fits with that sense of self. There is a unity between how you think and feel inside, and what you say and do outside. That's what being authentic, being 'true to yourself' actually means – what we used to call 'character'. The opposite is the silencing of self that brings with it that deadening sense of hollowness and depression.

The opposite of autonomy is not dependence. It is feeling controlled. Feeling controlled runs counter to something deep in human nature. When you feel controlled by forces outside or within yourself, you are dissatisfied and unhappy, uneasy, anxious or resentful. Your functioning, your performance and your creativity in every domain of your life are undermined. If that sense of being controlled is chronic, you can become despairing of yourself and of your life.

You can, of course, feel just as pressured and controlled by forces *inside* you – by anxiety, guilt, perfectionism, harsh self-criticism, a desperate need for approval, or by compulsions or addictions of any kind. These inner pressures create an internal tyranny. Or they can be externalized into tyrannizing those around you. You try to control their behaviour as a way of managing your own pressurized inner state. The issue is not whether the rewards and pressures are external or internal – it's how controlled you feel by them. When you feel like that, negative things happen.

Your three needs – for closeness, competence, autonomy – are always present, but ebb and flow in intensity and urgency at different times and stages of your life. There is a natural tension between closeness and autonomy, between being deeply engaged with other people and being alone and free to focus on yourself. The attempts to resolve these conflicts, to bring them into some kind of balance, account for much of the activity and drama of development right through life and for the unique colour and flavour of each life stage.

In this book, I will describe how these three drives find expression in a series of ten developmental tasks, each task presenting itself as you come to the end of one stage of life and get ready to enter the next; and how through resolving each task your sense of self and personal identity develops. If you tackle these developmental tasks successfully, you feel happier and more satisfied with the way your life is going. You feel that your life is in progress, that it is not suspended or stagnating. You see yourself as doing, in some general way, what you were put into this world to do.

The aim is to provide you with a psychological framework within which your own development as a person can be more deeply understood, a grid on which you can locate key events in your life that have an emotional resonance and linger in your memory. It will help you trace how you became the person you are as you negotiated each stage and turning point of your life and met its challenge.

In my last book, *Flourishing*, I set out the ten evidence-based strategies that increase happiness and well-being. It was, if you like, a way of examining your life in cross section – looking at how the brain works, how you think, how emotions play out, what gives meaning to your life – and how all these factors shape or undermine your happiness. This book is different. It is a *developmental* account of what shapes you as an individual, and how at each stage of life you set down patterns that will shape your capacity for happiness and success at the next stage.

This kind of developmental account takes full measure of your past, which is a rich resource – a way to understand and change the patterns of your unfolding life, and to predict how you are likely to react to the challenges and possibilities of the life stages ahead. You can't control all that life throws at you, but you can meet it on your own terms. Far from being a passive victim of your past, *you* are always the author, interpreting and reworking your lived experiences into an evolving narrative. So, at any point, you can also revise your interpretations, reassess the past, reframe the present, reimagine the future, and reset your development on a new course. There is always a new chance to heal old wounds and to deal with unfinished business – and to do it better this time.

Entering each new stage of life is a predictable life crisis, shared with your own generation, the cohort of people who were born around the same time as you, and who move through the life course with you. But some crises and turning points are silent and private. Cumulatively, this means that your life is always a mix of stability and change, a function of the experiences that have shaped you and the new circumstances in which you find yourself. But at every stage, and most acutely at points of transition, the opportunity opens up again to find a new balance, a better resolution of an old developmental task.

The key point is this. At any stage, you are never fully formed. The story is never over. The story is *always* of a life in progress.

PART ONE

This Is Your Life

1. Navigating the new life course

You have one wild and precious life – just one. One opportunity to live that life in your own way. One chance to live through each stage of your life, and with no chance to rehearse, so you want to make that life count. Understanding yourself is a critical starting point – how you came to be the person you are, and the basic psychological needs that drive your development over the course of your lifetime.

When we think about the course of a lifetime, most of us divide it up into different stages that start and end at particular times, each stage having its own agenda. Getting through these stages was once a relatively straightforward journey. You were expected to achieve the big milestones in your life at a particular stage and in a particular sequence – finish your education, find a job, marry, settle down, rear a family, retire. But the contours of the life course have changed radically in the last hundred years. You no long travel along a well-signposted road towards the expected three-score-and-ten. In the twenty-first century, you live your life on a high-speed motorway, with multiple lanes, intersections and exits, and with the destination a lot further away – and you have no updated psychological route map to help navigate your course.

Consider just two paradoxical changes.

More years were added to the average life expectancy in the twentieth century than in *all* previous millennia combined. In the blink of an eye, says Laura Carstensen of the Stanford Center on Longevity, the length of time that we are living has doubled.[1] You are now living in the era of the hundred-year life.[2] Most babies born since the year 2000 in developed countries can expect to live to be a hundred or older. If you've already made it to adulthood, and are in reasonably good shape, there's a good chance of living into your nineties. And whether you do or not, you must live and plan as if you will.

Yet, for all the extra time you have to live, you have become time-poor. 'How are things?' you ask someone, and the answer is likely to be, 'Busy, busy, busy.' The period extending roughly from your late twenties to sometime in your early sixties has now become the 'rush hour of life'[3] – when you establish yourself in work, find a soulmate, settle down and raise a young family. No sooner have you done all that than you find yourself facing the onset of middle age – and all the questions, challenges and opportunities that life stage brings with it.

Now put these two realities together. The amount of time you have to live has doubled, yet a full third of your adulthood is now a 'rush hour'. That's just one of the many changes and challenges you face in the new life course.

The new life stages and their time frames

This stretching of the life course has created two new life stages and changed the timing of the rest.

The new life course	
Life stage	*Time frame*
Infancy	birth–two years of age
Early childhood	two–six
Middle childhood	seven–eleven
Adolescence	puberty–late teens
Emerging adulthood	late teens–early 30s
Young adulthood	early 30s–late 40s
Middle age	50–late 60s
Late adulthood	late 60s–late 70s
Old age	80 and onwards

Reaching adulthood takes so long that you have to negotiate a new in-between life stage, emerging adulthood, which extends from the end of adolescence to the late twenties, or even early thirties. This new stage exerts an upward pressure on the timing of all the rest, which now start and finish later. Young adulthood does not properly begin until your early thirties and extends well into your late forties, which in turn means that middle age does not begin until around the age of fifty and then lasts into your late sixties.

And then? Well, there's a long way to go until old age, so there's another new in-between stage. In the USA, nearly half of those aged sixty-five to sixty-nine and one-third of those in their early seventies consider themselves to be middle-aged – for want of a better term.[4] I have called it late adulthood – the stage of your life when you know that you have definitely passed the midway mark but you certainly don't feel 'old', and being called a pensioner is very much out of step with your lived experience because your desires, motivations and the way you want to live your life are subtly different from what they were in middle age, or what they will be in old age.

Old age does not begin now until near eighty, or at the onset of physical frailty or prolonged ill health. But while the onset of old age is later, it also lasts longer, and how independently you can live at that stage has become an urgent and pressing issue.

The factors that influence you at each stage

This new life course is quite different from what came before, presenting you with a different set of choices, decisions and challenges, so it requires a deeper understanding of yourself, and also of the internal and external factors that influence how you develop at each stage.

FOR A START, YOU ARE DIFFERENT

Compared to your parents and grandparents, you are healthier, more educated, with better cognitive functioning, and you outperform them on a range of intelligence measures. You are better travelled, more connected to the wider world, both real and virtual. You see fewer constraints in how you live your life and pursue your goals, and you have more freedom to mobilize the resources you need to do all that.[5] So as you negotiate the big transitions in the life course, you are not marching in the same lockstep as they did.

YOU HAVE MORE PERSONAL FREEDOM AND CHOICE

This applies at each stage, so your life has become more fluid and individualized. The commitments you make at one stage are more reversible. You can change jobs more often. You can leave and re-enter education multiple times. You can more easily divorce and remarry. If you are a woman, you have more control over your fertility and you no longer labour under the constraints that prevented your grandmother continuing her career after she married.

Decisions about how to share the role of provider and caretaker are made by you and your partner, although there are still strong expectations that women should be the main caretakers. Lone parenthood, while rarely easy, is more common and enjoys more social support. In some western countries, if you are gay or lesbian you can marry, have children, and live openly as a family, and those who identify as transgender, non-binary or gender-fluid are asserting their right to be recognized and treated equally.

But having more choices is not cost-free. You are also held more personally responsible for the choices you make. The success is all yours if your choices work out – as is the failure, if they don't. You have to defend the choices you make, not least to yourself; for example, whether to stay at home to care for your children or go back to work. You can no longer hide behind the shield of tradition or social obligation.

In a consumer-saturated society, having so many choices risks creating a fetish of choice about everything. Having multiple options for every trivial decision creates cognitive overload, depletes your mental and physical energy, and uses up the intellectual resources you need to do anything that requires attention, concentration, focus and problem-solving – and that's pretty much everything important in your life.[6]

THE BAR FOR WHAT CONSTITUTES SUCCESS
IS BEING RAISED NOTCH BY NOTCH

This is true in every domain of your life; 'getting it right' is the new pressure. Once, just 'being' in a particular role – a wife, husband, a parent, a teacher, a leader – was enough to secure your self-esteem and garner the respect of others. Now it's how you personally perform the role that matters. So you are under more pressure to do things 'right', and there are more consequences if you don't. The pressure comes from outside, but also from inside yourself. Your sense of personal worth is more closely tied to how well you do things.

You expect more from your personal relationships – more intimacy, more equality, more support to keep growing and developing – and are correspondingly more dissatisfied when those expectations are dashed. It takes a lot more time and personal investment to rear happy, resilient and successful children, and it goes on for a lot longer than you thought it would. At a day-to-day level, all of these pressures are increasing the number of goals and micro-goals in your day-to-day agenda.

YOUR ATTENTION IS UNDER SIEGE IN A NEW WAY

You are living your life in a digitally saturated world. We are just waking up to the alarming discovery that our attention is being hijacked by heavy use of smart phones and social media, designed to make it easier to respond addictively to the content they provide. Many of your 'choices' are controlled by powerful algorithms that know more about your preferences and habits than you may do yourself – a very modern threat to autonomy and control, because it doesn't work by coercion but by seduction. The lure of technology is convenience, the new uber-value.[7] Finding easier, faster ways to do anything is meant to free you, but often ends up making your decisions for you and overriding what you say you really value, such as face-to-face interaction or time to think.

In this open, digitally networked world, privacy, closeness and belonging are being radically redefined. Once, we defined ourselves in smaller, more bounded communities. Now, your 'community' is exponentially expanded by access to the internet and social media – but that very freedom can create an individual and collective sense of insecurity.

AGE IS NO LONGER THE MARKER IT ONCE WAS

Outside of childhood and advanced old age, chronological age now predicts the *least* about someone and how they live their life. It's more a proxy or shorthand for changes you observe in yourself and your lifestyle.[8] For example, if you are now in your fifties, you may have recently taken on a demanding new work role or have just taken early retirement. You may be securely anchored in a long-term marriage. You may be divorced, or embarking on a second relationship.

You may still be rearing teenagers, or already have grandchildren, or have just become a dad again, courtesy of a new, younger partner. You may have recovered from your first real health scare, be training to run a marathon, or both. Whatever your age or circumstances, you now have more power to set the agenda of your life than ever before in history.

YOU HAVE MORE CONTROL OVER THE
TIMETABLE OF YOUR ADULT LIFE

When you think about your life, says biologist John Medina, you automatically assume the presence of an internal clock. At birth, it's set at zero, and then it ticks away incessantly for the rest of your life.[9] You 'clock' yourself against an expected social timetable, when major events like getting married, settling into a career and having children are 'meant' to happen, and when they happen 'too early' or 'too late' it has an impact on your happiness and well-being.[10] That timetable used to be largely set by your chronological age, and reinforced by strong social expectations. Indeed, your social class still has a bearing on these timings.

Social class is now largely defined by how long you spend in education. If you leave before completing secondary school, you are more likely to get married, have children and retire earlier than your middle-class counterparts. More significantly, you think of yourself as older. How old you think you are is not a trivial thing – it has significantly negative implications for your health and well-being, increasing your risk of heart disease and other illnesses. But whatever your class, you now have more power to set the timetable yourself, and being 'too late' for anything is now very generously defined.

Being as young – or as old – as you feel

How you think about time is important. Time and the passage of time shape us in important ways – how we think, how we feel, and what we put most value on.[11] Monitoring time is a basic part of being human. From the moment you are born, your biological clock starts ticking, setting an unconscious rhythm. Day to day it affects your circadian rhythm and over a lifetime it sets the rough timetable for your aging and your development. So time, development and aging are intimately linked, and as we progress through each life stage, our relationship with time changes.

How you think about time matters – a lot. At one level, when you think about time and your own life, you see time as flowing in a constant, linear motion, the implication being that once it has passed, you can't get that time back. This can lend itself to a kind of age determinism – feeling that your chronological age not just influences but determines your capacities and the possibilities in life. If you think and feel like that, it has a host of negative outcomes – poorer physical and psychological well-being and, not least, reduced longevity.[12]

Age determinism is not some abstract philosophical stance. It reveals itself in a day-to-day belief that chronological age determines your physical, psychological and cognitive capacities and so dictates what you can and cannot do. Older adults are at the sharp end of such stereotyping, not least the idea that aging is associated with inevitable physical and psychological decline. This kind of persistent stereotyping threatens the value you put on yourself. It undermines your motivation to be proactive about your health and your determination to stay open to life, to new opportunities, and to possibility. Serendipity does not stop when you reach sixty.

The opposite of age determinism is believing that age is just a number. There is usually a gap between chronological and subjective age – how young or old someone feels. By the end of their thirties, over 70 per cent of adults say that they feel significantly younger than their chronological age. This more dynamic view of age is not just some harmless vanity – it really matters. It is associated with higher self-esteem, less stress, more optimism, better physical health and cognitive functioning, higher levels of psychological well-being and increased longevity.[13]

When you feel younger than your chronological age, you are more hopeful and positive about your life and therefore more likely to manage it in a more proactive way. You look after your health, rather than going into avoidance mode; when you encounter a health set-back, you increase your efforts to get back on form as quickly as possible; and you are motivated to preserve your autonomy and strive to live as independently as possible for as long as you can. This has a knock-on positive effect. Take just one study of people aged fifty and older: compared to those who held a negative view of aging, those with a more positive view of aging lived 7.5 years longer.[14]

In addition, feeling younger than your age is strongly linked to being more open-minded, more curious, more interested in new ideas and experiences, ready to approach new and unknown situations, and able to adapt flexibly to changing circumstances.[15] You are also aware that not all time is equal – that there are 'anchor periods' in your life that hold outstanding meaning because they were the happiest or most difficult times of your life, and you use these as reference points to which all other periods of your life are compared.[16] And contained within these anchor periods are bespoke lessons to be learned and applied to how you live your life now.

This view of time opens up the possibility of reworking our relationship with time and the opportunity to throw off the tyranny of believing that chronological age defines us, and instead to realize that at every stage of life, the trick is to feel young in the right way – full of curiosity, open to life and eager to learn. And to feel old in the right way – wise in your way, as someone who has a unique story to tell. Adopting that more dynamic mindset about time will not just make you feel happier and more fulfilled – it will imbue your life with an enlivening purpose. That mindset opens you to possibility, to a robust optimism about your life and a determination to make the very most of the time left to you.

As a result of these changes, the traditional paradigm of human development has changed. The old understanding was that life was neatly divided into three stages. In childhood and adolescence you developed. In adulthood you matured. In old age you declined. But a mounting body of research about human development throughout life has fundamentally changed that understanding, and the new paradigm is simple and dramatic. Aging and development are not opposites, they are synonymous – you are aging *and* developing, from the moment you are born to the moment you die.[17] How liberating an idea is that?

So whatever your stage in life, you are a generation in transition. This is making big calls on your psychological resources: on your capacity to keep changing and adapting; to form and maintain high-quality relationships; to take responsibility for your own life and drive it forward; and to do all that at a high level of competence. All of this requires a much better understanding of yourself, and of the fundamental desires and needs that must be met so that you can keep growing and developing at every stage of life.

Identity: your life story

At each stage of life, your sense of self and personal identity finds expression in the story you tell about yourself and the story significant others tell about you. That continual and evolving self-narrative is a fundamental way to understand yourself; to bring together the different parts of yourself; and to organize your important experiences, past, present and expected, into a coherent story. Therefore, self-narrative and identity are tightly meshed.[18]

Your personal coherent story is your way of maintaining a sense of personal continuity as you change and as your life changes: *this is who I am; this is what made me the person I am; this is what I expect from life; this is what gives meaning to my life now.*

You ground that story not just in your biographical details but in experiences and turning points that were particularly important to you. In childhood, your identity is centred around specific events and experiences that are usually shared and co-remembered with a parent – that is why, as an adult, it is sometimes hard to separate out what you actually experienced from what you were told you experienced. In adolescence, and again at midlife, your identity deepens and widens, your story extending over a larger segment of time.

You engage with your story in a deeper way as you try to respond to a new imperative – you want to make your life amount to something, to identify its purpose and its larger meaning.[19] You begin to see recurring themes in your life, extending further back in time and into the future. You begin to see more clearly your place in your family and social group, and even in historical time – a process that emerges during young adulthood and becomes particularly pronounced at midlife. As you become conscious of time left, you interrogate your past to better understand where you are now, in order to cast some light on what is possible for the future.

The attempt to understand and engage with your own story opens a window into the complexity of yourself and your evolving life. It makes you knowable to yourself in a more compassionate way. But most of all, it reminds you that you are the author of that story, continually interpreting and reinterpreting what is happening inside and outside yourself – and that you can also reset your story and direct your development on to a new course.

As you do that, you free yourself from the common illusion that our lives proceed in an orderly, sequential way. Instead, you begin to see that your life, like every life, is not linear. Instead, it is characterized by advances and setbacks, lapses and gains, and that they are all part of the developmental process that made, and is still making, you the person that you are.

The life course may be changing but our fundamental drives remain constant

You don't come into this world psychologically naked. You come ready equipped with three fundamental psychological drives:

- the need for close connection with other people
- the need for autonomy, and
- the need for competence.

A sense of autonomy, the right kind of closeness, and feeling effective in your life – these three drivers are the big engines of personal development at every life stage and the non-negotiable requirements for a happy, fulfilled and successful life.[20]

- *Closeness*: The drive for closeness takes three forms. The first and most intense expression is your need to form an attachment to at least one person who will protect and support you, especially when you are vulnerable. The second is the drive to form close relationships that bind you to friends and allies, providing a sense of belonging. The third is the drive to care for offspring, for those you love, or for someone who is vulnerable or in need of help.

- *Autonomy*: The drive to be an active agent in your life, to govern yourself, and to shape the direction and organization of your life. You want to explore the world around you, and inside you, so you can keep growing and developing into the fullness of who you are. There are many givens in life that you can't control: such as your innate temperament; the family and life circumstances in which you were reared; and random events (the lucky breaks and unpredictable setbacks). Yet, the nature of being human is to be an actor, and to exercise what control you can over your life. That sense of autonomy is what gives you the inner authority to claim your own choices and to own your own experiences. This is how you stake out the core of your individuality.

- *Competence*: The drive to master things, to be good at what you do, to manage the different domains of your life, and to rise to whatever challenges life throws at you.

How these fundamental needs are met is woven into your identity – the ongoing narrative that you construct about yourself, and which in turn shapes what you expect of life and how you choose to live it.[21]

The nature of autonomy

It's easy to grasp why closeness is a fundamental human need, and the world leaves you in little doubt about the demand for competence, but autonomy is somewhat of an orphan need. The word tends to provoke a small frown, as if it carries a whiff of selfishness about it. It is an essential component of character and growth, and yet it is often

misunderstood. It is important to understand what autonomy is –
and is not. Here are three myths about autonomy.[22]

MYTH 1: AUTONOMY IS AN EXTREME FORM
OF SELF-SUFFICIENCY

Being independent-minded, able to stand on your own two feet and
be responsible for your own decisions are all part of being autonomous. But none of that implies that you hold yourself apart and
separate. It does not mean that you refuse to depend on others for
support or allow others to depend on you. In fact, truly autonomous
people find it *easier* to depend on others, and experience much less
psychological conflict about it.

MYTH 2: AUTONOMY IS THE ENEMY OF CLOSENESS

No, it is not. When you are autonomous, the relationships you form
with your parents, friends, partner and work colleagues are happier
and of a higher quality. You take care of others willingly, not because
you have to, and the care you give is more effective. It has a more
positive impact on the person you are caring for, and on you.

MYTH 3: AUTONOMY IS AN EXPRESSION OF A WESTERN
BRAND OF HYPER-INDIVIDUALISM AND DOESN'T HOLD THE
SAME SWAY IN OTHER CULTURES

In fact, in countries with more collectivist cultures and attitudes, which
stress duty and dependence on each other, there's an even stronger link
between autonomy and well-being. The more autonomous people are,
the happier, more satisfied and personally fulfilled they feel.

The function of closeness, autonomy and competence[23]

Your innate need for closeness, autonomy and competence are the psychological equivalent of your biological needs for food, water, sleep
and sex. They are essential, and you cannot thrive without them. But
they work differently from your biological needs.

In the case of your biological needs, the set point is satisfaction.
When you are no longer hungry, thirsty or sexually aroused, you feel

satiated. But in the case of your psychological drives, the set point is not just satisfaction, it is growth and development. After each satisfactory experience of closeness, of autonomy, or of acting competently, you feel that you are more fully yourself. This motivates you to seek out more: you want a deeper engagement in a relationship; you want to set the direction of your life in a more active and confident way; you want to expand and develop your talents and abilities. That is why meeting all three needs is the main driver of development and happiness at every stage of your life.

The fundamental drives to meet your closeness, autonomy and competence needs are not just 'feelings'. They influence the neural circuits in your brain, activating the hormonal and operating systems that influence motivation, behaviour and stress response.[24] They are deeply rooted in your instinctive behavioural systems, and it is their instinctive nature that gives them their psychological power.*

---

* You are born with five instinctive brain-based behavioural systems, designed to help you survive and thrive in the world, and to interlock and intersect with each other. *The Attachment System*: the instinct to form a strong emotional tie first with one person, and later with others, to provide the protection, security, love and encouragement you need to grow and develop. *The Exploration System*: the instinct to venture out on your own, to explore, play, learn, create and master the world around you and inside you. The drive for autonomy helps you do that and, in combination with a *Secure* attachment, helps you do all that completely. *The Social System*: the instinct to form social bonds – banding together with others for companionship and help. You seek out friendships, one-to-one relationships with particular others, and a group that gives you a feeling of belonging. To maintain those bonds you have to become socially competent and develop a strong sense of personal identity that will help you find a unique and secure place in your friendships and in the group. *The Sexual System*: the instinct to find a mate who sexually and psychologically attracts you, and with whom you can potentially have children. But sexual attraction is not enough to keep a couple or parents together for the time it takes to rear a child to near adulthood. So after the initial attraction phase, you need to develop an attachment bond. *The Caretaking System*: the instinct to provide care, comfort and help to those who are dependent on you, or are temporarily in need. This is most strongly triggered by becoming a parent. From the moment of birth, babies have evolved desires, preferences and behaviours designed specifically to trigger this urge in parents, but also in others. Parents, for their part, have evolved a system of desires, preferences and reactions designed to synchronize with those of their babies. Just to be on the safe

In humans, the instinctive systems don't operate in the rigid patterns evident in other species. They are more flexible, designed to function in very different personal, cultural and social contexts. But it is this very flexibility that makes them prone to going wrong. For example, if your needs for closeness and autonomy are frustrated, you can still become competent, but it will be at a higher cost to yourself and to your relationships. Your competence will have a driven quality about it – more anxious, draining and oppressive – and what you achieve is never quite enough.

These three psychological needs are not separate items to be checked off; one is embedded in the other, and if one is chronically thwarted, it will exact a heavy toll on your happiness, well-being and success in life.[25]

From the very beginning of your life, your drive for autonomy is shaped and nurtured within your close relationships. It is achieved not at the expense of closeness, but with the assurance and confidence that stem from closeness. The more secure your close relationships, the less compromised your capacity for autonomy. When both these needs are met, your drive for competence is strong, energizing and liberating.

To use a simple analogy – the comfort and support of your close relationships is the vehicle that carries you safely through each stage of your life. Autonomy is the fuel that propels it. And competency is the route map or navigation system that will get you efficiently to your desired destination.*

These three psychological needs are present at every stage of life,

_____

side, the caretaking system also triggers a general desire on the part of parents and non-parents alike to leave something worthwhile behind them, to make the world a better place for the next generation.

* The kind of *balance* between closeness and autonomy that is most satisfying to you is influenced by your inherited temperament. Some of you came into the world as 'yes babies', on the extraverted side of the continuum, drawing your energy from engaging with others, tolerant of being passed around to friends and relatives to be hugged and kissed, wide open to novelty, ready to give everything a go, and adapting easily to change. Some of you are 'no babies', on the introverted side, with a strong sense of your own boundaries, overstimulated by too much interaction, cautious about novelty, and choosy about what to expend effort on.

although expressed differently at different times. They are like internal tides, currents tugging you one way and then another. But they can get out of balance. If the closeness you experience is too overwhelming, you begin to drown. Striving too hard for autonomy will isolate you, and you drift too far from shore. Too great a need to show how competent you are, and you exhaust your strength. Too little effort, and you never learn to swim at all, just stay paddling in the shallows.

Your life, then, is a series of transitions that you must negotiate in order to grow and develop. Through every stage, you are driven by your needs for close relationships and love, for the ability to actively direct your own life course, and for the knowledge and skills that come with investing in and succeeding at the various roles in your life.

2. The drama of development

Each life stage has its own psychological agenda, what psychologist Erik Erikson described as 'developmental tasks', forming a series of 'crises' or specific challenges that must be addressed.[1] The developmental tasks encapsulate the way you need to meet your basic drives for closeness, autonomy and competence at that particular stage. How you try to resolve their inherent tensions accounts for much of the activity and drama of development.

The developmental tasks identified by Erikson in 1951 are still resonant, but they need to be expanded and updated in light of the changes in the life course and the significant advances in knowledge about human development since then. This is my updated version.

The ten developmental tasks of the new life course

Life stage	Time frame	Developmental task
Infancy	birth–two years of age	trust or mistrust?
Early childhood	two–six	autonomy or self-doubt?
Middle childhood	seven–eleven	belonging or isolation?
Adolescence	puberty–late teens	identity or confusion?
Emerging adulthood	late teens–early 30s	self-responsibility or dependence?
Young adulthood	early 30s–late 40s	intimacy or loneliness? initiative or passivity?
Middle age	50–late 60s	generating or stagnating?
Late adulthood	late 60s–late 70s	purpose or decline?
Old age	80 and onwards	integrity or despair?

Each developmental task is triggered by different cues: by changes in your physical, cognitive, emotional and social functioning; by your own changing desires; by social cues from family, friends, peers and the world in general about what you are expected to do at particular points in the life course, so that you keep maturing and find a satisfying and viable place in the society in which you live.

At both extremes of the life course – early childhood and advanced old age – physical changes are the important triggers, while at most other stages psychological and social factors are more salient. Whatever their source, the message from these triggers is unmistakable: this is what you need to do *now*, this is the developmental task that confronts you and that must be resolved.

Once a particular developmental task is activated, it affects what preoccupies you. It influences how you think, how you feel, how you behave and what you remember. For example, if you are asked to recall memories from each decade of your life, apart from very big or unexpected events, what stands out are memories that relate to the major developmental task of that stage. When you recall your twenties, memories of falling in love, or your early experiences of sex, or the break-up of a big romance tend to be most vivid, while becoming a parent or a high point in your work may predominate in your memories of your thirties or forties.[2]

Each life stage begins when a particular developmental task is triggered and ends when that task is resolved. The 'old' task loses its prime position in your thoughts and feelings and goes into the background as a new task emerges that will define the next stage of development. The old task is not less important, it's just not written in bold any more, it's greyed-out. This happens quite naturally. For example, the strong desire for autonomy is the prime task in your second and third year of life; it goes into the background during middle childhood, then resurfaces with renewed force in adolescence as you try to establish your own identity. It emerges again as a key concern at midlife, and again in old age.

For every developmental task, there is a polarity, a dynamic tension between the two opposite poles. For example, the desire for trust is rooted in the fear of being abandoned or rejected, the urge to make friends is rooted in the misery of isolation. The spectre of stagnation motivates you to make your life count for something.

The nature of life is that you keep moving between the two poles, and the task is to find some way to balance and integrate them. When that resolution is satisfactory, you move towards the positive pole, and that becomes your steady state, readying you to move on to the next stage with confidence. When the resolution is not satisfying, you drift towards the negative pole, compromising your capacity for the next task. That is why each developmental task is a 'crisis' or turning point. It sets you on a particular trajectory, with significant consequences for your happiness, well-being and success.

You are never fully formed

There is a large overlap between one stage and another – a new stage is already beginning as the old stage is coming to an end. Life stages are not like a stack of boxes arranged in a determined order, but more like phases. It is in this more fluid and non-linear sense that the idea of 'stage' is used in this book.* Neither is psychological development a linear process, but rather a series of transitions, turning points and transformations.

On the basis of his research into adult life, Daniel Levinson, a former professor in Harvard and Yale universities, found that adulthood unfolds in a sequence of relatively stable life periods lasting between seven and ten years.[3] During the stable period, you build a life structure that centres mainly around your close relationships with family and friends, your work and, for some, around a deep personal interest or commitment to something.† These are the elements of your life in which you invest most of your time and energy, which influence the

---

* Some researchers have abandoned the idea of life stages. This is largely in response to the failure to find fixed pre-determined patterns. But most people still think of their lives as unfolding in a sequence of stages or phases, and it is that more fluid definition of stages that is used here, a useful way to organize what we know about human development as it unfolds over the life course.

† A community of interest could include a professional or sporting association, a social movement, a political party, or a religious group that you are deeply committed to. For many people in Ireland, for example, the GAA becomes a way of life.

way you engage with the world for this period, and which define the character of your living.

At the beginning of each stage, you make choices. These choices allow you to give expression to certain parts of yourself, but they also require you to put aside other choices you could have made, and other sides of your personality, at least for now.

Each stage is book-ended by significant transition periods, lasting between three and five years, a large boundary zone in which you get ready to end one stage and enter another. That means you spend nearly *50 per cent* of your life in transition, changing, or thinking about changing some aspect of your life, assessing whether the life structure you have created is still viable. Is it still satisfying, or does it need to be changed in the light of new needs inside yourself, or new demands from outside?[4] As you will read in Chapter 18, the transition to middle age is particularly significant in this respect.

As you approach the end of one decade and the beginning of another, you think more deeply about where your life is going, about its meaning or purpose, or the lack of either. The link between how satisfied you are with your life and your physical and psychological well-being is stronger during these transitions than at other times.[5] That's why the beginning of each decade, turning any of the 'Big O' birthdays, has particular significance for many people.

These transition periods are key times for transformation and development, when you have the opportunity to loop back to repair earlier unfinished business. For example, you get three shots at getting autonomy right – in very early childhood, in adolescence, and again in midlife. If you are a parent, as you help your children to develop a basic trust, to become securely autonomous and competent, any wounds you have can be healed in the process. This is what early psychoanalysts refer to as the second edition of childhood. What over-arching principles can guide that process? This is something we will explore throughout the following chapters. Over the page, I set out the basic psychological principles for a life well lived. These principles are not limited to any one stage in life, nor are they separate injunctions. Rather, they are embedded one in the other. In later chapters we will carefully tease out how these principles of living emerge at each life stage, relate to each other and, crucially, what you can learn about yourself now by thinking about them.

The principles of a life well lived

Life stage	Time frame	Developmental task	Psychological principle
Infancy	birth–two years of age	trust or mistrust?	Be trustworthy
Early childhood	two–six	autonomy or self-doubt?	Be bold
Middle childhood	seven–eleven	belonging or isolation?	Be generous
Adolescence	puberty–late teens	identity or confusion?	Be authentic
Emerging adulthood	late teens–early 30s	self-responsibility or dependence?	Take the initiative
Young adulthood	early 30s–late 40s	intimacy or loneliness? initiative or passivity?	Invest and commit
Middle age	50–late 60s	generating or stagnating?	Create something of lasting value
Late adulthood	late 60s–late 70s	purpose or decline?	Seize the day
Old age	80 and onwards	integrity or despair?	Be wise

When we think about our lives, we tend to loop backwards and forwards, trying to figure out how the past has influenced who and how we are now, and what we expect and hope for the future. This book is designed to help you interrogate your past in order to understand who you are now, why you made the choices you made, and how you may be, or want to be, in the future.

I have set out nine life stages, with ten corresponding developmental tasks that you must address in order to progress from stage to stage. This is the nature of the life course, and our work here is to survey our current life stage from the perspective of what has gone before and what is yet to come.

In this regard, middle age is particularly important. Halfway through any journey or project, there is a natural pause, a calculation as to what progress you have made and what is still to be done. So, too, as you approach midlife. You become acutely aware of the time you have left and feel a new and pressing urgency to make your life count for something. The sense of being halfway between the start point and end point is a powerful incentive and driver. This is when you set your own agenda for the second part of your life. It is a moment of self-realization that reaches into the past and extends into the future, allowing you to understand your life prior to this and plan your life after this. It is for this reason that our survey starts at this pivotal point.

3. The prime of life

It may elicit a hollow groan from some, but it is true to say that in middle age you are in your prime. Your cognitive and emotional functioning improve, your sense of self and personal identity become stronger, and your body is still relatively youthful and capable. You are 'comfortable in your skin', more confident and self-assured.

You will need these attributes, because midlife is a significant turning point in the life course, challenging you in many ways. You are coming to the end of what might be called the first agenda of life – the dreams and plans that were gestated during adolescence and set in motion in your twenties.

Now, you pivot to the second agenda – what to do with the next half of your life. The first agenda was heavily influenced by the hopes and expectations of your family and society, but the second agenda is generated by you. As you reflect on what you want your one and only life to amount to, at midlife you can rewrite your personal narrative and make the choices and decisions that will shape the direction of your life in the decades to come.

What makes this the prime of life? Well, in middle age you have a more assured mastery of the world you operate in, and you function at a high level of competence. Your cognitive executive functioning improves significantly. Your vocabulary is richer. You are better at reasoning. You possess a rich store of the irreplaceable, tacit knowledge that comes from experience. You make better use of time. You feel more in command of yourself. Most of all, there are striking improvements in your judgement. You know when to consult other people, and when you have to make a decision yourself. Even your spatial memory is better – you are better at finding your way around the world, in all senses of the word.

There are some losses in the mechanics of cognition. You are not as fast at processing rapidly incoming stimuli as you were in your twenties, so are unlikely to beat your teenage children on a video game or at badminton.[1] You can live with that. You are more adept at using higher-order cognitive skills to compensate for any declines – you have enough life experience to quickly spot complex patterns in how things are unfolding. You have a better grasp of realities, are better at judging what works, and does not work, in most situations and can more easily identify recurring patterns and risks. You are sensitive to the highly complex worlds of family, work and social contexts in which you operate, and you feel that you can handle them competently.

Your new sense of mastery is matched by a new status and authority in the different domains in your life. The younger generation may be fizzing with inventiveness and technological innovation, the media and society still youth-obsessed, but even in this red-hot technology-driven world, overall it's the middle-aged who hold most of the institutional and political power and make the major decisions that shape how people live and work.

The power of resilience

In middle age, you are at the peak of your capacity to learn from past experiences and to manage your present circumstances. Just as well, because the downside to having achieved a certain seniority in the different domains of your life is that you have also accumulated the responsibility overload that goes with that. As a consequence, you are more likely to experience an acute sense of crossover stress as simultaneous and competing demands from different parts of your life become harder to juggle. These pressures can trigger a feeling of angst, a sense that you can't escape the demands of those around you and those who are dependent on you.

It takes a long time to fully acknowledge and adjust to what's happening. Middle age, as the joke goes, is feeling that if you only had two weeks free from pressure, you could sort out the whole lot and get back to normal. But, finally, it sinks in. This *is* the new normal, and will be for a long time to come. You are now the person that the

younger and older generations in your family and at work increasingly see as the go-to person when a problem arises.

You also have your own problems. As middle age progresses, you
are likely to face some predictable losses, like the death of a parent or
other close relative. You may develop health problems, like hypertension or arthritis, and the negative effect is magnified if you consider
that these have happened to you 'too early'. There may be problems in
your family, in your work, or in your finances. Too many setbacks
compressed into a short time frame can put strains on even the most
resilient individual.

Despite the upward trajectory in life satisfaction and emotional stability at midlife, there is also a paradoxical increase in rates of depression,
anxiety and sometimes serious distress, particularly amongst women,
those who left school early, those who are struggling financially and
those who identify as LGBT. Rising rates of obesity, a more sedentary
lifestyle and low levels of physical exercise are also posing threats to the
physical health of middle-aged people.[2]

On the other hand, moderate levels of hardship that are well managed enhance your skill and confidence in managing adversity and
losses, now and in the future. Resilience in middle age has its own
profile.[3] It comprises:

- an ability to manage uncertainty
- persistence and grit
- a positive view of the future
- an objective view of what aging entails
- a sense of purpose
- a sense of humour, and
- a broadly spiritual perspective on life.

Most of you can manage some combination of those coping skills,
and a sizeable minority of you excel in all. But what *most* clearly distinguishes high and low levels of resilience is having a more philosophical,
spiritual perspective – the ability to see yourself and your life as part of
a wider cycle. The way you look at issues is broader and more balanced.
Even as you confront your own mortality, the positive backwash is the
realization that you are kept afloat by the good things in your life, by

the battles won and the lessons learned from those you lost, and most of all by those who love and care about you.

You are now at the peak of your capacity to learn from those past experiences and to manage your present circumstances, so you are well positioned to experience stress-related growth. This is the belief that you have grown and developed as a person not *in spite* of any adversity you have endured but *because* of it. When you reflect on the way you dealt with it, got over it and learned from it, you feel that it's made you a better, wiser and more compassionate person.[4]

A new stability

Middle age brings a new sense of confidence and a broader sense of well-being.[5] Your life is more settled, and you feel a new stability. The combination of being settled and experienced is regarded as one of the best bits of being middle-aged. Over 70 per cent of you feel that this stage of your life is exciting, enjoyable, a time when you have more personal freedom, when changes are still possible. Over half of you believe this is the time in your life for focusing more on yourself and finding out who you really are.[6] At a deeper level, there is generally a closer fit between the way you are and the way you would like to be. You are still optimistic, but it's tempered by realism about what's possible. You know yourself better and are better equipped to utilize your inner resources to pursue what's important to you. As your responsibilities decrease, this is a trend that will pick up pace as you enter your sixties and succeeding decades.

Yet, even if you find middle age pretty stressful, it's a mixed state that could be described as 'happily stressed'.[7] Your capacity for emotional regulation improves markedly. You can manage your feelings, your moods and stress responses more effectively, and are not as easily thrown off your stride. You've learned to find more ways to use your strengths and manage your weaknesses. You've figured out what works best for you – a great training ground for the emotional regulation you will need in order to manage the rigours of old age. You have a better sense of what can and cannot be done in most situations and the really important things to focus on. You are more skilled at buffering yourself from troublesome people and needless annoyances.

You are confident enough not to hold back when you think you have something to offer. You still make mistakes, but you are less likely to beat yourself up after each one.

> I was always a perfectionist. I can't blame my parents, they never put any pressure on me, it's just the way I was. I liked to achieve things, to do things right, but inevitably I went over the line. I'd put myself under enormous pressure, and then would beat myself up if the slightest thing went wrong. I'm still like that, but I've noticed recently that I've got better at managing it. At a certain point of self-flagellation, I catch myself up and I say, 'Orla, stop it! You've learned something from this. You will always be learning and that's good.' And that always consoles me.
>
> Orla, 51

You are less tempted to compare yourself to others. You know now that people's lives, including your own, are complex and not always as they appear on the outside. You are less worried by other people's reactions. As you contemplate the prospect of your own mortality, you adopt the ironic and self-deprecating style character-istic of middle age – a kind of hard-earned, knowing, almost defiant confidence. You aren't perfect, but that no longer bothers you. You're learning to live with who you are.

Coming into your own – if you're a woman

While men and women both enjoy the benefits of being middle-aged, the emotional gains are particularly sharp if you are a woman. In mid-dle age, women score higher than men on most measures of well-being.[8] You feel that you are making big strides in your development, that you have come into your own. Far from feeling washed-up and unattract-ive, you have a more favourable body image than younger women do, and you rate your sexual attractiveness and overall physical condition pretty high. What influences your body image now is not your actual age, but your *subjective* age – how young or old you feel and judge your body to be, and how concerned you are by aging.[9]

Negotiating the menopause is challenging. Hot flushes, broken sleep, unexpected bouts of tears, strange aches and pains are no fun. You may experience a loss in libido and have more trouble achieving orgasm. These stresses temporarily soak up your attention and may make it harder to focus on your life.[10] But for most women, menopause is nothing like the crisis it was once thought to be, delivering a dismal menu of anxiety, depression and lack of purpose. The loss of fertility is not an assault on your core sense of self, although you may mourn it for a while, especially if you could not have a longed-for baby. But it also marks the beginning of a new independence and sexual freedom.

A newfound sense of confident power is one of the most marked psychological changes in women in middle age.[11] You feel more personally powerful than at any other stage of your life. Your self-esteem increases. The heavy-duty years of young adulthood are over. You are still busy but are beginning to carve out what you longed for back then – more time for yourself. You are less prey to feeling anxious, unappreciated, resentful. Your desire for autonomy surges. You want to reacquaint yourself with yourself. You are less defensive, more open. You *possess* yourself in a new way.

You have a more assured sense of your life expanding. You can better integrate the rational and emotional parts of yourself, so you make better decisions. You are less reactive, more in control of your life. You feel more authentic as you make your way steadily towards becoming the person you always wanted to be.[12] Some of you may now consciously translate the personal insights you have gained from your own life into activism in the public arena.

My community is what matters to me now. I understand a lot about families and what they need. I left school early, I never had a proper job, and just drifted into a very early marriage that did not work out. I ended up rearing three children on my own. I think I know what needs to be done to help girls like that, so I'm involved in a local support group for lone parents that is funded by the health service as a counsellor. I think I can make a difference, make it better for them, even in a small way.

May, 55

That combination of personal insight and commitment to future generations gives women a powerful sense of their own efficacy and is associated with high levels of well-being. This is borne out by the exuberant perspective of a senior manager in a large company.

No question. This is the very best time of my life so far. I know it sounds like a cliché, but I have found myself. Over the last fifteen years I have worked hard in my family and in my job. And that's not easy when you have two children that you want to really care for. But it has been worth it. The kids are fine, they are happy, they have friends, and are doing well at school. And I've discovered that I'm really good at what I do. That gives me huge confidence. I am at the top of my game now and I feel I can go further in my career, and I feel confident enough to say that now. I didn't have that confidence when I was younger. I invest a lot in developing the people who work for me. I had one boss who really went out of his way to help me in my early career, I owe him a lot, so I feel I'm giving back now. I have a good family life, very good friends, a good job, and a pretty nice life actually.

Eileen, 56

Another woman who gave up work to care for her children was equally positive.

I've a great sense of liberation now. I look back at my thirties and it's a blur. We had three children very quickly, that's what we wanted. My husband has a very demanding job. I worked after our first child was born, went part-time when the second came along, and with the third, it was all becoming more stressful so I pretty much gave up work then to take care of the kids – but also to have time with them and enjoy them. My mum worked full-time and she often says that she feels that she missed out on watching us grow up. She was actually a great mother to us, but she was always rushed and under pressure and it must have been hard on her. Being full-time at home has been very rewarding for me, but it was a lot of work. It's such a relief now not to be running around bringing the kids to school or sports or whatever. I relish the freedom from all that. I'm back working part-time now but I'm planning to go back to college next year to train as a social worker. I think I'd be good at that kind of work now, especially working with kids with problems. I think I understand better now what kids need. So, yes, it's a very good time of my life.

Tessa, 56

Finding your true identity in midlife

In middle age you become more reflective. You think more about yourself, about the person you have become, and how that is reflected in your identity. You've accumulated many roles and versions of yourself, in your family, with your friends, at work. These multiple identities are like layers of skin. The more you have immersed yourself in one or more of these roles, the less sure you may be of what is underneath them any more.

You feel an urge to be in your own skin, to start shedding all these versions of yourself, like a snake sheds its old skin to reveal the fresh, glistening skin underneath. When you do, you will still occupy most of the same roles as you did, they remain part of your identity, but you won't feel obscured by them.

I gave up my career to look after my kids full-time. My husband's job meant we had to move several times in the first ten years of our marriage, so we felt that it was important that I was there for them to help the kids settle into a new environment and have a sense of stability. I have no regrets at all about that. We had a good family life. But there were times when I felt invisible. My whole life revolved around my husband's and the children's routines. I felt that I was always seen as someone's wife or someone's mother. My own identity as a person was just submerged really. Then, things began to ease off in my late forties, and I went back to my own job as an accountant. Then I became myself again. But, it's interesting, it's not like not my old self. It's different. I felt stronger in myself, more confident.

Isabelle, 55

Carl Jung describes the individuation process, the process of becoming more fully yourself, as involving a rebalancing of four opposing tensions.

- Young vs old
- Doing vs enabling
- Outer vs inner investment
- Creation vs destruction[13]

As you make the transition from one life stage to another, particularly at midlife, you become more acutely aware of these polarities, and as they are rebalanced, the new resolutions are incorporated into your developing identity.

Young vs old

Your awareness of your own aging raises fears that your youthful self is ebbing away, that your vitality is drying up, and that you are no longer in the full flow of life. You may feel jaded, more cynical or sceptical of new initiatives, like there's nothing new to learn any more.

> I hear myself saying things to younger people that I never thought I would, like, 'Been there, done that. Didn't work then, won't work now,' and I'm slightly appalled. It's such an echo of what older people used to say to me when I was young and eager about some idea, and I hated it then. But I can't seem to stop myself. I don't know what's changed in me to make me like that.

Larry, 55

To resolve those fears, you have to find a way to be young. You can't be physically young any more. Most of you don't want to *be* young again. You are relieved that feeling naive, junior and inexperienced is now behind you, or at least more artfully disguised. But you do want to *feel* young, to remain enthusiastic, optimistic, daring and game for life. You want to stay attuned to the abundance and possibility of life, and to the potential in yourself to meet that possibility.

I can certainly attest to this from my own experience. For a long time I had dreamed of accompanying my great friend Anne, an intrepid traveller, on one of her adventures. So that's what I did at midlife. Four of us set out to trek in South-East Asia. Anne, having little time for any hint of a package holiday, insisted on us travelling gap-year style. 'It's meant to be an adventure, not a holiday,' she told us sternly, 'and that means leaving your comfort zone.' So we lugged our big backpacks around, travelling on buses and trains. ('You meet more people.') There were some hairy moments, and an occasional heated argument about what Anne meant by 'basic' accommodation. At one point, we found ourselves sleeping on mouldy mattresses in ramshackle bamboo huts on an isolated island in the rainforest. But it was exciting, eye-opening, profoundly liberating. For me, the strangest moment was when I dreamt that I had started smoking again. I had given up smoking in my early twenties and had no urge to start again. So why was I dreaming about it now? And then it struck me. I last smoked in my early twenties, and the way I felt then was how I was feeling now – delighted by the possibilities life held, and free as a bird to go after them.

Finding a new way to be young is just half the story, however. You must also find an affirming way to take on being old – experienced, authoritative, accomplished, far-seeing, compassionate, and wise in your own way.

Doing vs enabling

At midlife, you are still striving. There are important things yet to do and to achieve. But you also become more attentive to the inner voice of satisfaction, and as you progress further into middle age, that voice becomes more audible, more worthy of attention. You are more conscious of the staleness of slogging, of one demand followed inexorably by another, of feeling in harness, and you want to invest more time and energy in things that you enjoy and think are worthwhile, or that have some personal meaning for you.

You are also more aware of the complexity of things, and the limitation of what one person alone can do to make big changes, as well as the satisfaction that comes from *enabling* things to happen by investing in others. Now, alongside the satisfaction that you get from achieving something yourself, you recognize the satisfaction that comes from enabling others to act, and the pleasure in not always 'doing' but 'being' with things as they unfold.[14]

This rebalancing also plays out in your gender identity.[15]

Despite some loosening of gender stereotypes at midlife, men and women are still expected and encouraged to each operate on a certain end of the 'doing' and 'enabling' spectrum. If you are a woman, you are expected to enable others by being receptive and responsive to their needs. You are encouraged to achieve, but with certain limits. Being perceived as 'power-seeking' or 'dominant' attracts strong disapproval and dislike; the word 'careerist' is reserved for women only.

If you are a man, you come under different pressures. You are expected to be tough-minded, dominant and in control of your feelings. Showing vulnerability is frowned on. There has been some easing of this. You are now encouraged to show your 'softer' side, but there are strict and subtle rules about how *much* softness is permitted. For example, sadness reveals your caring side. It's okay to tear-up, to show what's called 'the moist eye', after a significant loss or setback (or after a major sporting achievement when you have proved your toughness). But if a tear actually *falls* from your eye, you lose status, because this is seen as a loss of self-control. The ideal male emotional display is a kind of 'passionate restraint', subtly letting others know that you are feeling strong emotions, *but* you are able to control them. This show of passionate restraint improves your status.

In middle age, you begin the process of breaking loose from these gender constraints and feel freer to express your 'other side'. This shift is more marked in women than in men, and it has been observed in very different cultures. Why now? The shift may have evolutionary roots. In young adulthood, women and men are subject to what's called the 'parental imperative', that mix of cultural and maybe biological pressures to suppress one side of themselves and express the other.[16] Women are under pressure to suppress their own immediate self-interest, their wildness and, most especially, their anger, and to focus on being nurturing and emotionally responsive. This readies them to care for babies. For their part, men are under pressure to 'man up', to suppress doubts and feelings of vulnerability, so that they can compete with other men for whatever resources are available, protect their interests and provide for their families.

At midlife, as children get older and more independent, that pressure lifts. Women feel freer to focus more on themselves and are more at home with their own power. The seniority, status and increased confidence that comes with middle age also lightens the pressure on men to maintain 'face'. They feel less emotionally constricted, free to express their feelings more openly.

> I always knew my dad loved us, and he was always very proud of our achievements. But he never told us directly that he loved us, like Mum used to. In fact, the first time he said it openly was when I graduated from college. He came up to me after the ceremony and shook my hand, quite formally, then completely unexpectedly, he said, 'I love you, son,' and then kind of choked up. I was flabbergasted, and a bit choked up myself. All I could manage was, 'Thanks, Dad. I love you too.' Then we immediately started talking about something else, as if nothing happened.
>
> Eamon, 45

Outer vs inner investment

In young adulthood, you are very engaged in managing the world around you, and in responding to others' needs. You are involved, plugged in, busy, always adapting to multiple demands, and you know what it is to feel overwhelmed by the demands of others. If you are a woman, the tension between meeting your own needs and the needs of others is more acute. In early middle age, you are still doing a lot of managing and responding, but in your sixties there is the beginning of a turn inwards, to your own needs and feelings. It is only the tip of the iceberg, though. The more significant rebalancing towards yourself will happen at the next stage, in late adulthood.

Creation vs destruction

By midlife you are unlikely to see yourself, or anybody else, as perfect. You have experienced and witnessed enough human weaknesses, setbacks and mistakes to knock the edge off any careless optimism. You have seen how disappointment and grief over lost opportunities, or anger and guilt about betrayals, play out in ways that are destructive to others, or to yourself. Coming to terms with destructiveness is never easy, but you must do so, otherwise you won't be able to free your energies to create something good and worthwhile from these accumulated and irreplaceable life experiences, which can give you a new capacity for empathy and compassion for other people, and for yourself. This is the beginning of wisdom.[17]

4.   Is this it?

Approaching midlife is full of portents, messages from the universe that you are aging. There are cues from your body, reactions from the people around you, from your position in life. Turning forty still counts. 'I'm forty,' you say, bemused. You get a few jokey cards about 'The Big 4-O'. You might throw a party. Then you pretty much forget about it. After all, you're *busy*. You are still doing your juggling act with work and family responsibilities, so being forty seems like a seamless continuation of young adulthood. Anyway, you don't feel middle-aged. '*Me?* Middle-aged? No way!' Still, the messages keep coming. You're not quite there yet, but you are definitely on your way.

The Big Dip

The first sign of impending middle age is not reassuring. You begin to feel low. This takes different forms – a general sense of stress and strain, more worries, a loss of confidence, feeling that it's going to be hard to deal with any difficulties you have, more problems sleeping, maybe a spike in depression. You are in the Big Dip, when happiness and well-being temporarily drop to their lowest level in the life course, outside of advanced old age.

The Big Dip happens around the world, irrespective of the state of the economy or a country's culture.[1] It happens to men and women, to rich and poor, to those who have children and those who don't. The timing varies from country to country. In developed economies, where people live longer, midlife and the dip come later than in poorer countries, where both come earlier. In developed countries well-being is at its lowest at the age of forty-eight, and in very prosperous countries a year earlier.[2] But there are other variations. For example, American women's well-being bottoms out at the age of forty, while American men are at their lowest a full ten years later. But, eventually, everybody starts to recover.

Does the Big Dip constitute a midlife crisis? This was an idea that took hold in the 1970s and has lingered on because it has a certain melancholy allure, even a tinge of excitement that *something* might be happening to change your whole life, or at least relieve the 'been-there, done-that' tedium that may be afflicting you.

For one in four of you, the dip does develop into a crisis but, on further probing, that usually happens only when you are also experiencing a setback in your life, like getting divorced, losing your job, combatting financial or health problems, things that cause distress at any stage of life.[3] For most of you, the Big Dip is more likely to mean a time-limited period of emotional churn.[4]

What triggers the Big Dip? Your first real intimation of mortality. You have an unmistakable sense that you are aging, moving up the line. The first signs are in your body. Your hair is greying or getting thinner. You notice a few pounds going on. The youthful preening in the mirror gives way to a more appraising scrutiny, the laughter lines look more like wrinkles. You find yourself squinting to see your face more clearly. *I need glasses*, you think. Meanwhile, you buy a better mirror. You notice slight glitches in your physical performance, so you make more heroic efforts in the gym to compensate.

> A few weeks ago, I was going for my usual evening run in the park, but I was a bit later than usual and the gate was locked. So I stepped on the gate and swung my leg over in what I expected to be one smooth action – except it wasn't. My leg didn't quite clear the gate and I stumbled. I was quite put out actually. I don't normally think much about my age, but I did then. I really will need to get back in shape.
>
> Terry, 47

It's not just changes in your appearance that are cueing you into your aging – you also notice that your peers are aging. You bump into someone you haven't seen for a while and you think, 'God, *she* looks old,' or, 'He's really aged, I hardly *recognized* him.' But any little surge of self-contentment is instantly followed by the realization that, of course, you must look older too. Or you hear that a friend or colleague has been diagnosed with a serious illness, or someone you knew at school has died, and you suddenly feel more vulnerable, but you repress that feeling fast.

These intimations of mortality trigger a more significant change – your sense of time flips.[5] Up to now, you've measured time as 'time since birth'. As a child, you carefully tracked every movement forward. ('I'm not *six*. I'm six and a *half*!') In your twenties and thirties, you track time in a more immediate way: am I keeping up with my peers or falling behind? But at midlife, your sense of time flips from 'time since birth' to 'time left'. This awareness of 'time left' is different from knowing in a rational way that you, like everybody else, will die eventually. Now, you become aware of this in a very personal, visceral way. You can envisage your own eventual death somewhere down the line, still a long way off but there, immovable. It's like reaching the top of a hill and seeing, for the first time, in the far distance, the end of the road ahead.

And then, the questions start. Is this it? Is this my life, and what exactly have I achieved? Now what?

These questions trigger a period of stocktaking. The Big Dip can feel depressing, but it is also a driver of action. It forces you to review your life so far, where you are and where you thought you'd be at midlife, and also to picture the rest of your life. What do you want the agenda of the second half of your life to be? It is necessary to experience this dip, this trigger, so that you are moved to thought, then to action, to plot out the direction of your next stage.

Pulling back so you can make a better jump

Stocktaking at midlife involves the three Rs:

- reassessing your life to date
- reviewing the progress you have made, and
- revisiting the unlived parts of yourself.[6]

Like an athlete facing a high jump, this period of stocktaking allows you to pull back in order to gather your resources so that you propel yourself forward with enough momentum – what the French call *reculer pour mieux sauter*, pulling back so you can make a better jump – in your case, to meet the challenges in the second half of life.

Reassessing the past and the agenda that has driven your life

By midlife, you've clocked up a lot of hours. With time no longer stretching endlessly ahead, you are assessing the agenda that has driven your life up to now, and how much of what you had hoped and planned for has materialized or evaporated. That agenda was first formed in adolescence, or in your early twenties, influenced by your parents' expectations and what your family put most value on. Or sometimes, as in my own choice of career, it was shaped by a chance encounter.

My plan when I left school was to study English literature in university. In those days, you just registered for the degree you wanted to take. But just before I registered for the course, I was in a queue, chatting to a girl I did not know, who told me she was going to study psychology. 'What's psychology?' I asked. She told me, and it sounded so interesting that, there and then, I decided to study psychology too. My parents, who had no idea what this might qualify me for, were appalled, and a big row ensued. But I persisted, and it was one of the best decisions I ever made.

This is the agenda that you pursued in your twenties and shaped into a personal enterprise in your thirties. By midlife some of you are nearing the end of successfully completing the first tranche of that agenda. Some of you have abandoned all or parts of it because it didn't work out, or it lost the allure that once gave it energy, or you just let it drift away for reasons you don't fully understand.

By now, the boundless optimism and self-belief that launched you into the adult world have also taken some knocks against the wall of reality and you have to let go of some illusions about yourself, and about what's possible. Although, like most, you still like to believe that what you're good at is pretty unique; that you have more control over things than you have; and your view of the future is slightly more optimistic than is warranted by the facts. Just as well. If you lost these slightly over-positive illusions, you might be mildly depressed. Too much reality is bad for you.[7] The only way to avoid illusions, Daniel Levinson observes, is not to desire anything too much. But if you can't muster a desire for something, it robs you of the enthusiasm and motivation to try anything.[8]

Reviewing your life structure

In young adulthood, you organized your life around the triad of your closest relationships, your work, and your personal interests. Now, you reassess how good a fit there is between that life structure and where you are now. Is it still viable? Is it still satisfying? These are two very different kinds of judgements. Viability is about whether something is working or can work in the world. Satisfaction is how you feel about it.

For example, the dream you had of running your own business or making it as an actor may still animate you, but it's not paying the bills. You still love the person you married, but you can no longer live with their heavy drinking. These are issues of viability.

Your job may be providing financial security and status, but it's crushing your spirit. Your marriage is stable and functional, but the intimacy between you has been hollowed out. These are issues of satisfaction.

Around one in five of you arrives at midlife having failed to build any viable or satisfying life structure, drifting from job to job, unable to make a commitment, or to maintain a long-term romantic relationship. As you enter middle age, you see your life as having little impact on others and experience a feeling of deep disappointment – in yourself, in other people, or in life itself. Now, as you face middle age, you feel a growing panic, or despair, about where your life is heading.

Revisiting the unlived part of yourself

At every stage of your life, especially at key transition points, you have to make choices. You decide to pursue some options and to abandon others; to express some sides of your personality and to set aside or suppress others. Every choice sets you down a particular path and closes off another that would have taken you in a different direction and developed a different side of you. At midlife you are reviewing the choices that you made, and how they have worked out. But you are also reflecting on the choices you did not make, the parts of yourself that you set aside or neglected. Like a stick surfacing in a stream, this unlived life begins to surface into your consciousness. You start to listen to what writer Truman Capote called 'other voices, other rooms'.[9]

The more pressure you were under in your adolescence and your twenties to make the choices that you did, or the fewer choices that were open to you, the louder and more insistent those 'other voices' become. The *what ifs* tug at your attention and preoccupy you in a new way, and you feel a growing need to explore that unlived life, to discover new parts of yourself, to recapture a sense of wholeness and authenticity. Searching and finding, feeling lost and then found, are major themes at midlife.

> My father died suddenly when I was seventeen. He was self-employed and had no proper pension, so on top of the shock of losing him, we were left in pretty dire financial straits. I was the eldest and my mother depended on me a lot. So I had to leave school after my Leaving Cert to help out financially – so that was the end of my plans to go to college. Effectively, I became the man of the house. The rest is a long story. I found that I had a head for business, I worked hard, and one thing led to the other, so I've ended up with a successful business and made a good bit of money. I'm very proud of that. But recently I came across some old photographs of me as a kid. I was grinning in the photos, not a care in the world. And I felt suddenly very sad that when Dad died, I had shut down a part of myself, I closed off something that used to be there, some joy in life, being carefree. Is it still there? I don't know. That's what I have to find out, I suppose. I'm forty-seven now, I don't want to be walled in to being this serious person I've become, for the rest of my life.
>
> Patrick, 47

There is a pull inwards now, you think about the past more, searching for a better, more nuanced understanding of yourself, of how you became the person you are. As you do, you rework your narrative about yourself, using it as a way of exploring what's possible when heading into the future. That story about yourself houses your identity, combining the private way you feel about yourself and the public self you present to the world.

The story you tell yourself about yourself

As you proceed through life, your narrative about your own life – the story you tell yourself about yourself, and the story that significant people tell about you – continues to evolve.[10] This narrative is not something that you possess in a passive way. On the contrary, it is constantly shaping what you perceive, what you expect, what you think is possible, and what you do.

As a child, you are a character in your own narrative, but the story is strictly in the present tense. In adolescence, you are the hero of your story, you take more ownership of it, and it extends well into the future. This process continues in your twenties and takes on a new complexity and depth in young adulthood. In middle age, you are right in the middle of your story, and it extends further into the past and into the future than ever before. You enter it in a deeper way, consciously using it to strengthen your sense of self and your identity, to make space for your own desires and hopes, as well as those of others you care about. You use it to rehearse different scenarios and play out their likely consequences, a form of imaginative exploration.

At midlife, this narrative breaks in two ways – into stories of redemption or of contamination.[11] If your life up to now has gone well or you've managed to overcome significant difficulties, you feel redeemed, blessed, and your story is correspondingly full of positive meaning, strengthening and amplifying your sense of self, motivating you to be generative, to pay back, or pay forward.

If your life has been consistently hard, or you have not recovered from a major setback, you may be beset by feelings of failure and help-lessness. You feel stymied, your life and hope spoiled, contaminated by what happened to you. Your internal narrative becomes truncated, cut off from your inner resources. You are unable to play out more hopeful and realistic scenarios, obscuring any potential turns in the road that could hold the possibility for change, or generativity.

Constructing and reconstructing your identity is a lifelong enter-prise, but at certain stages of life, certain moments of potential change, you encounter the task more urgently and dramatically. There are three crucial turning points. The first happens in your sec-ond year, when you experience your first, distinct sense of self and your first recognizable identity, although that is still deeply embed-ded in the close nexus of your family relationships. The second happens in adolescence, when a similar but far more complex step in individuation occurs, a precursor of your adult self. The third hap-pens at midlife, when you reassess and rework that identity to prepare for the next half of your life.

At midlife, whatever you are feeling about yourself or about how your life has gone, there is now a real opportunity to re-engage with your own story of how you became the person you are, and who you can become.

Reviewing the past can sometimes be painful, but it is also full of promise, an irreplaceable source of self-understanding, wisdom and moral growth. It is a solid platform on which to build a more sustain-able and compassionate happiness. It is a way to greatly increase the chances that when you look back on your life, you will judge it to be successful in the way you wanted it to be.[12]

PART TWO

Life in the Rear-view Mirror

Midway upon the journey of our life
I found myself within a forest dark
For the straightforward path had been lost . . .

Dante Alighieri, *The Divine Comedy*
Translation by Henry Wadsworth Longfellow

At midlife, you have to go back in order to go forward – to find out what made you the person you are now, to revisit the significant turning points in your own development. You are now positioned to review the past equipped with all the life experience you have accumulated, to identify as best you can how you experienced each stage of your development, how each developmental task was resolved, and how you feel about the outcomes.

How easy is it for you to trust?

How liberating or intimidating does it feel to decide to take your life into your own hands? How competent do you feel to do that?

What are the big lessons you have learned to date – and do these lessons reassure you or plunge you into self-doubt?

However you feel, one thing is indisputably true: you know more now than you did at earlier stages of life, because at your disposal is a rich store of memories, some conscious and well elaborated, others hovering at the edge of your consciousness – fleeting memories, images and fantasies, and dreams that seem to linger in your mind.

Some memories are triggered by day-to-day events that generate anniversary reactions. You watch as your children or younger colleagues pass through a particular familiar stage in life, and suddenly there is a rush of images and feelings that, like a time machine, transport you to an earlier time in your own life. It comes alive vividly, but the person observing, reliving and internally narrating the story is your current adult self. You are the producer and director of the life story spooling out in your mind.

In this part of the book you will read about each of the life stages that have brought you to midlife, teasing out the delicate developmental work that goes on in each of them as if happening in real time. When considering your life as you've lived it so far, you need to pay particular attention to the impact of your initial experiences of attachment, the first and most intense expression of your instinctive drive for closeness, autonomy and competence. Attachment is crucial to every aspect of how you are as a person. It is explored in detail in Chapter 5 and is at the heart of the chapters that follow.

Please treasure this spontaneous process of remembering. If you pay attention, you will learn a lot about yourself, about the challenges you faced, and about the reserves of resilience that got you through. Stay open, not fearing what you may find, because in the story that unfolds, you will find at least some of the answers you need to the vital questions that midlife poses – for example, why you are the way you are.

Approach reviewing your past boldly and with curiosity. Because, however happy or unhappy you were or are, you are still standing – and half of your life awaits you.

5. *Infancy:* Finding someone to rely on

It is ironic that the most consequential task of life, figuring out your first experiences of trust or mistrust, begins when you have no language to encode what happened. Instead, those vital earliest memories are non-verbal – sensations in your body or images in your mind that are nonetheless strong and enduring, still influencing the basic trust in yourself and in other people that you need to get through each stage of your life.

The profound truth about trust is this: it's our way of dealing with uncertainty.[1] If we were a hundred per cent certain about how things would turn out, why would we need to trust at all? But life and the future are inherently uncertain, and never more so than in infancy. Hardly surprising, then, that the very first developmental task or crisis in life is to find one person that you can depend on, someone you can trust.

By the end of your first year, if you have found that you can depend on one person, someone who really cares for you and responds willingly and with love to your basic psychological needs, you will have laid down the deep nucleus of basic trust: emotional security. If you haven't, your basic trust and the emotional security that comes from it will be compromised. This is the psychological base factor in all our lives: attachment. The type of attachment we first experience, we first learn from; it colours our view of the world, our place in it and our ability to move through it successfully.

At birth, you are instinctively primed to attach yourself to your mother, or whoever cares for you most day-to-day. You search for her – crying, rooting, sucking, nestling and clinging. You prefer her smell, gazing at her face above all others. Soon, you smile and coo at her, closely tracking her every move, mirroring her expressions. Then, you want to break free, absorbed by some distraction, preferring to follow that. But after a while you cry for her again, craving her touch, her voice, her comfort. When she responds to your signals, you have your first experience of control, of competence. Thus begins the little drama of attachment and separation, reunion, separation again, doing, resting and learning. This is a search for closeness and autonomy, equilibrium and wholeness. And this is a search that will repeat itself in multiple ways as long as you live.

Attachment

Attachment is the first and most intense expression of your instinctive drive for closeness, autonomy and competence. How that system works was first identified by John Bowlby, a child psychiatrist at the Tavistock Clinic in London, and his long-term collaborator, Mary Ainsworth, a professor at Johns Hopkins University. Together, they revolutionized our understanding of the fundamental role of attachment in human development.[2] Bowlby was the first to see that the nature of a child's attachment to its mother is not just a sentimental tie but an instinctive response, rooted in our evolutionary past, and that the attachments we form at every stage of life are a powerful and consequential force in human development, from the moment you are born to the moment you die.

You are primed to seek closeness with the person who is most available and responsive to your physical and emotional needs and has the most emotional investment in you – or as near to that package as possible. It is with that person, your major caretaker, that you form your first and primary attachment. Why one person? Because from a survival point of view, it's not adaptive to waste time dithering about who to turn to in situations of danger and risk.

For most children around the world, that person is likely to be their mother. When a mother is not physically or psychologically available, the infant can readily form its primary attachment relationship with someone who is prepared to be the major caretaker – their father, an adoptive or foster parent, a grandparent, an older sibling or other family member. However, rather than use a precise but technical term like 'major caretaker' throughout the book, I will use 'mother' – but take 'mother' to mean the person who is a child's major caretaker.

Your attachment system is instantly activated at any sign of danger, or a feeling of exhaustion or distress, triggering an instinctive set of behaviours that Bowlby suggested were regulated by a control centre in the brain that links your emotions, memory and physiological stress response – an understanding now validated by modern research in neuroscience.[3] But even in the absence of danger or distress, the attachment system is always 'on', scanning the environment to be sure it is safe.

When you make satisfactory contact with your mother, your face lights up with relief and joy, even as you are still crying big fat tears. You have restored your sense of 'felt security'. Only then will the alarm bells quieten down. As you get older, it may be enough to get verbal reassurance from her, or just to know that she is *psychologically* available, the lines of communication open and fluid. That knowledge is enough to restore your sense of 'felt security'.

The four phases of an attachment relationship

There are four observable phases to an attachment relationship.

- *A strong desire to be physically and emotionally close to your mother* : this is the first step in building a pathway towards an exclusive attachment with her.
- *Separation distress* : you protest more loudly and insistently when you are separated from her, becoming anxious and agitated. Nobody else will do when you feel very frightened or distressed. It's highly adaptive to keep close to your special protector.
- *Safe haven* : your mother becomes your safe haven, the person you automatically and urgently turn to when you need to be comforted and reassured.
- *Secure base* : towards the end of your first year, and particularly in the second year, you use your mother as your secure base. You venture out to explore the world immediately around you, armed with that special and untroubled confidence that comes from knowing that someone is 'at your back', available

to help and rescue you when needed. This frees you to give your full attention to exploring more widely, to learning, playing, and mastering your little world. When that secure base is threatened in any way, you are deeply unsettled, on high alert, anxiously looking back, your attention divided, your energy conflicted.*

These four phases will be repeated in adulthood when you fall in love and form a long-term romantic attachment. Closeness, separation anxiety and safe haven are highly visible during the infant's first year of life, and again in the first phase of a romantic relationship. The sense of secure base comes into its own in the second year of life, and again in the 'serious' phase of a romantic relationship. Having a secure base in a relationship operates almost below the radar. It is a background feeling, and often you only really notice it when it's threatened or gone.

For the vast majority of people, all four elements of attachment are usually found only in the relationship between a child and a parent, and between partners in a long-term romantic relationship, or occasionally an exceptionally close friendship or sibling relationship. But you don't form an attachment with your child – the attachment bond is between a child and a parent, not the other way round. Parents and children share deep emotional ties, but parents can't turn to the child to provide security and protection. And if they do, it's never good news. It signals psychological problems in the parent and causes them in the child. The only exception is the attachment to a frail and aging parent, when they may turn to an adult child to provide emotional security.

* As young children develop and get on busily with their lives, a parent's role as secure base may become less obvious. But any threat to that secure base – a parent becoming ill, leaving or threatening to leave, serious marital conflict – and a child will become immediately anxious and preoccupied. This will affect their concentration, their physical and psychological health, and sometimes their progress at school. In adulthood, even when a couple has decided to separate, the loss of their once secure base can disorganize their functioning for quite a while, disrupting their attention and performance at work.

In childhood, forming a primary attachment is most easily done in your first year. It can happen after that, but if a child is grievously deprived of consistent one-to-one caretaking in that first year, such as happened in some Romanian orphanages,★ the attachment system can break down.[4] Behavioural systems like attachment and caregiving are designed to be flexible in humans, so they can break down under certain conditions of high stress.

The quality of attachment

Virtually all children form a primary attachment, but it was Mary Ainsworth who discovered that the *quality* of that attachment differs. Specifically, some children form secure, high-trust attachments with a parent; for others, their attachments are insecure. The quality of the attachment relationship has significant and long-term effects on the child's development.

Ainsworth made this discovery through an ingenious experiment that replicated how an attachment relationship works. She called it *The Strange Situation*. It has been shown many times that how a child behaves during this experiment is a powerful predictor of the quality of the child's attachment relationship with a parent, of many aspects of their current and future happiness, and of their development throughout the life course.[5]

Imagine the scene. You are aged between twelve and twenty months and you and your mother arrive somewhere new, where you are greeted by a 'friendly stranger', most often a young woman, who shows you into a pleasant, toy-filled room. Over the course of the next twenty minutes, your mother will leave the room twice for two

★ Some of the children who spent their early childhood in bleak Romanian orphanages, deprived of any opportunity to attach themselves to any one person, became 'attached' to objects, like a mobile hanging over their cots. But if they were deprived of any opportunity to form an attachment with one person, and if this continued for a long time, it had catastrophic effects on their brain development, and gave rise to profound emotional and behavioural difficulties. Many of the most severely deprived children were subsequently unable to form any attachment, even with the most caring adoptive parents.

very brief separations, lasting in total no more than two minutes. The first time she leaves you with the friendly stranger, the second time you are left alone in the room. When your mother returns after each brief separation, the only instruction she receives is to greet you from the door and respond to you as she thinks fit. This experiment is designed to trigger the attachment system, the brief separations acting as a cue to danger for the child. The purpose is to observe the attachment system in action. Ainsworth discovered that this little drama plays out in three very different ways.

In the first scenario, you play happily until the arrival of the stranger and the departure of your mother, which are natural cues to danger and immediately activate the attachment system. When your mother returns, you try to move closer to her, your safe haven. Once reassured, you return to play. This behaviour corresponds to what Ainsworth called a *Secure* attachment, a fluid balance between your drive for closeness and your drive to pursue your own agenda and explore autonomously. About 67 per cent of children have a *Secure* attachment – and in families that are stable, the percentage is even higher, about 80 per cent.

In the second scenario, you avoid closeness with your mother, apparently reacting only minimally to the cues to danger. There is no emotional response to her departure and you accept the presence of the stranger matter-of-factly. Neither is there an emotional response to your mother's return. Throughout the whole episode, there is little emotion on display, and your expression and demeanour remain neutral. This exhibits an *Avoidant* attachment, a pattern shared by 20 per cent of children.

In the third scenario, you show little interest in exploring the room or playing with the toys. Instead, you stay close to your mother, fretful and fussy, or just sitting passively at her feet. She encourages you to play but your play is shallow and frequently interrupted by a return to her side. When your mother leaves, you cry angrily and move away from the friendly stranger. When your mother returns, you cry even harder and cling to her legs. But if she tries to lift and comfort you, you struggle out of her grasp, but still cling on. This little drama is as unsettling as the last one, a story of distress, anger, frustration and ambivalence, with no resolution and no happy ending. This exhibits a *Resistant/Anxious** pattern of attachment and it is observed in 12 per cent of children.

These results have since been replicated in many hundreds of studies worldwide.[6]

Types of attachment

There are three 'basic' types of attachment – *Secure*, *Avoidant* and *Anxious*. It is important to note that, in childhood, the quality of attachment is specific to a particular relationship. For example, a child can be insecure with one parent, but *Secure* with another.

As her work developed, Ainsworth and other researchers, like Mary Main of the University of California at Berkeley,[7] found that some children were behaving so oddly in the *Strange Situation* that they fell into none of the three main attachment categories. These odd behaviours were signs of what became known as an insecure *Disorganized* attachment.†

---

* *Anxious* attachment was originally called *Resistant*, or *Ambivalent*, and some researchers still use these terms. So for clarity and continuity, I will use *Anxious* rather than *Resistant*.

† In the *Strange Situation* experiment, a child who has a *Disorganized* attachment alternates between staying anxiously close to the mother, or wandering aimlessly around, not fully engaging with the toys but unable to shift attention away from her. When the stranger enters the room, the child looks apprehensive, but instead of coming nearer to the mother, may back away against the wall. When the mother returns after the brief separations, the child may crawl towards her crying, but then stop suddenly, freeze and fall silent, looking at the mother in a fearful way, but simultaneously smiling. If she tries to pick the child up, the child may react in an odd way, raising its hands to its head, or crawling to the stranger, looking to be picked up by her, rather than the mother. These confusing episodes may last only a few seconds, require expertise to identify, but signal an overwhelming fear, and are the markers of a *Disorganized* attachment, a pattern shown by 15 per cent of children. A child with a *Disorganized* attachment has a basic underlying attachment, most often an *Anxious* attachment. For that reason, and because most of the research has been done on the three basic types, especially in adulthood, I will focus on them in this book.

The patterns described here are prototypes, patterns displayed by children at the extreme end of each type. But some *Secure* children show some *Avoidant* or *Anxious* behaviours, some *Avoidant* children do not show such an extreme aversion to physical contact, and the exploration and play of some *Anxious* children are not quite as compromised. However, the key difference between them is that in the case of a *Secure* attachment, the attachment system is working optimally.

How different attachment types are formed

Ainsworth and other researchers found that the *Secure* or insecure quality of a child's attachment was strongly predicted by how their mothers responded to and cared for them, physically and psychologically. Mothers differed in five key ways in how they did this.[8]

I. SENSITIVITY − INSENSITIVITY

Babies with a *Secure* attachment had the most sensitive mothers, quick to pick up their baby's signals, adept at reading and interpreting them, and responding to them promptly. They were attuned to the baby's preferences and 'ways', able to see and understand things from the baby's point of view. Being understood is a fundamental part of intimacy, trust and emotional security. When a mother ranks high in sensitivity, she is also very likely to be high on the other four dimensions. Sensitivity emerged as the bedrock quality that makes for a *Secure* attachment in a baby.★

In contrast, the babies with *Avoidant* or *Anxious* attachment had mothers who scored low in sensitivity. Those geared their interactions and responses to their own needs and moods, interpreting the baby's signals in line with what they themselves wanted to do. For example, they interpreted whatever the baby was doing as meaning the baby 'needed' to eat or sleep, if that was what they wanted them

---

★ When babies and their fathers are observed in *The Strange Situation*, the father's sensitivity is linked in the same way to *Secure* attachment, although fathers may express sensitivity differently to mothers.

to do. If the baby looked lonely or distressed, they often ignored it, or seemed not to notice it at all.

2. COOPERATION — INTERFERENCE

The most important marker of cooperation was respect for the baby's autonomy, seeing the baby as a separate person, with its own needs and wishes. If the baby was happily engaged in something, their mother rarely intruded or interrupted.

At the opposite end of the scale, the least cooperative mothers treated the baby's own wishes or preferences as having no validity. When they were caring for the baby or interacting with them, they were more likely to physically intrude on them, to be 'at' them, rather than meshing their behaviour with the baby's needs.

3. ACCEPTANCE — REJECTION

The mothers at the high end of this scale not just accepted but delighted in the baby. Delight and pride are not the same. A mother may be proud of her baby's 'achievements' or appearance, but delight is about the baby's very being. These mothers accepted the responsibility that being a mother entails in a generally cheerful way, even though caring for the baby had inevitably limited their own activities. They got frustrated and irritable occasionally, but they didn't 'make an enemy' of the baby.

In contrast, the least accepting mothers were often angry and resentful, sometimes voicing rejection of the baby, and of being a mother, and these feelings seemed to overwhelm any enjoyment they got from the baby.

4. BEING ACCESSIBLE — IGNORING OR NEGLECTING

The mothers whose babies had formed *Secure* attachments with them were the most psychologically accessible, even when in another room or distracted by other demands.

Mothers at the low end of this scale were either so remote or preoccupied by their own concerns that they didn't pick up the baby's signals, or deliberately tuned them out. They ignored the baby's efforts to communicate that they wanted to be picked up, or played with, or talked to, noticing them only when actually doing some-thing with them, or when they became too insistent to be ignored any longer.

5. AVERSION TO PHYSICAL CLOSENESS
AND NEGATIVE FEELINGS

Mothers at the high end of this scale showed a marked aversion to close body contact with the baby. For others, the signs were more subtle. Some were openly intolerant of any expression of anger or sadness by the baby. Others reacted in a more disguised or indirect way.[9]

Each dimension – physical and psychological – influences the other, interacting to produce different patterns of caretaking, which in turn are linked to whether a child develops a *Secure* or insecure (*Avoidant* or *Anxious*) attachment with its mother.*

What about your early experience of attachment?

You can't go back in time to observe how you were cared for in infancy, although you may have some scattered memories of your very early childhood, and much clearer ones from the age of four onwards. But the way you feel about your childhood experiences with your parents – the memories and images that are most vivid – is a good guide, because the most vivid and enduring memories are of experiences of intense emotion, whether positive or negative. These emotionally charged memories are stored in a powerful way by the same neurochemicals that are involved in the 'fight-or-flight' response.[10]

---

* Just as there are degrees of difference in the quality of children's attachment, there are also degrees of difference in caretaking patterns. Mothers of *Secure* babies are not saints, and mothers of insecure babies are not 'bad' mothers. The profiles described here are of mothers who score on the extreme high/low end of these caretaking patterns. These are general descriptions that try to capture the flavour of the three different 'states of mind' about attachment, so the examples cannot be seen as diagnostic in any way.

Secure

When a baby has a *Secure* attachment relationship with its mother, it creates a fluid and free space where the child can express a range of positive and negative emotions, in turn providing a constant flow of information to the mother, which guides her responses. This gives the baby a feeling of control that lays the foundation for a *Secure* attachment and a sense of autonomy and competence in close relationships. This is evident as early as twelve months of age.

In contrast, babies who have an insecure attachment, who are *Avoidant* or *Anxious*, have more difficulty in forming close relationships, and in other aspects of their development too.

Avoidant

If your attachment to your mother was *Avoidant*, your day-to-day experience in the first year of life has a different quality.

Your mother may generally look after all your physical needs, albeit without much evidence of pleasure, but she does not respond readily or quickly to your cries, tuning them out, or delaying as long as possible before responding. As a consequence, in the first few months of life you cry more frequently and for longer than *Secure* babies do.

She feeds and changes you regularly, but in a kind of businesslike way. There is an absence of tenderness, her expression is often unsmiling or neutral. You try to get her attention by looking at her intently, gurgling, smiling, but she responds minimally, or appears not to notice.

When she describes you, her tone is matter-of-fact, but offers little that gives a 'feel' for you as an individual. Her observations have a detached quality about them, as if she is describing a baby she is caring for, not 'her' baby. She often seems irritated by your demands, responding with barely disguised impatience. Or she may adopt a more long-suffering stance, complaining about the burden of being a mother.

The most striking thing is her discomfort with physical closeness.

She kisses you, but usually lightly, on the head, often with a kind of pecking motion. There are few spontaneous cuddles or affectionate touches. When you touch her, she may stiffen slightly. When she holds you, it is at some distance from her body, arching her belly away, although the movement is very subtle. When she carries you, she may hold her arms stiffly, straight in front of her, as though transporting you on a tray. You can't mould or 'sink' into her body, making it hard for you to get any comfort or pleasure from the contact, leaving you frustrated and unsatisfied.

When you approach her and make a bid for physical contact, she may try to distract you by offering you a toy, or a snack. She may reject your bids for contact outright, openly acknowledging her dislike of physical closeness, saying things like, 'Stop hanging out of me!' When you are rebuffed by her, you look visibly distressed and seek contact with her even more actively. When you look sad, she subtly withdraws from you, looking or moving away from you. She may describe you as not a 'cuddly' baby, but this is belied by the many attempts you make to be picked up and cuddled by her.

As the months progress, you spend more time playing away from your mother than a *Secure* baby does, often moving out of her sight. She may ignore you for long periods. When you get very frustrated by something, like a toy that won't work, your mother may briskly interfere and solve the problem for you, rather than with you. She has little tolerance for angry outbursts, and will often respond with irritation, sharply telling you to stop fussing or she will take the offending toy away from you, despite your cries.

This constant rejection of your bids for closeness also makes you angry, and that anger leaks out. By nine months, your mood is often angry and defiant. Sometimes, when she holds you, you may lightly hit her, but in a disguised, fearful way. Your bids for attachment have been rejected so often, you now seem to feel angry and fearful in situations that normally arouse love and longing.[11]

Rebuffed again and again, you become discouraged. You gradually school yourself to avoid the sharp pang of rejection by decisively shifting your attention away from the urge to get close to her – you look away, lean away, move away. Instead, you focus your attention on exploring and playing on your own. It's your way of dampening down, or trying to switch off, your needs for physical and emotional closeness. But the way you explore and play has a driven and defensive quality about it, showing little of the joyful curiosity that is evident in a *Secure* baby. By the time you are one year old, your *Avoidant* behaviour has become a mirror image of your mother's.

Anxious

If your attachment with your mother was *Anxious*, the most striking thing about your day-to-day life is how unpredictably she responds to you. Sometimes she is responsive, fussing over you, holding you in her lap for long periods, cuddling you, although in a distracted way, or as a way to comfort herself rather than you. But, unlike the mothers of *Secure* babies, who remain consistently physically affectionate, her cuddling will have tailed off considerably by the end of your first year.*

She shows no discomfort with physical closeness, yet of all the mothers her handling is the least tender, and the most inept. You cannot seem to get a firm grip on her, or mould into her body, leaving you frustrated and unsatisfied. You respond very negatively when she won't pick you up or tries to put you down, throwing a tantrum, or crying disconsolately.

Her lack of a firm physical grip on you is paralleled by her poor understanding of you. Her descriptions of you and your reactions are often vague and confused, constantly meshed into long accounts of her own childhood, or her own reactions. She shows little awareness of you as a separate person, with your own plans and desires. Her attitude to you is ambivalent, sometimes she is warm and affectionate, more often irritable and exasperated. She may describe you as 'a

---

* A child does not have the same quality of attachment with everybody in his hierarchy. He can be *Secure* with one parent and insecure with the other – although in the majority of cases, the two attachment relationships tend to be similar. Whether a specific attachment relationship is *Secure* or insecure depends not on the child, but on the quality of the interaction with that person.

very demanding baby'. She often seems preoccupied, her mood low and irritable.

She shows little sensitivity to your signals or natural rhythms. She appears not to notice when you are getting restless, tired or distressed. Consequently, there are many conflicts between you, and your relationship is volatile. Her feeding routine is often erratic. She tends to force food into your mouth, or coaxes you to eat more than you want, and feeding is often a battle of wills. The same intrusive pattern is evident in the ways she plays with you. She rarely initiates play, but if she is in a good mood, or interested in what you are doing, she may play with you, but often in a way that interrupts or intrudes on what you were already doing.

She ignores you for long periods, especially if she is preoccupied or having a long conversation on the phone, paying no attention to your crying, shooing you away irritably. She alternates that with being overprotective. As you begin to move around and explore, she often discourages you, issuing a stream of warnings. When you run into difficulties, she is quick to intrude and berate you, but offers little practical help.

Her unpredictability and frequent mood changes mean you have to keep your attention on her, so you are anxious, vigilant, reluctant to move away from her. You react strongly to any minor separation, yet you seem unable to communicate your distress clearly. You are often cranky and fussy, other times you lapse into passivity, exploring little, apart from looking around. When you are ignored, you sit listlessly, repetitively pulling at your hair, or chewing on a toy. But you alternate that passivity with defiance, refusing to comply with her instructions or requests. The more negative your mood, and the more defiant your behaviour, the more irritated and stressed and helpless your mother becomes, but also the more she responds – an unhappy vicious cycle. By the end of your first year, your mood and demeanour are a mirror of your mother's – preoccupied, conflicted, passive, helpless.*

---

* These *Anxious* and *Avoidant* strategies mirror how children react in very high-stress situations where they are separated from their mothers for prolonged periods. In the 1950s, John Bowlby and James Robertson did a study on children who were

The effect of attachment on autonomy

While the mothers of *Avoidant* and *Anxious* infants seem to be mirror images of each other, their caretaking has this in common – it is intrusive, a quality that will prove damaging to a child's autonomy. Intrusive means playing in a way that ignores the infant's signals, not appearing to notice their attempts to control the pace and intensity of the interaction, or disregarding those attempts. When the baby was enjoying whatever they were doing, they took it as a cue to escalate the stimulation even more, overstretching the baby's capacity to respond, and stressing them.

When babies are stressed, they try to control their mounting physiological arousal by increasing self-comforting behaviours – putting their hand to their mouth, sucking their fingers, touching their own or their mother's body, clasping their clothes or blanket. They look at their mothers less often, and when they do, their expression is neutral, rather than happy. If that fails to dampen their arousal, they look or turn away. They often break off eye contact, turning their heads away, and when they do, their heart rate lowers.[12]

The mothers' intrusive behaviours were often as subtle as the babies' responses – micro-movements, fleeting expressions. They

---

separated from their mothers for a long period because they had to be hospitalized or were put into care. (See Bowlby, J., Robertson, J. & Rosenbluth, D. 1952. 'A two-year-old goes to hospital'. *Psychoanalytic Study of the Child,* 7 (1), 82–94.) Because of the severely restrictive visiting rules of that time, these two- to three-year-olds saw little or nothing of their mothers for weeks or months at a time. What Bowlby and Robertson observed was harrowing. At the beginning, the children showed intense distress and misery, crying incessantly for their mothers. But soon, they gave up their fruitless protest. Instead, they lay listless and despairing, grieving silently. Finally, they seemed to enter a stage of detachment, and appeared to be indifferent to their mothers when they visited. Even when the children returned home and were reunited with their mothers, the problems continued. Some clung intensely to her, showing great distress at even the briefest separation, and this could continue for weeks, months, or even years. Others remained detached, rejecting any closeness with the mother, treating her as if she were a stranger. For some, this detachment was temporary, for others it became permanent.

differ in only small ways from the behaviour of the other mothers and babies. Yet, these subtle differences are consistent, and consequential for the baby.

The way stressed babies try to get control over their emotional reactions, by turning away and appearing neutral, biases them to 'tune out' their own physical and emotional reactions in a more general way. This inhibits their expression of the full range of feelings, thus compromising their future ability to connect and engage in close relationships. The outcome is a kind of defensive self-sufficiency, not real autonomy. By twelve months, many of them have developed an *Avoidant* attachment.

How do you get your needs met?

Whether your relationship with your mother is *Secure*, *Avoidant* or *Anxious*, you are still attached to her – insecure attachment is still attachment. The *quality* of your attachment reflects the strategy you use to get your attachment needs met as best you can. If you are able to follow your instinctive attachment urges, you can follow the primary attachment script – staying close enough to your mother, your secure base, to allow you to explore and play safely, and turning to her as a safe haven when you are frightened or distressed.

If, on the other hand, your mother has set severe limitations on how close and psychologically available she is to you, the message you get is, 'Don't bother me unless you are in serious trouble.' You then have no option but to develop a second-best strategy, like avoidance of closeness, or anxious clinging and fussing, to manage those limitations. You have to readjust your natural attachment response so as to keep your mother as close as she will allow, and that way you hope you can still reserve her as a safe haven in times of real danger and stress. But an insecure strategy such as this will be at a big cost to yourself. (These strategies are not conscious, of course, they simply represent your responses to the situation you find yourself in.)

To maintain an *Avoidant* strategy, you have to bury your feelings. As your feelings of longing, distress and anger cannot be safely expressed, the burden of dealing with them is placed on your small shoulders to resolve. So you shut out those feelings, where they lie untended, frozen, compromising your capacity to form close and intimate relationships. But this strategy of strict control and deactivation is not entirely successful. In *The Strange Situation*, for example, you may seem unconcerned when your mother leaves you with a stranger, or completely alone, but your body tells another story. You show the same elevated heart rate and other physiological symptoms of stress as *Secure* babies exhibit during separation from their mothers, when they are overtly distressed. But unlike *Secure* babies, your heart rate and cortisol levels stay elevated throughout the session, even when your mother returns.[13]

An *Anxious* strategy exacts a different cost. Ramping up your distress and demands, as a way of trying to get your needs met, risks you becoming overwhelmed by your feelings, unable to easily switch them off. Your longing to be close, and your anger when you can't, means that anger and closeness become hopelessly entangled in your mind. Being constantly preoccupied by your attachment to your mother – becoming entangled with her needs and treated as if you are not a separate person – soaks up your energy, blurs the boundaries between you and your mother, and seriously compromises your autonomy.

6. *Infancy:* The power of early attachment

As you revisit and reassess your own experiences of attachment in childhood, you may become aware of echoes in your most intimate adult relationship, a characteristic way you feel and act, especially when you're vulnerable and stressed, because it is those feelings that activate your attachment system and reveal its workings.

Of all the roles your parents play in your life, how they respond to your attachment needs has the most long-term and pervasive effects. A *Secure* attachment connects you to life in a more abundant way and is associated with a host of positive outcomes.[1] It influences how you explore, learn, play, and master the world around you; how harmonious and happy your relationships are with your parents, siblings and friends; how well you do in school; how you cope with the pressures of adolescence; how you negotiate intimacy and autonomy in your romantic relationships; and the quality of the commitment you bring to your work, and to your life. But most of all, it influences how you will care for your own children.

Your primary attachment relationship is where you learn the foundational skills for well-functioning close relationships: sensitive attunement to another person's signals; synchrony, the ability to coordinate your responses with another's; and reciprocity, the ability to give and take. These are the core skills you will need to make friends, to find a place in a peer group, to negotiate intimacy with a partner, and to care for a child in a way that builds their emotional security. A *Secure* attachment with both parents will anchor you even more securely in the world, undergirding the robust sense of autonomy and resilience that you will develop.

The power of early attachment to shape your life

It may seem extraordinary that your early experiences of attachment should have such a profound effect on such a wide range of outcomes over your life course. There are three reasons for this.

- First, it shapes your capacity for self-regulation.
- Second, it substantially affects your happiness.
- Third, it forms your inner model of what a close relationship should be.

Your ability to manage your emotions

The attachment system is designed not just to keep you safe from external dangers but also from the debilitating effects of distress and stress. Your primary attachment relationship is where you first learn how to regulate, or, more accurately, to co-regulate your own stress reaction, with your mother becoming your co-regulator. The brain has evolved to accommodate this kind of co-regulation as a way of conserving resources. But if a young child is forced to try to regulate itself, the brain develops and functions in non-optimal ways, absorbing and depleting the energy needed to explore and master the world.[2]

This kind of co-regulation will allow you not just to stay calm, but to keep your thoughts and behaviour organized and to stay focused on the task at hand, even as frustration and stress mount. In the process, you internalize the way your mother responds to you when you are distressed, and this becomes the way you manage your own distress and how you respond to the distress of others. The way a *Secure* attachment works is the model for successful self-regulation. You know how to steady yourself, and when you need guidance or help from someone else. After a stressful episode, you regain your composure quickly and resume what you have to do, with the least disruption to your functioning. You get back into a positive mood faster and stay in that mood for a longer period. Each time you succeed in managing your reaction to stress, it strengthens your self-regulation muscle. You learn that stress is not overwhelming or endless, it has a cycle, and you have learned how to manage that cycle. Moreover, you are able to soothe and help others.

An insecure attachment, on the other hand, puts an added burden on your capacity for emotional regulation. During the first three years of life, especially in the first year, if your need for closeness, physical comforting and reassurance is chronically frustrated, the effects are incorporated into the fabric of your nervous system, affecting the circuit wiring in an area at the front of the brain that modulates your emotional responses.[3]

Your capacity for joy and happiness

If you are securely attached to even one parent, your natural capacity for love, for interest and excitement, for good humour and wide-eyed wonder at the world is unfettered and amplified. This regular experience of positive emotions isn't just a 'feel-good' factor – it is a survival factor. Positive emotions serve a very specific survival function – they are designed to broaden your perspective, to open you up to others, to novel experiences and to opportunities. That ready positivity primes you to approach life in an open and positive way that will systematically build your personal and social resources.[4] This increases your store of resilience.

Insecure attachment, on the other hand, is rooted in the regular and daily experiences of anxiety, rejection, frustration, distress and the cognitive burden of building defences against these attachment wounds. Your natural zest for life, the urge to explore, to learn, to be exuberantly yourself, is undermined by self-doubt and anxiety. You worry, with good reason, about the likely absence of reliable support if you stumble or fail in your endeavours. This exacts a heavy cost on your capacity for joy and happiness.

Your blueprint for how relationships work

On the basis of your experiences in each attachment relationship, you form an internal model of that relationship that serves as a rough blueprint, a set of 'if-then' rules, about what is likely to happen if you seek closeness or try to exercise your autonomy. The blueprint includes which strategies are likely to work best, and which actions are likely to end well, or in anxiety, sadness or anger. On that basis you work out a set of default riding-instructions, so you don't have to work out each time how to react. This provides you with a certain sense of predictability and control.

Constructing an internal model is not a 'cold' mental process – you don't assemble all the facts and come to a cognitive judgement. The experiences you pay most attention to are 'hot' – those that arouse strong emotion when they happened, positive emotions like joy, relief, exhilaration, but also, and most particularly, those experiences that aroused fear, distress, sadness, anger, disappointment and betrayal, emotions that signal a threat to your relationship with someone who is crucial to your survival and well-being. That's why your brain registers them so strongly.[5] So your internal model pivots on *emotional* experiences – that is how it is laid down, and how it is activated.

Once organized, your internal model operates automatically and largely outside your awareness, acting as a lens that frames what you expect, what you seek out, what you avoid, and how you interpret and react to new experiences. Any new information tends to get fitted into your existing model – you 'see' what you expect to see. This means your internal model shapes the very stuff of self – your memories, your beliefs, and your assumptions about who you are, what to expect from other people and how close relationships work.

Each time you become aware of any stirring of desire for closeness, each time you are stressed or face a challenge, this is the dense network of memories that is triggered and that shapes your response. When what you expect is not good, it prompts you to mobilize your defences in advance, which then shape what you see and experience.

If you have a *Secure* attachment relationship with your mother, constructing an internal model of that relationship is an uncomplicated process. You communicate your needs to her, and she responds effectively. You incorporate these experiences into your internal working model, creating an expectation that in a close relationship, your needs are likely to be met; that it's okay to examine your own feelings, and safe to express them; and that you can be yourself without fear of rejection. You don't need to devote a lot of mental space to putting up defences to screen out, repress or 'forget' negative experiences and feelings. Instead, you can use all your psychological energy to invest in your relationships, and to get on with the work of childhood – exploring and learning.

You readily turn to others when you are stressed, under pressure, or in need of guidance and perspective. But you can also retreat to a solid core of security in yourself, be your own safe haven and secure base. That nexus of basic trust, that solid core of confidence, ease and openness, is the blessed legacy of a *Secure* attachment in childhood. Long before you have language or a capacity to think, the memories of that relationship are embedded, not just in your brain, but also in your body, your senses, your reflexes, your physical movements and body rhythms, priming you for emotional and sexual intimacy in adulthood.

This is not what happens if your relationship with your mother is insecure (*Anxious* or *Avoidant*). Constructing an internal model of that relationship is altogether more complicated. The first casualty is what happens to your own lived experience – what Bowlby described as knowing what you are not supposed to know and feeling what you are not supposed to feel.

On knowing what you're not supposed to know and feeling what you're not supposed to feel[6]

If your relationship with a parent is insecure, you are confronted by a troubling dilemma. You have learned that your bids for closeness or reassurance are routinely rejected, ignored or manipulated, and that the anxiety, sadness and anger that you then feel cannot be safely expressed without jeopardizing whatever closeness is allowed. You know you must repress these dangerous feelings, or disguise them as something else. As a result, you cannot construct an internal model of that relationship that is open, flexible or coherent. Instead, your feelings, and your body's physical reaction to those feelings, memories and what you are thinking and intending, are all separated off from each other.*

But the mental distortion does not end there. A parent who is insecure, wittingly or unwittingly exerts covert but strong pressure on you to deny or distort your own lived experience, and instead to impose their reality, their version of themselves as a parent, their version of you and the relationship between you. This is the only way they can preserve their own defences, by selectively attending to only certain signals that you send and ignoring those that would challenge or disturb their own idealized or confused version of themselves, and the defences they have built against the painful reality of their own experiences in childhood.[7]

This false view of reality eventually submerges your own and becomes the dominant inner model that you consciously operate from, even though your own reality still surfaces in troubling, confusing memories, in symptoms of extreme distress, and in sudden outbursts of anger. In time, it becomes your 'prototype' internal model of all close relationships, or your state of mind about attachment, your default position, especially when you are stressed and you revert to your earliest learning in life. And it is powerfully activated when you become a parent yourself, or in the deepest reaches of intimacy with a partner in adult life.

That's not to say that other working models you generate have no effect on your development. Even if your primary attachment relationship is insecure, a *Secure* attachment with your father, grandmother, or other caring adult, can provide a particular kind of confidence that can surface in specific contexts, or offer some protection against stress and adversity. Even if your security is compromised, there is this one island of security, a trace memory of how things could be.

---

* If your attachment relationship with your mother is *Disorganized*, you are unable to process or integrate your experiences of extreme fear. This disorganizes your mental functioning more generally, so it is virtually impossible to construct any coherent internal model of yourself, of the frightening parent, or the relationship between you.

Whatever happened, change is always possible

The *Secure* or insecure (*Avoidant* or *Anxious*) primary attachment you form in early childhood is not destiny, but it does set you on a particular path and continues to exert a powerful influence. However, the links between early attachment and later development are neither simple nor straightforward. What can be said with confidence is this: right throughout the life course, what happens at one stage of life has the strongest and most direct impact on the next immediate stage, and then gets modified by the experiences you have at that stage. There is always a tension between the forces for continuity, like your internal inner model, and the forces for change in your life.

The *circumstances* of your life can change, and *you* can change.

You get another chance in adolescence that opens up the possibility of becoming *Secure*. As a child you have little power to change the circumstances of your life, or how your parents care for you. And you don't yet have the cognitive capacity to examine, revise and update your internal working model in the light of your experiences in other relationships. But cognitive developments in adolescence, particularly the ability to think in a more abstract way, potentially enable you to do that, allowing you to compare your own family experiences with those of your friends and peers, to see patterns in what once seemed unrelated events. The same is true in adult life, if you find someone you can solidly depend on to love and support you and respond sensitively to your attachment needs.

The longer the history of an insecure attachment with a parent, the harder it may be to change the internal model, or your more general 'state of mind' about attachment. But change is. *always* possible, especially during periods of rapid change and transition in yourself, or in your closest relationships, or with skilled intervention from a professional psychotherapist who understands the workings of attachment.

The role of trust in your life

By the end of your first year, you have accumulated enough experiences in your primary attachment relationship to answer two fundamental questions that are dynamically related to one other:

Can I trust myself? Am I lovable enough, worthwhile enough, for the person I am most attached to now, and for others I may get close to, to be accepted and loved?

Can I trust the person I am most attached to now, and others I may get close to, to respond to me, especially when I feel vulnerable?

If the answer to both questions is a confident yes, then you have laid down the nucleus of a basic trust in yourself, and a readiness to trust others.

This is important for your development for a number of reasons.

- You are more likeable and more trustworthy – trust engenders trust, the classic positive spiral.
- A disposition to trust does not make you gullible – high-trust people react strongly and swiftly to being let down.
- You are readier to take calculated risks – trusting someone always means taking an initial risk because there is no 100 per cent certainty in life. The more practice you get at taking risks, the more you learn about yourself, and about other people, and the more opportunities you create for yourself.
- Trust helps you build a broader network of relationships, and that network then offers you more protection from being exploited – the more you reciprocate and engage with others, the more you come to believe that other people can be trusted, and the more trustworthy you become.

Trust, trustworthiness, taking a risk and engaging with others are deeply interlinked, and together create the perfect virtuous cycle.

But what if you cannot answer yes to the trust questions? Or what if your answers are hedged, contingent? Yes, you say, I will be accepted, *but* only *if* I am constantly trying to please people, or am always successful at what they think important, or if I never stumble. In this case, your disposition to trust has been compromised and replaced by mistrust.

It's adaptive to be 'on guard' with someone who has let you down. But mistrust, or chronic distrust, exacts a high cost, absorbing cognitive and emotional resources that you need in order to grow, develop and succeed in the world.

Mistrust carries with it a host of adverse consequences.

- You are viewed more negatively by others – you are seen as less likeable and less trustworthy, making your relationships more difficult. You come across as tense and guarded, on high alert for hidden agendas, betrayal or exploitation. This is off-putting.
- You are unwilling to take risks – until you get clear evidence that someone can be trusted, you are very reluctant to take a risk. So, you only 'trust' when you are 100 per cent certain – but in that unlikely circumstance, there is no risk, so there is no need for trust.
- You substitute control for trust – in the absence of trust, you try to control how other people behave. You are intolerant of any disagreement that you perceive as threatening that control. You try to control them by making insistent and excessive demands to prove they care about you, and you threaten major emotional upheavals if your demands are not met.
- Low trust makes you more gullible – this is one of the paradoxes of low trust. You have little practice in taking risks and learning how to judge trustworthiness and are less embedded in a network of relationships, so you run a higher risk of getting it wrong and of being let down. This is the experience you most dread, seeing it as an irreversible catastrophe, not as something that you can learn from.

A life well lived – what we learn from infancy

The principles of a life well lived – infancy			
Life stage	*Time frame*	*Developmental task*	*Psychological principle*
Infancy	birth–two years of age	trust or mistrust?	Be trustworthy

In Chapter 2, I set out the ten developmental tasks you undertake throughout your life course, as well as the guiding principles that emerge if things go well at each stage. In infancy, that's becoming open to the grace of trust, so it's a particularly vital stage. Your accepted belief with regard to trust or mistrust writes the first rough draft of your narrative about yourself and your life. Even though that rough first draft is based on your earliest experiences of attachment, and even though you have no conscious memory of them and no language in which to frame them, this first chapter of your story will become a core part of how you understand and manage yourself and your close relationships, and of how you think and plan for the future.

But you are also continually constructing and reconstructing your sense of self and your identity. You are not just moving yourself through the life course like a sealed package, you are also rewriting that narrative, and with it your sense of self.[8]

The quality of your early attachment relationship has shaped the quality of how you trust, especially in your close relationships. You can't make yourself trust, or stop a feeling of distrust – they happen spontaneously in the brain. But if you struggle with trust, there are steps you can take that, in time, will open you to the grace of trust.

Mistrust is different, however. It's a stance on life that develops from cumulative experiences of being rejected or manipulated by those you depended on. And that *can* be changed. It can change if you are lucky to be in a close relationship with someone who is worthy of your trust. It can also be changed by focusing on your own trustworthiness.

For anyone who struggles with trust, distrust or mistrust, it is important to understand that trustworthiness is a set of *behaviours*, and how you behave is under your own control. Being trustworthy works a kind of alchemy: the more you act in a trustworthy way, the more your own trust grows.

How to be trustworthy[9]

You can choose to practise the following behaviours in your day-to-day life.

BE PREDICTABLE
Be reliable and dependable, especially in situations where the stakes are high or someone feels vulnerable.

ACT WITH INTEGRITY
Be as good as your word, be credible when you make a promise. Do what you say you will do.

BE AUTHENTIC
Match what you say with how you think and feel – the audio synching with the video, as it were.

BE CARING
Care for someone and their concerns. It's hard to trust someone you feel has little interest in you or what matters to you.

BE COMPETENT IN A WAY THAT COUNTS
It's not possible to fully trust someone who lacks the specific ability that is critical to a particular situation, for example, a parent who is chaotic, or a professional who doesn't know what they are doing. And for those who *really* depend on you there are further requirements with regard to competence.

- *Be sensitive*: be attuned to their needs and bids for connection.
- *Be responsive*: be ready to respond to those needs whenever possible.

- *Be a safe haven*: be reliably there for those who feel vulnerable and in need of reassurance, protection or comforting.
- *Be a secure base*: be solidly at their back, so that they feel they can get on with their lives with confidence and energy.

TAKE YOUR CUE FROM HIGH-TRUST PEOPLE

Be ready to trust when there is no strong and compelling reason for not trusting someone. In the absence of such warnings, give them the benefit of the doubt, the chance to demonstrate *if* they are trustworthy, and maintain that trust until there is clear evidence that they *can't* be trusted. Then react immediately and strongly: withdraw your trust, so they are left in no doubt that this has jeopardized their relationship with you. And set the bar higher for regaining your trust.

STOP CONTROLLING

If you learned early in life that you could not trust those you most depended on, you may have substituted control for trust. It's a poor substitute. Trying to control other people has a chilling effect on close relationships, creating anxiety and conflict and ultimately undermining whatever trust is there. It's hard to catch yourself in the act of controlling because it's often disguised as an act of care, or a demand to be cared for. One clue is the intensity of your urge to control – the rapidly rising anxiety when you think that someone you depend on is moving out of your ambit of influence and withdrawing from you. Another clue is their reaction – the degree of anxiety or rage expressed by the person who feels controlled by you. The *only* way to stop the urge to control is to learn to control your own anxiety and understand its origin.

Sigmund Freud once remarked that it's not the original psychic pain that holds us back from life, it's the defences we develop to shut out the pain. Unless you find out what's beneath the scar tissue and locate the root of your pain, you will remain static.

7. *Early childhood*: Discovering your will

The major developmental task of early childhood is to develop a robust and secure autonomy, a confidence and ease in your developing self and in your capacity to manage the challenges ahead. That autonomy is nested and shaped within your ongoing attachment relationships with both your parents. You will rely on each of them to anchor you securely in yourself and in the world, as you change and things around you change. How they respond to that will teach you your first lessons on autonomy. How freely and confidently can you explore? What control can you exercise over the things that matter to you? How safe is it to openly express the torrents of anxiety, anger or disappointment that wash over you when your efforts to manage yourself or the world end in frustration?

There is a lot at stake. If you achieve a secure autonomy, you are ready and confident to tackle the twin challenges of learning and competence. If you don't, you are beset by shame and self-doubt. That is the major developmental task that now has to be resolved. The battle begins.

Becoming autonomous happens in overlapping waves, with key changes occurring through the ages of two to three years.

You discover yourself

At the moment of birth, you physically separated from your mother's body. Your psychological birth has to wait until your second year.

Towards the end of your first year, if you are put in front of a mirror with a dot of lipstick on your nose, you will not recognize the face in the mirror as your own, so you won't react to the dot. As far as you are concerned, you are looking at a baby with a funny dot on its nose, nothing to do with you. But when you turn two, you

recognize the face in the mirror is your *own*, and immediately touch the dot on your nose – '*Look, that's me!*'[1] This first experience of self-awareness coincides with your new ability to lay down your first conscious memories – the first building blocks of your identity.

Your capacity to resist develops

The capacity to resist is the first active expression of autonomy, and its last redoubt. Even when you cannot actively resist, you can resist the imposition of someone's will, at least in your mind. As an infant, you resist unwanted intrusion by stiffening your body and by looking and turning away. But when you are two, something exciting happens – you discover the magic power of the word 'no'. 'No' really makes things happen, it stops adults in their tracks. The word 'no' is rapidly followed by 'me' and 'mine', with equally gratifying results, allowing you to stake out your first little personal domain, although if you have siblings this is subject to frequent incursions.

Your will emerges

Resistance is good but will is brilliant. Consciously exerting your will makes its first appearance early in your second year. Now, when you want to do something, you are capable of turning that desire into an intention to act. The stronger your will, the more committed you become to making it happen. At the beginning, you are still amenable to high-quality distraction on your parents' part, but not for long. Now that you have the hang of this will thing, you want to put it to full use.

The experience of will is no small thing. It's the psychological equivalent of recognizing your own face: an intense experience of self. Without the experience of will, the very notion of self cannot be understood.[2] Hardly surprising, then, that you greet any parental opposition to your show of will as an unendurable affront to your new, but fragile sense of self. Will is central to a robust sense of autonomy. That does not mean that you are not open to influence. Autonomy lies in your capacity to freely accept that influence or reject it. But at the age of two, you are still practising how to do that.

You seek to exercise control

A sense of control over your life is at the core of autonomy. You exercise control in two ways. Your preferred strategy is exercising *primary control* – directly making things happen and trying to influence the people and events that are important to you. But the world does not always cooperate with what you want to happen, and then you have to switch from primary to *secondary control* – controlling yourself. You cannot achieve the goal you want, so you decide to switch to another, or you change your expectations, or your attitude – that is how you adapt to the reality that you face. Exercising secondary control is not passive acceptance or giving up, it's an active strategy to minimize losses and maximize your capacity to take up a new opportunity that *is* attainable.[3]

Throughout the life course, as your capacity and power increase, your ability to exercise primary control increases, peaks, plateaus, and then gradually decreases in advanced old age. So starting in middle age, you become steadily more willing to use secondary control. At every stage of life, striving for primary control but being able to switch to secondary control when needed maximizes your chances of happiness and well-being, and of success in life.[4] There are great rewards for persistence, but none for beating your head against a stone wall.

Resistance, will, choice and control are fundamental to autonomy. The task now is to learn to use each in a fluid and confident way, free from fear and self-doubt. To hold on to your sense of 'me' and 'mine', to govern yourself, while at the same time cooperating in this grand enterprise of being a member of a family and, in time, a society.

The arrival of the social emotions

In infancy, you are equipped with just the basic emotions of survival – fear, anger, joy. That's enough to signal: 'I need urgent help', 'You are frustrating me', 'This is making me happy.' In your second year, you develop the capacity for social or self-conscious emotions, designed to make group living possible: guilt, shame, empathy.[5]

Guilt

Guilt is the feeling triggered by knowing that you have done something you shouldn't have done, or failed to do what you should. It's your *own* judgement on your behaviour, either when you realize that what you've done is wrong or when somebody else points it out to you. Guilt can range from a feeling of mild regret all the way up to full, anguished self-blame. It is a heavy, painful feeling, designed to motivate you to change your behaviour, or to make amends. This 'after-the-fact' guilt is the most common form of the emotion when you are really young.

In time, you will develop the capacity for another kind of guilt – *anticipated* guilt. This is designed to work in advance, to stop you giving in to your worst impulses, because you can already imagine how bad you will feel if you do. It can also motivate you to start your first efforts at self-improvement, because you can also visualize how good and virtuous you will feel if you succeed.

Shame

This is triggered by *other people's* negative judgement of you. The harsher and more public the judgement, the greater the shame. Shame ranges all the way from mild embarrassment to burning humiliation, a feeling of being exposed, stripped naked, degraded. You feel 'small' – diminished and powerless. Shaming is the nuclear option, designed to punish somebody for behaving in a way that the community as a whole judges to be particularly destructive. It makes you feel excluded from the group. That's why being shamed evokes the most fundamental of all human fears – being isolated and abandoned by others. Unlike guilt, which is feeling bad about your behaviour, shame is more primitive, more fundamental. It's distress about your whole self, a feeling that you are a bad person, a 'failure'. It's an attack on your core identity – you 'lose face'. The resulting distress is more total, more overwhelming. And the reaction to shame is not to try to make amends but the strong urge to just disappear, to hide away or melt into the background.

Empathy

As a child, you have a lot of natural empathy, the ability to understand the emotional state of another person in a *feeling* way that triggers a sympathetic or helpful response. That makes empathy one of the most powerful and effective ways to teach you how to behave well with others, and how to have long-lasting and fulfilling relationships.

A toxic mix

Guilt, shame and empathy are powerful emotions. Parents use them to socialize children, but they come with a big health warning. Most parents report using 'after-the-fact' guilt to help a child understand the negative effect of their behaviour on others: 'David is crying because you hit him. You made him cry. It's not nice to hit people.' Delivered with moderate feeling and without too much anger, and combined with a call on a child's empathy, a small dose of guilt-induction can foster their understanding and sympathy. At too high a level, guilt can paralyse them.

Shame should never be used to punish a child, especially a young child, because it evokes the threat of being abandoned and isolated. When you are so utterly dependent on your parents to survive, you are acutely susceptible to any such threat. Shame also makes you feel dejected, helpless, alone, preoccupied by yourself. It cuts you off from other people. As a child, you can't process these feelings, so you withdraw, or you act out your distress and anger, creating new problems for yourself, and for your parents. And it crushes your confidence.

As a young child, shame and guilt are often triggered simultaneously. When you feel guilty about something, you are likely to own up, try to fix the problem, or make amends in some way. But when guilt and shame get mixed, it interferes with that response. You are more inclined to try to hide what you've done, delay owning up, or try to get away with it altogether. As a young child, your level of guilt and shame may be way out of proportion to any actual bad behaviour, and in high-stress situations you may even blame yourself for problems that have nothing at all to do with you, like a parent's illness, death, divorce or their abuse of you.

If your parents frequently make you feel guilty or ashamed, it creates a simmering resentment that will undermine your long-term relationship with them. Worse, it can chronically undermine your ability to distinguish your actual intentions from their negative judgement of what you intended – a key component of autonomy. If you are a girl, you are at particular risk of chronic guilt, especially if your mother suffers from depression. You are likely to blame yourself for her sadness or irritability, and for your inability to make her feel better. Your mother is also likely to blame herself for feeling depressed and for not being able to respond to you, modelling a self-blaming response and further compounding the problem.

Even empathy for others must be moderated and balanced by compassion for yourself. If your natural empathy is manipulated by a needy parent, and you happen to be a competent child, too much empathy can cause you to adopt a compulsive caretaking response that over a long period will undermine your well-being. If you have a more fragile temperament, an excess of empathy to a parent's distress may evoke a matching and disabling distress in yourself and blur the boundaries between you and them.

If this becomes a pattern, it can lead to a form of self-silencing – swallowing your own feelings in an attempt to maintain harmony and avoid conflict in relationships.[6] This pattern can become well established by late in middle childhood, and continue into adolescence and adulthood, making you highly susceptible to false beliefs about your responsibility for other people's problems, or problems in your relationships, a tendency that can dog you right throughout your life, confusing what is happening and wearing you down.

Chronic experiences of guilt, shame and excessive empathy are a toxic mix, powerful internal pressures that can control you and that are harder to resist than external pressure. They emerge in many forms – in patterns of debilitating anxiety, perfectionism, harsh self-criticism, chronic need for approval, compulsions or addictions. These forces are not just controlling you, it is possible you will use them to control other people, as a way of managing your own pressurized inner state.

Doing what you like to do, and doing what you have to do

Early childhood is when you get to grips with the two powerful motivational systems that determine a large part of what we do.

- *Intrinsic motivation*: doing something because you find it inherently interesting and enjoyable.
- *'Carrots-and-sticks' motivation*: being incentivized by the prospect of reward, or the avoidance of sanctions.

Autonomy is key to the optimal functioning of both.

Intrinsic motivation is the Rolls Royce of motivational systems. When you do something just because you find it interesting or enjoy the challenge, it's an exercise in autonomy, but it collapses if that sense of autonomy is undermined by any efforts to control or improve what you are doing. That's a big loss, because intrinsic motivation leads to higher quality performance and achievement in every domain of life, including school and work. You learn and master things more effectively and are more pleasurably absorbed in the task. It is central to creativity, and to happiness, well-being and a stronger sense of self. Being intrinsically motivated is a form of optimal human experience, and a major source of enjoyment and vitality at every stage of life.[7]

But not everything in life is inherently enjoyable or interesting, at least initially. There are things you have to do for your own safety and well-being, and rules you have to follow to make group living possible, your first group being your family. That is where the second motivational system comes in, 'carrots-and-sticks', driven by *external* incentives – the prospect of a reward, or the avoidance of disapproval, loss of privileges, or punishment. And the least effective 'stick' is physical punishment.[8]

Why physical punishment doesn't work

Physical punishment carries a host of problems. For a young child, punishment may *look* like it's working. The child may cry and promise they will never do the bad thing again, but they are capable of only the most fragile kind of self-control. In the moment, temptation, anger or competitiveness can trigger misbehaviour *before* they make the cognitive link to the likely consequences.

The second problem is that punishment breeds resentment, fear and anger towards the punishing parent, so a child is not likely to internalize the values that the parent is trying to instil. Instead, they may internalize the parent's aggression. This can lead to them behaving aggressively towards other children, acting out with their parents and at school, and can lead to chronically low self-esteem.

While it may achieve immediate compliance, this is at a big cost to a child's developing autonomy and sense of self. Being hit or manhandled is a grievous loss of bodily autonomy.

But surely mild physical punishment like a smack on the bottom doesn't do much harm? You may ask. The problem is that one parent's definition of mild punishment is another's definition of abuse, and when sufficiently enraged or stressed, what started as mild punishment can get out of hand.

Do carrots-and-sticks work?

Aside from physical punishment, yes, they do work – most of the time. Incentives are powerful motivators. But carrots-and-sticks and intrinsic motivation turn out to be very uneasy bedfellows. Once the prospect of incentives is introduced, the vital and creative force of intrinsic motivation is undermined, or even destroyed.

Once incentives are introduced, you are being driven by something external, and not by something autonomous that comes from inside you. The incentive is now *controlling* you, and it kills off your inherent interest and enjoyment in the activity. Feeling controlled kills off autonomy, and without autonomy, intrinsic motivation collapses. Your attention automatically switches to the outcome, so your focus becomes more narrow and urgent – finish the task and pick up the reward.[9] As a consequence of that narrowing, it is harder to think laterally and to 'break set' – a critical component of innovation and creativity.

The ability to motivate yourself to do things, not just because you want to or have to but also because it is the right thing to do, is a key step in becoming your own autonomous person, capable of committed action – taking charge or 'owning' what you do and seeing it through. That commitment is the basis for the kind of vital engagement that drives the highest quality learning and performance – in school, in sport and in work. What was once prompted by external has now been fully transformed into self-determined self-regulation. When autonomy wins the day, you have set the scene for the growth of competence.

Controlling and scaffolding

In early childhood, you start the business of learning to become competent in a way that readies you for the world outside the family, and you rely heavily on your parents to help you do that. When people try to help others to learn something, they tend to adopt a controlling style or a scaffolding style – the difference between the two hinging on the level of respect accorded to autonomy.

Controlling

A controlling style is characterized by intrusion. This does not include the normal stream of parental requests, instructions and warnings that children are remarkably adept at screening out. The more damaging kind of intrusion is being directed and controlled in a way that needlessly ignores your own will and choice, and disrupts the natural flow of learning. If your mother adopts a controlling style, a lot of what she says to you is directed at getting you to comply.* She frequently interrupts what you are saying, and imposes her interpretation on the experiences you are describing. She is critical of the way you do things, fussing about mistakes you make. When you sense you are failing at

---

* Most of the studies in this area involve mothers and children, reflecting the fact that mothers are most likely the major caretakers day-to-day.

something, you become nervous and less coordinated and decrease your efforts. It's counter-productive because controlling undermines a child's motivation at *all* levels of ability. More generally, a mother's urge to control is less a response to a child's need than to some need in herself.

Most often, a mother adopts a controlling style because she believes that she has to push you to succeed and becomes ego-involved in what you are doing. Every success and failure, in her eyes, becomes a judgement of her own worth – how intelligent or incompetent she is, how good or bad a parent she is. Her self-esteem is at stake and her urge to interfere and control is her effort to ward off that threat. The paradox is this: she is now *less* likely to succeed because her focus has shifted to herself, and she is less attentive to you or the task at hand. When you are struggling with a task, or she feels under scrutiny from other adults, she becomes even more controlling, and more likely to intrude and direct your learning. You are likely to describe her as 'always telling me what to do', not encouraging you to make your own decisions. This creates a lot of tension for her, and for you.[10]

Scaffolding

If your mother adopts a scaffolding style, she tries to minimize the need to intrude. She encourages the choices you make, and your attempts at mastery. She is more attuned to your needs and preferred way of doing things, allowing herself to be 'led' by you. She converses with you differently. She listens to what you are saying and tends not to interrupt. When you run into difficulty or look for her help, she responds by offering information that will help you, or makes a constructive suggestion.

She tends to ask questions that are open, enabling: 'What do you think?', 'Can I help you in any way?' She acknowledges your opinions and perspective, and praises what you've done. But she says that only *after* you've done it well, affirming your own efforts to achieve the desired result. Your interactions have a positive, relaxed, mutual tone.

As you advance into childhood, a scaffolding approach promotes your capacity for deep learning.[11] Research shows that being put under pressure diminishes the quality of a child's learning. In one study, a group of school-age children were asked to read a passage from a book. Some were put under pressure by being told they would be asked to recall what they had read and answer questions about it. Others were not told that. When tested later, there was no difference in what the two groups of children recalled, but those who were *not* pressured showed superior conceptual learning. They had a better understanding of the main points of what they had read and, weeks later, had retained more of that information. Pressure to perform narrows your focus to the *detail* of what you are learning, which undermines deep learning. Again, this early experience of how you absorb information is something that may be shaping your life to this very day.

8. *Early childhood:* The gift of autonomy

In early childhood, attachment is still a work-in-progress. Whereas, in infancy, it was mainly about developing a secure closeness, a basic trust in at least one person and in your own worth, attachment in early childhood is about using that closeness to build a secure autonomy — a robust confidence in yourself, in your ability to explore, manage challenges, and find the optimal balance between risk and caution as you do. Your attachment relationship with each of your parents is the arena in which you learn to do all that, and the quality of each attachment will shape the quality of your developing autonomy, how much you relish and enjoy the enterprise, and how competently you conduct yourself.

Autonomy is not just about *outer* exploration of the world. Sometime in your third year, it's also about *inner* exploration — exploring your feelings, particularly your negative feelings. As a child, you are completely dependent on your parents to help you do that, particularly the parent immediately at hand when the upset happens. For most of you, that is likely to be your mother, and mothers are generally seen by children as being better at, more interested in, this kind of emotional co-regulation.

You rely on her to step in before your mounting frustration or discontent overwhelms you, tipping your attachment system *away* from exploration and towards seeking safety in closeness. If that becomes a pattern, it will undermine your need to develop the optimal and fluid balance between autonomy and closeness that you need to become competent.

If your attachment with her is *Secure*, your play is enthusiastic, engrossed, marked by long bouts of concentration.*

* Note that the descriptions here of *Secure*, *Avoidant* and *Anxious* attachments are prototypes or 'pure' types, with many children and mothers interacting in less

If your attachment with your mother is *Avoidant*, you explore and play independently, but with little ongoing interaction between you. You are often using play as a way to distract yourself from your untended feelings of sadness and anger at the lack of a satisfying closeness with your mother.

If your attachment with her is *Anxious*, your exploration and play have a passive, listless, aimless quality. You choose activities that require less cognitive complexity to master. When you run into difficulty, you give up more easily. Your mother is generally too preoccupied by her own needs to notice when you need help or to show any sustained interest in what you are doing. When she does respond, her focus is on your frustration and distress, or her own, rather than encouraging you to solve the problem. She complains that you are making too much of a fuss, saying things like, 'Oh stop playing with the blocks if you are getting that upset about it.' She rarely encourages you to explore and constrains you by issuing frequent warnings that direct attention back to herself and her own needs: 'You won't be able to do that and then you'll want me to come over and do it for you and I've enough on my plate with everything else going on around here.' Her responses do not encourage or promote competence.

Loving dangerously

As you and your mother wrestle with the challenges of autonomy, with perfect timing your father assumes a new role and importance in your life. The more psychologically accessible your father is, the more positively and warmly he engages with you, the more you will benefit. And yet, the precise role of fathers, apart from being a 'good provider', remains opaque.

In many areas, your father and mother behave in much the same way in how they interact with you. Fathers can be as attentive and

---

extreme ways. The degree of sensitivity, intrusion on autonomy, and rejection, is the key differentiator between *Secure* and insecure forms of attachment.

responsive to your needs as mothers can, equally affectionate and engaged, ready to praise, willing to teach you how to do things. They can show the same readiness to cooperate, to see things from your perspective, to provide information attuned to your level of cognitive development, to motivate you by suggesting things you are likely to accept. But your father and mother can also match each other in their level of insensitivity; in being intrusive and controlling and pressuring you to achieve; in ridiculing your efforts; or being coolly detached, indifferent, critical, punitive and rejecting.[1]

Despite the many similarities, a father's role is different from a mother's in subtle but important ways, and his effect on your development is unique. Most of all, fathers play with you. Right across cultures, when fathers spend *any* time with their children, they play with them, rather than do more routine caregiving. And their play is different from a mother's – more challenging and physical, more vigorous, more rough-and-tumble compared to the quieter, more verbal play of mothers. They issue more direct orders, tease you more, encourage you to compete and take risks.*

Fathers, the psychoanalysts used to say, love dangerously. Their expression of love is more contingent, you have to work harder to achieve it. When they see you do something well, that love brims over in a kind of inarticulate pride and delight. They seem to sense that, in the safety of their presence, it's satisfyingly exciting for you to do things that your mother might consider too rough, or even dangerous. It's harder to read the relationship your father has with you, and its effect may only become clear to you in adulthood.

In the case of your father, it's the quality of your attachment to him in your second year that counts. The best overall predictor of a *Secure* attachment in later childhood and adolescence is the combination of a *Secure* attachment with your mother in your first year, and with your father in your second.

When fathers are supportive of their autonomy, their sons make

---

* Fathers have always encouraged their sons to 'act like a boy'. Nowadays, when men have daughters, many become more attuned to the whole issue of gender, and more supportive of their daughter's competitive instincts.

greater progress in their development between the ages of four and eight, suggesting that fathers' relationship with their children, particularly their sons, is critical as they make the transition from the family to the wider world. The more fathers serve as sensitive, supportive and challenging companions to their children, the more emotionally competent their children will become, the greater will be the gains in their self-reliance right up to the age of nine, and the higher will be their achievement in reading and maths.

A father who is sensitive, supportive and challenging encourages you to act autonomously. This has a significant and unique effect on your achievement in school, especially if you are a boy, predicting greater increases in self-reliance, right up to the age of nine.

What if you are not reared in a traditional 'Mum and Dad' family? The attachment discussions for heterosexual couples apply to all parents – gender and family make-up don't matter – it's all about availability, support, the right basis for attachment.

Autonomy or self-doubt?

As this second stage of your life comes to an end and you enter childhood proper, you can now answer two more fundamental questions.

Am I the kind of person who can cope with life competently, and is worthy of support and help?

Are my parents, and other people, likely to give me that support and help?

If the answer to both questions is yes, then you have built the inner core of a secure and flexible autonomy that will give you the confidence and resilience needed to face the challenges ahead.

If the answer is no, the result is an inner core of self-doubt, a chronic second-guessing of your own capacities and experiences.

If the only support on offer was controlling and intrusive, you retreat to a lonely self-sufficiency. Or, alternatively, you become confused about the limits of your own power, developing a false bravado, a controlling style, believing yourself to be more powerful than you are, yet remain beset by a chronic fear that you will be exposed and shamed. If that intrusion was combined with overprotection, you may lapse into a pervasive sense of passivity and powerlessness.

If your autonomy has been nurtured, your own way of doing things valued, and you have been encouraged to set your own direction, you are now in a strong position to keep growing and developing. You trust your own decisions more, you take the initiative, and you are more creative. You are more capable of mobilizing and organizing the right emotions when faced with a challenge, which is the essence of self-motivation.[2] You have learned, with your parents' support, to integrate your negative emotions into uninterrupted, concentrated bouts of exploring and learning, carrying on even when in a relatively poor mood. You can put in the effort required. You have learned the rudiments of taking the initiative boldly, but safely. All of these skills position you well for the challenges ahead in middle childhood and adolescence.

The gift of autonomy

Autonomy, like trust, is the gift that keeps on giving. It has numerous benefits that enhance your life and relationships throughout all future stages of the life course.

YOU ARE HAPPIER

When your need for autonomy is met, your day-to-day mood is more positive, even if the external circumstances of your life are difficult.

You are more vitally engaged in your life, your self-esteem is higher, and your health and emotional well-being increase. You are more empathic, ready to respect others' autonomy, so your close relationships are happier.[3]

YOU HAVE A SENSE OF INNER FREEDOM

You feel free to think your own thoughts, and to choose whether or not to express them. You are better able to resist your impulses.

If you cannot resist the urge to do something, because you are susceptible to crippling guilt, or anxiety about disapproval, or agitation, then your response is compulsive, not free.

YOU ARE MORE ENGAGED AND
COMMITTED TO WHAT YOU DO

Because you are self-directed, you have a stronger sense of agency and ownership. When you make a commitment, you are more whole-hearted about it, approaching it with unconflicted energy.

You believe that your individual contribution matters. This is the best antidote to the boredom and alienation that hollows out enjoyment in your work.

YOU LEARN MORE EFFECTIVELY

Not only do you learn more effectively but the learning is deeper, more conceptual and longer lasting: your thinking is more open and flexible, and your capacity for problem-solving is better.

YOU ARE BETTER AT SELF-CHANGE

When you act autonomously, your efforts to change your own behaviour – for example, to lose weight, develop better habits, or recover from addictions of any kind – are more persistent and successful.

YOU HAVE A STRONGER, FLEXIBLE SENSE
OF YOUR OWN IDENTITY

You are more open and ready to question your assumptions, more open to new information about yourself, and more active in using that information to help you direct your life. You see what unites you to other people, but also what makes you different and unique. You become a self-explorer, better at making strategic decisions about your life, more proactive.

YOU ARE MORE AUTHENTIC

Autonomy is a pre-condition for authenticity, because being autonomous means there is unity between the inside (how you are) and the outside (how you act). You stand behind what you say and own what you do, so your actions are in tune with what you genuinely feel, believe and value.

In some situations, where you have little power, you may have to disguise your real feelings, but if you have to do this too often, the psychological price is high. You feel angry and powerless, with a lurking sense of shame about betraying yourself.

YOU ARE MORE CREATIVE

Not only are you more productive, but the quality of your performance is higher: this has been demonstrated right across the world of work – in the arts, in education, in sport, in business, in technology.[4] For example, if you are an athlete, autonomy is associated with high performance, more determination and persistence in training, especially after suffering a setback, more positive mood, more energy and vitality, and you run a lower risk of burnout, depression, eating disorders and other stress-related symptoms. And you stay longer in the sport.[5]

YOU CAN BETTER WITHSTAND GROUP PRESSURE

If you find yourself under intense pressure to act in ways that you do not believe are right, or you are personally attacked, rejected or isolated by others in a group situation, the stronger your sense of autonomy, the better able you are to withstand the pressure, detach yourself from the toxic dynamics and survive without psychological damage.

Autonomy is at the heart of your moral compass. It steadies you up, allowing you to keep an 'inner hold' on yourself when under sustained group pressure.[6]

YOU HAVE A STRONGER SENSE OF PURPOSE

If you are autonomous, you feel you are driving not just the organization of your life but its overall direction, and that is what gives meaning and purpose to your life, connecting you to something bigger than yourself.

Maybe there is a trace memory of that primal unity of once being part of your mother's body, because it seems to be written into our deep nature to seek that experience again – in a purpose, a cause, an idea, a mission, or a spirituality that is bigger than us.

YOU CAN DEAL MORE EFFECTIVELY WITH ADVERSITY

Autonomy is your ultimate defence against the inevitable losses, setbacks and crises you will face in life. Even in the midst of the most extreme suffering, it is what Viktor Frankl, the psychiatrist and concentration camp survivor, called the 'last freedom'. Everything can be taken from you, he said, except the human freedom to choose your attitude and how you respond in any given set of circumstances.[7]

In contrast, if your sense of autonomy is weak, you are more influenced by what others expect of you, readier to conform to what you regard as 'normal'. This kind of conforming identity is associated with a high need for structure, a low tolerance of uncertainty and ambiguity, and more avoidance of problems and challenges. None of these self-defensive strategies equip you to thrive in the new self-directed life course.

A life well lived – what we learn from early childhood

The principles of a life well lived – early childhood			
Life stage	*Time frame*	*Developmental task*	*Psychological principle*
Early childhood	two–six	autonomy or self-doubt?	Be bold

If everything goes reasonably well in early childhood, the key psychological principle you learn in the course of completing your second developmental task is to be bold.

Your sense of autonomy, be it strong or weak, puts you on a particular developmental track. But as with all life stages, at *any* point in your development you can change trains. How you are is always embedded in a particular pattern of interaction between yourself and the people who are most important to you, and you stay the same only as long as those conditions also stay the same. If your parents learn to support your autonomy, the pathway changes. When it comes to developing a secure autonomy, even if things did not go well in childhood with your parents, other opportunities will present themselves – particularly in adolescence, and again at midlife.

Autonomy and risk-taking are conjoined twins

There is rarely certainty in life, so the only way to live and grow into the fullness of who you can be is to take a calculated risk. Otherwise, your life will be governed by anxiety and self-doubt; you will miss opportunity after opportunity; and you will never learn to manage your life competently.

Will taking some risks make you feel anxious, exposed and vulnerable? Yes. But taking a risk is the only way to release yourself from the isolation of avoidance or the mental muddle that comes from trading your own autonomy for the doubtful gain of avoiding disappointment or criticism. The longest-lasting regrets in life are not about doing things that didn't turn out as well as you'd hoped, they're about not doing the things you could have done. Fortune favours the brave.

TAKE THE LEAP

Open yourself to someone you can trust, a willing partner or a friend, or book a few sessions with a therapist. Will you experience a rush of anxiety? You will. But to borrow a phrase: feel the fear and do it anyway.[8] The moment of acute anxiety will pass, and your pent-up longings will gush out, sometimes in a torrent of sobs, but often in a huge sigh of relief.

RESIST BEING CONTROLLED

Sometimes you are being controlled by someone you depend on who uses disapproval or coercion to shut down your opinions or stop you expressing how you feel. In a relationship with someone who is controlling, you are being bound by *their* rules, and when you break a rule, the threat is rejection or exclusion. As a child, you have little power to change those rules, but in adulthood you do, if you learn the 'if-then' rules.

In every relationship there are 'if-then' rules that play out in four moves.

- *If* I do this (A)
- *Then* this is their reaction (B)

- And this is how I feel (C)
- And this is what I do (D)

For example, if you say something that displeases someone else, then they react angrily, then you feel anxious or full of self-doubt, then you try to retract what you said – you are being controlled by their anger and your need for their approval. You can't change A unless you extinguish your autonomy, and you can't change B. You can't do much about C. But you can change D – you can resist and stick to your guns. That depends on learning to tolerate your own anxiety about their reaction or losing their approval.

A controlling sequence is a tightly choreographed dance, but it takes two to tango. So change your moves. Dust off your capacity to disagree respectfully, to resist calmly, and to assert your own view with confidence. You have nothing to lose but your fear. (This is assuming that you really don't have anything to fear, like a violent or abusive partner. If you do, you need to seek help, *now*.)

When you feel under pressure or full of self-doubt, visualize someone who really cares for you and has your interests at heart: that simple mental action has an immediate effect – your motivation increases, you concentrate harder, and you persist longer in trying to solve the problem facing you.[9]

RESPECT THE AUTONOMY OF OTHERS

Like trusting others, this also works a kind of alchemy. The more sensitively you respond to someone else's need for autonomy, the more attuned you become to your own autonomy needs. Be open to challenge from those who depend on you, so they feel free to disagree with you and argue their point. The most frequent complaints adolescents make about their parents are that they don't listen and they give too much unasked-for advice. Instead, listen attentively to the raw material of adolescent experience, and help them shape it into an authentic and coherent moral framework. Try asking open-ended questions. Allow them to make their own decisions in a way that matches their developmental stage, and when they mess up, try giving feedback without criticism.

Above all, don't take their opposition personally. Think of it as a necessary and legitimate contest about domains of influence, otherwise they will never learn to make their own decisions and form their own values. The mistake is to take fright, to be shocked by the first stirrings of rebellion and take it as a rejection of you or what you hold dear. Instead, hear it for what it is: 'How about not making assumptions about me, because I'm changing?' Use it as an opportunity to test your own assumptions about yourself and what you believe and value.

9. *Middle childhood:* Joining the company of children

Between the ages of three and five, your vital interest in friends and peers coincides with a dramatic acceleration in your social and cognitive competence. Your play becomes more organized and social, and you begin to master the rudiments of friendship and belonging. You get better at relating to other children, one-on-one and in small groups. Your thinking becomes more complex and flexible, and you develop a new cluster of cognitive, social and emotional skills.

You can now marshal your feelings, thoughts and behaviour into a reasonably effective course of action. You can make simple plans with a companion, and carry out your plans, but you still struggle to see around corners so it's hit-and-miss a lot of the time. You acquire more self-understanding and self-control. You compare yourself to others. And as your imaginative capacity develops, your sense of 'This is who I am' is amplified by 'This is who I could be', usually along the lines of stronger, more beautiful, better at football, or a character in a far more royal and dramatic life than yours.[1]

The spurt in your social and emotional capacity will prove as important as your cognitive advances in determining your readiness for school. The more socially and emotionally competent you are, the more positive your attitude to preschool, and later 'big school'; the more successful you are in adapting to the demands and routines, the better your relationship with teachers and schoolmates, and the higher your academic achievement.

Between the ages of five and seven there is a further acceleration in your development. By the age of seven, you are ushered into the wide, peaceful plains of middle childhood.

For most children and their parents, middle childhood is a golden era. This used to be a stage that was fairly insulated from the wider world. Now, you have access to TV, and at some point may have access to a smart phone or the internet, so the boundaries that once separated childhood from that wider world are thinner; by the age of ten, many children are already fantasizing about becoming celebrities.

This is the stage of childhood when you develop what Erikson called 'industriousness' – a term that captures the *busyness* of this stage, and the deep pleasure of feeling useful.[2]

You already see yourself as an apprentice, an adult-in-the-making, although adulthood is still a distant, foggy prospect. You like being near people who *know* things and who know how to *do* things. You identify with them and try to imitate them. But most of all, you want to make things, and to make them perfectly. Outdoors, you build elaborate structures with pieces of wood and debris. Indoors, you create whole universes of Lego, Little Pony, Barbies. When you survey your work, you experience a burst of pride, and a contentment that is new. As you develop, you like to play games that require strategic thinking and elaborate rules that you can play alone or with a group.

You come to understand that emotional reactions are not just caused by events, but by how they are interpreted, and that people can have different emotional reactions to the same event. You become aware that you can experience mixed emotions and can be simultaneously happy and sad, angry and nervous. You can distinguish what you really feel inside from what you decide to show outside, and the difference between real and pretend emotion. When you and a sibling are in dispute and a parent intervenes, you are not above faking crying to boost your side of the story. But you are also getting better at seeing things from someone else's perspective. In short, you are now ready to join the 'company of children'.[3]

Friends and peers

The 'company of children' has two divisions: friends and peers.[4] Peers are those you identify as 'people like me', usually defined by age and gender. Friends are a sub-category of peer relationships, those with whom you share a special kind of mutual liking and closeness.

Friends and peers are alike in many ways, sources of invaluable advice about the laws and rules in the republic of children. Both are tuned in to things that parents think unimportant, or that are forbidden. Both provide the opportunity to develop your thinking, social skills and your ability to express and manage your emotions. Both require ongoing negotiation about closeness and status – the two underlying dimensions in every important relationship.[5]

During all but the briefest social encounters, your brain is automatically monitoring two things: closeness and status. Is the other person interacting with you in a way that is building closeness, conveying liking, understanding or appreciation, and decreasing the emotional distance between you? Or are they pushing you away? You are also monitoring status. Is the way they are interacting with you conveying respect, treating you as an equal? Or is it conveying disrespect, contempt, putting you in a 'one-down' position? The more important the relationship, the more vigilant the monitoring of closeness and status. Whatever judgement you make sets in motion a chain of positive or negative interactions that will have an immediate effect on the outcome of the interaction. If repeated often enough, it will eventually affect the quality and endurance of a relationship.

In the normal course of events, when things are going reasonably well, we are generally prepared to give someone the benefit of the doubt. Once negativity begins to mount, however – when there are too many tense or disappointing interactions – the ratio of positive to negative behaviour falls below 3:1, and we are readier to place even ambiguous behaviour into the negative box.[6]

In friendships, particularly female ones, you are more attuned to closeness than status and monitor it carefully, quickly picking up any decrease in that closeness, any signs of emotional distancing. You are adept at measuring the emotional temperature in a friendship, like a friend becoming 'cool' towards you. But with friends, concerns about status are never far below the surface, the tension surfacing in increased competitiveness.

In peer groups, everybody is more attuned to status, although closeness is still significant. The measure of closeness is having an assured place in the group, a feeling of belonging. The measure of status is popularity and acceptance, based on the *opinion* the group has of you. When you socialize in groups, there is more intense rivalry and competition. Reciprocity is strictly monitored. You do things for each other, but you keep a close eye on ensuring there's an equal balance in the exchange of favours. Moving from strict exchange of favours to a more generous give-and-take is a sign of growing trust, that you are investing in a more long-term close relationship, a process that will become crucial in your love relationships in adulthood. But most of all, it is with your close friends that you understand and learn about the importance of reciprocity, mutual dependence, influence and support. Those four inter-related elements constitute the 'deep structure' of friendship.[7]

'Like me' and 'not like me'

You learn a different set of social skills in a peer group than you do in your friendships. You could say that peers teach the honours course in group skills: how to read social signals and respond appropriately; the right way to enter a new peer group and learn its rules, codes and special language; how to avoid social embarrassment; the acceptable limits of teasing; how to cooperate and how to stand up for yourself; how best to exert influence; the importance of allies and the art of coalitions.

As your social network expands, you learn how to negotiate different group norms and how to move flexibly between groups. You will discover, often the hard way, which thoughts to keep private and which to share with peers, what's okay to say at home and what should be kept strictly within the peer group. As you move well into middle childhood, you begin to try out new roles or personas in different peer groups, a key part of finding your own identity.

Peer groups answer the basic human need for belonging, the need to feel part of a group 'like me'. But there is also a corresponding wariness of the 'out-group', those you judge as 'not like me'. At every stage of life, we instinctively organize ourselves into actual and mental groups of 'people like us'.[8]

We identify with and form an actual or mental group on every conceivable basis with people who look like us. Who are the same age or gender, who come from the same ethnic group, or the same town, city, county or country. Who support the same sports team as we do, or have a common interest or grievance. This feeling of 'groupness' can be created on the flimsiest basis, for example, with fellow passengers delayed at an airport.[9] Once formed, the group then begin to exaggerate anything that distinguishes them from other people, and there is a growing pressure to conform to group standards. They may go on to discriminate in favour of *their* group, and against the out-group.

The safety, solidarity, mutual help and comfort that come from feeling part of a group is the upside. The downside is the hostility often shown to the out-group.

Separate worlds: Me Jane. You Tarzan. Keep out!

Children's mutual attraction to children of the same gender, and the corresponding wariness of the other, starts early.[10] From the age of two, girls show a strong preference for the company of other girls, and by the age of five that preference is even stronger. By the age of three, boys are starting on their separate journey.

By the time children attend playschool, over 80 per cent are spending nearly three times as much time with same-sex friends as they do with opposite-sex friends. By the age of six, they are spending *eleven* times more time with them, and rarely venture into a mixed-group without the safety net of a same-sex friend.[11] And this strict segregation won't change until the age of eleven, or the onset of puberty.

When it comes to explaining the way boys and girls opt to segregate themselves from each other like this, there is much scratching of heads. There is no evidence at all that parents or teachers encourage them to avoid each other. Moreover, even when they actively intervene and encourage them to 'play together', the avoidance persists. This segregation may have evolved as a way to avoid premature sexual relationships, or as the way for boys and girls to learn and practise gendered behaviour. Or it may simply reflect the fact that they like to do different things.*

---

* Individual and group differences observed in how boys and girls behave are a matter of degree. The gender spectrum is very wide. Most boys tend to cluster at

It's not just boys' rough play that girls don't like, they are also averse to their frequent bids for dominance. The way girls successfully influence each other and achieve dominance simply does not work with boys, as we will see shortly. When girls find themselves competing with boys for a common and valued resource, they often lose out.

This segregation into in-groups and out-groups has been observed by social scientists in all cultures, although the degree of separation varies, depending on the culture.[12] The only circumstances in which it does not happen is when there aren't enough children in an area to permit gender preferences. In this case, children will settle for whatever playmate is available. When a social group of boys or girls is formed, each consolidates and forms a distinct group 'culture'.[13]

BOY CULTURE

Boys' style of interaction is constricting, designed to get the other boy to concede a point or withdraw, which has the effect of shortening the interaction, or derailing it altogether. Their overriding motivation is not to show weakness or be put in a 'one-down' position in the status hierarchy, thus jeopardizing whatever idea or territory is being defended. Yet, despite all this, boys greatly enjoy each other's company, function well in a group, and the group works effectively. Their networks of friends and peers are more integrated than girls'. In their peer group, they are all more likely to be friends, or to become friends with each other.

GIRL CULTURE

Girls organize themselves into small groups of two or three close friends. They play in smaller, more private spaces, their play active but not rough. They prefer interacting one-to-one. The ability to maintain close relationships, to display interdependence, is a central part of their self-definition. They use 'we' or 'let's' a lot – signalling togetherness and equality. Compared to boys, they make more suggestions and

---

one end of the spectrum, most girls on the other. But there are many exceptions, and gender behaviour is always a matter of probability, likelihood.

agree with each other more. Their style of interacting is *enabling*, designed to keep the interaction going, and thus develop closer and more intimate relationships with each other.

Girls try to influence each other but rely more on persuasion than force. They rarely issue direct orders to each other, behaviour likely to provoke an accusation of being 'bossy'. When girls are hostile to other girls, it usually takes the form of negative gossip and exclusion rather than outright aggression.

In girls' and boys' groups, the highest status child is the one who is listened to most, who takes the lead, who is good at organizing and gets things going. There the similarity ends. In boys' groups, the highest status is at the top. In a girls' group, the highest status is in the *middle* of a tight network, having the most connections and close relationships where they can exert influence.

The alpha girl is the one the other girls confide in most, and most often ask for advice. For the other girls in the group, their status is measured by how emotionally and socially close they are to the alpha girl. But that kind of subtle emotional and social closeness is liable to change, so girls' hierarchies are less stable than boys' are. Social power and influence can increase, or ebb away, with no obvious outward conflict, a source of much female anguish – and Schadenfreude. Bids for dominance create more tension than they do in a boys' group.

THE PRICE OF DOMINANCE[14]

In one experiment, a group of boys and a group of girls aged between four and five were observed as they played with a toy film-viewer that showed cartoons. The viewer was designed in such a way that only one child could view the cartoons at a time, and access depended on securing the cooperation of the others. In both groups, a dominant child soon emerged, and got to spend the most time looking at the cartoons. But the way that dominance was achieved was quite different.

Most often, boys simply physically pushed each other out of the way. Girls pushed each other out of the way too, but they did it verbally rather than physically. Although they were no less determined than the boys were.

Another, intriguing difference emerged. Apart from getting access to the viewer more often, the dominant boy does not differ much in other ways from the other boys – *all* the boys behaved quite dominantly and submitted less often to the alpha boy's control. In contrast, the dominant girl behaved dominantly in a more general way, not just when she wanted to see the cartoons. She tried to control the other girls. Consequently, there was more tension in the girls' group than in the boys', who smiled and laughed much more often than the girls, and in general seemed to be having more fun.

Why this difference? Because a bid for dominance is a more fraught issue for girls, less accepted than it is in boys' groups, where it's regarded as legitimate and normal. When they later enter the world of work, and a lot more is at stake than getting access to cartoons, girls will relearn that lesson, painfully.

Separate worlds: *We do things differently here!*

There's no consensus on the root of the behavioural differences between boys and girls.[15] What is clearer is what does *not* cause them. They have little to do with individual personality, or how stereotypically 'masculine' or 'feminine' a child is.

IS GENDERED BEHAVIOUR BIOLOGICALLY BASED?

Maybe. Gender differences in behaviour and preferences may reflect brain-based differences that have evolved as males and females specialized in different tasks to ensure survival. Men primarily found territory and defended it; competed with other males and groups for mates and scarce resources. They fought and hunted in groups, organizing themselves into a hierarchy to make this more efficient, but also to regulate aggression and competition and to maintain order in tense situations. The role of women was primarily to bear and rear children, which was done in extended family groups, where maintaining intimate and cooperative relationships provided the glue that held them together and encouraged mutual dependence and support.

It's important to note that gender differences are not manifested in innate behaviours, but in tendencies or preferences to act one way and not another in particular circumstances – and there is a lot of individual variability. Not all girls are cooperative, not all boys are competitive. The gender spectrum is very wide, with a minority wired towards the extreme ends of the continuum, and the rest occupying more moderate positions.

ARE GENDER DIFFERENCES IN BEHAVIOUR
A RESULT OF UPBRINGING?

To some extent, they are. Children are born into a world that is gender-saturated. From the moment of birth, girls are socialized into a pink world, and boys into a blue one. Parents respond to these strong cultural cues, and they get incorporated into how they socialize their children and how they interact with them, although this varies considerably from culture to culture and from family to family, and evidence of direct gender socialization by parents is not consistently found in all studies.

In general, apart from very traditional cultures where boys are favoured, mothers' day-to-day interactions with their children have little to do with the child's gender. Fathers tend to treat children in a somewhat more gendered way. They exert more control over sons than daughters, but this may be in response to more aggressive behaviour in boys. This is not the case for mothers, whose attitude to their sons has no obvious link to how boisterous they are. And if they adopt an overly controlling style with boys, it can result in a simmering resentment towards women in adulthood.[16]

As children develop into middle childhood, parents' behaviour changes. Mothers begin to interact with their daughters more in the way they relate to other women, and their relationship becomes more intimate and reciprocal. Fathers also increasingly relate to their sons the way they do to other men, engaging in the kind of friendly rivalry and banter they use with other men.[17] They like to do traditionally 'masculine' things together, like playing or watching sport, but this is already changing as girls become more active in sports.

The links between nature and nurture are complex, and it's not yet clear if parents are *causing* gendered behaviour, or simply *responding* to it.

ARE GENDER DIFFERENCES A FUNCTION OF CONTEXT?

There is consistent evidence that boys are generally more competitive than girls. But there is also growing evidence that gender differences, like risk-taking, negotiation and readiness to compete, are influenced by subtle cues from the environment. When those cues are changed, these differences narrow, or even disappear.[18] For example, girls are much more competitive when they are competing against themselves and trying to better their performance than when they are competing with others, a type of competition boys relish.[19]

Let's do this, will we? No, we'll do this[20]

Girls primarily use polite suggestion to try to influence other girls. Boys prefer to use direct commands. But here's the rub – while girls are mostly responsive to boys' suggestions, boys only listen to each other. Between the ages of three and five, this difference intensifies. In mixed groups, boys increasingly get to make most of the group decisions. Even when the girls issue direct orders, the boys ignore them. If two toddler girls or boys are having a dispute about a toy, the one who is grabbing the other's toy will usually stop when ordered to by the rightful owner. But when a boy and girl have a similar dispute, the offending girl will stop grabbing the toy when told to by the boy. But the offending boy won't stop when told to by a girl. And this is *before* they are three years old!

You can see how this might play out later, in the world of work. The advantage lies with the boys – all that practice in arguing and jockeying for position helps them to keep their eye on status and climb the hierarchy more easily. This advantage is also what makes trying to achieve equality in personal relationships, especially in the distribution of household tasks, a perennial source of tension. Women get fed up with all the arguing, and often end up just doing the task themselves.

Whatever the reason, boys and girls show distinctly different preferences in how they play, and in how they organize themselves socially, and prefer to do this with their own gender.

Why friendships and belonging really count

Your relationships with friends and peers will occupy a large part of middle childhood, and how they work out will have a significant impact on your happiness and well-being.[21] When children are asked about the kinds of things that stress them day-to-day, they frequently mention being teased by friends and peers, having no friends, or feeling isolated by their peer group. If children are excluded by the peer group, they show significantly higher levels of cortisol than children who are more popular, and the rise in cortisol does not follow the normal daily rhythm – rising in the morning, gradually declining during the day. It stays high throughout the day, disrupting the normal pattern of stress regulation. This disruption weakens their immune system and impairs their learning and memory.

The effects of rejection by a peer group are even stronger if combined with having few close friends, or none at all. You are at higher risk of loneliness, social anxiety and depression. You are more likely to act out or try to avoid school. But the most telling, and heartbreaking, evidence of the vital importance of a peer group is this: being victimized by peers has a *less* disruptive effect on your stress regulation system than being isolated or rejected outright by them. Rejection and exclusion deprive you of all contact. Whereas being victimized, cruel as it is, constitutes some kind of social contact.

The loneliness and stress of being deprived of a peer group is marginally more manageable if you are more introverted, and content with your own company. But if you are naturally sociable and extraverted, your longing for the company of peers is visceral. Your feeling of loneliness is so intense that you want to burst out of your own skin to relieve the agitation inside you.

10. *Middle childhood:* Stocking up for the road ahead

As you advance through middle childhood, you spend more and more time away from your parents, at school and at play. They are your secure base and, like a tired warrior, you return each day to that base to replenish your reserves. So what happens at home, and the quality of your relationship with your parents, will continue to play a decisive role in your emotional and social development, and in turn will influence how successfully you deal with your friendships and peer relationships. You still need your parents to be psychologically available, ready to listen and talk to you about the events of your day. You rely on your mother to know you well enough to say, 'You're very quiet today. Is everything okay?' And then it all spills out, a raw and unprocessed narrative, and you know she will help you put some order and meaning on it.

Your parents can help you hone your social skills and get a better handle on the ups and downs with friends and peers. At the end of his long career as a leading researcher in child development, Uri Bronfenbrenner came to this conclusion: what every child needs, he said, is the enduring, irrational involvement of one or more adults to care for them, and do things with them. 'In short, somebody has to be crazy about that kid. '[1]

As we saw in Chapter 9, in middle childhood, your emotional and cognitive capacity increases. You start to understand that your own and others' emotional reactions are not just caused by things that happen, but by how those things are interpreted. You learn that people can have very different emotional reactions to the same situation. You have the ability to see things from another person's perspective.

Your emotional coaches

Your parents play a very significant role in that emotional development, by modelling how they handle emotion and by becoming emotional coaches, helping you to make sense of and manage your own and other people's emotional reactions. Long before you arrived on the scene, each of your parents had a well-developed set of attitudes to emotions, and ideas about how they should be handled.[2]

Some parents believe it's unnecessary to pay much attention to emotion, and shy away from or even disapprove of emotional displays of any kind. This will not do you any harm, once you know that, in their own buttoned-up way, they are 'at your back' and are rock solid in their support of you. However, it does limit the opportunities to explore your feelings more fully, to trace their origin, and see that there are other ways to manage them.

Other parents put a lot of value on emotions and open emotional displays. They pay attention to their own feelings, and to how others are reacting. What counts is how skilled they are in how they do this. It's a big advantage when your parents are comfortable and skilled at identifying and expressing different emotions, and encourage you to do likewise, particularly if they see your negative reactions as an opportunity for intimacy, a teaching moment, in which they can help you identify what you are experiencing, and why, and help you come up with constructive solutions. This is the way they can scaffold your emotional development, and it pays off.

There is a strong link between the quality of the coaching parents provide, how well you can handle negative emotions, and the quality of your relationships with friends and peers.[3] You are better at regulating your own physiological stress reactions when in the grip of potentially disruptive negative emotions – when you feel frustrated, angry, sad, disappointed. Being able to safely contain these emotions, to modulate and soothe them, makes it easier to stay calm, to focus your attention, to listen more attentively, to think more clearly, and to resolve conflicts more effectively.

If you receive that kind of coaching, by the age of eight you are more socially competent; have more satisfying friendships and peer-group relationships; enjoy better physical and psychological health; and are doing better at school.[4]

But, as in most things, there is a sweet spot. Too little emotional coaching and support, and you risk becoming overwhelmed in stressful situations. Too much, your parents intervening too early or being overly placating, deprives you of the opportunity to use situations that are emotionally challenging as a way to learn how to manage them yourself in your own way, and undermines your autonomy. A moderate amount of emotional coaching and support works best – a parent who adopts an empathic, calm approach that allows you to regain your composure and try to manage your own upset feelings, and who intervenes only when it's clear that you can't do that. This is what will build your confidence in your own ability to cope.

Between the ages of eight and eleven, girls become more aware of the overwhelming cultural and social pressure to be 'nice', which in their case means kind and self-sacrificing, and the conflict that often creates with their own desire to be emotionally honest in their close relationships. Boys, for their part, are engaged in their own struggle between the pressure to be tough, stoic, never showing vulnerability, and their own desire to be more open about their softer feelings of hurt and the effort of bravado.

The emotional and social skills that your parents teach are not formulas that can be applied to managing your relationships with friends and peers. The advantage they confer is a more general kind of social competence – you are more emotionally savvy, better able to adapt to a variety of social situations. If your parents are sensitive to the conflicts that you are experiencing between the desire to be 'like the others', and the desire to 'be myself', it strengthens your autonomy, and readies you for adolescence when these cultural and social pressures become much stronger.

Having a 'difficult' temperament

Emotional coaching and support are even more important if you are temperamentally prone to negative emotionality,[5] reacting strongly to anxiety, worry, guilt, sadness and anger.* You struggle to focus your

---

* A 'difficult' temperament may make you more susceptible to ADHD, attention deficit hyperactive disorder, a neurological disorder with a strong genetic component, or a variant condition called ADT, attention deficit trait. What they have in

attention and are distractible, except when you are really interested in something, when you are capable of a kind of hyper-focus. In middle childhood, this kind of temperament can take different forms. You may be predominantly anxious, worrying unnecessarily about things that turn out to be unimportant, or have trouble sleeping. Or you may get angry quickly and easily, overreacting to frustration, your mind racing a mile a minute as you try to control the spiralling out-of-control feeling.

ADHD, or some variant of it, may not be a random, trouble-making genetic glitch. Such a temperament is as much part of the human make-up as other kinds of temperamental traits, like being extraverted or introverted.

Some scientists and writers view ADHD as a genetic residue of the nomadic hunters we all once were, before we evolved into farmers.[6] A genetic variant associated with ADHD has been found to be more common in populations who are nomadic and have to keep adapting to new environments. It's speculated that the hyper-focus aspect of ADHD, along with your capacity to be distracted by what might be better opportunities, would also have given you a big advantage as a hunter, roaming far to find the best game. But these kinds of abilities are not well adapted to environments that are highly structured and rule-driven, except in specific situations or contexts.

For example, your tendency to hyper-focus can help you to get urgent tasks done, to do (very) last-minute preparations, or to bring projects to the finish-line. You get so absorbed that you hardly notice that you are skipping meals, missing sleep and hardly attending to your other needs. But if you do this too often, your health and relationships will suffer. All of this is still speculative, but it is a welcome antidote to the current fad for turning normal variants of human behaviour into 'syndromes' and disorders.

There may be other advantages, too. The reason we have negative emotions is to alert us to danger or threat, so it's conceivable that people wired on the more extreme end of emotional reactivity act as

---

common is difficulty controlling your attention, distractibility, impatience, difficulty in setting priorities, staying focused and managing time.

a hypersensitive alarm system for the group. They may often 'go off' unnecessarily, but they also do the lion's share of worrying or agitating in a family or group. Great poets, artists and actors are not always 'difficult' people, but they often are. The upside of that kind of temperament may be an increase in sensitivity, not just to the sorrows and brutality of the world, but also to its beauty and fragility, a sensibility that can find creative expression in the arts.

Nonetheless, having such a temperament makes it harder to manage your relationship with friends and peers. You are bewildered by the negative reaction you sometimes get from other children who think you are loud or aggressive, or just too complicated. When you are rebuffed socially, you tend to withdraw or react angrily. That can make it harder to make and keep friends and fit into a peer group, and can create a great deal of unhappiness in childhood. This is very hard on you, and on your worried parents. But every bit of emotional support and coaching you get from them helps you to manage things better. Every bit.

Making friends – it's all about attachment (again)

The quality of your attachment to your parents runs like a red thread through your life, continuing to influence how you feel about yourself, and the quality of your close relationships, including your friendships and peer relationships.

Secure

If your attachment relationship with one parent is *Secure*, you have a head start, and you are even better off if your attachment with both is *Secure*.* Your mental model of yourself and of others is solidly based on trust and all that goes with it.[7] You are more emotionally positive,

---

* This effect is stronger in relation to a child's attachment with their mother, rather than with their father. But this may be due to the fact that there are fewer studies on the effects of child–father attachment on children's social competence.

which acts like a magnet to other children. You expect to be liked and treated well by other children.[8] This doesn't mean you're not nervous approaching children you don't know, just that you are willing to give it a go. You can take the initiative, confident that you can probably manage any challenges that arise, and if you encounter difficulties, you can turn to your parents for support and advice. You are ready to cooperate, sensitive to the need to find a good balance between your own needs, preferences and opinions and those of other children. But you are also better able to withstand undue pressure from more dominant children, and to remain more truly yourself.*

There are also more specific mechanisms that account for this link between *Secure* attachment and social competence. For example, if you are securely attached to your mother at the age of three, by four you have better language and social skills, and by the age of seven you have closer friendships. Why? Because within that early attachment relationship with her, the communication between you is open, fluid and non-defensive, based on her intimate knowledge of who you are, what you like and what you find difficult. You internalize that capacity for self-disclosure and openness, which is central to high-quality friendships.

Insecure

In contrast to the open flow of intimate conversation that happens between *Secure* children and their mothers, mothers of insecure children use a more closed and controlling style of interaction. The lack of openness and tolerance of negative emotions means that you have to try to make sense of things on your own – there is no one to help you figure out why another child upset you or would not play with you. As a result, upsetting experiences lie there, undigested, creating a

---

* Social and cognitive competence is also shaped by your natural intelligence, your special talents, the quality of school you attend, and many other factors. But a *Secure* attachment is a separate and significant factor, helping you reach the top of your potential range of cognitive and social competence, whatever your level of intelligence and social context.

pervasive negativity. This negative, distrusting attitude leaks into your interactions with other children, souring the relationships. This has a particularly adverse effect on boys, and on their peer relationships, because boys rely more on their mothers to help them understand and deal with their anxiety, anger and sadness to allow them to foster harmonious relationships with their friends and peers.

Consider this study[9] in which a group of young children are shown a series of pictures that depict ambiguous social situations: for example, a child tripping over another child; or one child being hit by a ball or having juice spilled over them by another. Each child is asked what they think is happening in the picture.

The children who are securely attached to their mothers are more likely to explain what is happening as an accident, not intended by the other child.

In contrast, the children whose attachment to their mother is insecure are more likely to say that the action of the other child was hostile, intentional. This tendency to attribute hostile motivation to other children is rooted in their own experiences with their mothers, who often misread their intentions and attributed more hostile motives to them. They are lonely and want company, but their immature bids to get that attention are often interpreted as deliberate attempts to annoy her or being 'demanding' or 'selfish'.

If you are insecure, making friends is harder. You struggle with trust and harbour more self-doubt. Your autonomy and sense of self are shakier. You fear getting too close and dependent on friends in case, when they get to know you, they reject you. Or you are over-eager to be liked, swinging between being too placating and too demanding. Your insecurity may leak out in outbursts of anger or compulsive attention-seeking that put other children off. You attract more negative reactions from teachers. If you often look sad, this may puzzle other children, who may eventually shun you.[10]

If you are insecure, your emotional demeanour is generally more negative. You come across to other children as 'not nice' – their umbrella term for being difficult, argumentative, angry, or attention-seeking – so it's more likely you will be disliked and avoided by them. You tend to get into more conflicts with other children, and when you do, you have more difficulty disengaging and are less empathic. To compound your suffering, you are also more likely to attract more negative reactions from teachers.[11]

AVOIDANT AND ANXIOUS

If your attachment with your mother is *Avoidant*, you engage in less elaborate pretend play than *Secure* children or, in more extreme cases, show an almost total absence of fantasy play involving people. You are wary of becoming too dependent on friends, preferring to keep your options open, which other children find unpredictable. You often feel outside of things and lonely.

If your attachment is *Anxious*, you are prone to getting stressed. You lose emotional control more easily, reacting in a helpless and dependent way. When it comes to bullying, *Avoidant* children are more likely to be the victimizer, *Anxious* children to be the victims. *Secure* children are less likely to be either.

Friendship and belonging – or isolation?

At the end of middle childhood, the child you were when you took your first tentative steps outside the family has been transformed. If all has gone well, you are more assured and immensely more competent, cognitively, emotionally and socially. Your personality, character and identity are more consolidated. You have a secure network of friends and are embedded in a peer group. You have experienced a kind of intimacy that is different from the intimacy of family, and you have learned from it. You are more emotionally stable, able to integrate your negative emotions into uninterrupted, concentrated exploration and learning, carrying on even when in a relatively poor mood. You feel a new sense of contentment and pride in yourself. You have achieved a sense of mastery. You know you are capable of mobilizing and organizing your cognitive and emotional resources when faced with a challenge.

You feel more on top of things, have a buoyant sense of momentum and of vital engagement in your life. When you have to exert sustained effort to achieve something big, you are not daunted, you respond with a determination and grit that, you note with some sly satisfaction, often surprises your parents. You now know how to find goals that are worth striving for. You have learned to take the initiative boldly, but safely. You stand prepared on the final threshold of childhood. You have packed psychological provisions for the crossing to adolescence.

But for some of you, things may not have gone so well. Your childhood may have been troubled by chronic stress, conflict between your parents, alcohol abuse or other issues. You may have left for school in the morning already worried what you would find when you got home in the evening. Some of you have endured physical and sexual abuse, bringing your childhood to a traumatic end before it even began. Deprived of consistent support from your parents, you had to enter the world of peers alone, psychologically naked, and may have found that world to be a lonely and isolated place.

You may have struggled to get the closeness and support for your autonomy that you needed from your parents, compromising your attempts to become competent. You don't feel so good about yourself. When your need for mastery is frustrated, and you struggle to make friends or find a place in the peer group, you are deeply disappointed, beset by a feeling of inadequacy, of something missing or lacking in yourself. At the end of childhood, your confidence in your own effectiveness is shaky, easily undermined. You are prey to feelings of inadequacy, of not being 'enough' in yourself. As you face the crossing to adolescence, provisions are low. But you haven't given up hope.

A life well-lived – what we learn from middle childhood

The principles of a life well lived – middle childhood			
Life stage	*Time frame*	*Developmental task*	*Psychological principle*
Middle childhood	seven–eleven	belonging or isolation?	Be generous

Middle childhood is when you understand how to show generosity to other people and the world around you. Its developmental task – learning to make friends and get along with peers – sets you up for life. Perhaps you learned to navigate the world of friends and peers in middle childhood. But if you didn't and it's something that worries you, there are steps you can take at any stage of life to learn how to make friends. The basic requirement is a positive readiness to act in certain ways.

- *Be ready to initiate* a social interaction or respond positively to an initiative from a would-be friend.
- *Be ready to self-disclose:* at the very start, keep it brief, light and not too personal. Then, stop to give the other person a chance to reciprocate. Don't force the pace. For a real friendship to develop, you have to let go of your outer shell, your public persona, and reveal your softer, more private self, your deeper feelings, including your fears and anxieties.
- *Be ready to give and ask for support:* to help a friend work through their thoughts and feelings about a big decision; to listen as they blow off steam about problems they are having, and cluck in sympathy; to know how to cheer them up when they are feeling low; to try to see things from their perspective in an empathic way; to offer advice in a way that is not intrusive; and to express in words or actions how much you appreciate and care for them as individuals. But you must also be ready to reach out for support yourself, otherwise the friendship becomes unbalanced.
- *Be ready to hold your own:* friends are human, and sometimes overstep the mark. You have to make it clear when something they did or said has bothered or upset you, and discuss it in an honest but constructive way, without resorting to personal attack or angry accusations. You have to put aside resentment while you listen to their side of the story, and be ready to accept that their view is different from yours, while still honouring your own experience. And you have to return the favour and allow them to do the same – and be ready to admit when you are wrong and ask for their forgiveness.

But those are just the basics. The deep structure of friendships and belonging is founded on *equality* and *reciprocity*. In every relationship there are temporary imbalances when one of you is more in need of support than the other. But overall, you want to feel that what you are getting from the friendship is roughly equivalent to what you are putting into it.

There is a lot of 'noise' in close relationships – crossed wires, unintended consequences of a well-intentioned act, the usual quota of irritation and disappointment, the occasional bout of envy and jealousy. The only and best way to deal with that 'noise' is to act generously. When you respond generously, and it is seen to be sincere and not in the service of buying favours, it elicits a reciprocal generosity in your friends and a desire to be helpful and cooperative. This is good for you and good for your friends. Your self-esteem increases, so does your friends', and you both enjoy higher levels of physical and psychological well-being. This is a great strategy, not just for your friendships, but also as a training ground for your romantic relationships.[12]

II. *Adolescence:* Figuring out the person you are becoming

Between the ages of nine and fourteen, the mighty force of puberty is bringing your childhood to an end and ushering in a momentous series of physical and psychological changes that will transform you physically, mentally and emotionally.

The span of adolescence is modest, less than ten years, but the agenda is *big*. You have to make the transition to secondary school. You have to become more independent. You have to manage a new peer group, more unstable emotional states, and get your head around the whole business of dating and sex. And if that's not enough to be getting on with, there is a new urgency about becoming competent, with unambiguous signals from family, teachers and wider society that you have to up your game. You are left in no doubt that what you do in adolescence *really* counts, opening up or shutting down your options in adulthood. This realization comes dropping slow into the adolescent mind, but in the pressurized, hyper-competitive world you now inhabit, it gets hard to ignore.

Your need for autonomy surges now – and that will be the wind at your back, the psychological equivalent of your new sexual drive, sharing the same intensity and undeniability. You make a quantum leap in how you exercise every element of that autonomy. Your explorations of yourself are deeper. You think and act more independently. You become more unpredictable. You like to say and do things that surprise people, and sometimes yourself. It's your way of resisting being controlled by their expectations.

And in the middle of all this, you have to figure out what kind of person you are becoming – the major developmental task of adolescence.

Creating the story of who you truly are

As you cross the great divide between childhood and adulthood, forming a new, more complex identity is your prime developmental task.[1] As a child, you take your identity as given, unquestioned. Now, that identity is revisited and reworked to meet the demands of adolescence, and you have to answer some fundamental questions.

- What kind of person am I?
- How can I fit this new sexual me into the way I always was?
- How am I the same as other people, and what makes me unique and different?
- What has really changed about me, and what has stayed the same?
- What qualities are central to the core of who I am?
- What gives value and meaning to my life?
- What dream of life is awakening in me?

Identity is what allows you to bind up the different parts of yourself – your experiences, beliefs, values and aspirations – into a coherent whole, what Erikson refers to as the style of your individuality. It represents your sense of inner sameness and continuity over time, but also your capacity to change. You use your identity as an inner template against which you test your actions: is this something that a person like me does? It guides your choices and your behaviour, and firms up your commitments; it steadies you up, motivating you to behave in a way that is consistent with the way you think of yourself and what matters to you.

The first time I became really conscious of my own set of values was in boarding school when I was about fourteen. There was a lot of bullying there, which I hated, but I didn't say anything because I was scared I'd become a target, or that people wouldn't like me. But I was really ashamed of myself. It went against something very deep in me. I thought: 'This isn't the person I am, or want to be.' So I started challenging it. It made me unpopular for a while, but I felt better about myself, stronger.

Barbara, 54

You feel a new urge to consciously differentiate yourself from your parents, siblings, friends and peers. How you do that bears a remarkable resemblance to what happened in your second year, which is why adolescence is called the second edition of childhood.[2] At the age of two, you ventured out into the wider world of childhood, curious, expectant, slightly apprehensive, all the while keeping a weather eye on how close and available your parents were. At the end of childhood, you venture out in the same way into the wider world of adolescence, and you use much the same tried-and-trusted process.

As a young child, you discovered the world by exploring and experimenting, by trial-and-error. You asserted your emerging self by saying no, by opposition, by going to excess, by testing yourself, and the patience of everybody else, to the limit. That was the only way you could learn how things worked, and the limits and scope of your own power and competence. In adolescence, you do the same thing, but in a more conscious and deliberate way. Rebellion, resistance and argumentativeness are the adolescent equivalent of the toddler 'no'. You know what you no longer want, even if you're not yet sure what you do want. You try and then discard provisional identities, and what might be grandly called 'life philosophies'.

You have to figure out how to balance your longing to be unique and different with your equal longing to be accepted, to have an assured place in your peer group, and to maintain a close relationship with your family and a modicum of peace at home. Asserting your opinions too stridently risks constant conflict, marginalization or rejection; submerging them risks being overlooked, taken for granted or, worst of all, being boring.

The process of forming an identity is often messy, and rarely easy. You zigzag between the old sense of self and the new one emerging. You often feel alone and marooned, equally far from the safe shore of childhood and the still invisible destination of adulthood. You are occasionally gripped by dread that you will be left behind, and that spurs you on.

If all goes well in adolescence, the prize at the end is great. You will have formed the template for your adult self and staked out the core of your individuality. Along the way, you will experience moments of intense self-recognition, full of surprise and delight, and occasionally a corrective sense of dismay. But while you are doing all this, you have only the vaguest idea of what is at play. You are just a teenager, for God's sake. You only know, at crucial moments, that something has shifted inside you and is moving you on in your life.

Your busy brain

In adolescence, your brain is still developing. There are changes in your prefrontal cortex, the area of the brain involved in motivation, seeking out new information, setting goals and exercising cognitive control – the neurobiological underpinnings to the process of form- ing your identity.[3]

You also take another cognitive leap – you can now think in terms of possibility and have a whole new set of cognitive tools to do that. You can question, speculate, hypothesize, fantasize on a much grander scale than you could before. You can build elaborate theories about love, life, morality and, of course, yourself. This allows you to soar above the middle childhood limitation of thinking that is practical and grounded in reality. Now, you can subordinate that limiting reality to the far more exciting, if sometimes alarming, realm of the possible.

You can suspend your knowledge of reality at will and ponder the impossible and the hypothetical, hence the endless, exhausting and exhilarating arguments about how the world could or should be if you had any say about it. You can reflect on your own thoughts. You can argue against your own beliefs and self-interests, just for argu- ment's sake. You can modify your own position when persuaded by the merit of an argument. In other words, you are now gleefully engaged in the game of thinking.

Accompanying all this cognitive pyrotechnics is a pull inwards. You spend more time alone with your thoughts. Your gaze becomes more self-reflective, turning towards the internal, private aspect of yourself, now couched in the new language of abstraction. Your sense of self is more permeable. You more easily absorb the opinions that other people have of you, making you more realistic, and more vulnerable.

You become more egocentric and self-absorbed. You construct an elaborate fantasy of some glorious destiny that awaits you, unconstrained by the trivial matter of what this might actually require of you. In the fevered hub of your adolescent mind, you stride the social stage, unique and central, an imaginary audience witnessing your every act. That's why you no longer simply go in and out of a room – instead you make an entrance and stage an exit. For the first time, you become capable of deliberate, strategic self-presentation. All of this, the imaginary audiences, the elaborate fantasies, serve a real purpose: opening up a space where you can try out new identities, and start writing the story of who you truly are.

The story of your many selves

In adolescence you become aware, in a more complex way, that you have many selves. Your self with your mother is different from the one with your father, siblings, friends or teachers. There is a difference between your private self and the public self you present to the world, and between your ordinary self and your ideal self. In adolescence, these different and often contradictory selves must be sewn together into a stable and coherent identity, a more complex and differentiated 'true self'.

This process of self-construction is intensely private. Yet it is also a reflected self, negotiated, moulded and affirmed in the context of constant social interaction with the people who are significant to you. As it's subject to regular revision, it's also volatile. But there is an irreducible and deeply private core that is formed from within, like a crystal.

You can now see causal links between different things that happened to you, how one preceded or succeeded the other, and their broader implications.

I was very close to my dad, but he died when I was seven. I didn't just lose him, I think I lost a bit of myself. I was a different person with him than I was with anybody else. That self just disappeared when he died, and it didn't emerge again until I was well into my thirties, but not in the same way. I often wonder if I might have developed differently if he had not died then: would I have been a different person?

Nell, 65

You can interpret events, but also recognize that they are open to more than one interpretation. You can offer a summary of your life, or parts of your life. You can see broad themes in your story, experiences and reactions that keep recurring. All of this enables you to transform the facts of your life into a story that is uniquely reflective of you as an individual, your particular version of the oldest human stories: a hero on an epic journey; a slayer of dragons; being lost and then found; rags to riches; frog to prince; princess finally found.

All of those changes allow you to construct a more elaborate narrative about yourself, an indispensable part of constructing your identity.[4]

The evolving narrative

In middle childhood, you began to construct a story about yourself, about the kind of person you are and the qualities that distinguish you from other children. In adolescence, that story takes on a more elaborate form. For the first time you become capable of forming a coherent account of your life story.[5] You can now link the past, the present and the future, and begin to see how you became the person you are and who, in time, you might become. You can place when significant events in your life happened more accurately. You have a better understanding of why they happened, what may have been motivating you, or other people. You begin to identify recurring themes in your life, to see that there were significant turning points, embedded in memories that stand out more vividly than others.

This evolving narrative becomes a stable holding space, a grid that confers structure, order and meaning on your experiences, and on what is happening in you and around you. It gives you a way to understand what motivates you, what links your thoughts, your feelings, and how you act in the world. It binds together the continuities and discontinuities in yourself and in your life, allowing you to integrate the old you and the fledgling new you.

Oh God – the moods!

In adolescence you experience the full emotional negative continuum: high anxiety, bouts of irritability, deep gloom, loneliness, lethargy, envy. You feel overwhelmed, bored, agitated, unable to concentrate. Then you sample the full menu of positive emotions. You are happy, engaged, interested, excited, enthusiastic about (certain) challenges. You knock a lot of fun out of things. You bask in pride when you do something really right. You are swept away by new consuming passions, some quickly discarded (have a look around the attic), some settling into a more enduring interest.

The transition to adolescence puts a heavy strain on your capacity to organize and manage yourself and your life, and your happiness and self-esteem take a hit. You feel less in control of your life, more harassed by the demands being made on you. You often feel self-conscious and awkward, and very alone. You jump from one task to the other without finishing things. You put things off. You react more extremely to setbacks and failures. Occasionally you feel plain depressed.

You are more susceptible to mood swings, less anchored in the middle ground, more vulnerable to unexpected events. You get upset by things that may appear trivial to adults. A stupid mistake, an awkward moment with someone, saying something that came out wrong – these things can threaten your precarious sense of self. It's hard to summon the emotional reserves to persist after screwing up again. You have an acute sense of disappointment when your high expectations are dashed. You often feel overwhelmed. So, when you occasionally explode and announce dramatically, 'I can't *stand* this,' it is a powerful statement of what you are feeling. This negativity reaches a peak by mid-adolescence and then begins to decline as you finally get a handle on things.*

---

* As always, there are individual differences. If you experienced depression or emotional turmoil in childhood, or struggled with poor self-control, your risk of problems in adolescence is higher.

But you still have your moments. At times of high emotion, you are convinced that what you are feeling is unlike what *anybody* else has ever felt. You have big insights, you are full of strong convictions and then, like ice melting in a sudden thaw, your certainty collapses and you are overtaken by a kind of existential dread, gripped by a fear that nothing is certain any more. But although you veer easily into despondency, you are also more likely to experience euphoria, and occasionally you catch a glimpse of the world as perfect.[6]

You are painfully conscious of the discrepancy between the way you want to be and the way you are; between the way you want the world to work, and the imperfect way it does. The intransigence of parents and schools is a constant irritant. But when things quieten down, or nothing much is happening, you start to worry that life is passing you by. Nonetheless, for most of you, this emotional lability and high-wire dramatics is not a sign that you are fundamentally unhappy or maladjusted.

You feel most negative when you are in places structured by adults – in class, in church, doing chores. It's harder to concentrate. You are less willing to mobilize your energy. Compared to children or adults, you are much more likely to feel alienated from what you are doing and wish you were doing something else.[7] Adults feel motivated and interested in what they are doing about 40 per cent of the time. You feel that way only 25 per cent of the time.

Where do you feel most highly motivated and engaged? When you are furthest away from adults, hanging out with friends, in school corridors, in cafés, in the park. You and your mates are like an underground political movement, only happy when hanging out with your fellow oppressed, well away from the tyrannical regime.[8]

Girls at the crossroads

The gendered relationship styles and ways of dealing with stress that you developed in childhood intensify in adolescence, and their impact is greater on your happiness and well-being.* Adolescence is a particularly stressful time for girls. Harvard psychologist Carol Gilligan describes the transition to adolescence as a crossroads, the meeting place of girls and women, where girls are at risk of 'drowning or disappearing'.[9]

At the end of middle childhood, girls are able to speak freely and honestly about their feelings. They stay connected to their own experiences, to what they know. But as they enter adolescence, as they try to forge new, more adult relationships with their parents, friends and boyfriends – relationships that are authentic – they have their first acute encounter with a dilemma that will continue to haunt them in young adulthood: how to care for others in their close relationships, but also to care for themselves. They veer unsteadily between being 'good', selfless, sacrificing themselves to the needs of others, in the traditional way expected of women, or being 'selfish', focusing only on their own needs, but compromising their need for closeness and hurting those they care about.

They try to solve that dilemma by caring for others, hoping that they will be cared for in return. These erstwhile 'stalwart resisters', ready to say directly what was on their mind, begin to compromise the untroubled authenticity that shone from them in late childhood.[10] At the very moment when their sense of identity is so dependent on exploring and knowing themselves in the context of close relationships, they become disconnected from themselves, losing confidence in whether their own feelings and experiences are a valid guide to what is happening in close relationships. The attempt to be honest and authentic becomes more fraught; there are more conflicts and evasions.

If you're a girl, throughout adolescence your self-esteem drops twice as much as boys' and does not begin to recover until the end of your twenties.[11] The drop is particularly steep for girls who mature early. Body image becomes a central concern. You are acutely aware that how you look will loom large in how you are judged by boys,

---

* As noted earlier, the gender spectrum is wide, and how typically gendered your behaviour is varies widely and is shaped, as well, by particular circumstances. For example, an only girl in a family of boys may have developed a more 'male' style of discourse.

and by other girls. How satisfied you are with your appearance is the single biggest predictor of your self-esteem in adolescence.

An acute fear of disapproval, and anxiety about others' distress, can lead to 'self-silencing', suppressing your own thoughts and feelings, especially anger, in the interest of maintaining closeness and harmony in relationships.[12] If this self-silencing becomes chronic, you feel a powerless anger, a sense of entrapment, shame and self-betrayal that gradually diminishes your sense of self. It undermines your right to own and voice your own experiences, and weakens your autonomy.

'Tend-and-befriend' is the female style of stress response. When you are stressed, you turn to a friend to get help and support, and you, in turn, are highly attuned to their stress. Your concern extends beyond your own circle of friends to girls in your wider network of peers who are going through a hard time, and you discuss their plight with other girls. This very female way of managing stress usually involves an extensive discussion of issues and feelings, speculation about possible causes and consequences, and a *lot* of advice. These kinds of supportive and open discussions increase your feelings of closeness, build a special kind of intimacy and result in very high-trust, high-quality friendships.

But you are also more vulnerable to internalizing the distress that others are feeling, experiencing in yourself the sadness and hurt you are witnessing. You are more given to rumination, alone or with friends. You revisit the same problems over and over again, with the same exhaustive exploration of all the issues and negative feelings involved. This kind of co-rumination can exaggerate the problems, your distress magnifying with each discussion, putting you at higher risk of internalizing problems, and experiencing low self-esteem, anxiety and depression.[13]

Boys and the pressure to conform

If you are a boy, you continue your more autonomous style of relating to your friends and peers. But you also become readier to confide in each other more, to discuss the issues and problems that you are confronting – but within strict emotional limits. Expressing feelings of hurt carries the risk of appearing 'babyish', so feelings of vulnerability are often suppressed, the male version of self-silencing. You sometimes ruminate about problems, but much less frequently than girls do. Occasionally, an intense discussion with a friend about a problem can veer into co-rumination but, unlike girls, this does not have the same negative consequences. This may be because it happens so rarely that it's taken as a sign of an especially close and high-trust friendship.

Boys' response to stress is likely to be 'fight-or-flight', responding with anger or withdrawing from a relationship when there is tension or a lot of conflict. When you are together in a group, there is more teasing, mock (or sometimes real) threats of physical aggression, exacerbated by the increase in testosterone. Unlike girls, you do much less cognitive processing of your negative feelings, so feelings of hurt, disappointment or insecurity are often channelled into anger.

You are also much more likely to distract yourself from stress by trying to laugh it off with your friends. Boys are good at generating fun and excitement, an important element in how satisfying your relationships with friends and peers are. However, relying on distraction can also turn into denial, letting the problem grow and fester, and depriving yourself of support. This general style of stress response puts boys at higher risk of externalizing their problems, acting-out, aggression, antisocial behaviour, or problems in school.

The pressure to conform to gender stereotypes intensifies in adolescence. Boys remain constrained by the 'boy code', under pressure to maintain an image of being tough, emotionally stoic, invulnerable. That is beginning to change, but very gradually and privately. Some of you are willing to admit to feeling a sense of loss and disconnection from yourself. You would like the opportunity to reveal your feelings of uncertainty and vulnerability without the risk of appearing 'girly' or 'gay'.[14] But as you progress through adolescence, that resistance to the boy code fades in the face of strong peer pressure. If you have at least one parent who is emotionally engaged and offers a safe space to discuss your thoughts and feelings, you can better manage that pressure to conform and, as a result, you are at lower risk of depression, have higher self-esteem, higher-quality friend-ships and are more engaged in your academic work.[15]

Friends – *your primary audience*

Friends play a key role in your efforts to build an identity and con-struct the story of yourself. They, rather than your parents, are now your primary audience. Your discussions about yourself with them are more open, elaborate and free-ranging. You look to them for confirmation that you are unique, but not weird. The more respon-sive and agreeable they are as listeners, the more confidence you have to expand your new sense of self. Compared to parents, friends ask more questions, they make sympathetic noises, are more willing to follow where you want to go with your self-narrative, and they don't try to shape it to their own agenda.

On the other hand, whereas parents may be selectively responsive to specific aspects of your story about yourself, when friends are unresponsive it tends to be about the *whole* story. Parents also have a more consistent style of responding, so you know what to expect, whereas your friends may be responsive on one occasion, but not on others. Girls enjoy an advantage here as, like women in general, they construct more elaborative narratives and are more responsive listen-ers. That's why both boys and girls prefer to talk to girls about personal matters.

Consistent unresponsiveness, from parents or friends, has the effect of silencing a particular aspect of your identity, and if you can-not find a more responsive listener, it may shut it down permanently, constricting the process of becoming more truly yourself. You can-not explore and share experiences that are important to your emerging sense of self. You are forced to suppress the factual details of your experiences. This act of suppression is important because facts ground the interpretations you make, are less vulnerable to manipulation, and so help to steady your sense of self.

12. *Adolescence:* A time of emotional crossover

Up to now, your need for closeness was twin-tracked: you turned to your parents to meet your attachment needs, and to your friends to meet your need for companionship. Attachments and friendships are two different systems, they work by different rules and are attuned to different rhythms. But starting in middle childhood, the two systems begin to merge, as some elements of attachment get transferred to close friends, and later to a romantic partner. This gradual transfer continues right through adolescence and into your twenties, and is only finally completed when you establish a serious romantic relationship. It takes place in a number of steps.

- *The desire for physical and emotional closeness*: starting in middle childhood, you spend more and more time with friends and peers. In adolescence, that accelerates and your friendships become more emotionally intimate.
- *Separation protest*: by early adolescence, you mope and fret if you're away from your friends for too long and are flooded with relief when you are joyfully reunited with them. By mid-adolescence, the disruption of a close friendship is a source of significant distress. Yet, the absence from friends rarely provokes the level of distress and disorganization that a prolonged absence from your parents would.
- *Safe haven*: gradually, your friends become your preferred safe haven for *some* things, a source of advice and reassurance about issues like maintaining your image, not being 'weird' or boring, and managing the intricacies of dating, issues which you believe they understand better than your parents do.
- *Secure base*: this final element of attachment is rarely transferred to friends and has to wait until you are in a long-term romantic relationship, when your partner

becomes your new secure base. But even in early adulthood, parents often remain the default secure base if you have no one else.

There's a lot of emotional crossover between family, friends and love relationships, and you import much of what you've learned in one domain to the other. The quality of your attachment relationship with your parents will influence the quality of your friendships, and both together will influence the quality of your romantic relationships.

This transfer of attachment means that the function of your attachment with your parents also changes. You are less dependent on them for your survival than you were in childhood, and no longer turn to them for help with quite the same urgency as you once did. You try to deal with stress yourself, or you turn to a friend. This striving for emotional autonomy is a hallmark of adolescence.[1] But when you feel vulnerable or a bit lost, you still rely on their experience and intimate knowledge of you to give you the right advice about conflicts with friends or problems with love. And their role as the secure base in your life remains crucial.

How attachment changes during adolescence

The nature of attachment changes in adolescence.[2] Sometime at the end of middle childhood or during the transition to adolescence, the individual attachment relationship you have with your mother and with your father consolidates into a more general 'state of mind' about attachment. It is likely to match the state of mind of the parent who was your major caretaker and reflect how secure your relationship was in infancy.[3]

Secure

If your state of mind is *Secure*, your sense of self is strong and your psychological boundaries are flexible enough to embrace the new experiences of adolescence. You are emotionally open, ready to explore your own feelings and motives. You are better able to take account of someone else's perspective, yet also able to take your own side, to see yourself as an autonomous person with the right to your own beliefs and opinions and your own valid perspective on things.

Your solid sense of trust in yourself and in other people, and the more assured sense of autonomy that goes with being *Secure*, is a big bonus in adolescence. Your values are more fully internalized so you can better withstand the inevitable pressures, especially from high-risk peers. You are less likely to make decisions out of fear or misplaced guilt, less likely to appease as a way of getting approval, so you experience less internal conflict. You are more self-motivated. You find it easier to move from 'have to' to 'want to'.[4] Your North Star is steady.

Despite the emotional volatility of early adolescence, your mood is generally positive. Compared to someone who is insecure (*Anxious* or *Avoidant*), you process positive and negative information differently, especially in stressful situations. For example, when you have a conflict with someone you are close to, not infrequent in adolescence, immediately afterwards you can recall more positive than negative things about your relationship with them, so you try hard to reconcile and get things back on track. This positive bias becomes part of your 'broaden-and-build' strategy, building up your emotional and social resources for the challenges ahead.[5]

Insecure

If you are insecure, adolescence is more of a struggle. Your sense of self is more brittle and defensive, especially in your close relationships. You have fewer emotional reserves to cope with the new demand of forging your unique identity. You have greater difficulty and are less interested in investing energy in your own development, in intimate relationships, or in helping others, setting the stage for relationships with your parents and with your friends that are likely to frustrate you and them.[6]

Unless there has been a change, your parents are likely to lack the sensitivity to be attuned to your changing needs, especially for autonomy, continuing their habit of intrusiveness and control, pressurizing you to think, behave and make decisions consistent with their needs and motivations rather than your own. If you resist, the resulting conflicts can strain the already compromised closeness of your relationship. Everyday disagreements become freighted with old wounds and can spin out of control. You have little confidence that you will be heard.

You are often intensely angry with your mother, refusing to cooperate with her, even when she is trying, in her own way, to help you.[7] If your relationship with your father was always insecure, your anger at him can sometimes burst into open and aggressive conflicts. After a conflict with either parent, you find it hard to recover your equilibrium. You recall your hurt and angry feelings more vividly and hold on to them longer. They seep into how your feel about the relationship more generally, creating even more tension. Nobody has much capacity to soothe the resulting anger, hurt and helplessness.

This ongoing stress makes it hard for you to regulate and manage your emotions and mobilize your energy. Instead, your attention is depleted trying to manage the chronic anxiety, anger and sadness that often beset you, and to maintain your defences against those feelings, putting you at higher risk of smoking, drugs and early, high-risk sexual relationships.[8] These are the general consequences of being insecure, but there are also more specific problems associated with a particular style of insecurity.

- *Dismissing:* if your state of mind is *Dismissing*, you are too fearful, too emotionally unschooled to open up long-repressed feelings in case you are overwhelmed by them. You try to shrug off your anger and sadness, but this is belied by your intense physiological arousal, so you withdraw instead. Your relationships with friends, or a romantic partner, are chilly, distant and transactional. But your suppressed anger surfaces in unconscious or unintended ways. You project your angry feelings on to them, ready to accuse them of hostile motives. As a result, they are more likely to describe you as hostile.
- *Preoccupied:* if your state of mind is *Preoccupied*, you remain too confused and mired in ambivalence, too frequently

overcome by helpless anger to extricate yourself from your enmeshed relationship with your parents, and you carry this style into your friendships and romantic relationships. You are hypersensitive to any hint of rejection, overreacting to every setback, becoming emotionally overwhelmed and needy, making for fraught and volatile close relationships.

Despite the storms, this is a time for positive change

Attachment is not destiny, though, particularly in adolescence, when it's more unstable. The stress of adolescence can make a previously *Secure* adolescent temporarily insecure, or exacerbate the problems of insecure adolescents. For example, if your parents get divorced or some other stress befalls the family, you can be plunged into insecurity. However, it's not the adverse event itself that causes the problem, but the extent to which it undermines a parent's capacity to be attuned to your needs or embroils you in their psychological currents.

Some families weather the storm of divorce in a way that manages to protect their child's security or, even more impressively, in a way that can result in a once insecure child becoming *Secure*. How? Amidst all the disruption, these families find a way to balance the needs of each person in the family with the more general need to keep the family going.[9] They work out a way that allows each family member to safely and comfortably express their feelings and opinions, and yet get on with the business of cooperating closely together to get the family tasks done well and keep the whole show on the road.

Apart from the ups and downs of family life, adolescence also offers the real possibility of positive change. In childhood, you are embedded in an unquestioned pattern of interactions within your family. You assume that all families behave like yours does, and even when you notice differences, you can't analyse them or imagine them transposed to your own family. This changes in adolescence. You are now capable of seeing yourself, and your parents, as separate individuals, allowing you to stand back a little more and question your relationship with them. You become more aware of their frailties and contradictions, more perceptive about any disparity between what you see and what you are told by them.

If you are insecure, these new capacities open up the possibility of positive change. Add to that your wider network of friends and mentors, who can open up your perspective on yourself, allowing you to re-examine the way you think and feel about yourself and your relationship with your parents. For the first time, you may glimpse the possibility that things could be different. The surge of autonomy now coursing through you may further widen that window of opportunity, giving you the courage to break free from how they see you and relate to you, and to earn for yourself the security that always eluded you. And when you do, you are better able to accept the reality of the parents you have, and to manage the limitations of your relationship with them.

Becoming more *Secure*, and more autonomous in your thinking, eases the passage to adolescence. But does that mean it will be a smooth and orderly process? No, it does not. Very little in adolescence is smooth and orderly. But in less than a decade, by the time you are a newly minted adult, you will probably better understand why your parents are as good or bad as they are. You will appreciate, at least in your head, their stoic tolerance, or the difficulties they faced in their own lives, although working out your feelings of rejection, hurt or confusion is another matter.

Life with your annoying family

If the physical onset of adolescence is reliably signalled by puberty, then the equivalent social signal is an increase in conflict in the household. From your vantage point, it's like a veil has been lifted on your parents, revealing deep flaws that somehow escaped your attention earlier in your life. Now, everything about them irritates you. How they talk. How they dress. The noise they make when they are eating.

If you were asked in real time what you are thinking about when you are with your family, negative thoughts outnumber positive ones by about ten to one.[10] But what bothers you most of all is what you see as their intolerable invasions on your privacy.

> My parents are, like, always on my case. My mother just won't let me alone. Like constantly going on about what I wear: 'You're not going out in that, are you?' Or commenting on my mood, like: 'What's wrong with you today?' My father's big thing is how long I spend in the shower. He once actually timed it. He said it was twenty-five minutes. I mean, like, so what? Can you believe that?
>
> Ger, 14

Underlying the surface conflicts is your struggle to become independent. Broadly, you and your parents want the same thing – for you to become more independent and responsible, and for the relationship between you to become more equal, mutual and adult-like. But the agreement pretty much ends there. You are firmly focused on the independent side of the equation. They are firmly focused on the responsibility side.

Here's the key issue to understand: you can be independent and dependent in an autonomous way, or in a way that is pressured and controlled. What matters is how you *feel* when you are making the decision.

What your parents bring to the table

How parents handle all these conflicts ranges along a continuum, and in the normal course of things, as adolescence progresses, parents gradually allow more autonomy.[11] At the very beginning, parents control all-important decisions. As you mature, they make the decisions, but only after talking to you. This is followed by you and your parents deciding together. Then you progress to making decisions yourself, but after talking to them. Finally, you make decisions by yourself.

This progression towards full autonomy should depend on your age and the progress you are making towards self-motivation. But it's also deeply coloured by the way your parents have always responded to your need for autonomy, how traditional or liberal their views about childrearing, and how *Secure* or insecure their own state of mind about attachment.

ENCOURAGING DEMOCRACY

Some parents actively encourage and support your autonomy, approaching family decisions in a democratic way.

- They believe that adolescent children have a right to be part of family decisions in which they have a legitimate interest and perhaps even some expertise.
- They show a readiness to let everyone in the family air their view, argue for their preferred option, and disagree without fear.
- They make an honest attempt to integrate everybody's ideas into the final decision or plan.
- Mothers tend to express their own ideas directly and coordinate family discussions so that everybody has the opportunity to express their own opinions and negotiate disagreements.
- Fathers tend to comment on others' suggestions rather than first offering their own views, but are also ready to disagree.
- For girls, if both parents encourage them to explore different options and assert their own views, the greater their autonomy. For boys, how fathers handle disagreements holds special significance, especially a readiness to tolerate or encourage their assertiveness.

When autonomy is encouraged, family relationships are closer, warmer and more open. You feel free to talk to your parents about anything that is concerning you, and you are more open to considering their advice and guidance. These lessons in autonomy transfer to your other close relationships. Your approach to resolving conflicts with a friend, or later a romantic partner, is warmer, more relational and collaborative, and the quality of those relationships is correspondingly higher.

The added bonus is a double crossover effect. Close and autonomous friendships at the beginning of adolescence predict high-quality romantic relationships at the end of adolescence, which in turn predict higher-quality friendships in your twenties.

EXERTING TOO MUCH CONTROL

Other parents stay clustered on the more controlling end of the spectrum. When parents exercise a lot of control over your decisions, your reaction is rebellion, disengagement or submission – or some toxic mix of all three. Rebellion is fine, as long as it's fuelled by your fierce desire to be autonomous and not a disguised form of dependence, a compulsive urge to *always* do the opposite of what your parents want. Submission and disengagement can work as a short-term tactical manoeuvre to gather your resources or get support from someone. But if submission becomes chronic, it spells trouble, breeding a sullen resentment that will undermine your long-term relationship with your parents. If disengagement becomes a permanent strategy, it triggers a more decisive withdrawal, a habit of compulsive self-sufficiency that signals trouble in other close relationships.

Crucially, being over-controlled undermines your effort to resolve the big task of adolescence – finding and forming your own identity. Autonomy fundamentally relies on the freedom to disagree, to express your own views without fear. That is your first step in setting new boundaries between you and them, and you need to be assured that this necessary process of becoming yourself will not jeopardize your ongoing need for closeness and support. If the price of asserting your autonomy is rejection, you are faced with a no-win situation that will set the stage for more long-term estrangement, or more mentally entangled and enmeshed relationships.[12]

WHEN EMOTIONS ERUPT

Sometimes, in even the most secure of families, the normal and temporary distancing between adolescents and their parents takes a more intense turn, triggering a crisis of identity that can erupt between girls and their mothers, or boys with their fathers.

As a boy, a dominant competitive father can undermine your attempts to carve out your own identity. Nothing is ever enough to secure his affirmation or praise, as if there is only so much to go around – and he has to hoard it, to shore up his identity.

As a girl, if your relationship with your mother is exceptionally close, this can make the struggle to form a separate identity more urgent and complex. You fiercely resist the pull of the old intimacies and assumptions about you, and your mother is likely to react with bewilderment to this changeling in her midst.

> I thought that I knew what to expect when my eldest daughter became a teenager. We were always very close, so I thought I could deal with the moodiness and all that. But the year she turned fifteen she started to fly into these rages at me for absolutely nothing, or at least what seemed like nothing to me. One day I was so upset I said to her, 'What's happened to you, Celia? You were never like this!' And she said, 'You know nothing about me, Mum! You think you do, but you don't.' And then she burst into tears. I was flabbergasted. But we kept talking at least, and I gradually got to understand that these blow-ups were her way of shaking me out of thinking that I knew everything important about her. And of course I didn't, she was changing. She was right. So I had to get to re-know her on her own terms. We get on great now. But it was absolutely nerve-wracking at the time.
>
> Stephanie, 57

Siblings – the good and the bad

Start with this thought: your relationship with your siblings will be the longest-lasting relationship of your life. At all stages of life, sibling relationships revolve around two poles: support, love and loyalty on one side; competition and conflict on the other. All that varies is the intensity of the conflict and the extent of the support on offer. Some competition between siblings is inevitable, a residue of the childhood need to get access to the most precious resource – your parents' attention.

Your relationship with your siblings remains important in adolescence, but it's less intense than in childhood, and more egalitarian.[13]

Older siblings can't dominate you in the way they did in childhood, although that does not stop them trying. You and your siblings can band together occasionally to resist the excesses of parental oppression. You can pick up a thing or two from older siblings that will ease your passage into adolescence.

The bad news is that the relationship with siblings also becomes more fraught, and conflicts are even more frequent, and more intense, than those with your parents. The main point of contention is how the resources, privileges and prime space in the house are distributed by parents. Accusations of unequal and preferential treatment, real or perceived, are rife.

Your attachment style affects the quality of your relationship with your siblings, a spillover from the relationship you had with your parents in childhood. If your state of mind is *Dismissing*, you are more avoidant and defensive in how you interact with your siblings, you express little warmth, or open affection. If your state of mind is *Preoccupied*, your relationship with them is volatile and often marked by angry outbursts.[14]

The joy of no siblings

What if you are an only child?[15] The common perception is that you are probably lonely, spoiled, overindulged, overprotected, and likely to become an unhappy, poorly adjusted, selfish person. Parents regularly say that one of the reasons they want to have a second child is to ensure that their firstborn is not an only child. There is little psychological evidence for such negative views of only children.

For the most part, only children are not distinguishable from their peers who have siblings in terms of their psychological well-being, character or sociability.

The most consistent differences are that:

- they are likely to score higher on intelligence
- they are strongly motivated to achieve
- they are successful in school and stay longer in education, and
- they hold more prestigious jobs in adulthood.

They feel grateful that they didn't have to share their parents' time and attention or endure conflict and competition from siblings. They valued their time alone as a child, and felt it facilitated more creative play. In childhood, their relationship with their parents is generally close, and they feel that they were more mature than their peers with siblings.

The sexual self

As puberty advances, the fuzzy sexuality that characterized late childhood ends and the target of your sexual interest becomes *much* clearer as an opposite-sex or same-sex peer begins to exert a sexual fascination. As you engage with that, you begin to add a new and significant layer to your identity – thinking of yourself as a sexual person and a romantic partner. Developing that identity necessarily involves exploring your own sexuality and, for some, sexual orientation or gender identity. Whatever your identity is, you've got to work out how to enact it in the highly competitive world of adolescence, finely attuned to what your peers regard as 'normal' or will accept, and to what feels right for you.

This is more complex if you are gay, lesbian or transgender. You have to come to terms with what that means in a very personal way, and then try to integrate your public and private sense of self, often in the face of strong cultural pressure to deny it. Having a *Secure* attachment to a parent, or even one close friend, is a huge resource, allowing you to disclose your sexual or gender identity earlier, to develop more positive attitudes about yourself, and to resist pressure and discrimination.[16]

At some point, you fall in love. Apart from all the other joys, this consolidates your gender and sexual identity. A girl feels like she has become a woman, and delights in her femininity, while a boy feels a new pride in his masculinity, a process that is mutually encouraged, both wanting to fit together like jigsaw pieces. For gay, lesbian, bisexual or transgender adolescents, the process of consolidating a sexual identity, of 'assigning' a different or complementary identity to the lover, has to be worked out in a more individual way, without the benefit, or constraint, of gender stereotypes. But in early adolescence

especially, this process may be burdened by the anxiety of not knowing whether your sexual orientation is a permanent or temporary
phenomenon, and the lack of a supportive context in which to discuss
your most intimate concerns.

By late adolescence, everything has steadied up. The notion of
being a romantic partner is now embedded in your identity, and you
have experienced a new kind of love. Three great psychological currents begin to merge, as a precursor of what will happen in adult life:

- the sensual affection of childhood
- the sexual power of adolescence, and
- attachment.

A life well lived – what we learn from adolescence

The principles of a life well lived – adolescence			
Life stage	*Time frame*	*Developmental task*	*Psychological principle*
Adolescence	puberty–late teens	identity or confusion?	Be authentic

Adolescence is when you become your authentic self. While it can be
stormy, when all goes well you will reach the other side ready to
embrace adult life with a strong sense of who you are and what matters to you. That is the fundamental task of adolescence.

A robust and secure identity holds you steady in life. But what if
the process of becoming your own person was short-circuited at key
points in your life – by external circumstances, or pressure from your
parents to conform to their demands, or as the result of your identity
being submerged by a dominant personality in your family or an intimate relationship?

You are always a work-in-progress

There is no end point in identity. From start to finish, your sense of self
and identity are continually changing. So, if your identity formation

was short-circuited, you can now give yourself a second chance to start the open, free-range exploration of yourself and what you want from life, and the necessary trial-and-error that is part of the process of forming your own identity.

GIVE YOURSELF THE RIGHT TO DISAGREE WITH THE ASSUMPTIONS OTHERS HAVE ABOUT YOU

The developmental root of identity is the freedom to disagree. You first discovered who you were and what you liked by knowing what you were not and did not. The first step in asserting that identity is giving yourself the right to say: 'This is *not* the way I feel or think. This is *not* the kind of person I am.' The next step is the freedom to argue your point so you can find out just how important your feelings and opinions are. If you never got the chance in adolescence to say, 'How about not making assumptions about me?' then say it now. Will this unsettle people? Maybe. But after some initial surprise at this change in your style, people will get used to it, and each time you do that, it boosts your confidence in your own identity.

LISTEN TO YOUR INNER DIALOGUE

The constraints of becoming your own person were once external. Now, they are internalized. You need to start by listening to your inner dialogue. When we are having a conversation with somebody, there is always an inner dialogue that parallels the actual dialogue – what you are thinking or feeling but are not saying because you assume it would be met with disagreement, disapproval or disinterest.

Everybody does some filtering like this, but if your sense of identity is weak or confused, you are much more likely to filter. If you frequently walk away from conversations that leave you feeling low and dissatisfied because you didn't register what was important to you, or even register yourself, then think of a recent conversation like that and try this exercise.[17]

- Divide a page placed lengthways (or two pages taped together) into four columns.

- In the far right column, write down what the other person said as accurately as you can remember.
- In the column next to that, write down what you said.
- In the next left column, write down what you were thinking but not saying (in other words your internal dialogue).
- Read the conversation through and mark everywhere in the conversation where there was a mismatch between your external and internal dialogue.
- In the far left column, find a constructive and measured way to express the thoughts and feelings that you inhibited. *This* is the conversation that would have left you feeling that you acted with strength and authenticity.
- Now, ask yourself a series of questions.

    o Why did I not say what I was thinking or feeling?
    o What was I trying to accomplish?
    o Did it work?
    o What assumptions was I making about the other person?
    o Does this happen only with this specific person, or is it a more general pattern?
    o What do I gain from this?
    o What do I lose?
    o Is the gain worth the loss?

- Honest answers will reveal the internal model you laid down early in your life, the set of assumptions about who you are and how other people are likely to react to you. Your internal dialogue is an echo of long-gone conversations with those you depended on. But you are no longer a child and the person you are talking to is not your mother or your father. It takes time and practice to change this pattern, but the pay-off is worth it – a more secure and assured sense of your own identity.

KNOW WHAT YOU STAND FOR AND THEN STAND FOR IT ALL THE TIME

It's easier to hold to your principles 100 per cent of the time, says Clayton Christensen, a former professor at Harvard Business School,

than it is to hold to them 98 per cent of the time.[18] A secure sense of
who you are and what you believe and value is the guiding light that
keeps you on a steady course.

Through the adolescent years, you have made a rough cut at answer-
ing the big questions posed at the beginning of adolescence. You
now use those answers to cobble together the core of a new identity,
or at least enough for you to say: 'This is who I am. This is where I
belong. This is what I want to do.' In short, you have created something completely new. What you've done is not extraordinary. It's
just normal. But it's still amazing.

   However you find yourself at the end of adolescence, the process
of forming your identity is not over, and now spills over into the
deeper, broader exploration that happens in the next stage: emerging
adulthood.[19]

13.   *Emerging adulthood:* A taste of freedom

may my mind stroll about hungry
and fearless and thirsty and supple
and even if it's sunday may i be wrong
for whenever men are right they are not young

e. e. cummings

Your twenties are what Professor Jeffrey Arnett calls the 'volitional years', when you are most free to make choices about who you are, who you want to be, and how you live your life.[1] You want to have a good taste of life before you settle down – to have finished your education, lived independently, travelled, held a job for a few years, and lived with your partner for a while. Arnett described this life stage as 'emerging adulthood'.

- *The age of feeling in-between*: a time when you no longer feel adolescent, yet not a full adult either.
- *The age of exploring your identity*: trying out various possibilities in love and work, working out some view of your adult self and of the world you live in, and moving bit by bit towards making more enduring choices.
- *The age of instability*: a time of frequent changes in education, work, romantic partners and living arrangements.
- *The self-focused age*: the time of your life when you will experience more personal freedom and less social control than you have ever had before in your life, or are likely to ever have again, once you take on the more enduring commitments of adulthood.
- *The age of possibilities*: the time when you are most likely to feel full of optimism about the future and how your life will

eventually work out, even if your current prospects are less than perfect.

The most striking external feature of emerging adulthood is that those in their twenties are more likely to be still living at home than ever before. Across the EU's member states, including Ireland, nearly 50 per cent of you still live at home, with rates differing from country to country.* This pattern is mirrored in all developed countries and big urban areas. In the USA, for example, where traditionally most young people left home early, about 34 per cent aged eighteen to thirty-four now live at home. In Canada, the rate is 42 per cent, in Australia 38 per cent, in Russia 51 per cent, in Japan nearly 50 per cent.†

In addition, 'leaving home' does not mean what it used to. You leave home to move in with friends, or a romantic partner; you get a job and move out and live alone for a while; you leave to go back into education or training or take a gap year; you go back home again; then you move out again. About 40 per cent will boomerang back at least once.[2] All that's constant is your email address.

Why? A mix of reasons. It's taking a lot longer to prepare for adulthood, to get the qualifications, training and experience necessary for a job market that is highly competitive and precarious, where most jobs require a high level of competence. (In fact, most of you are still in education – over 40 per cent in the EU and nearly 70 per cent in the USA.)

The process of developing that competence looms large in your twenties. If you are in college, it's a hard, competitive slog, and you

---

* In southern and eastern European countries, where living at home has a long tradition, the rates are highest – 67 per cent in Italy, 65 per cent in Spain. In the UK it's 34 per cent, and only 18 per cent in Denmark – perhaps because in Scandinavian countries there are generous state payments to young adults to enable them to live independently.

† These figures are taken from a variety of official sources, including Eurostat, EU-SILC survey, Pew Research Centre surveys and the UK Office for National Statistics. Figures can vary from study to study, depending on the methodologies and age ranges used.

are likely to be accumulating substantial student loan debts. If you leave school early, you are likely to work in a low-paid job in the service sector, with little security or future prospects. In Europe, unemployment rates for your generation are more than double what they are for other age groups. If you are at work, the jobs are often low paid, and rental accommodation is expensive in big cities, so most of you remain financially dependent on your parents to some degree.

There's more to it than that, though. It's also taking longer to prepare *psychologically* to meet the demands of adulthood. In the workplace, more people work in teams than ever before, and managing those relationships requires a high level of social and emotional competency, although that's nothing compared to what's required these days to maintain a successful personal relationship. In both areas, you are expected to take individual responsibility to keep things moving forward. You have internalized these new expectations, and they are reflected in the way you define what feeling like an 'adult' means now.

The new markers of adulthood

In previous generations, the markers of adulthood were external events – leaving school, getting a job, getting married, setting up a household, having children. These markers now rank at the *bottom* of what signifies feeling adult – bar becoming a parent, which immediately catapults you into adulthood.* Instead, the top three markers of adulthood – in specific order – are psychological:

- feeling that you are ready to accept responsibility for yourself

---

* While becoming a parent ranks low in importance for emerging adults, for emerging adults who become parents, Arnett notes that it is often enough to decisively mark the move into full adulthood. It not only restricts exploring many options, it shifts the focus from achieving self-responsibility to becoming responsible for others.

- feeling confident that you can make independent decisions, and
- feeling financially independent.

This combination of economic necessity and changed psychological focus is what drives the need for the extended period of exploration and maturing in your twenties. You are laying the groundwork that will ready you to make the binding commitments of adulthood. Living at home simply gives you more freedom and flexibility to do that.

The prime developmental task of emerging adulthood is to become responsible for yourself and for your life, so that you can take on the binding commitments of adulthood. In adolescence, you formed some dream of the life you hoped for; in your twenties, you try to turn it into reality. But first, you want to enjoy a period of freedom and independence, to find out by a process of trial-and-error what you are good at, what you find interesting and satisfying, and to figure out how viable your plans are, how likely they will work in the world you inhabit.

In this way, your explorations into yourself go wider and deeper, expanding and solidifying the sense of personal identity you began to build in adolescence, and which will form the structure for your later development in adulthood.[3] But you are ready. Your drive for autonomy is surging, a wellspring of energy, zest and curiosity that will flow into virtually everything you think and do.

The purpose of this exploration is to find the right path, to get ready to make the commitments that will give you a secure foothold in adulthood, but that will also allow you to keep growing and developing. Range too narrowly in your explorations, and you risk foreclosure – making premature choices that may stall your development, limit your potential and, at midlife, come back to haunt you. Range too widely and for too long, and it becomes a way to avoid taking on the commitments of adult life.

In every era, what happens in your twenties counts, a lot. Later in life, if you are asked to recount your memories from different stages of your life, the most frequent and vivid memories are likely to be from your twenties, because what happens at this time is consequential: your options are still open, very little about the future has been finally settled.[4] This is when you consolidate your identity, when you say yes to certain parts of yourself and no to others. But you won't fully grasp the import and consequences of those decisions until midlife.

The friend zone

A few close friends and a network of trusty companions provide the ballast needed for the unmarked crossing between adolescence and the steadier terrain of full adulthood. Your network of peers provides the breadth of social contact you need to help you see where you might fit into the world. Your close friends allow you to do that too, but in a more private and intimate way.

The quality of your relationships with friends and people in your wider social network will constitute a large part of your happiness in your twenties. When your need for friendship and belonging is frustrated, you are prey to the toxic brew of anxiety, depression, envy and loneliness that affects your psychological and physical well-being.[5]

Loneliness and social isolation are two different things. You may have peers with whom to socialize, but still feel lonely if you don't have a close relationship with a friend you can trust to be there for you. You enjoy an intimate relationship with a romantic partner but feel very isolated because you have no network of friends and peers to meet and have fun with. Chronic loneliness or social isolation puts you at significant risk of anxiety or depression, which may interfere with your ability to concentrate on your studies or at work. Most of all, it hampers the process of exploring yourself, which is a key marker of this stage.

You and your friends serve as mutual sounding-boards, counsellors and consolers.[6] You help each other to think things through and deal with the day-to-day hassles as well as the bigger stresses, like the break-up of a romantic relationship, a setback in college or work, trouble at home. Friends are great, but they also create their own set of stresses. They make demands on your time. They get on your nerves. It's often hard to get the right balance between your need to belong and your need for autonomy; between maintaining a special friendship and maintaining contact with your wider network of peers.

The social whirl

If you are *extraverted*, you are strongly motivated to socialize with friends and peers, ready to initiate friendships, to make things happen socially, and to join in whatever activity is being organized. You thrive on all this interaction and are energized by it.

At the more extreme end of extraversion, you like to exercise a kind of soft power. You like being in charge. You like to make an impact socially and to continually expand your network. Others rely on you to get things going, to make plans, to organize activities, to persuade others to join in. Generally, you enjoy all this, though you may complain about the work and frustration involved in trying to organize the group. You may also have to put up with the occasional resentment and push-back from your friends when they feel they are being over-organized or controlled by an excess of leadership. And your closest friends may feel neglected by this swirl of social activity.

If you are more *introverted*, your need for sociability is lower. You like having friends and socializing, but in small doses. You cherish time on your own and can feel overstimulated and overwhelmed by too much social interaction. You are slower to initiate friendships and may rely on a more extraverted friend to do that, or to persuade you to join in social activities. While you may strongly feel that you don't need all this social contact, when you are forced to be more outgoing you usually find that you enjoy it and it boosts your mood.

If you are *shy*, socializing is more difficult. You are more inhibited and nervous in social situations and more physiologically reactive. Your palms may sweat, you blush easily, making you even more self-conscious. You rarely initiate social interaction. If you do and you cannot overcome your initial anxiety, you withdraw too quickly, leaving the person you are talking to wondering what happened. That kind of social anxiety tends to lessen as you mature and learn a few critical social skills. And when you settle into a stable romantic relationship, particularly with a partner who is more naturally sociable than you, you can coast along happily in their social wake.

At the more extreme end of introversion, you are not nervous about socializing, you are just less interested and may actively avoid social occasions.

Managing your relationships with friends, peers and romantic partners requires the same set of basic social competencies. Being able to:

- *initiate* a relationship
- *disclose* important things about yourself at the right time
- *provide* helpful emotional support
- *assert* yourself in the right measure, and
- *manage conflicts* effectively and constructively.[7]

In addition to temperament, self-esteem affects your capacity to make friends. In the normal course of events, when you meet someone new your instinctive response is to put your best foot forward to make a good impression. But this does not happen if your self-esteem is low. Instead, you are more focused on trying to avoid revealing what you see as your flaws, rather than drawing attention to your strong points. This self-protective, defensive stance can come across as aloofness or arrogance.

Loneliness

Getting to know somebody involves two people gradually revealing more personal, private and important things about themselves, but this process must be reciprocal. Loneliness gets in the way of doing that.

If you suffer from loneliness, you exhibit a particular pattern of self-disclosure.[8] When you are talking to someone of the same sex whom you don't know well, you tend to start at too high a level of self-disclosure, for example, by launching into an account of a very personal and upsetting experience you had. This might make a great beginning to a short story, but it's not a great way to start a conversation in real life because, depending on what you reveal, you risk coming across as needy, or odd. It makes it hard for the other person to reciprocate in kind. This shaky start is not helped by the fact that you then say very little else about yourself as the conversation proceeds.

When you are talking to somebody of the opposite sex, you do the opposite, beginning at too low a level of self-disclosure, sharing virtually nothing about yourself. You stick to topics that are so neutral, they invite equally neutral replies. After this unpromising start, you stop talking, leaving it up to the other person to keep things going, so the conversation eventually peters out. However, at the end of the interaction, *you* feel that the other person now knows you better – the trouble is, they don't feel that way. You haven't picked up the lack of intimacy, and this discrepancy has a dampening effect on any future interaction between you.

How your attachment style works for and against you in your twenties

In your twenties, your attachment style shapes how you approach the main tasks facing you: becoming responsible for your own life, establishing and deepening your close relationships, and managing your life in an autonomous and competent way.

Secure

You face these challenges with a substantial advantage. Your sense of self is strong, stable and coherent.[9] That inner strength and resilience is reflected in the confident way you explore your inner and outer worlds, in your readiness to take calculated risks and in your ability to set and pursue goals for your life. You are able to leverage the full value of being young, curious and optimistic because being *Secure* nudges you in the direction of happiness. You have learned that feeling happy is a valuable signal that you can move forward with confidence.

Positive feelings are not psychological accessories. Their fundamental purpose is to alert you to opportunities.[10] When you feel happy, you're more open to new ideas, readier to approach new people and new experiences. You can think of more things to do and are more motivated to actually do them. You are more attuned to the big picture, to possibility. All of this helps you to connect to others, to experiment, to be creative. In the process, you build networks of support and personal resources – a good strategy at any stage of life, but pure gold in your twenties as you struggle to get a foothold in adult life.

The cumulative experiences of being loved and supported attune you to the abundance of life. You are on familiar terms with joy and contentment. Loving and being loved come easily to you. You find it easy to be grateful, and to take delight in your achievements and the achievements of those you care about. You have the ability to approach and pursue things with unconflicted energy, not second-guessing yourself or holding back.[11]

This capacity to regulate your emotions, to resist becoming emotionally overwhelmed in the face of frustrations, setbacks and failure, will prove a key resource.* You are able to easily access your store of good memories. You have a clear sense of what you expect and believe to be essential in a good relationship, and you are direct and constructive about confronting a friend or romantic partner who lets you down. That way, you sidestep many otherwise painful and destructive experiences and can resist falling into prolonged bouts of rumination and resentment. All of this gives you a generally optimistic view of the world, a more balanced view of threats and opportunities, so you can tolerate the ambiguity and uncertainty of this in-between stage of life more easily.

Avoidant

Your sense of self is more brittle, your self-esteem held in place only by excluding from your consciousness your feelings and memories of vulnerability or weakness. You have to be on guard, therefore you

---

* If your temperament has compromised your capacity for self-regulation, the accelerating demands to become competent and manage your life can take a heavy toll on you emotionally. Being *Secure*, and having a reliable, secure base in a relationship with a parent, close friend or romantic partner buffers you from the worst of the stresses. You will struggle most in contexts that are unstructured, so establishing solid habits and routines in your day-to-day life is critical.

have little sense of ease, especially in close relationships. You rate yourself much higher on qualities than those who know you would, and if you do acknowledge any weakness, you dismiss it as unimportant. You try to sustain this image of yourself by exaggerating your achievements, or by fantasies of self-perfection and power.

You assiduously avoid situations of intimacy and self-disclosure that threaten your defences. You try to repress worries about rejection and separation. Yet, negative thoughts and images of yourself break through. When you describe a problem in a romantic relationship or the kind of dreams you have, what emerges is a sense of yourself as closed-off, distant, alone, afraid and angry.[12] But somewhere in your consciousness, you always know what you don't appear to know.

This deactivation strategy works when you are dealing with everyday stressors, like setbacks in your studies, work or personal relationship. But when you are faced with major stressors that involve reorganizing your routines, plans and hopes, your deactivating strategy can collapse.[13] Your physiological arousal rises rapidly, as does your blood pressure, and you experience other stress symptoms that interfere with getting enough oxygen to the muscles of your heart, raising your risk of hypertension and heart disease in the long term.[14] But even then, your mind is slow to activate thoughts of turning to the person you are most attached to.

Your happiness also falls victim to your deactivating strategy. Repressing your negative emotions dampens down your capacity to fully experience positive emotions. You guard yourself against a surge of affection or raising your hopes of love in case it might draw you into a risky closeness to someone. This general constriction spills over into your approach to self-exploration, which is restrained and shallow, and it lends a compulsive and rather joyless quality to your drive for achievement.

Anxious

You hype up your distress in an effort to get the care and reassurance you need. Your sense of self is more fragmented and unstable, your self-esteem shaky and volatile, too dependent on others' approval or on some immediate sense of achievement. This uncertainty about your own value is the residue of a long history of frustrating, unpredictable experiences with parents who were too caught up in their own needs to care for you, leaving you vulnerable to self-doubt and harsh self-criticism. It undermines your sense of yourself as a separate and autonomous person, with the right and the capacity to live your own life. You become confused about the reality or validity of your feelings and experiences, especially in a conflict situation, and try to repress them in case they court disapproval.

You are easily overwhelmed by distress when things go wrong, struggling to calm yourself or regulate your stress response. When you experience love, affection or hope, you try desperately to hold on to those feelings. But memories of past disappointment or loss are vivid and intrude into your consciousness, one memory setting off the other like a bushfire. Yet, during interpersonal conflicts, the level of your expressed distress is not reflected in your heart rate, unless the distress reaches a very high level, suggesting that you are exaggerating the genuine distress you feel. Trying to manage all of this absorbs a lot of your resources, making it hard for you to take the risks and confront the challenges that face you in your twenties.

How your attachment style is impacted by strong emotional experiences

Secure, *Avoidant* or *Anxious*, these are the strategies that play out in your twenties, especially in your close relationships with family, friends and lovers. But your style of attachment can also be affected by what happens in those relationships. Severe family stress, a very upsetting romantic break-up, a particularly bruising first year in college or in your first job can temporarily undermine your *Secure* style.

Correspondingly, an insecure style can be transformed by a 'corrective emotional experience', a powerful re-experiencing of an old fear or trauma but with a different ending. This time, you find what you were hoping for instead of what you dreaded.[15] These 'corrective emotional experiences' can happen in a serious romantic relationship, or in a close, supportive relationship with a friend, a mentor, a therapist – somebody who is in some way 'older and wiser' and has your interests at heart.

Stress and your attachment style

By adulthood, one of the major distinctions between being *Secure*, *Avoidant or Anxious* is the strategy you use in response to threat or stress. If you are *Avoidant*, you try to deactivate your stress response; if you are *Anxious*, you hyper-activate it; if you are *Secure*, you do neither.[16]

Secure attachment and stress

If you are *Secure*, you mainly use the primary, default attachment strategy – when you feel vulnerable, you turn to the person you are most attached to for comfort, reassurance and encouragement. You can see that automatic 'turning to' when couples in an airport are saying goodbye to each other. Compared to couples who are travelling together, they draw closer together, gaze at each other's faces, talk more intently to each other, and touch each other more often.[17]

You have learned that stress and distress are manageable, and that you are likely to get help and support from those you are attached to. You can explore things that trouble or upset you in your close relationships, without that distress automatically and uncontrollably spreading into other aspects of the relationship. If you find yourself under severe stress, you may temporarily resort to a *deactivating* or *hyper-activating* strategy, but not in the automatic or compulsive way those who have an insecure attachment style do.*

Avoidant attachment and stress

If you are *Avoidant*, you adopt a *deactivating* strategy. You try to repress that urge, suppress your distress and distance yourself mentally, emotionally and behaviourally from the source of the stress by

---

* As before, the descriptions here of *Secure*, *Avoidant* and *Anxious* attachment represent the 'pure' types. In the less extreme cases, the associated attitudes and behaviours may be less pronounced, but the essential dynamic remains the same.

diverting your attention to something else. This shuts down any deep mental processing of what caused you to feel anxious, angry or sad. Therefore, your memory for what made you stressed is poor or inaccurate, and what you recall is emotionally shallow and lacking in insight.

Anxious attachment and stress

If you have an *Anxious* style, you adopt a *hyper-activating* strategy in response to stress or any perceived threat. You are hyper-vigilant for any sign of rejection in your close relationships and respond by exaggerating your resulting anxiety and distress, setting off a rapid negative feedback loop. Your mind floods with worries and doubt, and with memories of previous painful experiences, one negative memory automatically setting off another in a chaotic way, disorganizing your emotional equilibrium, and deepening your distress.

You make all-out, recurring attempts to get the person you turn to for support to respond immediately to your signals of overwhelming distress. You try to reduce the physical and psychological distance between you with a mix of pleading, demanding, clinging, controlling, and bouts of intense anger, when you don't get the response you want. You may try to regain control by threatening to end the relationship, but are then overcome with distress, provoking more attempts to get support, and further weakening your position.

Why attachment is so important to how you cope with stress

In your twenties, there is no shortage of threats and upsets – a conflict in an important relationship; the break-up of a big romance; trouble at home; disappointing examination results; negative feedback at work – or a more nagging sense that something is not right, that you're not moving on with your life in the way you should. Whatever the source of the threat, a pattern of thousands, or even millions, of neural responses in your brain has already automatically triggered a specific set of memories, physiological reactions, feelings, thoughts and behavioural reactions in response. This is a mix of wordless, sensory experiences, physiological reactions and automatic reflexes that are beyond your conscious awareness.

'Look,' your brain is saying, 'here's a read-out of all the data concerning what happened in your early life when you sought closeness, comfort and reassurance from the people you were most attached to.' The data comes in flashes of very specific and vivid images and sensations, including the name or visual image of the person you are or were most attached to, and is accompanied by an automatic and urgent desire to make some form of contact with that person. There are three stages to this stress/threat reaction.[18]

- **Stage 1:** The first stage happens in your pre-conscious mind, not yet in your conscious awareness. This pre-conscious process has been replicated in laboratory experiments.

  Imagine you are watching a computer screen where strings of letters appear one after the other and you have to identify as quickly as possible how each string can be made into a word. The speed of your response is an indication of how accessible your thoughts are about that word. Some of the words are related to closeness, like 'love' or 'hug', some are related to loss of closeness, like 'separation' or 'rejection', some are neutral, like 'hat'.

  Before you see the string of letters, threat or stress words – like 'failure' or 'loss' – appear on the screen for only 20 microseconds, too fast for your conscious mind to register them, but your brain does. You then react faster to words related to closeness than to other words, triggering images, or even the name of the person you are or were most attached to. Unless you are embedded in a long-term romantic relationship, very often the person you think of first is your mother.

  In other words, your attachment system is instantly and automatically activated when you register any threat, and this happens whether you are *Secure* or insecure. If your attachment style is insecure, you already know that the person whose image flashes into your mind is unlikely to respond to you when you turn to them for support. But this does not stop you automatically turning to them in your mind when threat looms.

- *Stage 2:* The second stage is conscious: you start to think about how you will respond.
- *Stage 3:* The third stage is action: your physical reaction to the trigger.

When you were a child, one stage rapidly followed the other. In adulthood, apart from serious and very distressing experiences, you are better able to defer the second and third stages for a while. You have more alternatives than a child does, a range of other people lower down your attachment hierarchy that you can turn to for re-assurance and guidance. Or, if they are no longer available, you may turn to God, or some other spiritual source. In a highly threatening situation, you may temporarily attach yourself to whoever looks competent and caring – a doctor, nurse, fireman, a kindly official, or anyone you consider 'stronger and wiser' in that situation, and once they are close, you feel safe.

14.   *Emerging adulthood:* The mating season

Maybe you tasted love before now, an early blossoming. But once you enter your twenties, you have entered the mating season. Your sexual system is at full tilt and, like great herds of wildebeest on the move across the Serengeti, you and your peers start the search for a mate. You want to find 'the one', but not exactly *immediately*. You want to cast your net wide, and you date people you would never consider marrying.

The drama of falling in love will play out over four stages:

- attraction
- dating
- falling in love, and
- becoming attached.

What happens at each of those stages will shape whether this great romance will thrive or end in tears.

Falling in love tends to be an all-consuming experience, transcending everything else that is going on in your life. The descriptions of the experience are remarkably similar. You feel swept up in something over which you have little control. No wonder. The reward centres in your brain are in overdrive, your body releasing amphetamine-like substances that put you in a state of high physical and emotional arousal. Your sensory awareness becomes acute – you notice the slightest sound, touch, smell. You are physically and emotionally restless. You have less need for food or sleep. You are sometimes so high on hormones that you experience mild hallucinogenic effects. You are convinced that the object of desire, and the entire experience, is completely unique and special. You believe this relationship will 'last forever'.

As if that were not enough, falling in love also activates the areas of the brain associated with obsessive-compulsive disorders. You become obsessed, you want to know everything about the beloved, to possess them fully. There is an intense emotional and sexual pre-occupation with each other. At no other time in the human life course, outside of infancy, do you experience such intense physical and emotional intimacy as you do when you fall in love, especially the first time. The experience will linger wordlessly in your mind for a long time to come.

Eventually, your brain habituates to the cocktail of 'falling-in-love' chemicals, and the 'being-in-love' pair-bonding endorphins – oxytocin and vasopressin – take over. There is a growing sense of mutual caring, kinship and companionship.[1] It's broadly similar to what happens in a close friendship, yet subtly different. You have an overwhelming desire to make everything perfect for the beloved, to protect them, care for them like they have never been cared for before. Sex is exciting, and frequent. But you are still a relative novice. Most of you are past the awkwardness of early adolescent fumbling, but you still worry about your body, your desirability, your sexual performance. Working out the mechanics of smoothly coordinating your sexual desire and prefer-ences with a partner's takes time and effort.

Finding your 'safe haven'

It usually takes about two years to form a full attachment bond with a partner. The first stage is the increasing physical and emotional in-timacy. This is accompanied by the adult version of separation anxiety – a protest by one of you at what you see as the other's unwarranted absence, and negotiation about things like how much time each of you spends with your own friends. As the relationship becomes more established, your partner becomes your preferred *safe haven*, the person you turn to when worried or vulnerable. The final stage is when your partner replaces your parents as your secure base, the psychological anchor in your life, your number one.

All the while, your three powerful instinctive systems – sex, care-taking and attachment – are becoming united in this bond between you. The quality of the attachment bond will be jointly shaped by your attachment style and your partner's. You each bring your own story of what happened when you sought closeness in the past. That story has already shaped the tone and quality of many of your interactions to date, and in all the ambiguous spaces. And when you knew only a little about each other, you called on your own store of attachment experiences to fill in the gaps.[2]

Secure

A *Secure* attachment style doesn't make you, or your love, perfect. You come to love with the usual human quota of blind spots, frailties and annoying habits. But the overall package you bring with you is a big bonus. You are optimistic about love, you believe it's possible to find somebody you really love and who will love you, and that such love can last a long time. Your comfort with emotional closeness is matched by your ease with physical intimacy and your readiness to respond to your partner. Most of all, you bring a capacity to trust.[3] For you, trust comes easily, you are ready to trust, capable of being trustworthy, and prepared to work at building trust in a relationship.

Insecure

If you are insecure, you bring a bleaker package to your romantic relationships: entrenched concerns about closeness and dependence; chronic worries about being taken advantage of, rejected or abandoned. You lack the experience of the easy and mutual partnership that a *Secure* attachment style brings. Your mood is often low, making it harder to accommodate your partner's desires and goals and to manage the inevitable conflicts that arise.★

★ The patterns described here are of people with an insecure attachment but who can function in the world and have no major psychological difficulties. Those who do have mental health difficulties may also show these patterns, but there are other signs of maladjustment and difficulty coping with the demands of life.

AVOIDANT

If your attachment style is *Avoidant*, your aversion to emotional closeness has a dampening effect at every stage of a romantic relationship. Even in ordinary social interactions, you are vigilant about your personal space. You find it hard to tolerate somebody moving physically too close to you, especially if you are talking about personal issues. Every time someone steps over that invisible boundary, your body registers discomfort.[4] You have a certain insight about this. For example, you are aware that you can come across as unfriendly or indifferent, and that is how friends are likely to describe you. But you see this as how you *choose* to be, not attributable to any insecurity. You are lonely, but often fail to recognize the empty feeling as loneliness, describing it instead as boredom or indifference. And even when you do acknowledge your loneliness, you believe this is the way life is and that you may never get really close to anyone, an expectation that can become a self-fulfilling prophecy.[5]

You are sceptical about the existence of 'true love'. And even if you think it's possible, you believe it soon fades. For you, flirting and romance are a game to be played. You may have a lot of casual sex, one-night stands, clocking up sexual conquests that provide sexual satisfaction with the minimum of interaction, few displays of affection and often little regard for your partner's enjoyment. Afterwards, you may feel alienated and estranged from your sexual partner. If you are a woman, you may agree to unwanted sex as a way to avoid emotional intimacy or conflict.

Most of all, you find it hard to trust. You are suspicious of your partner's effort to build intimacy and trust, often seeing it as manipulative, an attempt to force you into a closeness you don't want.[6] You hold back on expressing your feelings, exercising strict control over what you disclose. You are more emotionally hidden, more secretive, sharing little of substance about yourself, reluctant to discuss personal things in any depth, quick to shut down conversations that get too close for comfort.

From the beginning of the relationship, you may be reluctant to commit, jealously guarding your 'space' and independence, wanting to meet less often and spend less time together than your partner does.

When you do spend time together, you often feel tense, bored and disengaged. When you start to date regularly, you complain about 'too many conflicts' with your partner; about 'too many demands'; about the relationship being 'too stressful', 'too emotional'. You react to upsets and conflicts by dismissing their impact and distancing yourself. Even when you do commit, you hedge your bets by investing little in the relationship; several months in, your commitment is still low, and you downplay any intimacy that may be developing.

ANXIOUS

If your style of attachment is *Anxious*, you strongly believe in 'true love'. You find it easy to fall in love, and you often do. You readily admit to how lonely you are, but it never quenches your hope that one day you will find a close relationship that will banish that loneliness forever. You see yourself as a very trusting person, but your trust veers dangerously close to gullibility. You long for the feeling of safety that eludes you, and obsessively search for it in a new relationship. You take flight from your anxieties about being hurt with fantasies of a perfect love that will meet all your needs. You may already have some awareness that you come across as demanding, emotionally volatile, unable to stand up for yourself, and therefore easily exploited.[7]

In the very early stages, your hopes and expectations are so high that it compromises your ability to form any accurate impression of your partner. You are on an emotional knife-edge, ready to jump to positive or negative conclusions on little evidence. You idealize, you adore, you plunge into despair. You attribute a lot of significance to any support they give you, seeing it as a good omen for the relationship, but are then easily disappointed when that support is not always available. You are unable to relax, fearing that unless you stay vigilant, you will lose your partner's attention and interest as unpredictably as you once lost your parents'. Your face often looks tense, even during your most tender and intimate moments. You are distraught when there is conflict between you, but even when a partner is abusive, you can persuade yourself that this is some kind of 'proof' that they really care about you. You miss danger signals.

You tend to disclose too much, too early about yourself, already assuming a level of intimacy that is not yet shared by your partner, then trying to push them into more disclosure by asking intrusive personal questions, feeling rebuffed and hurt if they are reticent.

You are also caught in powerful emotional currents that are flowing in different directions. The strong positive desire that propels you forward is exquisitely balanced by the intense anxiety it arouses. You desperately want this relationship to develop but worry about how to manage it. And even as the fledgling relationship is getting off the ground, you may be giving inconsistent and confusing signals about your intentions. Paradoxically, then, you can miss opportunities to initiate a relationship that might work out.

You put great store on the power of passion and become quickly obsessed, almost addicted, to the beloved. But your ambivalence keeps surfacing. You swing between being too accommodating and too demanding, worrying that without constant demands and scrutiny your partner will pay less attention to you, and may stray. You worry about asserting your own desires and demands. Day-to-day, this makes for frequent mood swings, bickering, and an often volatile and fraught relationship.

As your relationship develops, your chronic need for affirmation and approval can interfere with having satisfying sex. Your mood is affected by day-to-day fluctuations in how your sex life is going. If you are a woman, you may be vulnerable to agreeing to sex as a way to feel wanted, loved and cared for, so you are likely to be having more sex than you really want. Fearing disapproval or rejection, you may over-defer to your partner's preferences as to how often you have sex and their favoured sexual activities, even though what matters more to you is the affectionate side of sex rather than sex itself. When you have a conflict or are worried about the relationship, you use sex as a route back to safety.

If you are a man, you may be anxious about your body and your sexual performance, reluctant to press your desire on a partner, so you are likely to be having less sex than you would like. But as the relationship develops, you may increasingly pressurize your partner into having more sex, by sulking or inducing feelings of guilt.

When two attachment styles collide

A relationship is a two-way street. The quality of your attachment style affects the relationship, but so does your partner's. Most people, irrespective of their own attachment, are attracted to a partner who is warm, trusting, authentic, forgiving and prepared to invest in the relationship. Someone who is *Secure* is most likely to tick all those boxes, so is the partner of choice. Yet, there is a good chance that you may end up, temporarily or permanently, with someone who is insecure. Why? At the most simple level, only two-thirds of adults are *Secure*, so there just aren't enough to go around.

Of course, an insecure attachment does not mean that you are not attractive, likeable, charming, interesting, or even fascinating. Someone who is emotionally closed can provoke in their partner a determined effort to be the one who breaches their defences, revealing the 'true' person within. The desire to save a partner from themselves, to redeem them from their isolation or suffering, flows especially strongly in the female bloodstream.

> He was a very aloof person when I met him first, I never knew what he was thinking, but that kind of fascinated me too. I thought he was lonely and just needed somebody to love him. But very soon into our relationship, these rows started, almost anything could spark an argument. For a long time, I thought I was to blame, I learned guilt at my mother's knee! But, deep down, I think I also convinced myself that these rows were a sign of how much he cared about me. I thought it would resolve itself in time, but unfortunately it didn't, and we eventually broke up, but it took four years, and by then I was thirty-four, and very afraid that I had missed the boat. But eventually [. . .] I was lucky.
>
> Eleanor, 40

Physical attraction and sexual desire can also trump your conscious preference for somebody who is *Secure*. For example, in the very early stage of a romance, being beautiful or handsome can cancel out or blur the edges of the more negative aspects of the way someone interacts with you and make them 'equal' to a *Secure* but plain-looking date.[8]

Feeling competent to move on to the next stage

By your late twenties, as you exit the stage of emerging adulthood, nearly 70 per cent of you feel that you have finally reached adulthood. If things have gone well, you have a steadier sense of self, a fuller view of who you are and what you want in life. You are open-minded, self-reflective, less afraid of uncertainty and change, with a stronger sense of overall purpose in your life. All of this gives you a kind of 'transition competence' – a strong sense that you can make the leap into the next stage of your life.[9]

If things have not gone so well, if you have drifted through your twenties, your exploration constrained or half-hearted, you might not feel able to take on the responsibilities of adulthood. You can't drag yourself away from the passive dependency of childhood, or the freewheeling freedom of adolescence. Your inertia weighs you down, you can't seem to get yourself going and make the confident leap into the next, more demanding stage of life. Don't despair. This isn't the end of the line – remember, your life is a work-in-progress.

A life well lived – what we learn from emerging adulthood

The principles of a life well lived – emerging adulthood

Life stage	Time frame	Developmental task	Psychological principle
Emerging adulthood	late teens– early 30s	self-responsibility or dependence?	Take the initiative

Taking the initiative and assuming responsibility for yourself requires a three-way process. First, you need to explore your options before committing to certain courses of action. That's a delicate balance. If you keep too many options open, you risk getting lost in aimless exploration and your life has an unsettling provisional quality about it. If you take on commitments without any meaningful exploration of who you are or what you want from life, you can find yourself in harness, alienated from yourself and your creative energy. This is a dilemma not just in your twenties but during any period of transition.

Second, you need to lay down the foundational skills that will ready you for love and work.

Third, you need to become skilled at dealing with the inevitable frustration and setbacks involved in that process, and also become skilled at coping.

Managing all the elements of that three-way process requires a lot of initiative. When you take the initiative in anything, it engages you in the enterprise in a different way – it gives it a forward momentum. The necessary trial-and-error involved is less random and more planned. You are less distracted by trying to out-perform others, more focused on mastering the task and sticking to the plan. If you encounter a setback, you are more likely to remember where you were at the beginning and focus on the progress you've made, rather than becoming despondent at how far you are from the end point. Emerging adulthood is all about taking the initiative.

Take the initiative in managing your love relationships

When you fall in love, sexual attraction, romance, interest, fun and friendship all count. These positives are what draw you together as a couple, but they don't predict how your relationship will turn out. The *most* powerful predictor is how much negativity is expressed when you are trying to resolve a disagreement.

Negative and positive reactions are not equal-opportunity emotions – expressing intense negative feelings has five times the impact of expressing positives ones. Bad is stronger than good.

To make love work, each partner has to take responsibility for managing that positive:negative ratio and, when negativity intensifies, must make strenuous efforts to put things back on track. But don't wait for your partner to do that – take the initiative yourself. Approach love in the knowledge that expressing intensely negative feelings and saying hurtful things is a much more powerful risk factor than positive feelings are a protective factor. This does not mean that positives don't matter – they do. But negatives matter more.

Therefore, make a promise to yourself and take the lovers' version of the Hippocratic oath: *Primum, non nocere.* First, do no harm.

Take the initiative to prepare for the high-pressure world of work

To survive at work, you have to get through the ordinary stuff. To thrive at work, you have to aim higher. Before you take on enduring commitments, use the freedom you have to set yourself stretch goals.

STRETCHED, BUT NOT STRESSED

Pick a goal just above your current level of skill – far enough to stretch you, but not to stress you. That's the key precondition for going into a state of flow.[10]

When you take on that kind of challenge, it involves disciplined attention and concentration, but not in an effortful way. Once you commit to the challenge, what you do goes into an automatic rhythm, yet you are laser-focused on the next move without having to consciously pay attention to each detail of the execution. Like a skilled athlete, you are totally and pleasurably absorbed by the rhythm of the game, yet hyper-alert to every opportunity and threat. This is the sweet spot between work and play. The more experiences of flow you have, the more committed you become to what you do, the more you sustain that commitment, the more it draws you further into the flow experience, and the more you come to enjoy the experience of making progress in that way.

MASTER THE ART OF PEAK PERFORMANCE

Become more aware of how your day-to-day functioning fluctuates.[11] Much of the time, you are ticking along in an average way, sometimes you are well below par, but sometimes you are performing at the peak of your abilities. There are eight elements to peak performance:[12]

- focused attention
- positive thoughts
- a challenging view of the task
- determination
- confidence
- control
- enough energy from nutrition, rest and recovery, and
- optimal level of arousal to allocate the right amount of energy to the task.

Each of these eight elements depends on your capacity to manage yourself under pressure. This, in turn, requires six psychological skills.[13]

- *Managing the right level of physiological & emotional arousal to get the task done*: this involves knowing how to calm and energize yourself, sometimes in rapid succession.
- *Cognitive restructuring*: knowing how to stop rumination, to increase confidence, to correct a bad habit, to sustain attention, and to prepare for performance.
- *Imagery*: being able to create vivid images in the mind's eye for mental preparation and practice of desired behaviours.
- *Setting goals*: setting 'outcome goals' and 'process goals' – and knowing when to switch focus from one to the other.
- *Controlling your attention*: knowing when to adopt a wide or narrow focus, and balancing the attention triad – self, other, context.
- *Routines and rituals*: having a set of predictable physical, mental and emotional routines that keep you centred, free up cognitive resources to stay focused on the task, and trigger the right mindset before, during and after you perform.

Take the initiative in learning to manage yourself under pressure

How well you manage your life is closely tied to your capacity to regulate your stress reaction, and what coping strategies you use to do so. The following table sets out a range of common coping strategies, both positive and negative.[14]

Common coping strategies (positive and negative)

Strategy	Positive/negative
Planning	Coming up with a strategy or plan to deal with the tasks you have to do and to address the challenges you face
Active coping	Taking direct action to solve a problem
Focusing	Putting aside other activities in order to concentrate on finding a solution
Timing	Holding back from acting until the time is right and not making matters worse by acting too soon
Seeking practical support	Asking someone for advice, information or practical *help*
Seeking emotional support	Turning to someone for sympathy, *understanding* and support
Constructive thinking	Looking for something good in what is happening, trying to learn something positive from the experience, and to grow as a person
Acceptance	Accepting the reality of what has *happened*
Seeking spiritual support	Turning to God or other spiritual source for *help*
Venting	Focusing on how upset you feel and giving vent to those feelings
Behavioural disengagement	Giving up trying to solve the problem
Emotional disengagement	Switching off by doing something else that will distract you – work, TV, daydreaming or sleeping
Relying on alcohol or drugs	Drinking or taking drugs to relieve the stress

The least effective strategy is drinking or taking drugs, neither of which addresses the problems you face and might end up creating new ones. Venting is not much help either. Contrary to belief, letting loose on just how bad you feel does not dissipate your frustration or anger, it just magnifies your distress.

There is no single best strategy. In a general way, engaging actively with an issue is productive as long as you have some control over the situation, however small. If you have no control, your focus needs to switch to some combination of strategies that will help you to manage your feelings of distress or frustration, so that you conserve your resources and stay calm enough to deal with the problem facing you – in other words, you switch from primary control to secondary control.

Overall, since life has a way of throwing up an unpredictable array of challenges, it's best to have a wide range of coping strategies to call upon. So take another look at coping strategies you don't habitually use, and practise using them when you face the ordinary hassles of life. That practice will stand you in good stead for any problems or pressures ahead. The higher your temperamental physiological arousal level, the more susceptible you are to becoming overstimulated and stressed, and the more important it is to learn how to regulate your stress reactions. This work on yourself and your methods of coping will pay off throughout your life course.

15. *Young adulthood:* The rush hour of your life

Sigmund Freud was once asked what a 'normal person' should be able to do well. 'To love and to work' was his answer. That pretty much sums up the dual developmental tasks of young adulthood: building intimacy and agency. This is the only life stage that involves twin tasks. And they are twinned, because they are interdependent and equally important. Building intimacy is not passive, it requires agency – using the power you have to act on the world, to exercise control and make things happen so that you can move your life forward. In turn, a robust agency depends on the sustenance provided by intimate relationships.

The rush hour of life has started. You are busy, busy, busy. Your biggest source of stress is having too much to do and not enough time to do it all. The demands in work and your personal life intensify simultaneously. This is probably the first time that you are in a job you will stay in, or want to stay in, for five years or more, so the level of investment and commitment required increases.

If you are not yet in a long-term relationship, you have to get serious about finding someone, if that is what you wish. As you advance into your thirties, this is not as easy as it was when the field was wide and open, and you had more time. If you are in a relationship, expectations of a more long-term commitment loom large. Once settled into a long-term relationship, there are inevitably more obligations. You are under more pressure to make joint decisions, and to coordinate your plans and activities. There are financial pressures, too, especially as you attempt to get a foot on the property ladder.

Once you become a parent, the demands on your time become relentless. Your life is suddenly full of meetings – parent-teacher associations, swimming committees, school fund-raising, coaching junior teams, professional networking events, voluntary organizations. Membership of associations rises steeply in your thirties, peaks at the age of forty, and then gradually declines over the rest of the life course.[1]

Big decisions must be made about how your children will be cared for, and how caretaking will be shared. For both partners, work–life balance now becomes an acute and chronic issue, especially for dual-career couples, often creating ongoing tension in your relationship.

Unless you want to risk exhaustion and burnout, you cannot pursue every goal with equal fervour. Most of you can easily identify what you most value in life – family, friends, work, fitness, good health, all feature high on most lists. The trouble arises when you find yourself pushed and pulled by competing demands from different domains in your life, and at the same time. Often, the urgent trumps the important. Rearing young children by its very nature is full of consistent but also unpredictable demands. So most of the time you just fire-fight, rapidly switching priorities in response to the most urgent demands, always on catch-up, often feeling you're not giving enough time and attention to any aspect of your life: to work, to family, or to yourself.

The technical term for all this busyness is 'role immersion'. You are more preoccupied, more absorbed in planning and doing what needs to be done to manage everything. You live feverishly in the moment, but you also have to keep an eye on the new set of pressures coming down the line. Is all this pressure making you miserable? Remarkably, no.

A new perspective

In young adulthood, your sense of self becomes more stable, you are better able to think about your earlier life and the things that shaped you, opening up the possibility for change and development. By the age of thirty, your childhood memories are more accessible than ever before and you can describe them more fully, more autonomously, and see things from your own perspective. You can separate out your account of childhood from what your parents tell you, but you can also see things from their perspective.

Observing your own children can unearth long-repressed memories and feelings. If that's painful, you can tolerate it better, especially if you have the vital support of a partner or a close friend who is prepared to listen as you untangle the threads of your experiences.

> We have a little fellow who's five now, and I see the way he relies on me to encourage him and glory in his little achievements, and I'm very painfully reminded of my own father who had no patience at all with us. He was very intelligent, but would come down like a ton of bricks on us if we didn't get something right. And he could be cruel, even though I don't think he meant to be. He once made fun of me in front of all my friends, and it really undermined my confidence as a child. Even now, when I make a mistake I feel pretty cut up. I still get angry when I think about that. I think he was trying to help us in his own way, but he had no understanding of children. I don't think my generation of fathers are like that. I hope not anyway.
>
> James, 40

Overall, the sources of day-to-day enjoyment in your life generally outweigh the stress. You are more settled psychologically, less self-absorbed, less likely to feel as anxious and depressed, and more contented than you were in your twenties.[2] You are vitally engaged in your life, so there's not much time for existential crises. Most of you are hopeful, optimistic and excited about your lives.

Not all of you are, however. Up to 30 per cent of you are struggling, to some degree or other, in either your personal life, in work, or sometimes in both. But you still have big dreams and are fairly confident that you will eventually achieve what you want from your life.[3]

Encounters with intimacy

At first glance, the main domain of intimacy is with a love partner. But intimacy has a deeper substrate, a capacity for mutuality, what Erikson described as 'an expansiveness of generosity'.[4] That generosity is what opens up the internal space for high-level responsiveness and cooperation in your close relationships. The opposite pole to intimacy is a feeling of alienation – of being untouched, of aloneness, constriction and loneliness. But it is also that lonely alienation that motivates your search for intimacy.

To be intimate is to reveal your innermost self, to make the very core of yourself known and understood, although a part of you will always remain mysterious, even to yourself. The longing to escape your own boundaries and separateness is part of being human, maybe driven by some trace memory of once being physically part of another person. Moments of deep intimacy allow a kind of self-transcendence.

You can experience intimacy in the wordless routines and rhythms that you share with someone you know so well that their familiarity is no longer noticeable, and in whose comforting presence you can enjoy the deep contentment of being alone, under no pressure to talk or to register yourself. But an encounter with intimacy can happen with a friend, or even with someone you don't know very well, if you are deeply immersed in a common activity. Or it comes by way of a gift, in those special experiences that stand out from the every-day and linger in your mind for a long time. When people describe such experiences there are distinct features.[5]

- An action, gesture, facial expression or touch that is better than a thousand words because it transcends the potential confusion of language.
- An awareness of someone's 'essence' – in you, there for you, with you.
- A distinct memory of when the experience began – the moment when you first became aware of the wholeness of the encounter – and the moment when it ended and you resumed the flow of normal interaction.
- The removal of boundaries, an opening of a door so each can enter the other's experience.
- An acute awareness of your own and the other person's body, although not necessarily in a sexual way. A sense of physical release, of muscles relaxing, as you let go of some psychological weight.
- A sense of transformation, a feeling of anticipation and excitement that something important is being revealed, that

you are moving towards some insight or idea that will change you, or the nature of your relationship with the other person.

• A combination of surprise and destiny, a sense that the experience is natural and spontaneous, yet was also meant to happen, ringing a bell somewhere deep inside you.

Standing guard over the solitude of another

Intimacy is at the heart of closeness in marriage.* Intimacy and trust work together, enabling the complex desires and needs of two people to be smoothly coordinated, softening the edges of the inevitable friction of close-up living. Without intimacy, you risk becoming self-absorbed, boxed into loneliness and isolation, an internal exile in your relationships.

The paradox of intimacy is that it's not possible without autonomy. It's hard to open yourself to intimacy unless you have a strong sense of yourself as a distinct and separate person. If you don't have that, intimacy feels like intrusion and risks overwhelming you. The highest task of a bond between two people, says poet Rainer Maria Rilke, is that each should stand guard over the solitude of the other.[6] That capacity for autonomy-in-closeness is what psychoanalyst Donald Winnicott called 'composure' – a capacity to be alone with yourself in the intimate presence of another.[7]

Marriage makes big calls on intimacy, and never more so than now. In less than a hundred years, it has been transformed, even revolutionized. Once, getting married was the gateway to full adult status, to setting up home, having (legitimate) sex, and having a family. Sociologist Andrew Cherlin of Johns Hopkins University puts it this way: marriage used to be the foundation stone of adult life, now it's the capstone, a way for a couple to publicly demonstrate what they have achieved by their joint efforts – a committed intimate relationship, personal maturity, and the financial security needed to sustain a household

---

* Most young adults marry, or have a stable, long-term relationship. I will use 'marriage' to refer to both.

and a family.[8] You don't marry now to conform to what's socially expected of you, but as a public affirmation and celebration of that achievement. That's the public status that most of you – straight, gay or lesbian – aspire to and build up to.

There's been a sea change, too, in how success in marriage is defined. The traditional marriage was strictly governed by economic realities, a trade-off between partners, the husband doing the financial providing, the wife doing the caretaking, and the success of the union was largely defined by how well or badly each partner performed their allotted roles; love and affection were a lucky bonus. Then, love, affection, romance and companionship became part of the essential package, softening the iron grip of obligations and duty. A spouse was meant to be your friend as well as your lover. Later, an expectation of more equal sharing of provider and caretaking roles joined the equation and further upped the ante.

Gay and lesbian couples want much the same from their relationships as straight couples do. And the things that predict the success and happiness of gay and lesbian long-term relationships are the same as those that characterize thriving heterosexual relationships:

- sustained intimacy
- commitment
- sexual exclusivity, and
- constructive problem-solving.[9]

As in heterosexual relationships, the honeymoon of early love ends and over a five-year period there are the same declines in relationship satisfaction and higher risk of break-up, and for the same reasons. Women consistently report providing and receiving more support than men, but in gay and lesbian couples the pattern of support is more equal.

The soulmate marriage

The latest iteration of marriage has crept up on us more recently – the belief that a partner should be a soulmate, someone who shares the dreams you have about your life, helps you make space for those dreams, and encourages you to develop that part of yourself that animates them. That way, each of you keeps growing individually, and so does your relationship. The soulmate revolution puts the desire for autonomy right up there with the desire for intimacy.

It's a noble aim, and a tall order. The result, according to researcher Eli Finkel of Northwestern University, is the 'all-or-nothing marriage'. Average marriages are now less satisfying, and the best marriages are becoming more personally fulfilling than ever before.[10] These higher expectations are not just psychological candyfloss. How they are met largely determines the quality of a marriage, which in turn affects your personal well-being. And that link is stronger now than it was in previous generations. But the soulmate marriage is high maintenance. It requires a loving bond, mutual insight, and a *lot* of personal and psychological investment in the relationship. But therein lies the problem. The irresistible force of high expectations is meeting the seemingly immovable force of another modern phenomenon – being time-poor. Nobody, least of all young adults, has any spare capacity.

Before they had children, your parents' generation had about thirty-five hours a week to spend alone together, eating their main meal together or just relaxing with each other. You have only twenty-six hours. After they had children, the time they had together decreased to thirteen hours. But you have even less time: just nine hours. That's less than ninety minutes a day. That lost time now mainly goes on work, especially if both partners work full-time, and also on a more intensive, involved style of parenting.[11]

But it's not just time. You also have less mental bandwidth – fewer cognitive and psychological resources to pay close attention to each other without distraction. At work and at home, you are often multitasking, subject to information overload and interruption, and the constant distraction of social media.[12] All of this deprives your relationship of the extra oxygen needed for the higher mountain you are trying to climb in the soulmate marriage. So, it's difficult. You have set the bar high. But then, so is the pay-off if you succeed.

The hard work of managing desire

Most of you consider sex an essential element of intimacy in your relationship. In many ways, deeply satisfying sex is a template for the demands and delights of intimacy. Full physical and emotional release requires a subtle and complex knitting together of desire, sensitivity, excitement, skill, playfulness, responsiveness and engagement. Each of you has to learn to coordinate your desires and needs with the other's, yet not become self-conscious. Sexual desire, or even time for good sex, is the first victim of the familiarity of domestic life, yet it never quite manages to dampen your sexual hopes.

Sustaining sexual excitement and novelty in a marriage depends on learning how to find a flexible balance between closeness and a certain alluring distance, a judicious use of ambiguity and unpredictability. Otherwise, it just becomes part of the bedtime routine, like having a warm drink, or setting the alarm. You fall back on reliable routines and habits that get the job done, but gradually dampen down desire.

In a busy household with young children, managing desire can be hard work. You do the first shift at work, the second begins when you get home in the evening, and the third begins when you (finally) get to bed. Yet, despite all this, most of you manage to be sexually active, and are more satisfied with your sex lives than your single or separated peers.[13]

At the early stage of love, good sex is a major contributor to the emotional quality of a relationship. In a marriage, it's more often a reflection of it.

Heterosexual, gay and lesbian couples report similar levels of sexual satisfaction, but also similar levels of decline in how often they have sex as the relationship progresses. Gay men generally want and engage in more sex, especially in the early years of a relationship, and are also more likely to have sex with someone other than their partner, but often with their partner's agreement. They like having a partner with complementary sexual preferences, for example, one partner liking a more active role in sexual activities, the other a more receptive one. This complementarity increases sexual satisfaction because it makes it easier to coordinate sexual activity.

In general, lesbian couples have sex less often than heterosexual couples but engage in more sensual and tender sexual activities – kissing, caressing, hugging and cuddling – activities that are not directly aimed at achieving an orgasm but aimed at achieving high levels of intimacy. As with women in heterosexual relationships, lesbian couples try to align their mutual desires, and are more focused on the emotional connection between them during sex. But gay – and especially lesbian – couples are more concerned about maintaining equality in sexual activity than heterosexual couples.

16.   *Young adulthood:* When two
attachment styles merge

When you enter into a committed relationship you bring your attachment style into the partnership too. As we have already seen, your attachment style is the internal model you have of yourself, of other people, and of how close relationships work. Unsurprisingly, then, virtually every element of marriage, and of parenting, is shaped by your attachment style and your partner's, and the security of the bond you build with each other.*

Separately and together, your attachment styles will affect how you respond to each other and how *Secure* or insecure the attachment bond between you will become. But that bond can, in turn, reshape your individual attachment style, especially during periods of transition. For example, during the two-year transition to marriage, or the nine-month transition to parenthood, you are both likely to become more *Secure*. Conversely, if transitions are highly stressful, it can make a once *Secure* relationship insecure, at least temporarily.[1] Yet, life has a way of returning to the mean, so the chances of becoming *Secure*, the way the majority of people are, are actually higher.

Secure attachment in a committed relationship

A *Secure* attachment means your memories of being cared for in childhood are easily evoked, and you process information about your partner more positively.[2] When your partner is supportive, you notice and appreciate it, and you are able to maintain a stable view of your partner, even after a significant conflict. You may be temporarily angry

* The distribution of attachment in adulthood is roughly similar to childhood, about 60 per cent of people are *Secure*, 20 per cent *Avoidant*, and 20 per cent *Anxious*.

and disappointed, but it will take a lot more for you to change your generally positive view of them.

You are ready for intimacy, to open up in a deeper way, and encourage your partner to do the same, but you are not intrusive, you are attuned to cues, better at judging the right moment to do things. If your partner is insecure, all of this gives them an opportunity to gradually drop their defensive style, if they are ready to take that risk. Being *Secure* in your relationship and remaining open go together. For example, if your partner behaves in a way that surprises you, or is inconsistent with your expectations, you recall it better, but are also more inclined to interpret it in a positive way, and to revise your view of what happened.[3]

This ease with emotional and sexual intimacy pervades your whole relationship, and minor upsets in one domain will not unbalance the other unduly. Sex with your partner, especially if a *Secure* partner, is generally mutually gratifying.

Insecure attachment in a committed relationship

An insecure attachment style makes it all much harder. Memories of past pain and betrayals are easily aroused. You are too quick to read negativity in a partner's expressions and have a low tolerance for any expression of negative emotions, becoming quickly stressed by disagreements. You are more guarded, unwilling to trust and not skilled at judging trustworthiness, so you report fewer day-to-day experiences of your partner being that way.

The lack of trust is the most egregious long-term legacy of being insecure. Your anxieties have no resting place, they prey on your mind, never resolved. You turn to control as a way to contain that anxiety. This may seem to work in the short term. Early in marriage, still in love and hopeful, your partner may try to make things work by complying with your demands, hoping that trust will grow. But as their effort to build that trust fails, it inevitably breeds a deep resentment that will erupt in bitter conflicts or withdrawal, provoking even more sustained efforts at control. This dysfunctional dynamic becomes a source of great mutual suffering and chronic problems in a relationship.

If you are insecure, your mood is often low, affecting your level of sexual arousal, intimacy and pleasure. There is less open communication of your sexual needs, resulting in less sexual satisfaction, not least because sex gets caught up in your way of handling stress and distress.

Avoidant attachment in a committed relationship

If you have an *Avoidant* attachment style, you have fewer emotional resources to call on in yourself – that store of positive experiences that's so readily available to those who are *Secure*. You pay little attention to relationship cues that may signal your partner's good qualities or intentions, and often fail to notice their positive behaviour towards you. Even when you do, you mentally process the information in a shallow way, so it's easily forgotten. That's why you can maintain a critical view of your partner, even in the face of disconfirming evidence.

When your partner opens up to you, sharing their deeply personal thoughts and painful experiences, you dismiss their concerns. 'That's all in the past,' you say. 'Forget about it. What's the big deal?' Ostensibly, you may encourage a partner to be self-sufficient, affecting indifference to what they do. But the indifference masks a fear, even despair, that your partner will lose interest in you and leave.

Your discomfort with closeness reveals itself in what happens in discussions about your relationship.[4] You avoid looking at your partner's face, and your own facial expression remains closed and guarded. You show little interest in the conversation, and you decide when to end it, often leaving your partner frustrated and dissatisfied.

> Yeah, he'll talk all right, but only about stuff he is interested in, kind of neutral things. He sighs when I try to bring up more emotional things between us, and says 'Why do we have to always talk about this kind of stuff? It's boring and it goes nowhere.' But it goes nowhere because he clams up. If I persist, it ends up in a row, and he walks out of the room. He knows this upsets me, but it's his way of punishing me for trying to get closer.
>
> Tess, 29

The mirror-image of that negative view of your partner is your defensive view of yourself as strong and self-reliant. To maintain that view, you have to find a way of excluding any self-threatening information from your consciousness. You do this by projecting all the blame for problems and conflicts on to your partner – you are always right, your partner is always wrong. You are readier to attribute malign motives to them, to make personally offensive criticisms, and markedly less forgiving than someone who is *Secure*.

Sex and love remain more detached. You have sex less frequently, and you often have sex to make yourself feel better. Afterwards, you show little interest in physical affection and may experience a feeling of estrangement and alienation. When there is a conflict between you, you don't use sex as a way to try to repair things. Instead, your desire for your partner may drop and you withdraw, part of your distancing strategy when stressed.

Anxious attachment in a committed relationship

If you are *Anxious*, your own boundaries are fragile, easily engulfed by your partner's personality and needs. You are threatened by their autonomy, and you respond by constant demands, anxious scrutiny, and intrusion on what they are doing, thinking and feeling. Your partner becomes impatient, irritable, accusing you of being too demanding, too controlling. You panic, provoking even more distress and clinging, alternating between angry attacks and pleading. You create a lot of conflict, but also take the blame for it, even when you are not at fault, leading to simmering resentment that unsettles you further and provokes yet more conflicts.

When a partner does open up, your attention is often distracted by your own preoccupations. You think of yourself as someone who is very sensitive to other people's emotions, but your sensitivity is often more attuned to how your own needs are being met, compromising your ability to accurately read what your partner wants. For example, when your partner opens up about some concern, anxious to signal your understanding and empathy you say, 'Oh, me too. That happened to me once' – and launch into a long account of your experiences, unable to resist the opportunity to move the attention on to yourself.

You are hyper-alert for any signs that your partner's feelings are cooling, or their commitment waning. You overreact to anything your partner does that pleases you or upsets you, attaching too much significance to it. You are beset by constant rumination. You swing between passivity, expecting to be cared for like a child, and lavishing attention and care on your partner, but with the open or unspoken expectation that this will be reciprocated in full. If it isn't, you are bitterly disappointed and resentful. Your anxious search for closeness and acceptance may interfere with your concentration, compromising your day-to-day plans and long-term interests.

If you have an *Anxious* style, sexual and emotional intimacy are more conflated. Upsets in one area unbalance the other. When there is a conflict between you, you use sex to try to make things right, but are less likely to enjoy it. You often use sex to give yourself a boost if you feel low. If both partners are insecure, sex is particularly fraught. For example, a partner who is *Anxious* sees sex as a barometer of security in the relationship, and you seek sexual contact as a way of reducing any distress.[5]

The hard work of handling conflict

Attachment influences how you deal with conflict.[6] When you are *Secure*, you generally approach disagreements in a constructive way, are prepared to have open and difficult conversations, and feel confident about your ability to deal with the feelings that arise. You acknowledge when you feel angry or distressed and are not easily derailed by your partner's anger. Your intention is to repair the relationship by trying to solve the problem between you, so your anger is the 'anger of hope'.[7] You try to temper your criticism and rarely make personal attacks. You are willing to admit when you get things wrong and can tolerate criticism of your own behaviour.

If your style is *Avoidant*, you may refuse to engage with your partner's complaint and when you do, you are defensive. You deny your own angry feelings and may instead project them on to your partner, attributing hostile motives to them when none are present. This repression of anger is automatic and deep-rooted.

In an experiment conducted by Swedish researchers, participants were shown pictures of happy and angry faces on a screen. As they watched, their reactions were measured, specifically the changes in facial muscles involved in emotional expression. When the images were flashed subliminally, for just 17–53 milliseconds, too fast to register in conscious awareness, those with an *Avoidant* style of attachment reacted to the angry faces by frowning. But when the angry faces were flashed for long enough to register consciously, they reacted differently, adopting a false 'smiling' expression – an automatic defensive strategy to block out their unconscious negative reaction.[8]

You angrily reject criticism but criticize your partner bitterly and are much less forgiving. You defend yourself by inflating your own goodness and exaggerating how difficult your partner is. You often refuse to negotiate. You disengage or stonewall, everything about your expression and posture saying, 'I don't want to see you or hear you. I don't want to be here.' This is a way of silencing your partner. It enables you to keep control but results in putting further psychological distance between you. This is what you are aiming to do, but it has a very adverse effect on your partner, and on your relationship.

> He just refused to listen to me any time I tried to explain why I was upset about something he said or did. He would just walk out of the room. It was like a door being shut. My experience, the intimacy of telling and listening was just off-limits, you couldn't go there. And then it would happen again and another door shut, and then another, until we were only operating on a small platform of 'safe' topics. But it eventually killed off any real intimacy between us. I'd forget about it sometimes until we were having sex, and then I would remember, and it made the whole thing empty and sad.
>
> Pat, 38

If your style is *Anxious*, you are easily roused to anger during a disagreement, but often it's an 'anger of despair', rooted in your own sense of powerlessness. You have little confidence that your partner will respond to you in an understanding or caring way.* Your ability to negotiate is weak, undermined by your anxiety and confusion about your own right to your feelings. You try to suppress your anger, but it surfaces easily in intense bouts of anger, leaving you ruminating angrily for hours, or even days.

Your attachment style shapes how you care for your children

Just as your attachment style follows you up the aisle, it also follows you home from the maternity ward. How you care for your children is directly influenced by your own attachment style.

If you are *Secure*, you treasure the close relationship with your children. You have a long and rich experience of being cared for, have internalized your own parents' warm and responsive caretaking style, therefore can bear the burden of childcare without too much stress.

If you are insecure, caring for children is likely to be a bigger struggle.[9] However, rearing your children offers you a second chance if your own childhood attachment was insecure. Witnessing their vulnerability can evoke your own repressed memories of your childhood, and a corresponding tenderness and sensitivity in how you care for them, increasing your chances of becoming *Secure*. So too will a partner who is very supportive during your pregnancy, especially if you are *Anxious*. If you can't get that support and have to cope with the new baby on your own, you are at higher risk of developing post-partum depression.[10]

It's hard, too, if you are *Avoidant*. You may never have expressed much interest in becoming a parent or, if you did, expected it to be

---

* Sometimes, of course, your fears mirror the reality of an unresponsive partner. But even when you do have a partner who is willing to be loving and supportive, insecurity makes it harder to see that or benefit from it.

onerous and to get little satisfaction from it. Already uncomfortable with any demand for closeness, the prospect and reality of intimately caring for a dependent baby may put you under severe pressure, and you experience less closeness with your newborn. Mothers with this style of attachment tend to see the baby as interfering with their lives and are preoccupied with re-establishing their independence and personal control as quickly as possible. But, in general, a mother who is *Avoidant* seems to adapt to the transition to parenthood more quickly than a man, perhaps buffered by her sense of competence in the role.[11]

Avoidant mothers and sick babies

A strategy of avoidance depends on repressing and controlling feelings of anxiety and vulnerability. During periods of ordinary stress, you can do that. But when faced with major stressors, this deactivating strategy can collapse and your anxieties can surface, disorganizing your thinking and behavioural reactions.

When the baby is well and healthy, or has only minor health problems, a mother who has an *Avoidant* style is able to maintain enough emotional distance to manage her own feelings of anxiety or stress. But this strategy breaks down under severe stress, for example if the baby develops a serious illness.[12] She is then at high risk of becoming overwhelmed by her own distress, which exacts an immediate toll on her health, and six years on she is still showing signs of emotional distress and deteriorated mental health.[13] *Avoidant* attachment is also associated with high physiological arousal, increases in blood pressure and other stress symptoms that interfere with getting enough oxygen to the muscles of your heart, raising the long-term risk of hypertension and heart disease.[14]

Fathers who are very *Avoidant* find it hard to adjust to becoming parents. They dislike the pressure to be anybody's caretaker. Having to respond to the relentless demands of an infant makes it harder to maintain their normal psychological distance, so they have more difficulty repressing their resentment and anger, leading to more conflict with their partners.

A life well lived – what we learn from young adulthood

The principles of a life well lived – young adulthood (intimacy or loneliness)			
Life stage	*Time frame*	*Developmental task*	*Psychological principle*
Young adulthood	early 30s–late 40s	intimacy or loneliness?	Invest and commit

The big takeaway from thinking about young adulthood is that the core of happiness and well-being is a willingness to make commitments and invest in them. This applies to your personal relationships, your children, and – as we shall see in the next chapter – your work.

How to practise positive behaviour to sustain your marriage

For most of you the closest personal relationship you are committed to is your marriage. Staying intimately connected to your partner while trying to manage your responsibilities at home and at work takes a *lot* of commitment. Not just the commitment to be there for the long haul, but to build up the reservoir of positive behaviour necessary to sustain happiness. Building that reservoir happens primarily in the mundane, everyday interactions of married life.[15]

BUILD UP THE EMOTIONAL BANK ACCOUNT

Make a lot of deposits, however small, in your joint emotional bank account. Being positive is not like your 'good' coat, to be kept for special occasions. Say 'I love you' at unexpected moments. Find ways to express your affection and fondness, to say how much you value and appreciate each other. Okay, occasionally it will sound corny. But who cares? Nobody will complain.

ALLOCATE ENOUGH MENTAL ROOM FOR THE RELATIONSHIP AND FOR EACH OTHER

Keeping connected depends on building a rich store of information about each other's life, preferences and dreams, remarkably similar to the detailed and affectionate knowledge parents of securely attached children have about them. Without this mental map, you can't find your way into someone's heart.

BE A FIRST RESPONDER

Marriages are full of bids for connection. Respond as fully and positively as you can to those bids. Turn physically towards your partner, make eye contact, try to attune to the underlying emotion and respond to that in your reply. When it needs more than words, be ready with an affectionate or sympathetic touch. However brief the interaction, this constitutes a powerful connection. Correspondingly, 'turning away', ignoring or dismissing a bid for connection, looking away or moving away, is experienced as a strong disconnection.

These moments of intimate connection are how you each build a mental picture of each other as good people, and that perception then serves to 'override' specific negative interactions. You then have less cause to criticize each other or get defensive, and your efforts to 'repair' the disconnection during an argument work better because you are each more inclined to believe that the other is positively motivated. How you do that is trust in motion, working in the moment.[16]

Imagine you are asked to do this exercise: rate how much you trust your partner, then recall an experience of being disappointed or let down by them, and say why you think that happened.

If you rate your relationship as low in trust, this is how you respond: 'My partner let me down. But that's typical of the way he goes on, he's just a very selfish person.'

Your explanation focuses on the three P's. It's *personal* – located in a character weakness that is inherent. It's *permanent* – an enduring feature that cannot be changed. It's *pervasive* – it will affect the whole relationship. When you have completed the exercise, you rate your trust in your partner even lower than you did at the start.

Contrast that to what happens in a high-trust relationship. When you describe an experience of being let down by your partner, you don't try to deny or minimize it, but you *explain* it like this: 'That does not happen very often, because my partner is normally a reliable and thoughtful person, and I think it was because she was under a lot of pressure at the time.'

In other words, you attribute the lapse to a specific set of external circumstances, not to an enduring personal quality, therefore it does not affect your overall relationship. Even though you have just described an experience of being let down, you now rate your trust in your partner even higher. Why? Because the way you interpreted and explained it reminded you of the store of good experiences you have had together.

AVOID CROSS-COMPLAINING

This happens when one of you starts to describe how stressful the day was, and the other cuts in to say, 'You think *you* had a bad day, wait until you hear about *mine*.' Try to make the first encounter in the morning, or when you meet after the working day, a positive connection. Share the most positive event of the day, however minor. On a bad day, you will have to scrape the barrel, but it's a good practice to search for that moment of fleeting joy, or calm, or relief, or the little burst of pride in something you did well. Just recalling it will lift your mood, may trigger a corresponding memory in your partner, and you both end up feeling better. Then, as long as you take turns, complain away to your heart's content.

SET ASIDE REGULAR PROTECTED TIME TOGETHER

This is not easy, but it's vital to reconnecting with each other as individuals. Paying a babysitter is a lot less expensive than paying a therapist, and nothing when compared to the cost of paying a divorce lawyer. Include the cost in your rainy-day fund. Or if you are stony broke, beg someone in your family to babysit – and reciprocate the favour by offering to help them with something.

DO SOMETHING NOVEL

There is an inherent tension in a marriage between security and romance. Marriage is designed to provide the security and stability needed to rear children and run a joint household. But romance thrives on novelty, risk-taking, adventure, on delays, obstacles, separations and the heightened arousal that accompanies them. Being aware of that tension is what keeps a relationship dynamic and vital.

To counter the deadening effect of familiarity and boredom that domesticity can induce, commit to doing something new together on a regular basis, something you haven't done for a long time together or have never tried. Spending enjoyable and pleasant time together has a positive effect on a relationship, but not as much as doing something novel, active and challenging, anything that arouses a feeling of excitement, passion, interest or playfulness.

You will feel better about yourself, experiencing again that sense of self-expansion that accompanies falling in love. It's easy to forget the person you fell in love with. When you engage in a (mutually defined) novel and exciting activity for about ninety minutes a week for a few weeks, it restores a fuller view of your partner – and of yourself. You feel more passionate about each other, boosting happiness and satisfaction in your relationship.

The first victim of familiarity and boredom is usually sex. The best way to prevent and counter this is for partners to keep trying to hone their sexual skills, spend time finding out how to better pleasure the other, and stay open to a range of sexual activities. I cannot better the pithy advice of an American sex columnist: Be good, be giving, be game.[17]

How to fight fair

First, try to sign up to the marital version of the Queensberry Rules.

- *Practise editing*: there's no need to express every negative thought, every disappointment, every irritation that comes into your mind. Editing slows down the start-up of an argument, lowering the chance of a neutral state morphing into a negative one.
- *Avoid using words like 'ever' or 'never'*: they immediately and invariably invite a counter-argument.

- *Avoid personal criticism, contempt, defensiveness and stonewalling*: keep your complaints to descriptions of specific incidents that upset you: 'When you said this or did that, this is how I felt.' Then stop, and give your partner a chance to respond.
- *Make a practice of then asking, 'Is there anything else you would like to say?'*: there nearly always is. Ask again if you think there's more.

BE OPEN TO POSITIVE INFLUENCING

Conflicts are inevitable in any long-term relationship, but you can cut down their frequency if both of you are open to being positively influenced. Some couples try to influence each other a lot, others are content to make a more modest number of attempts, and some make hardly any. Whatever the number of attempts, each partner must feel that influence is *possible* without a huge fight.

Being prepared to be positively influenced is especially important for husbands. Why? Because from an early age, women are more practised in cooperation, and men are more practised in resisting attempts at influence. And bear this is mind: the partner who has the greatest reluctance to accept influence also has the most power to change the relationship for the good.

Positive influencing has its own choreography, as has its absence. Couples who have mastered the art of influencing positively behave in very specific ways.

- Each partner gets the opportunity to present their case, their views and feelings about the issue at hand. This sets the agenda for the next phase: arguing their case.
- Arguing is the tricky bit, because it raises the emotional temperature, but they strive to get back on track by punctuating a long sequence of disagreement with frequent attempts at repair.

  o Stepping out of the argument for a moment and drawing attention to what's happening – 'We're both getting too heated here.'

    o Seeking clarity – 'Explain again how you see this.'
    o Humour – but they pick their moment.
    o Trying to find common ground – 'Well, we agree about
       that.'
    o Appealing to the values that govern their
       relationship – 'We always try to understand each other.'

- They respond immediately to a positive overture, but do not reciprocate a negative remark. For example, they attend to the positive intent of interruption – as an attempt to get the discussion back on track or to clarify something.
- They strive for compromise – which is easier because they have moved through the argument in a systematic and generally affirming way.

Will they feel mightily pleased with themselves? They will, and they should.

RESIST NEGATIVE INFLUENCING

Couples who struggle to influence each other also fall into predictable patterns.

- One or both partners try to prevent the other from stating their case, so the agenda is only partially set or misunderstood, and they move rapidly to the arguing phase.
- During the argument there is a lot of negative reciprocity. Instead of responding to the positive intent of what a partner says, they respond to the negative tone or expression, real or imagined.
- There is virtually no positive reciprocity – something neutral or positive gets ignored or met with a 'Yes, but' response.
- They are less successful at de-escalating mounting negativity and use fewer repair mechanisms.

They are less open to compromise. When one partner makes a proposal, it is shot down by the other, who makes a counter-proposal, so the argument ends in mutual frustration, increasing anger and despondency.

KNOW WHEN TO STAGE A STRATEGIC WITHDRAWAL

If the argument is getting too heated, the only solution is to stage a strategic withdrawal. And don't worry about losing face. Hans Blix, the Swedish diplomat who acted as the UN weapons inspector before the 2003 invasion of Iraq, put the case for losing face in lofty rhyme: *The noble art of losing face will one day save the human race*. It might also save your marriage.

So try to stick to this rule. If one of you is becoming too stressed to think straight during an argument, call time – but then you must commit to setting another time to continue the discussion when you have both calmed down.

BECOME A THIRD-PARTY OBSERVER OF YOUR CONFLICTS

Set aside seven minutes every four months (yes, that precise) to write about a recent conflict in your relationship as if you were a neutral third party who wants the best for both of you. This is a surprisingly effective way to gain a broader perspective on the dynamic between you. If you do this regularly, it will have a significant and positive impact on your relationship and halt the process of psychological distancing and isolating.[18]

LEARN FROM OTHERS

Observe how other couples behave, in real life or in novels, TV programmes or films, and talk to each other about what you each regard as constructive or destructive about the way they relate. This kind of discussion requires switching from normal to a more structured kind of discourse, which initially may feel self-conscious and embarrassing. Almost inevitably, one partner (okay, it's likely to be the woman) is more enthusiastic than the other, who may be outright sceptical. But if a couple is regularly falling into frustrating and upsetting discussions that go nowhere, this switch from 'normal' discourse, no matter how artificial it may initially feel, is worth the effort. It builds the kind of relationship awareness that increases satisfaction in a marriage. In fact, the improvements are as substantial as those found from participating in well-designed marriage enrichment programmes that require much more investment of time, and money.[19]

The average couple wait about six years before seeking help for their problems – and that's in the USA, where going for counselling is more the norm. By then, negative patterns are well established and harder to change.

Invest in your children

Responding to your children's need for closeness, autonomy and competence is the priority and takes a lot of investment. As for the rest, there are no shortages of books and websites that lay down rules on childrearing. 'Parent' has become a verb, a performance, subject to bewildering fads and fashions. Here, I offer just broad overarching principles.

- *Keep your eye on the important things*: let your children's three basic needs for closeness, autonomy and competence be your satellite coordinates, guiding what you do, and you won't go far wrong in how you rear your children.
- *Practise the difficult art of undivided attention*: when someone really needs to talk to you, even when you're busy, try to give them your undivided attention, however briefly. 'I have only two minutes, but it's all yours.'
- *Children need structure and clear rules to keep them safe*: make rules, but only as many as you can actually supervise or enforce. Children are adept at figuring out when you mean business and when your warnings can be safely ignored. The rules should be few, crystal clear and non-negotiable. Focus on setting out the positive behaviours that are desired and the consequences for *deliberately* breaking the rules. But bear in mind that children's capacity for self-control is only emerging in their third year, and that understanding the 'if-then' link between bad behaviour and sanction is a *slow* process.
- *Help children understand the distinction between feeling and acting*: young children are easily overwhelmed by anger or envy and have more trouble resisting the temptation to act out

those feelings. You can't help how you feel, but you can have more control over how you express those feelings – although that control is paper-thin in young children.

In 'Little Hans', one of his most celebrated case studies, Freud described the first lesson in self-control.[20] Hans was a five-year-old who was being treated for a severe phobia. He was terrified of going outside because he feared that the carriage horses on the street would bite him. This fear coincided with the arrival of his baby sister. He was so jealous of her that when he saw his mother bathing her, he sometimes wished she would drown. Unable to tolerate or contain this frightening urge to harm her, he tried to distance it by projecting it on to the horses in the street. Freud famously advised: 'You may feel it, but you may not do it.'

WHEN DEALING WITH ADOLESCENTS, START WITH YOURSELF

Ask yourself the following questions.

- What do I know about the experience of feeling overwhelmed or feeling alienated from what I'm doing?
- Did I ever make stupid mistakes that were caused by lack of experience?
- What do I know about being disappointed or disillusioned?
- Did I ever feel frustrated beyond endurance by the intransigence of authority?
- Did I ever panic that life was passing me by?
- Do I remember the experience of having extraordinary hopes for the future and for myself, and how it felt when the world refused to cooperate?

If you can recall these experiences, you are halfway there with adolescents, and if you are asked, you might have a thing or two to say that is useful.

17. *Young adulthood:* The world of work

The second task to be addressed in young adulthood is to make progress in your work. Work is central to the lives of most young adults, the stage in your life when you are under the most pressure to make progress in your career. You are part of a cohort who has spent the best part of your twenties preparing for the world of work. Compared to your parents' and grandparents' generation, you are more educated, more tech savvy, more at ease working in a changing workplace and with a more diverse workforce.[1] Now, you are looking for a place in that world or busy trying to consolidate the place you have. The task is to mobilize enough agency to make your way in the world of work, to set your course and master the everyday tasks. Being passive in your approach to work never paid many dividends. It pays even fewer now as you try to manage the modern workplace.

The modern workplace is more competitive, pressured and fast-changing than previous generations would have experienced. There's more job insecurity, performance expectations are higher, and the demands on your time more pressing. The reaction to these changing conditions is a new devotion to work. It has become more psychologically central in your life, especially if you are a knowledge worker. For many of you, your job is no longer simply a way to earn a living or move up the career ladder, it's become a core part of your identity, a way to measure your worth. Fifty years ago, the status of your job was signalled by the clothes you wore, or where in the building your office was. Now, how busy you are, the number of hours you work, your *devotion* to work, are what signal the importance of your job.

The great distractions

Multitasking, rapid switching from task to task, constant interruptions and distractions are embedded in how we work. You are bombarded by emails, many of them cc'd and not relevant to your work, but you are still expected to read them. In the era of letters, a response was expected in about two weeks. When the fax was introduced, the expectation of a response decreased to two or three days. With email, you are expected to respond almost immediately, or you get another email asking if you received the first.

Then add the temptations of social media, checking in on your Instagram feed or Twitter account to relieve boredom. Many of you work in open-plan offices or on 'hot desks', designed to encourage more collaborative working. The trouble is that they also encourage interruption.[2] Interruptions are not cost-free. Each time you are interrupted, however briefly, exacts a toll on your ability to concentrate, and this effect lingers for a surprisingly long time.[3]

If you are a knowledge worker, and that pretty much covers everybody, you are interrupted every three minutes on average in the course of a normal working day. Now take that number and multiply it by 25, or by 23 minutes and 15 seconds, to be exact. That's how long it takes to return to full concentration after an interruption. Distractions don't just eat up time while they are happening, they derail your mental progress afterwards as well.

To compensate for the loss of time caused by interruptions, you have to work harder and faster when you resume, but this puts you under more pressure, increases your stress and lowers your mood. You have fewer cognitive and psychological resources to solve problems, to pay close attention to the task at hand, or to what a colleague is telling you, and your capacity for high-quality, creative thinking is compromised.

Work–life balance

More women than ever before are now in the workforce, including those with children, creating an unprecedented problem around work–life balance. The provision of paid and unpaid maternal and parental leave varies widely in European countries and is virtually non-existent in the USA.[4] The pressure is felt most acutely by women, but it's also becoming an issue for men, a reflection of a generational change – younger fathers want to spend more time with their children.

Workplaces, particularly in the private sector, are still struggling to find a way to deal with the demands for flexible working. Flexi-time, special career tracks for women and other family-friendly measures are usually introduced with little urgency or enthusiasm. And they sometimes face covert resistance from some senior employees who got to the top by making big sacrifices. Seeing younger colleagues getting breaks they never had can raise troubling doubts in their minds as to whether they've paid too high a price for success. For some, their attitude hardens: 'I did it, so why can't you?'

But there has been progress. At the top level, some public and private organizations have made the changes necessary to ease the pressure and build a bridge between home and work, with the newer notions of 'work harmony' or 'positive work–life spillover'.[5]

Teams – the fundamental units of work

Over the last two decades, the amount of time spent collaborating with others has increased by at least 50 per cent.[6] As organizations try to break down silos and work across traditional departments, work is devolved to teams. Of their nature, teams are interdependent, each member depending on the other to get the work done effectively. But how effectively teams work varies widely.

In 2012, Google initiated a major study involving 180 of their teams across the world to find out why some were much more

successful than others.[7] The teams varied widely in how they oper-
ated, had different structures, different mixes of professionals and
personalities, and worked in different organizational contexts. Yet,
despite that variability, the same five key things distinguished the
most successful teams.

1. They were dependable.
2. They had clear structures, clear goals, and members were
   clear as to their role in the team.
3. The work had personal meaning and significance for each
   team member.
4. Team members believed that the work they were doing had
   a real purpose and a positive impact on the organization.
5. They had a culture that promoted 'psychological safety'.

The factor that attracted the most attention was 'psychological
safety'. What exactly was that?

Amy Edmondson first identified the concept when she investi-
gated why a number of hospitals had experienced very different
outcomes when they introduced a new surgical procedure for cardiac
patients. This procedure was less invasive, less risky and less costly;
patients recovered faster so required less time in hospital. The surgical teams involved in all the hospitals had a similar case mix, similar
professional qualifications and expertise, and the same level of
resources. While some were successful in their adoption of the new
procedure, others had mixed success, and some abandoned it completely. Edmondson found that what distinguished the successful
teams was a culture of psychological safety.[8]

- The shared belief that the team is a safe place for
  interpersonal risk-taking.
- The ability to have difficult and emotional conversations.
- Team members have the confidence to admit their mistakes
  or near misses, or to raise difficult and sensitive issues with
  regard to their colleagues' practices, without fearing they
  would be punished or marginalized by the team leader or
  other team members.

- They felt they didn't have to be on guard all the time and were comfortable expressing their views without sacrificing a sense of closeness and belonging.
- They expressed genuine enthusiasm for the ideas of others.
- Their style of communication was relational, not transactional. They were interested in each other's lives and liked to chat casually before and after meetings, rather than just going through the motions to get the task done.

Team psychological safety is one expression of high trust in a workplace. Trust has always been important at work. When you trust your manager, your colleagues and the organization you work for, everything functions better. You are more engaged, more committed, more productive, and readier to cooperate.[9] But trust has now moved centre-stage in a different way because organizations are under constant pressure to change, and trust oils the wheels of change.

The complicated business of motivation

As organizations strip out layers of management, employees are expected to be more self-motivated, to take the initiative, make decisions and take ownership of their work. This is all good news for employees, most of whom want to exercise more personal control over how they work and react negatively to changes in their immediate work space that are imposed on them.

When you have reasonable autonomy in how you do your job, you are happier, more engaged, more emotionally connected to what you do and more capable of high-quality, creative and sustained performance. You are also less likely to suffer from stress or health problems like high blood pressure, high cholesterol or depression.

So, it's all okay then, everyone on the same sheet?

Well, no – less than a third of people feel they have any meaningful control over the way they work. Consequently, they are less engaged, and many feel bored and alienated from what they do.[10] Their day-to-day mood is lower, decreasing their motivation, and they find it harder to make sense of what is happening in a more general way in the organization.

Sometimes, the source of the problem is individual, like being stuck with a manager who likes to micromanage or is a fussy perfectionist. But the major culprit is hidden in plain sight – the common incentives that are designed to motivate you to work harder, like targets, goals and financial rewards.

Take financial incentives as an example. Increased pay or bonuses sound great, especially if your job is very routine or boring and a bonus motivates you to work harder. *But*, and it's a big but, financial incentives only work well if they are used as *background* motivators, a way to thank people after they have pulled out all the stops to get a particular project over the line or to help the organization meet a larger goal. Forty years of psychological research leave little doubt that using incentives as *primary* motivators, promised in advance and directly linked to performance, has very significant downsides.[11]

Many organizations, especially in the financial, banking, consultancy and legal sectors, use a combination of high targets and big bonuses to get people to work long hours, but this carries a host of adverse outcomes. It undermines autonomy, intrinsic motivation, creativity and the quality of performance.[12] Why? Because incentives encourage you to adopt a narrow focus, i.e. get the task done and pick up the reward, so your behaviour becomes controlled by the prospect of the reward – *extrinsic motivation* – undermining any inherent interest that you had in the task and decreasing the cognitive flexibility needed for complex problem-solving and deep conceptual processing of information.[13]

This is counter-productive when you are faced with a complex problem and the way to solve it is not immediately clear. As organizations try to change and innovate, most of the pressing challenges they face, the so-called 'wicked problems', involve dealing with many issues simultaneously and cannot be solved by following existing formulas.[14] They require more organic, novel solutions that can only be discovered by giving people the freedom and autonomy to experiment, to play around with new ideas, and to learn by trial-and-error.[15]

To be creative, you need to range more widely in your thinking, to focus on more subtle aspects of the task, allowing you to free yourself from the established way of doing things, to 'break-set'. That vital but fragile process disintegrates when your autonomy is compromised and you feel controlled.

The adverse effects of incentives based on *extrinsic motivation* – as opposed to *intrinsic motivation*, where the desire to do something comes from inside yourself – are many and very real.

Incentives increase stress and undermine physical and mental well-being

This is particularly the case if you work in an environment that is highly competitive and pressurized, where the potential rewards are substantial and the cost of failure high, where your performance is constantly under scrutiny and bonuses are linked to achieving very high targets, or where there is forced ranking of individual performance against peers. All of this makes for a high stress and chronic work–life imbalance, something that would be familiar to lawyers who work under the yoke of the 'billable hour', for example.

Incentives make for more negative and tense work relationships

When you approach any task as a 'job I have to do', you are more likely to adopt a high-pressure, tense and negative style of interaction. You are more demanding, more critical, and there is less collaboration. The focus is on 'getting the job done', so there is little room for playing around with different ways to do things better or more creatively. In contrast, when you focus on the inherent interest of a task, you approach it in a very different way, more autonomously, more like play than work. You are more relaxed, but you will actually spend *more* time 'on task' and be more engaged in learning to do it well. You are also less likely to intrude on the way other people are learning, therefore interactions are more personal, more freewheeling, and more exploratory.

Incentives encourage addictive behaviour and short-term thinking

When laboratory animals receive repeated stimulation of the reward centres of the brain, they literally work themselves to exhaustion, and eventually starvation.[16] But, hang on, you say, surely not human beings with their bigger, smarter brains? But even a cursory acquaintance with the research on stress, burnout, addictions and a variety of psychological disorders like anorexia suggest otherwise – we are all vulnerable to being derailed by strong incentives, some of us even more than others.

Incentives undermine ethical decision-making

A major cause of the global financial crash, and a host of business scandals before that, was the widespread use of big bonuses. Powerful incentives encourage short-term thinking and unethical short cuts because they flip the relationship between means and end. What you do is no longer just a *means* to an end – the end is so tempting that it increasingly justifies *any* means to get there. As you are laser-focused on the reward, you decrease or switch off your attention to what's happening inside you. The complex way your mind normally works – monitoring what you are doing, why you are doing it and if it may be coming into conflict with your beliefs and values – is short-circuited.

The mere *presence* of powerful rewards or pressures overrides and disrupts that whole process, crowding out any doubts or moral qualms you may have. You become 'entrained' – similar to what happens when you get involved in a heated row – and you get caught up in a chain reaction. This can set you down a very destructive path.

As lead researchers in how incentives affect human behaviour, Edward Deci and Richard Ryan have concluded that incentives, if powerful enough, 'get people to do almost anything . . . to forgo autonomy, act against needs, and neglect or destroy what they value most, from relationships to the environment'.[17] And they said that in 2006, two years before the global financial crisis.

The inner work life

More and more organizations are looking to social scientists to help them get the best from their employees. The best ideas have science behind them and align closely to the basic psychological needs for competence, autonomy and closeness at work.*

Teresa Amabile, a professor in Harvard Business School, and her collaborator Steven Kramer are exemplars. Their focus is on what they call *inner work life*. Day-to-day, your outer work schedule, what you are doing at any time, is paralleled by your inner work life, what you are thinking and feeling. In one study they asked 283 employees across a range of organizations to keep a daily diary for four months, including asking them every day to describe one event at work that stood out in their minds.[18] When their answers were analysed, they found that the events they experienced, the small 'uppers' and 'downers' that happen throughout the day, significantly affected their inner work life, how they reacted, thought and felt as they went about their day.

The most significant 'upper' is feeling that you are making progress in your work, a sense of steady forward movement, getting things finished, small wins, having little breakthroughs and insights. That depends on several things.

- On clear and unambiguous goals and knowing that what you are trying to achieve matters.
- On having some say in how you do your work, and not having the decisions you make about that carelessly overridden.
- On being given sufficient resources and realistic time frames in which to complete the work.
- On getting the right kind of help, from the right people at the right time.

* I reverse-order the needs to reflect their relative importance to being successful at work.

- On working in a culture that allows ideas to flow freely, and that learns from its successes and failures.

These are the factors that catalyse progress; and those that block progress are their mirror-image.

Inner work life counts. When your mood is positive, you are more productive, engaged and committed. When the team mood is positive, there is more solidarity, more cooperation and a *50 per cent* increase in the odds of having a good idea. This creativity effect lasts into the next day and, to some extent, the day after that. Building a team or organizational culture that enables people to make progress in their work in a positive way takes investment, but you get a big bang for your buck. What do you think any right-thinking organization would pay for a piece of technology that increased by 50 per cent the odds of a good idea that might lead to significant improvements in productivity or customer service?

However, when Amabile and Kramer surveyed hundreds of managers around the world about what they thought really motivated people, they found that a shocking 95 per cent fundamentally misunderstood what was involved. In fact, they ranked making progress in your work last in a list of possible motivators.

The key psychological elements of success at work

Being emotionally intelligent is generally defined as being able to get your head and heart to work well together – using your feelings as important resources that can improve your thinking, judgement and performance, and using your rational abilities to modulate your emotional reactions.* Emotional intelligence has been found to be a stronger predictor of success at work than traditional IQ, qualifications

---

* Emotional intelligence is defined in different ways, variants of head and heart working well together: a combination of self-awareness, including how you are thinking and reacting, and what motivates you; a corresponding awareness of others; the ability to manage yourself and your emotions; and being able to effectively manage relationships.

or technical skill.[19] Of all the competencies listed by employers as essential for any given job or role, two-thirds are emotional competencies and only a third relate to IQ and technical expertise.[20]

That's not to say that understanding abstract concepts, thinking rationally and being able to solve practical problems are not important at work. They are, but increasingly they are just *threshold* competencies – they get you in the door but once you are in, they account for somewhere between just a quarter and a third of your success at work.

Emotions are not an optional accessory, they influence what you attend to, how you perceive things, how you think and react and, most crucially, they are key to motivation. Facts convince. Emotions motivate. Facts can convince you to do or not to do something, but whether you act on that conviction depends on how you feel.

Emotions are not just inert feelings – they trigger action tendencies in the brain, each emotion having its own signature action. For example, interest, confidence, pride and hope motivate you to engage in things. Feeling sad or demoralized motivates you to withdraw or disengage.

Being emotionally intelligent means being able to mobilize the right positive or negative feelings, at the right intensity, to meet a specific challenge.

- Just enough excitement to engage you, but not so much that it disorganizes your thinking.
- Just enough anxiety to keep you on your toes, but not so much that it paralyses you.
- Just enough anger to confront bad behaviour and right a wrong, but not so much that you lose control or damage a relationship.
- Just enough envy to motivate you to up your game, but not so much that it distracts you from your own goals.

Being able to mobilize the right set of emotions is central to 'peak performance', a term imported from the world of elite athletes, and to being able to perform at a high level when under pressure.[21]

To get to Olympic level, every athlete needs to have an exacting level of technical skill, physical fitness and emotional control. Peak performance depends on building deep reserves of all three that you can call on when you need to pull out all the stops. Of these three 'readiness' factors, mental fitness is what most accurately predicts an athlete's final ranking in the Olympics. That kind of mental focus is more colloquially known as a 'big game mentality'.

Mental focus enables you to selectively attend to the essential elements of the challenge you are facing, to shut out distractions and allocate the mental resources necessary to make the right decisions at the right time. That's what translates skill into peak performance. This kind of concentration depends on a very precious and limited fund of cognitive resources that are easily depleted. If you lose mental focus, you forget the sequence of micro-actions that you have performed thousands of times before. You become physiologically over-aroused, your heart races, and your breathing becomes rapid and uneven. Your concentration is disrupted by an onslaught of anxiety and self-doubt, and your confidence falters. Despite their intense motivation to perform well, this is one of the major reasons why highly skilled athletes fail to perform to their full potential.

Grit, mastery and flow

At the core of competence is the ability to master a set of skills and understand a body of specific knowledge.* If you want to be *really* good at something, you will need to put in about ten thousand hours of practice.[22] But just to be good at your job requires a lot of effort and hard work.

Grit is what Angela Duckworth, a professor at the University of Pennsylvania, calls the mix of effort, determination, persistence, hard graft and stamina that's necessary to keep going in the face of

---

* Our overall capacity for becoming competent is also embedded in factors that are outside our personal control – our natural intelligence and talents, and the socio-economic context of our lives. But in any contexts, mastery is what determines how well we manage what we've got.

frustration, setbacks and failure.[23] Grit is a far stronger predictor of life success than intelligence or talent.

As an example of grit, Duckworth cites a study by George Vaillant. In 1940, when he was a professor at Harvard, Vaillant began a study involving a large group of male students, then aged twenty-three, who were followed up every two years throughout their lives. At each follow-up they were asked about their lives, marriage, family and friends, satisfaction at work, income, and how much progress they had made in their careers. Data on their physical and psychological health were also collected, including their level of fitness. All these measures were then combined into a score of how well adjusted they were to adult life.[24]

At the very beginning of the study, the students were asked to run on a treadmill for up to five minutes. It was set at a steep angle and moved rapidly. This was a test not just of their fitness but of their stamina and strength of will – what Duckworth would now call 'grit'. It turned out that how long they stayed on the treadmill in their early twenties was a surprisingly strong predictor of their overall adjustment and success right throughout their adult lives.

The *psychological grit* you need to get things done and see things through is usually at its lowest in your twenties, but then rises gradually as you move through young adulthood and middle age, reaching its highest in your sixties.

Mastery can also be achieved in another way, if your work puts you into a state of flow.[25] The experience of flow is triggered by taking on a challenge that is just above your average skill level. You may do this because the challenge is inherently interesting to you but going into flow does not depend on that. It depends on your willingness to give yourself to it. The task may be initially taxing, but it turns into enjoyment at a very particular point: the moment when you feel that your skills are equal to the challenge, when you are stretched, but not stressed. That is also the exact moment when work and play become fused, your attention totally and pleasurably absorbed by the activity. Your mind stops wandering and your usual preoccupations and doubts fade from awareness. Instead, you are focused solely on your next move, each action carrying you forward.

However, the balance between skill and challenge is inherently fragile. If the challenge begins to exceed your level of skill, you become anxious; if it gets too easy, you lose interest and become bored. When you are in flow, it delivers on all fronts. Your concentration is more sustained, your energy level higher, you persist longer in the face of setbacks, and you experience a high level of well-being. Afterwards, you feel more confident, more energized and motivated to take on a greater challenge next time.

Flow is a type of 'optimal experience'. The more you experience flow in your average week, the more likely you are to feel energetic, creative, motivated and happy. And surprisingly, going into flow is much more likely to happen in work than in your leisure time.[26] Yet, only 20 per cent of people report experiencing flow on a daily basis, and one-third say they rarely or never experience it. A work environment that disregards autonomy, is full of interruptions and uses powerful incentives kills off the intrinsic motivation that gives rise to flow.

Bringing your mindset to work

The mindset you bring to your work, or to your life more generally, also matters.[27] The relationship between your actual abilities and how well or badly you perform at school or work is far from straightforward. Mastery depends not just on your abilities but on whether you judge your capabilities to be set in stone, or capable of being grown and developed.[28] This is what Carol Dweck of Stanford University calls having a *fixed mindset* or a *growth mindset*.★

If you have a *growth mindset*, you don't view effort as some sub-par substitute for natural talent, you see it as what nurtures whatever talent you've got and turns it into real accomplishment. This makes you

---

★ A mindset is not a global view of yourself or other people. You can have a growth mindset about learning a new language, but a fixed mindset about learning to use technology. A fixed mindset about women, and a growth mindset about men. Or vice versa.

more motivated to learn, to look for feedback on how you do things and to use setbacks as a valuable learning opportunity. Any fear of failing is mitigated by the conviction that you can learn something from the failure that will allow you to improve enough to succeed next time, so you are more optimistic and confident and have a higher expectation of success.

If you have a *fixed mindset*, you are more likely to underestimate your actual abilities. You set goals to prove the level of competence you have, or to demonstrate that you are better at something than others are. When you feel that you are making insufficient progress, or have made a mistake, you interpret this as a sign that you don't have the ability to do a task. Unsurprisingly, this makes you feel anxious, vulnerable and stuck. You shift your attention away from trying to learn and improve, to attending to how you feel, and try to protect yourself by lowering your expectations of success, by procrastinating, or even by disengaging from what you are doing.

Bringing your attachment style to work

Making progress, emotional intelligence, peak performance, grit, flow and mindset all share one common element: they depend on your ability to regulate yourself, your feelings and your stress reactions. This ability is influenced by your attachment style. It will not have the same direct effect on your behaviour at work as it does on your personal relationships, but it will play a role in how happy and successful you are there.[29]

Secure

If you have a *Secure* attachment style, you bring a good package to work – a positive mindset, a basic trust in yourself, a disposition to trust other people and to act in a trustworthy way. You enjoy working with other people, one-to-one or in teams, and you feel you can rely on them for support and help. But none of this makes you gullible or careless about your own interests and welfare at work. You look out for yourself and have internalized a healthy self-protection instinct. When someone breaches your trust, you react decisively.

When faced with the inevitable stresses and pressures of work, you generally respond constructively. If something is not working, you are ready to challenge your assumptions, to admit when you are wrong, and change course without debilitating self-doubt, rumination or lacerating self-criticism. When negative emotions run high, you usually manage to stay calm enough, although everybody has their moments. You expend a lot of mental effort trying to get a better understanding of why something has gone wrong, to get a different perspective on it, allowing you to reframe the problem in a way that makes it less overwhelming, and easier to solve. When you have exhausted your own efforts to resolve the issue, you are not conflicted about asking others to help.

Avoidant

An insecure attachment style is no help at work. If your style is *Avoidant*, you may invest a lot of time in your work. As in childhood, you escape from your unease with closeness by immersing yourself in what Ainsworth called the 'neutral world of things'.[30] But the way you work is driven, often compulsive and joyless. Yet, your investment in work may be less than it appears, compromised by the way you psychologically distance yourself from it. You find it hard to muster up positive feelings about where you work, are less committed to staying in the job, and put little value on loyalty.

You may dislike working in teams and getting involved in group activities. You tend not to rate others' contributions highly, so you see little point to working in groups, preferring to rely on yourself, to keep your thoughts and ideas to yourself, and dislike having a group influencing what you do. Your attitude to colleagues tends to be cool and defensive, and your communication is guarded and transactional. This stance can create tension with colleagues, especially when they are dependent on you to cooperate with them to get the work done. Their irritation may unsettle you by arousing old fears about rejection, which may interfere with your performance. All of this makes it harder to function well in groups, and neither you nor your colleagues tend to rate your performance in a team positively.[31]

When you find yourself working in a team where closeness and interdependence are valued, this *increases* your discomfort and further interferes with your performance. A culture of psychological safety that facilitates difficult and emotional conversations presents particular difficulties. You cannot acknowledge your own vulnerability, even to yourself, so the prospect of having it exposed in a group arouses acute anxiety, which you disguise as a cool contempt for the whole enterprise.

The general strategy that you use to repress feelings of vulnerability can also dampen down positive emotions. You are guarded about open displays of happiness because you fear dropping your emotional guard. This may block the relaxed and enjoyable flow that is required for creative work. Your tendency to resist becoming excited by novel information may disrupt your sense of control, unless the information is technical.

Anxious

If you have an *Anxious* attachment style, your expectations of work are likely to be too high, you are easily disappointed, so you find it hard to sustain any initial positivity you may feel about the job or the organization. Much of your attention and energy are absorbed by your concerns about being accepted and approved of by your colleagues, disrupting your concentration and focus on the task at hand. In a team, you tend to promise more than you can deliver. You draw too much attention to yourself and override conversational turns. You miss cues that you are irritating people. If you do notice them, you are immediately emotionally disorganized.

You are more willing to reveal your doubts and vulnerabilities but find it hard to call others to account because difficult and emotional conversations fill you with anxiety. You are easily derailed by stress, so managing a new role or organizational change is more burdensome for you. You overestimate how hard things are going to be and react by making too many demands.

There is a yawning gap between the way you feel you 'ought' to be and the way you are, and your performance rarely lives up to what you hoped for. You let worry and doubt about one aspect of your performance leak into other aspects. You ruminate about mistakes and failings, find it hard to deal with setbacks and are susceptible to harsh self-criticism. You immediately look for emotional support, yet simultaneously doubt that you will get it. You are thrown off course by any ambiguity or confusion and may try to force a black-and-white solution when the timing is not right.

You see yourself as a parent once saw you: inadequate, unable to cope, prone to stumble and fall. Yet you feel compelled to strive for perfection, to set yourself unrealistic goals, or standards that are too demanding. Or you may take the opposite approach and, as in early childhood, become passive and helpless, choosing a doubtful safety rather than exploration and mastery. You have little sense of what you want, and few opportunities to test yourself.

A life well lived – what we learn from young adulthood

The principles of a life well lived – young adulthood (initiative or passivity)			
Life stage	*Time frame*	*Developmental task*	*Psychological principle*
Young adulthood	early 30s–late 40s	initiative or passivity?	Invest and commit

When we consider the place of work in young adulthood, we see that, again – just as in your personal life – in order to be fulfilled and successful in your work life you must commit to it and invest in it. Given the demands of modern working life, committing to work does not mean letting it take over your life and having work compromise your other priorities.

As much as possible you should try to adopt positive behaviours in the workplace and in your day-to-day interactions with colleagues.

- *Create boundaries* : try some of these suggestions in your office or workplace.

  o Turn off your phone for set periods.
  o Use what influence you have to persuade or ban having phones at meetings.
  o Use laptops only to make necessary notes.
  o Turn off the internet unless specifically needed.
  o In open-plan offices, have a recognized naming system for specific work spheres, for example: 'No interruptions'; 'Only interruptions related to a specific project you are working on'; and 'Only absolutely necessary interruptions'.

- *Resist the creep of urgent but unimportant work* : these tasks have a way of creeping into your daily schedule, bogging you down and slowly draining away a sense of meaning and enjoyment in what you do. This is the work that doesn't need to be done by a particular person, so it floats around like a dust ball until it lands somewhere. If it has a way of landing on your desk, figure out why you can't resist the impulse to keep doing this low-value work and why you feel you can't say no.

And remember, attachment is not destiny. Just as being *Secure* does not guarantee success, being insecure does not mean you won't be successful at work. For example, some organizations put a high value on the kind of 'lone wolf' performance that is the preferred mode of operation if you are *Avoidant*. Similarly, in some artistic or specialist service organizations that value a high-octane style of work, the emotional volatility and desire for approval that go with an *Anxious* style may be valued – or at the very least tolerated – and you may thrive.

PART THREE
The Road Ahead

Life should not be a journey to the grave with the intention of arriving safely in a pretty and well-preserved body, but rather to skid in broadside in a cloud of smoke, thoroughly used up, totally worn out, and loudly proclaiming 'Wow! What a Ride!'

Hunter S. Thompson

18.   Standing at the mid-life crossroads

At midlife, you move backwards to move forwards. Now that you have revisited, reviewed and reassessed your life up to this point, you are ready to move forward and possess yourself in a new way. You are ready to react to what you have learned about yourself and how you want to live the next half of your life. The Second Agenda of life lies before you.

Whatever sense of burden or freedom, satisfaction or disappointment you have registered about your life consolidates into three questions.

- Is this how I want to live my life?
- What changes are possible?
- How committed am I to making them happen?

Your reactions and conclusions will play out in one of four broad patterns.

- Integration
- Exit
- Breakout
- Blocked

Integration

You may feel broadly happy with how your life has gone, but have some dissatisfactions, some things that you'd like to change or improve. There are no pressing problems in your marriage, but by midlife some of the high shine may have come off your relationship. The pressures of young adulthood may have spun you off into almost parallel lives, or your routines and sexual relationship may have gone a bit stale, ground down by the relentless demands of domesticity. So, once again, you need to start renegotiating the terms of endearment.

You talk, you explain, you argue, you exhort. Your partner responds, sometimes reluctantly, sometimes with an eagerness that surprises or even alarms you ('You feel *that* bored?'). All going well, you both commit to revitalize things. You decide to spend more time together as a couple, to invest more in your relationship, to open up opportunities for more intimacy. Or you decide that you each need to carve out more time to see your friends, or pick up a long-neglected hobby, or do something new together. Or try to do the whole lot.

It's trial-and-error, but if you both persist, things get better. There is a rekindling of affection and interest in each other, your relationship feels more solid and renewed, the revitalization coming as much from the process of engagement with each other as the actual changes made. Your secure base in the marriage is strengthened, enabling each of you to venture more confidently into the world, to live out a new side of yourself, to try new ways of being and growing together.

Similarly, you may be broadly satisfied with your career and your job, but also feel that you need to make some changes. You decide to invest in a new work project or make a lateral move to a different area of work, or you put more energy into the people side of your job. In the process, you let go of some of your earlier aspirations and make space for new ones. As you liberate yourself from old pressures, it allows a different side of you to emerge.

> I'm very invested in my post-graduate students, and I always tried to give them the time and advice that they needed, but I've always related to them in a strictly professional way. I don't think any of them knew me as a person. That's changed now. I find myself telling them about my own experiences as a post-graduate student or talking to them more personally about their lives. I don't know exactly when this started, maybe when I started thinking about my own life and what it was like doing my own PhD. So I've become less a formal adviser and more of a mentor – although I still give them the direction that they need. They've responded really enthusiastically and I've found it far more enjoyable and worthwhile myself.
>
> Nicola, 46

But integration can also happen in less happy situations. You may be unhappy enough in your marriage or in your job that you would like to leave but are painfully aware that this would cause great hardship in the particular circumstances of your family or your life. So, you stay put, not because you have to but because you choose to. You can't change the reality of your life, so your only positive option is to make a renewed commitment to it, a conscious decision to take ownership of the life you have, however imperfect, and to make what you can of it. It will not deliver the kind of happiness you long for. But it's a good enough happiness to sustain you, at least for now.

> My situation is far from perfect. My wife and I have grown very far apart from each other, and I see no prospect of things changing. I've thought a lot about it, a lot, believe me. But the fact remains that I have my children to think about. The two boys have just started secondary school, and I don't want to disrupt their lives. My wife depends on me a lot, she suffers from depression, and I'm not sure how well she would cope if I left, and how that would affect the children. So, I'm going to stay where I am, at least for the foreseeable future, and make it work the best way it can. I couldn't live with myself otherwise.
>
> Tom, 46

Whatever your circumstances, as you work through the changes that need to be made and integrate them into your life, that life may not look very different from the outside, but *inside* it feels different. You feel happier, or at least more satisfied than you were, more renewed, more connected to yourself and to those you care about, more in charge of your life. You are back on track.

Exit

Some of you take the exit route. You decide to end your marriage or leave your job. When it comes to ending your marriage, you are not alone. There are variations in the divorce rate from time to time, but in most developed economies it is running above 40 per cent, and the most common time to divorce is your mid-forties – bar in the USA, where it happens earlier.

In Ireland, the divorce rate remains very low but is slowly increasing, and the peak age to separate or divorce is fifty-three.[1] Why now? Because you find yourself burdened by long-standing problems in your relationship that have piled up, and you are already a veteran of many failed efforts to improve the situation. By now, you are more pessimistic, more desperate, your commitment draining away. You may have drifted apart or fallen in love with somebody else.

The balance of psychological needs you first brought to your relationship may have changed. When you first met, you each found, or hoped to find, in the other a particular mix of security and familiarity, novelty and risk that matched or complemented your own. But it may not have worked out that way. The promised excitement and novelty that once attracted you may have delivered chronic instability and emotional upheaval.

> My husband is a free spirit, full of life, always up for adventure. I loved that in him when we met, and I still do in a way. We lived abroad for a few years, and we had a great life. At the drop of a hat, he would organize a weekend away for us, and we had fantastic holidays. He put a lot of store on spontaneity. But since we came back, he just can't seem to settle at anything. He has changed jobs three times in five years. A few months ago, he started talking about emigrating to Canada. But I'm just not doing that. Our two girls are settled in school, but he still thinks we can take off on holidays right in the middle of the school term, I mean he just never knows when enough is enough. That was all very charming once, but we are in our forties now, and I want an adult for a partner, not a child. I've really tried to make him see that, but it's no use. So it's wearing me down and I can't live with this instability any more. So, no, I'm not hopeful about our marriage.
>
> Deborah, 45

When it comes to your job, exit may also be the option you choose, because your work is no longer viable or satisfying, or was never what you really wanted for your life anyway. You upsized or downsized your ambition. If you now choose exit, you might finally take the plunge to start your own business. Or you take a hard look at your long-held plan to write a novel and finally realize that it's just a fantasy, because you have neither the driving interest nor commitment necessary to make it happen. Or you realize that the price of success is too high.

> I was forty-three when I started my MBA. I wanted to advance at work. I thought I had a good chance of becoming CEO in a few years when Dave was due to retire. I was always a high achiever in school. I think I've always felt under a lot of pressure to be successful. My parents and my two brothers did not go to third level, and have pretty modest jobs, so I was the big family success. But doing that MBA part-time nearly killed me. My job was already extremely demanding and I worked long hours. We had two young children, another on the way. The day I got my results, I went back to my office and I thought, 'That's it.' I'm not putting my whole life in hock again like this. If this is the price of getting to the top, then it's too big a price. So I left and got a job as a General Manager in a smaller company. The pay was lower, but the hours were better and work was interesting, so the whole move has proved very worthwhile, very satisfying. I've learned a lot from it.
>
> James, 48

Making an exit takes a lot of psychological energy. It's disruptive for you and the people around you. There are moments of acute anxiety, nights when you wake up full of self-doubt and wonder were you crazy to start all this? To see it through, you need a surge of autonomy and a lot of support from family and friends. But if well planned and carried out with diligence and care, exiting can leave you feeling happier, more invigorated, ready for the new track.

Breakout

Breaking out is not really a strategy, more an impulse to escape. You are aware that there are issues you need to face, in yourself, in your relationship, or in your work, but you can't bring yourself to do it. You are unable to confront your problems directly, or are afraid that it would reveal the confusion, ambivalence and uncertainty of your resolve to do anything. So, with little or no preparation or planning, you make a break for it. Breaking out brings an immediate rush of relief or exhilaration.

Having an affair is the most common kind of breakout. In the USA, where researchers track long-term changes in behaviour, the proportion of people having sex outside marriage has held steady at about 16 per cent. But since 2000, the percentage of middle-aged people who admit to being unfaithful has risen to 20 per cent, while it fell to 14 per cent in younger generations.[2]

Why now? If you are unhappy or unsettled in your thirties you may be tempted, but you are just too busy, too tired. 'The mystery to me about affairs,' sighs one 39-year-old, 'is not *why* people have affairs but where they get the time.' At midlife, you have more time, and things are in flux.

Maybe you feel bored, afraid of getting old, of everything drying up, all passion spent. 'I just can't bear to think I will never love to distraction again,' one woman told me wistfully. Maybe you feel neglected or want to take revenge on an uncaring or unfaithful partner, or have fallen out of love but are unwilling or unable to confront the issues directly. For most, the lure and excitement of an affair stays in the realm of fantasy. But at midlife you can drift more deeply into that fantasy of an uncomplicated liaison, although it rarely works out like that.

> I wasn't happy in my marriage. I kept planning to tell my partner that I wanted to leave, but I couldn't face the conflict and the whole guilt thing – I knew I would cave in. So, I had a brief affair with a colleague at work. It wasn't planned. He was married too, and had no intention of leaving his wife, so I knew it wasn't going anywhere. I knew my husband was bound to find out and that would be it. So I suppose it was my way of making a decision. But I'm not proud of myself about the way I did it.
>
> Anne-Marie, 46

Sometimes, the breakout is sudden and brutal.

It was just unbelievable. My husband texted me from Paris – he didn't even ring me. I thought he was at a conference, but he said he was actually there with a woman from work that he had fallen in love with, and that he was leaving us. Just like that. I had no idea. He had been acting normally, no hint that anything was wrong. I had to tell the kids myself. It was completely unreal. Our whole life was torn apart.

Clare, 49

Sometimes, the trigger for an affair is not unhappiness, but success. If things go unexpectedly in your life, there is a sense of self-expansion, of discovering a new part of yourself. And there is nothing as irresistible as meeting someone who responds to that new side of you.

When I was in my twenties, I had no confidence in myself, and no luck with women – I was just nerdy and awkward. Then I met Elaine. She was a very calm and caring person and she gave me more confidence. She was the first person I had a sexual relationship with. Our marriage was happy and we had three gorgeous children. My career went far better than I ever expected and I became much more confident in myself. I was travelling more for my work, and I met a very smart and sexy woman, and we fell in love. Marcia challenged me in a way Elaine never did – sexually, emotionally, intellectually. It was a totally new experience for me. We were careless, so inevitably Elaine found out and we split up. It was all very messy. She is very bitter about the whole thing, and the kids took her side. My relationship with the two younger ones has recovered, but my eldest daughter does not speak to me at all. Marcia and I are very happy together, but there has been a big price to pay.

Derek, 50

After the initial turmoil created by a breakout, things sometimes work out, but more by accident than design, and rarely without inflicting harm on those who care for you. And if the boredom, ennui, or loss of sexual interest in a partner that served to trigger breakout masked an inability to sustain intimacy or commitment, and if that remains unresolved, it's likely to chase you into a new relationship.

Blocked

Some of you feel stymied, bogged down in a dead-end or stressful job, a chronically unhappy relationship, or a self-destructive habit, but you feel blocked. You feel unable to move forward in relationships that have lost vitality and purpose, or trapped in a bleak cycle of work, or repeating patterns that you cannot escape. There is an overwhelming sense of lost opportunities, of squandered efforts.

> I've known for twenty years that I should have left this marriage. It's killing me. I have worked myself up to a pitch of leaving so many times, and then baulked at the last minute. I come up with some excuse, usually some version of, 'It's not the right time.' Now I know there will never be a right time. You just have to do it. The reality is that I'm too afraid that I'd make a mess of things, that my life would come crashing down around me. I know it's irrational. Other people manage it. And every time I fail to leave, I hate myself more. It leaves my self-esteem on the floor.
>
> Doreen, 44

You may have an overwhelming sense of lost opportunities, of squandered efforts, seeing your life as having little real impact on others. You have a growing sense of sameness, slog, loss of pleasure, a draining tiredness, a feeling that you are on a long march with no relief in sight.

> I used to work really hard at this job. But not any more. I just lost energy and interest in the whole thing. I see the young guys coming up and passing me by. I do my job now, don't get me wrong, but I only do what I have to do, no heroics. But to be honest, I'm bored. I find it hard to summon up any enthusiasm for anything. My wife says I'm depressed. Maybe I am, but going to a psychiatrist isn't going to fix my job. I'm too young to retire, and I couldn't afford to anyway. I think a

lot about myself these days, and what's going to become of my life. At this stage, not much I suppose. I've shot my bolt, you could say.

Richie, 46

Sometimes you come tantalizingly near to mustering the courage needed to change things, but an unexpected health or family crisis blocks you, gobbles up your attention, forcing you to muddle through, but with no real plan or renewed commitment to sustain you. More often, though, the blocks are within yourself – a lack of confidence, a fear of failing or of being alone, an inability to summon up the energy or commitment to take a risk, a habit of passivity. So the moment passes, and the opportunity is lost.

You are left with a deadening inertia, a kind of controlled despair. You give up.

The personal cost is great – a feeling of self-restriction, a stymying of development, and a big drop in your self-esteem. If you are unable to muster the energy to confront your problems, or to expand the scope of what you define as a good and a possible life, the effects may linger into middle age itself.

The pull towards change

Looking back over your life at midlife, there is a pull towards change, of one kind or another. Sometimes this is very much a conscious feeling, sometimes it operates at a lower level, pushing and pulling you this way and that, but you have no real sense of what's happening.

The four broad strategies set out above are common reactions, ways of coping with the emotional toll of your life and the outcomes of your choices. Which of the four you adopt is rarely a straight, one-off choice. You may try one, then switch to another, then revert back again. Generally, integration and exit are more positive choices, while breakout and blocked present a threat to your well-being.

A breakout can catapult you into a period of turmoil that may finally settle down into a more or less satisfactory way to live your life, but meanwhile it will soak up a lot of the energy that you need to manage the challenges of middle age and think through your future. Stagnation delivers little but despondency and self-loathing, and if it continues may spiral you into what can become a long-term decline.

A strategy of integration, or an exit that is well thought out and managed, generally brings a new sense of order, meaning and renewal in your life, no matter how hard won. It will regenerate your life in middle age, ushering in a new period of creativity and renewal, energizing you to face the challenges ahead, and contributing in a new way to the people and projects you most care about. You are well positioned to take full advantage of the big gains of middle age.

19. *Middle age:* The urgency of time passing and time remaining

The intimation of mortality at midlife does more than trigger a period of retrospection. It primes you for the crucial developmental task to be resolved in middle age: to create or stagnate.

Erik Erikson used the word generativity, an obscure and clunky word that he himself described as 'unpretty'. At its root, it means to generate, to bring something new into being that will in time become self-sustaining. It is in this sense that 'to create' is used here.

By middle age, Erikson said, a person 'must have defined for themselves what and whom they have come to care for, what they care to do well, and how they plan to take care of what they have started and created'.[1] The most universal expression of being generative is to have and care for children. But it's broader than that. It means to create or make something, to invest time and energy in it, to care for it so that it will survive and thrive beyond your lifetime.[2] It involves creating a personal legacy, not in the sense of passing on an accumulation of money or assets, but something that will serve the broader interests and welfare of the next generation, or generations to come. What you produce must be self-sustaining, capable of changing and innovating in unanticipated ways, without you being around to direct or support it.

The desire for generativity is found across cultures, and becoming generative is associated with a high level of well-being and meaning in your life. It has the same positive effects whether or not you have children.[3] It's generally low in your twenties, builds in young adulthood, peaks in middle age, and then levels off in your sixties. Its importance in middle age is underscored by the fact that it has a bigger impact on your happiness and psychological well-being at that time than it does at earlier stages. Like all developmental tasks, it's a mix of your own emerging desires, social expectations and an evolving understanding of life and of yourself. Being generative also has an action element, an active engagement and commitment to make it happen.

The opposite of generativity is stagnation. The spectre of stagnation lurks in the corner of consciousness at every stage of life, bar childhood. In adolescence, it's the fear of being left behind by your peers. In your twenties and thirties, it's the fear of being stuck, or in drift, as your peers pass you by. But at midlife, it's an existential threat. Half of your life has already passed, the future is racing towards you, urgent but featureless. This spurs you on to make your life count for something, to leave the world a better place than you found it. That hope for the future holds within it the shadow of your own death, and the possibility of transcending it.

Creating and shaping your personal legacy will not be accomplished until the end of middle age. How invested and successful you are at resolving that task will have a significant effect on your happiness and well-being, not just now but in old age, when you are faced with finding meaning and value in the life you've lived.[4]

Something valuable to leave behind

Start by counting up the gains. Most of you have a more secure and responsible place in the larger society. You are more tightly knitted into its structures and networks, more aware of how it works, and have a more developed view about how it needs to change and develop.[5] Your approach to what you do is tempered by experience. You have suffered some losses and have come to terms with things that did not turn out as you hoped. You can now use the wisdom that comes from those gains and losses to help you create something of lasting value.

You also have more to pass on to the next generation – the accumulated knowledge you have gleaned from your work, or rearing a family, or from your involvement in the arts, in sport, in volunteering, or social activism. You have nurtured the children you have brought into the world, or a project or idea that you care about. You now want to sustain that investment into the future. Whatever you want to pass on, it must be something organic to you, to the person you are, unique in a self-defining way: 'This is what *I* have to pass on to the younger generation.' It constitutes, in some more or less conscious way, what you deem to be your personal legacy, the footprint you will leave behind in the world.

The first step in becoming generative is to produce something that you believe is valuable and worthwhile. In middle age, most of you will do that. The second step is to give it away. The first is the powerful extension of the self that comes with mastery of your niche in life, however big or small. The second step is the ability to see yourself as part of the larger human community, so it relies on your sense of close connection to others.[6] If you are generative, it strengthens your connections to others, gives you the opportunity to rework old wounds, and to emerge with a more secure sense of mattering and belonging.

Some of you have a head start in being generative. Even now, halfway through your life, recalling a parent as warm, affectionate and responsive to you when you were aged five makes it easier to achieve what you hoped for in life, and to be open, generous and concerned about others.[7] Being *Secure* tilts you towards generativity.

> I had great parents. They could not have done more for us, especially me. I had severe asthma as a child, and I was constantly getting chest infections and had pneumonia a few times – I was hospitalized once, it was so serious. I think my poor mother and father spent half their time nursing me and worrying about me. Thank God, I am much better now. I am conscious that I was very lucky in my childhood, and I am determined to try to do my absolute best for my children, to pass on to them what I got from my parents. I also volunteer for two charities. It's just my way of giving back.
>
> Emily, 53

If you were not that lucky, you may still be struggling with a sense of scarcity and be more fearful of depleting your meagre psychological resources by investing in other people. You hold tightly to your defences, tacking close to what you've always done, unwilling to open up questions that might unsettle you.[8] But not always. Despite a bad start, some of you have achieved an earned security, and a strong desire to make life better for other people.

I had a pretty miserable childhood. My parents had to leave school early and it was always a big financial struggle. My mother was a very harsh woman. She beat the daylights out of us, and I never remember her being affectionate, although she did get better with the younger ones. I was the eldest and got the brunt of it. She seemed more relaxed as she got older. I got a scholarship to secondary school and joined the civil service where I did well. For a long time I pushed my own childhood into the back of my mind. As far as I was concerned, the farther away I got from the whole thing the better. But it's funny, about ten years ago, it started coming back into my mind, and I began to think that if doing well in school had made such a difference to me, then why couldn't I help other kids now? So I've become very passionate about education for children in deprived communities, and I do a lot of voluntary work with community organizations who are involved in educational projects in deprived communities. Sometimes I feel like I'm just sticking my finger in the dyke – you are up against so much. But my own experience drives me on.

Donal, 60

Your chosen legacy project can be small and private.

The most important thing I've done in my life is rear my four children. I'm immensely proud of all of them. I worked the family farm all my life and I decided to hand it over to my son in my early fifties, so he could make a living and I could still help him. When I see him and my other two children making their way in the world, I feel I have a small part in their success. My wife and myself help look after our five grandchildren, and we are very involved in their lives. So when we are dead and gone, what they do will live on long after me. I hope that the farm will stay in the family, so I like to think a bit of me will carry on in all of that.

Micheál, 66

It can involve a whole community.

I used to teach history earlier in my career. Now I'm a principal so don't get to do much teaching. But I am very involved in local history, and I recently started a project to research the history and folklore of the townland around here. Now, it's expanded into a kind of genealogy project. Some of the other teachers are very enthusiastic and have got the children involved in researching their own family histories, and a group of us are hoping to produce a small book, and an exhibition next year. It's been great, very interesting. It has highlighted for me that you just get a loan on life, or where you live, so you must look after it well, so it's there for the next generation.

John, 57

Or you may take on a larger, more long-term project.

I am absolutely passionate about advancing women's rights. I think it's one of the most important issues in the world now, ensuring that half of humanity has the same rights and opportunities as the other half. I am very involved in a women's organization here, and also with an organization that is trying to give girls in the developing world a chance to stay at school. I know I can't change everything, but I want to feel that I did my bit to move the agenda on.

Bridget, 61

As you near the end of middle age, some of you have done well. You have come to terms with the past and the dreams that may not have worked out and replaced them with new dreams and plans that are more modest and flexible.[9] You have shaped your own legacy and emerged with a stronger sense of self and personal identity, and more compassion. You have adjusted to the changing demands of your close relationships and of your role at work and are ready to move on to a new stage of your life.

Looking back, I'd say I feel happier and more settled in my life now than I ever did. I took early retirement and that was the best thing I ever did – I still have nightmares that I am back in that job – I killed myself at the job. I don't have children to worry about, like some of my married friends do. I have great friends, and all going well healthwise. I have plenty of time to do all the things I'd like to do before I die.

Susan, 64

For some of you, it's been a mixed bag.

I suppose I've done okay. I've a good wife and a good marriage, and our two kids, well hardly kids any more, seem to be doing well in college. I've a good job at senior level that pays the bills and all that, and a pension when I retire in two years. But at another level, I feel something is missing. I thought my life would be different, more exciting maybe. I'd like to have achieved something definite that I could point to and say, 'I did that.' I used to have this fantasy of building my own house. But it never happened. There were always reasons not to – no time, no money, afraid to take the risk. Now I think, at least if I had done that, I could point to that house as something I did, something that was mine. It would be there long after I died, and other families would be enjoying it. What can I point to? That I attended a thousand meetings?

Liam, 63

For others, the spectre of stagnation has become a reality. You feel your best days are behind you, with little left to beckon you into a hopeful future. You have little interest in sharing what you knew or in guiding the next generation, your energy absorbed by a preoccupation with yourself and your own concerns. You may have an acute sense of your own vulnerability, of time and energy draining away. But you don't turn to the comfort of close relationships, fearful that you might expose your vulnerability, or be overwhelmed by any demands they make on you. Instead, your own being has become the sole focus of your attention. You indulge yourself as if you were your own child, a lavishing of care on yourself that somehow fails to satisfy, leaving an underlying cynicism and irritability that surfaces easily.

Oh, I make sure to have a lot of 'Me time' nowadays. I'm sick of taking care of people. I feel completely worn out. People are so selfish. I feel that nobody really cares about me, so I decided, okay, I'll take care of me. I spend a lot on myself – a lot! And I'm going to keep doing that. I don't even want half the things I buy, but who cares?

Fiona, 63

At its extreme, you have an overwhelming sense of lost opportunities, of squandered efforts.

I think I bottled my life. I wanted to be a nurse, but instead I got pregnant accidentally and was under pressure from my family to get married. I knew even then that it was a mistake. It didn't work out. My 'plan' was to leave my husband and strike out on my own as soon as our two kids were done for. I was still young. There were plenty of jobs around. But I didn't. I kept making excuses. I just couldn't muster the energy or the confidence or something. Maybe I was afraid I wouldn't be able to manage on my own, or that I wouldn't be able to hack a real career. So I just settled for a part-time office job once the kids were at school and here I am there since. I'm retiring this year. So I've nothing much to show for my life. The worst thing about the whole saga is that every time I resolved to change my life, and then I didn't, I felt even worse about myself. Anyway, too late now. So I'm as much stuck with myself as I am with my life.

Ann-Marie, 61

A life well lived – what we learn from middle age

The principles of a life well lived – middle age			
Life stage	*Time frame*	*Developmental task*	*Psychological principle*
Middle age	50–late 60s	generating or stagnating?	Create something of lasting value

Middle age is a time of reckoning and a time when you turn your mind to what your life means and how you can create something of lasting value. In the ordinary course of life, you measure how things are unfolding in ordinary time. But at certain points, for example at midlife or when you emerge from a significant personal crisis, you

are jolted out of that time realm and into what Ancient Greeks called
kairos, a deeply personal sense of time, a realization that this is the
opportune moment when something needs to be done and can be
done. Often, this realization is rooted in a new sense of vulnerability,
an urgency about time passing and time left.

First things first

You want to feel that what you are doing with your life will amount
to something, and that you will leave behind something of lasting
value. Wanting and hoping are a good start, but they don't make
things happen. You have to define and shape that legacy. There are
things you have to do – like sticking around long enough to give you
time to do that, and to experience what you create as it unfolds.

PROTECT YOUR BRAIN BY LOOKING AFTER YOUR BODY

A major study that tracked the fitness level of over 30,000 middle-
aged people in Norway over 10 years found that some had entered
middle age out of shape and stayed that way, remaining in the lowest
20 per cent of aerobic fitness for the entire 10 years; others moved in
or out of fitness; and the fittest few remained fit. During a 20-year
follow-up period, the researchers then checked records from nursing
homes and specialized memory clinics to see which participants
developed dementia, and if their level of fitness affected their risk for
the disease. It did.

People who were fit throughout the study period proved to be
almost *50 per cent* less likely to develop dementia than the least-fit men
and women. Perhaps more encouraging, those men and women who
had entered middle age out of shape but then worked to get fit
showed the same substantial reduction in risk.[10] And if you are wondering about your current state of fitness, you can use their free,
online fitness calculator.[11]

SEPARATE THE URGENT FROM THE IMPORTANT

The problem with being busy, busy, busy is that the urgent often
trumps the important. Use the matrix on the next page, developed

by Stephen Covey,[12] to help identify how you are spending your time. Divide a page into four boxes, listing the tasks to be done under each heading.

The 'urgent vs important' matrix		
	Important	*Not Important*
Urgent		
Non-urgent		

Most often, you will find that you spend most of your time responding to the urgent – important *and* unimportant – and the tasks that are important but non-urgent get pushed to the bottom of your endless 'To Do' list. Yet, these are the very things that will create something of lasting value. Think down the line: how will you judge if your life has been successful in a way that is important to you? What do you hope your children will say about you as a parent, or someone will say at your retirement party, or at your funeral? What do you hope you will have created that is of lasting value?

Now, work backwards from there. What do you need to do *now* to build that personal legacy? You will still have to do all the urgent and important stuff, you can still have the pleasure of doing things that are neither, but you are extending yourself beyond that.

CURATE YOUR LIFE AND YOUR ACHIEVEMENTS

Don't evaluate your life like you would a CV; look at it with a wide and loving regard. That reflective gaze is what allows you to see what you can create that can be of lasting value. Depending on your circumstances, what you create can range from high-minded projects that will benefit thousands of people to the most private of enterprises.

Create a beautiful garden that will outlast you.

Plant a tree that will be there for the next family to live in your house, and the one after that.

Make a video of your parents or grandparents, or a favourite aunt or uncle, as they talk about their own childhoods and how they lived their lives.

Or create something more ephemeral, like occasions with family or friends that will linger on in memory long after the events are over.

Small feasts in the garden during the summer, eating, sipping wine and talking until the light is finally gone.

Make a big occasion of Christmas: put up a dazzling tree, even if it's too big for the sitting room; pack the house with food and family; swear that next year you will cut down on all this fuss, only to repeat the whole thing the year after.

What matters is that it's an expression of something that you value enough to want others to share it – and generosity is at its core.

20.   *Late adulthood:* Life's new in-between stage

Sometime in your late sixties, you enter a new stage of life, even if you don't quite know what to call it. You know you are past the midpoint in your life, but you certainly don't consider yourself old. Retiring and drawing your pension used to signal the entry to old age, but not any more. Being called 'retired' or a 'pensioner' may be technically correct, but it's very much out of step with your lived experiences.

Most of you actively resist the idea of categorizing yourself as 'old' and report feeling about ten years younger than you actually are.[1] You don't just feel younger, you think that you look younger than your chronological age, and that gap between how old you are and how old you feel tends to widen the older you get. For you, old age is still a long way off, sometime in your eighties, or associated with a steep decline in health.

So, like those in their twenties, you feel you are at an in-between stage or, in travel industry parlance, a 'shoulder season', a period wedged between the all-systems-go pace of middle age and the existential task of settling into old age.[2]

> I'm seventy-two, so I'm not young, but I definitely don't consider myself old, as in old age. I think it's completely different now than it was for older people before. If I can manage to stay healthy and active, I hope I have a good twenty years ahead of me and I want to stay active and make the very most of that time. That's how all my friends feel. We are a different generation.
>
> Janet, 72

> At this stage, I think of myself as an old geezer. Although, when I dream, I am always young, with a full head of hair, and it's black! But then, I look in the mirror and I see this old guy staring back at me!
>
> Mike, 68

There is no consensus on what to call this in-between stage. Take your pick – 'young-old', 'healthy old', 'third age', 'later adulthood'. As for you, nearly half of you aged sixty-five to sixty-nine and one-*third* of you in your early seventies consider yourselves to be still middle-aged, and many believe middle age extends to age seventy-five. In a recent *Financial Times* series about how people aged seventy-plus are redefining aging – continuing to run successful businesses, starting new enterprises, doing marathons or even skydiving – this stage is referred to as 'the next act'.[3]

I will use 'late adulthood' because I think it best captures the kind of 'what's next', rather than 'what's gone', approach your generation takes to life at this stage, a maturing of the process that started in early middle age.

In contrast to other stages in life, there are few social norms about what's expected of you, or how to structure your life, apart from pottering around in the garden, enjoying grandchildren, or 'growing old gracefully' – whatever that means. As a result, it's a particularly unstructured stage of life, a peculiar mix of freedom and dislocation. The responsibility to structure your time is left to you. As a result, there is a lot of individual variability in how you live your lives, and that variability increases with age. Nor is there any single standard of successful aging. In late adulthood, as at every stage, people are individuals, and their lives are not uniform.[4]

Redefining 'the next act'

Your generation is very different from previous generations of sixty- and seventy-somethings. You have more financial security, exercise more control over your life, enjoy more independence and personal freedom, have more choices, and see fewer constraints on what you can do, especially if you are a woman. You are most certainly redefining this stage and doing so with great vigour.

You are likely to live longer and enjoy more years of healthy living than your parents or grandparents did. In Ireland, at birth a male can expect to live to eighty, and a female to eighty-four. The odds become

Late adulthood: *Life's new in-between stage*

247

a bit more precise in later life. For example, a man of sixty-five can expect to live another 17.6 years, and at seventy-five, another 11.5 years. If you are a woman, your prospects are even better. At sixty-five you have a good chance of getting 19 more years, and at seventy-five, 13.3 years.[5]

But you are also aware that the risk of developing chronic conditions like hypertension, diabetes, cardiovascular disease or arthritis also increases. You get used to visiting the GP, the dentist, the out-patient clinic and other medical services more often. About a quarter of you will be admitted to hospital at some point. There is a big class divide, more obvious than ever as you age. The more educated and economically secure you are, the lower the health risks. A lifetime of disadvantage, and stress, catches up with you in later life.

On the other hand, what were once fatal or debilitating diseases, the kind that would have killed your parents or grandparents, are now better controlled. A heart attack, stroke or diagnosis of cancer is no longer a death sentence. Most of you take better care of your health, are less likely to smoke, and more likely to give up smoking at this stage than your parents' generation did, although if you are a former smoker, you may have lagging effects on your health. Most of you are also physically fitter. You go to the gym or swim, and more than half of you walk regularly. If you are physically active, you are also far more likely to be socially active, to rate your health as better, and your quality of life higher. If you are not, you are more than twice as likely to feel depressed.[6]

How old you are and how old you feel

The distinction between how old you are and how old you feel is not a trivial point. How young or old you feel – your subjective age – is influenced by how you judge the state of your health, how much stress there is in your life and, not least, how much you have internalized negative views about aging. Feeling younger than you are is not some harmless self-deception – it's a far stronger predictor of your health, physical functioning and psychological well-being than your actual age and, as we have already seen, has a small, but significant effect on how long you will live.

Why? Believing that age is just a number gives you an extended sense of the future, and that turns out to be highly adaptive.[7] When you were young, having an extended view of the future motivated you to set more long-term goals in your career and to work harder to achieve them. Now, it shapes your mindset and your approach to aging.[8]

If you have a more extended view of the future, you are more likely to believe that the negative effects of aging are modifiable and negotiable, to some extent at least. It motivates you to live more healthily and strengthens your belief that keeping physically active is important. You focus more on the potential gains that come with maturity and feel less threatened by getting older. It motivates you to keep setting new goals that will keep you growing and developing as a person. You are much less likely to think that age has changed your core sense of self, your essence as a person. It gives you a stronger sense of purpose and meaning, a determination to take control of your life. It makes you more psychologically open, more likely to focus on new and emerging possibilities in your life, and to approach new situations with optimism and curiosity.

In contrast, if you have a more restricted view of the future, you believe that chronological age determines the process of aging and that the negative effects of age are fixed and immutable. You are more focused on what you consider the inevitable losses, and more susceptible to internalizing negative stereotypes about aging. You take the view that trying to stay physically fit is not worth it or is risky for older people. After all, you're going to get sick anyway, so what's the point of trying to prevent it?

At every stage of life, you are conscious of the gains and losses that come with it. In late adulthood, the dynamic tilts more on the loss side, particularly in relation to your health, and, for some, the ending of full-time employment. But that does *not* define how you think about your life.

Your biological reserves are decreasing, but you match that with your enduring capacity to keep adapting to the challenges you face.

You are more aware of the biological boundaries of life and as losses accumulate, you know that chronological age counts more than it did when you were younger, but you don't allow it to determine your life. Instead, you are resolved to make the most of these bonus years of health and vitality, and any dissatisfaction you have about aging increases only slightly as you progress through your seventies.[9]

Joining the organ recital

The signs that things are changing come dripping slowly, and the first ones are not encouraging. You notice a new susceptibility to colds, chest infections, vague aches, pains and injuries. When Jane Fonda, the high-priestess of the fitness movement in the 1980s, was asked what it was like to be seventy, she simply said, 'Everything hurts.' It's a good summary. You notice that when you and your friends meet up, often the first item on the agenda is a brief health and injury catch-up, what Irish writer Maeve Binchy called the 'organ recital'.

> Before, when a bunch of us got together, we would all be into what happened since we last met, where we'd been, what we'd done. We still do that, but not before we've all given updates on our ankles, or hips, or backs, or whatever new injury we have, what new consultant we've been to, what treatment or medication we are on, and whether it's any good.
>
> Cathy, 68

Women talk more about their health to each other than men do with their friends. Their conversations, as always, are more personal and intimate. They are also more likely to suffer from ailments like arthritis that are painful or interfere with their day-to-day activities.[10] On the other hand, men are more likely to die sooner. So if women are not thinking about their own health, they are worrying about their husbands'.

> I worry about my husband's health more than my own. It is such a job to get him to see a doctor. He mentions a symptom that is obviously

worrying him, but then resists getting it checked out unless I keep
nagging him.

Judy, 74

Your new concern about health reflects a deeper psychological
change. By now, most of you have experienced the death of someone
close to you.

> My dad died twenty-one years ago, and my mother and last remain-
> ing uncle died in the last two years. So it was the end of an era, really.
> That older generation is now gone. But what has really bowled me
> over is that a great friend of mine died this year. For some reason, I
> never expected that. We were great mates. I suppose I thought we
> would grow old together. I'm still trying to come to terms with it.

Ciaran, 71

You, or someone you are close to, may have a health scare. There's
a flurry of tests, an anxious waiting for results, the words 'positive'
and 'negative' taking on a whole new meaning. It comes to nothing
this time, but the lesson sinks in. At your age, death is no longer
exceptional or caused by something external, like an accident, as it
was earlier in life. At this stage, death strikes from within, from some
invisible process happening in your body. By now, the actuality of
your own demise is more easily imagined. By the end of your seventies, about four in ten of your age group is dead.

But despite all that, nearly 70 per cent of you report no fear of
death. What you fear is the process of dying, and the pain and indig-
nity that might accompany that.[11] If anything, the acute sense of the
limited time left provokes an urgent determination to see how many
good years you can wrest from the time remaining, how much pleasure, how many new experiences you can pack into these years, so
that you feel you are still growing and developing, your life still pro-
gressing with hope and vigour.

You have (mostly) adapted to the ongoing effects of aging on your
body and appearance, although you may still sigh when you survey
yourself in the mirror or the shower. Yet, for all that, in terms of
everyday activities, well-being and concerns about aging, the

differences between the beginning and end of late middle age are not striking. And some of the most high-functioning late middle-agers are in their mid to late seventies.

> I see people of my age dropping dead around me, so the way I feel now is that every day is a bonus. I never thought I'd hear myself use that cliché. But it happens to be true. I'm in great health for my age and my life is good. I still play a good bit of golf and Marie is off playing bridge. We still get on great together. The only thing is that there's not much going on in our sex life now and I miss that. I still think about it, but it's not eating the leg off you like in the old days. When I think of all the wasted erections of my younger days! But you know, I manage my pleasures now.
>
> William, 77

Stumbling on the secret of happiness

You have better cognitive functioning and outperform earlier generations on a range of intelligence measures. The majority of you report no memory problems. As you advance into your late seventies, you may notice more problems with your short-term memory. It's harder to recall intricate details of when and where things happened. You rely more on lists and Post-its. Sometimes, this gives you a fussy air. Some of you are careful to modulate that in case it makes you look doddery.

> When I was younger, I was struck by how fussy older people get. They'd come into meetings with sheaves of papers and notes and they'd hold everybody up shuffling through them looking for something. So I was determined not to be like that when I got older. I'm on a lot of committees since I retired, and I use the one-sheet rule. That and listening carefully is all you need to be efficient.
>
> Conor, 69

One of the most consistent and consequential findings about late adulthood is that people are happier and more positive than at earlier stages of adult life.[12] You remember more positive memories than you used to, rather than negative ones. Your capacity for joy, contentment, good humour, interest and pride in what you have achieved in life is as strong as ever, although you may not experience the big surges of excitement as often as when you were younger.

The big change is not in your positive emotions, it is in your negative feelings. You don't experience anxiety, anger, boredom, envy, jealousy, contempt or disgust as often as you used to when you were younger, although when you do, the negative feeling is just as intense as it always was. But the difference is this – the feelings don't come in overwhelming surges, you are less reactive to them, and they don't last as long.

You experience significantly less anger. Why? Because when you are young, you are focused on the future, on achieving your goals, and when you see your efforts being frustrated or blocked, you have to fight your corner, so you benefit from the anger that motivates you to act to secure your position and see off rivals. By late adulthood, you are under less pressure and you want to enjoy your life, so getting angry on a day-to-day basis is increasingly maladaptive and is associated with an increase in the biomarkers of chronic low-grade inflammation and a number of chronic illnesses.[13]

You also have more control over your feelings and are better able to manage and improve your mood at will. You are less likely to let one stressful experience define your whole week – unlike younger people, who tend to anchor their judgement of how the week went on the basis of the most stressful day they had.[14] You can control your tendency to worry more effectively.

> I still worry about the usual things, but now I find that I just don't think about them as much, I can set my worries aside for longer periods. So I don't sweat the small stuff that used to drive me mad when I was younger.
>
> Geraldine, 74

Your memory is increasingly biased towards the positive. This may be partly due to a change in how the amygdala, the threat centre of the brain, works as you age. When you are a young adult, setting out in the world, the amygdala reacts more strongly to negative than positive things, whereas now it's equally reactive to both positive and negative experiences.[15]

You use more emotional intelligence in how you approach things. You are better able to integrate your cognitive and emotional capacities, modulating your emotional reactions by trying to think through all the issues, but also trusting your gut reactions more when you make decisions. You also pay closer attention to negative information than younger people do, and you put more weight on it when making a decision. That makes you more circumspect, more wary about taking risks, so you may miss a good opportunity. But, then again, taking risks has more potential pay-offs for younger people – they have to plan for an extended future, and they have ample reserves of physical and psychological energy to take the hit if things don't work out.

You don't have that extended open-ended future. And that is the paradox of aging. At the moment when you can most easily imagine the end of your life, you are happier than the middle-aged, or even the young.[16] The time left seems too precious to waste on anger or regrets. The ending of your life is more easily imagined. But instead of triggering despair, you stumble on the secret of happiness – that life is precious and sweet, and that every moment counts.

This shift in your thinking profoundly affects the way you think and feel and what now motivates you. As time becomes less open-ended, it becomes increasingly important to make the right choices, not to waste time on things that have gradually diminishing returns in the now limited future. When you are young you're prepared to put up with a lot of hassle, and even pain, because it holds the promise of some new experience, an opportunity to discover something interesting or useful to your future plans, so your strategy is to maximize possibilities. Now, you are relieved of concerns about a future where there is everything to play for and everything to lose. Your attention shifts decisively on to emotionally meaningful experiences, particularly with the people you most care about.

You change the way you process experiences in your relationships – you pay more attention to emotions. You recall the emotional details of an encounter more thoroughly than younger adults do. Someone's emotional qualities become more important in how you consider them, and the emotional quality of your interactions with them counts more. You have a finer sense of how context affects the way people feel and a more nuanced understanding of emotions. You understand how complex and subtle feelings are, and that you can experience a mix of emotions all at the same time. You are more aware that the most intense joy can be bitter-sweet and tinged with loss; that anger is often mixed with sadness or love – or even a certain amount of satisfaction that you have managed to discombobulate somebody who has annoyed you.

All of these changes have big implications for how you live your life. For how long you can or want to work. For the now very extended time you and your partner will live together, without child-rearing and paid employment to structure your time together. For the projects you want to try, or finish. You need to find a new configuration for your need for closeness, autonomy and competence.

The end of the 'rush hour' of life

Some of you look forward to leaving the burden of full-time work behind, but being forced to retire at sixty-five rankles with others, especially if you love your work, enjoy the camaraderie and feel at the top of your game. In Ireland, for example, more than one in five middle-aged people have no plans to retire at any time.[17]

In the US, between 60 per cent and 64 per cent continue to work during retirement, and 89 per cent would like to continue working full-time, even if they do not need the additional income. By 2022, it is predicted that 32 per cent of those aged sixty-five to seventy-four will continue to work after retirement, and 11 per cent of those aged seventy-five or older will carry on working after that, a trend that is particularly strong for women and those with education.[18]

In Ireland, only 13.6 per cent continue to work part-time, with men significantly more likely to work than women, particularly married women.[19] But whether that is because the rest don't want to or are unable to find part-time jobs is not clear.[20]

Most of you would prefer to retire more gradually – decreasing your hours, going part-time, moving to a less demanding position with fewer responsibilities, or finding a 'bridge job' to fill the gap between working full-time and giving up work completely.[21] In the USA, however, only one in five people say their employers allow any of those options, and even fewer allow changing to less demanding positions, and it's unlikely to be different here.[22]

Historically, when you retired you were firmly steered away from work, or the jobs on offer were poorly paid, with little recognition and few institutional supports, or a poor match for your knowledge and skills.[23] Nothing much has changed. This is a huge waste of talent and experience that could be put at the service of the whole community. Writer and social activist Marc Freedman has come up with an inventive way to fill this gap, what he calls the 'encore career'.

The idea of the encore career is a new phase of work that comes after retirement, when the skills, knowledge, experiences and insights acquired during your career can be put to use in another area that sorely needs that resource. Examples of such areas would be parts of the public service that are underfunded or under pressure, schools in deprived areas, the voluntary and community sector, or civic activities. This is a way to use the enormous untapped resource of the current healthiest, most long-living and educated generation.

The encore career allows you to do something of real value, to make a contribution to the common good, to boost your own well-being and, in some cases, to earn a modest income. This is a stage of your life when most of you have insights about what matters, as well as the motivation, energy and time to act on this accumulated wisdom.

Adjusting to retirement

Retirement triggers a cascade of changes – not just in your finances or how you spend your time, but also psychological changes in how you think and feel about yourself and it affects your close relationships. It's not a single event, more a process that unfolds over a period of time: the pre-retirement phase, when you do your planning; the transition phase, when you are adjusting to it; and the post-retirement phase, when you set a new agenda for living. Each phase is crucial in determining the success of the next – theoretically, that is.

In reality, a sizeable number of you do little planning, apart from joining or investing in a pension fund, and in Ireland 38 per cent don't even have that security and have to rely on qualifying for the state 'old age' pension. For example, most of you do little thinking about what expectations your adult children may have about giving or receiving financial or practical help, like childcare or babysitting, and how they match your own expectations and desires. And what about a now very elderly parent that you may be expected to care for?[24]

In personal terms, retiring has a small but significant impact on your self-esteem. It drops slightly in the five years coming up to retirement, stabilizes the month you retire, and remains stable for several years after, suggesting that it's the prospect of retirement and the transition that triggers the drop.[25] Why? You may be increasingly finding your job too tiring or demanding, or have trouble adjusting to new technology or frequent organizational changes. Or you are already worrying about how you will adjust to life after work. The more central work is to your identity, the bigger the hit on your self-esteem.[26]

Social invisibility

When you retire, you may encounter a new and distressing phenomenon – becoming socially invisible. This is one of the downsides of aging, especially after you retire. By your late sixties, you are no stranger to negative stereotypes about aging – the perception that you are slowing down cognitively and not quite up to par; that you are more rigid and set in your ways.[27] To add insult to injury, you are likely to be treated as asexual, especially if you are a woman. You are, of course, less likely to attract this negative stereotyping if you are very rich or continue to enjoy high status in your field. And if you are a male billionaire, this appears to confer a type of sexual magnetism that's not immediately obvious to anyone bar the upward socially mobile.

Agism is not likely to be expressed as open prejudice. For example, you are unlikely to be stigmatized like those who face sexism or racism. Rather, it takes the form of interpersonal invisibility. You are simply perceived as less relevant, less worthy of social attention, no longer in a position to either help or hinder people from achieving what they want, so they are less likely to pay attention to you or seek you out. Ouch.

How you react to retirement, and how it affects your well-being, depends on many things, such as your individual circumstances, the state of your health, how physically active you are, your finances, and your temperament. If you are extraverted, open, flexible, conscientious and find it easy to get on with people, you do better.

In general, women find it easier to adjust to retirement, maybe because work is less central to their identity, or they have invested more in their family and friends or have a wider variety of social activities. Crucially, how you adjust to retirement depends on whether you think of it in terms of loss or gain.[28]

If you think of it primarily in terms of loss – of an important social role that is also a core part of your identity; or of the sense of achievement and pride that comes from bringing home a decent wage – then it's harder to adjust. Add to that the loss of structure and the uncertainty as to what you are supposed to do with your time, and the process becomes more stressful.

I saw this with my own grandfather, who worked in the local distillery for his entire adult life. It was gruelling work, especially during the 'season' when the whiskey was being made. But he loved his job, and the camaraderie with his friends, and was immensely proud of the whiskey they produced. When he retired he seemed lost. He would potter around his small back garden, but we would see him staring over the back wall at the distillery stack, especially during the 'season', and he could tell by the quality of the smoke what stage of distilling was happening, and he would look so sad when he came back into the house.

If, on the other hand, you think of retirement in terms of gains – freedom from work-related stress; from the hassle of having to deal with awkward people day-to-day; freedom to spend more time on things you have always enjoyed or had no time to do – then your reaction is very different.

I'm an architect, and during the recession work dried up completely, and I thought I was completely washed up. But I was always really into music, so I decided to go back and do a four-year music degree. It's been a hard slog, but I loved every bit of that course. I soaked it up in a way I couldn't have when I was in my twenties. Back then, I lacked the patience and discipline that I have now. Everyone in my class was younger than me and I loved that. I've always felt more comfortable with younger colleagues than the senior guys who like to throw their weight around. On the course, I saw it as my business to help anybody who was interested in things I happened to be good at. I got on really well with all of them. They wanted me to be the class spokesman, but I wasn't interested in that at all. I feel I've done my duty there! I just wanted to open up their perspective on things, to help them understand the processes behind things and why they had to master them.

Doing the course postponed the retirement thing for me. A lot of guys seem to lose authority when they retire. It diminishes them. I still see myself cantering on. Now that I've finished my course, I'm conscious that I need to do something else. But I don't have any master plan. Maybe I'll go back to painting. I'm feeling quite positive about the future. I'm enjoying my life now. I feel I'm being selfish sometimes – doing all these things that I didn't have a chance to do before, like reading and watching films. I've no health problems. One thing, I probably don't meet people enough, I'm lazy about that. And that might be a problem.

Mike, 69

Whether you retire by choice or because you have to also has a big bearing on your adjustment. If you are forced to retire because of your age, or health problems, or because you have to care for an ill or disabled spouse or family member, you may find the whole transition more difficult. But if you choose to retire so you can spend more time on something you enjoy, you will adjust more quickly and positively. Similarly, if you choose to continue working because you like the structure or added financial security it provides, or because you want to be productive and feel relevant and useful, it boosts your physical and psychological well-being.[29]

For all these reasons, individual reactions are very varied. For some, it's plain sailing.

> Oh, I love my life now. I felt a huge burden lifting off me the day I walked out the door of that place. For the first time in my adult life, I have time to focus on myself. I've gone back to singing. I really wanted to be a professional singer when I was in my twenties, but I was afraid I wouldn't be good enough. I just didn't have the courage to give it a go. I've always kept up some singing, but there was never any time. I was so busy looking after the kids and in my job. Now, I've joined a choir. I'm going back for singing lessons. I'm walking a lot so I've lost weight and am fitter than I've been for years. This time of my life is really good, actually.
>
> Alice, 69

For others, it's a struggle to adjust, especially if you were successful, identified strongly with your work and enjoyed it.

> I had so much fun before I retired. I used to travel the world in my work. Retirement sucks, it was a big mistake. It used to be Cape Town or Cape Horn, it's all nappies and babysitting now. I'm exaggerating, of course. I'm a useless grandpa, even though I love them of course. But my wife and kids all worry that I need something to do – 'Here's an adorable grandchild to keep you busy.' Anyway. Over and out. I have to bring the girls to school tomorrow.
>
> Roy, 69

For a small number, being retired is crushing, and when combined with other problems can be the beginning of a long decline.

> I retired three years ago, three years and seven months to be precise, and it is awful. I loved my work, and nothing has been able to replace it. I have no interest in playing golf, I found it utterly boring, and that's all most of my friends do now. My wife is younger than me and still working, so are her friends, and when we socialize with them, I feel I have nothing interesting to say, like I'm this old codger she's dragging along, so I avoid that as much as possible. Do I think it will get better? No, I don't. Just more of the same.
>
> Kevin, 69

The thirty-year 'rush hour' of life may be coming to an end, but you are *busy*. One man I contacted to ask if I could interview him left me a voice message that managed to hit on all the big themes of late adulthood.

> Look, I'd be delighted to do an interview – apologies for not getting back to you sooner. Between the jigs and the reels, I haven't had a minute. I was weighed down for a while with a persistent chest infection. The problem is time, or rather timing. Marian and myself are heading off now for two weeks in France. Then when we come back we have a family commitment straight away – we have to go to London to look after our grandchildren, to give Alice and her husband a chance to take a break for their anniversary. But I'll contact you when I get back and we can fix up a date then, okay?
>
> Neil, 70

For Neil, the 'jigs and the reels' include serving on two boards and running a small consultancy practice that he set up when he retired.

A time of changes

Of course, not all of you are thriving. Some of you have had your life turned upside down by the sudden death of a spouse, are finding it hard to cope with living alone, the onset of a debilitating and chronic illness, ongoing problems or an upheaval in the life of one of your children. Some of you are still dogged by emotional difficulties you had earlier in life.[30]

However, for most of you, this is a rich and rewarding stage of your life when you reap the benefits of all you have achieved and learned in your life up to now. Most of you are conscious of how you have changed.

> Have I changed? I think I did change in my forties. I softened up a lot. I used to be quite abrasive and bolshie, very opinionated. But I don't think I've changed much since then. Looking back on it, I would say I was in my prime in my forties. That was a very creative part of my life. I came from a family of accountants and I always considered

myself slightly 'alternative'. I always loved music and painting – that was part of what attracted me to my wife Trish, she loved art too. I became an architect because I wanted to make things. In the early part of my career I had to do a lot of routine stuff, but in my forties I was finally able to get involved in much bigger and more creative projects. I'm happier in myself now.

Chris, 70

Apart from health, you expect that problems with family, work, stress and leisure time are going to lessen.[31] The only area where problems are expected to get worse is in relation to your health. And you are right on all counts. You are likely to be less stressed than you were at earlier life stages. You have a greater understanding and acceptance of the person that you are. You are warmer, more sympathetic, more dependable, more independent-minded, more grounded in yourself and perceptive about others than at any other time of adulthood.[32] There is a noticeable vitality to your life.

21. *Late adulthood:* A time to thrive

Your social network gets smaller as you age, not, as was once thought, because you become more disengaged or isolated, but because you begin to prune out your more casual acquaintances. You do this so that you can spend more time with those you feel closest to, your inner circle – usually a combination of a partner, your close friends, and one or two siblings. They are your social convoy, those who surround you and travel with you as you age and are available to you in times of need. They are the people who know you best, whom you can confide in and depend on for support. They possess an unrivalled capacity not just to support you but to affirm your sense of who you are.[1] This process of pruning starts in middle age and your social convoy, usually around eight people, remains much the same size as it was then.

You are less motivated to keep in touch with the larger, more expansive and diverse network that you wanted when you were younger. The die-hard extraverts with extraordinary energy and capacity for getting people together maintain a larger network of friends, but it now contains a larger proportion of close relationships. And for everybody, close relationships remain a major source of self-esteem.[2]

But here's the really good news – your relationships get better as you age.[3] You feel a new freedom to refind yourself in your relationships and are more likely to have high-quality ties with your children, your partner and your friends. You have fewer problematic and ambivalent relationships in your life, and fewer conflicts with people. And even when you do, you are less likely to blame them, you are readier to forgive, and your view of them remains positive.

Easier happier marriages

Nearly half of the average marriage is now spent after the children have left home, when your relationship with your partner comes into sharper focus.[4] Usually, there is a substantial improvement in the relationship between you, particularly for women.[5] You are happier and more satisfied together, you enjoy each other more, and there is less conflict. The marriages that have survived up to now are likely to stay stable; some of the most unhappy ones have been winnowed out by divorce.

Over four in ten of you continue to be sexually active.[6] You still think and fantasize about sex, but less often than when you were younger, and your fantasies are generally less exotically elaborated. But one-third of you report *more* sexual thoughts and activity than even younger adults. A lot depends on the state of your health, not being depressed, and the quality of your relationship. The more sexually active you are, the more satisfied you are with your life, the more positive your attitude to aging and the less likely you are to consider yourself old.[7]

Hovering over your relationship is your awareness that the time left together is limited. As you advance into your seventies, with every passing year the odds of you or your partner becoming ill or dying in the not-too-distant future are increasing. It's common to hear couples refuse to talk about the future or plan too far ahead. They might joke about it, but it is underscored by that deeper awareness.

You are determined to make the best of your time together. There is more humour, affection and validation in your day-to-day interactions. When an interaction is going well, you put more effort into keeping it going and making the most of it. You still make each other angry, sad or anxious, but you also make sure to express your love and affection for each other and the joy in each other's company.

Compared to middle-aged couples, even during a conflict you are more affectionate to each other, more neutral and positive as you hear each other out. You tone down your anger and are much less belligerent. Even when strong negative emotions are expressed, they are interwoven with affection and expressions of forgiveness. And afterwards, you rate the way your partner behaved as more positive than an objective observer might – a change from middle age when your rating was much nearer that of an objective observer – probably a benign form of self-deception, and a result of the general bias towards positivity that comes with age.[8]

Even in relationships that are not happy, where a partner is still difficult, tense or domineering, there is more reluctance to initiate an argument. When one partner is negative, the other is less likely to reciprocate. In short, you are better able to stop escalating a disagreement into a full-blown conflict. You have learned to leave well enough alone.

But late adulthood and the positive changes that come with it cannot fix long-standing problems in a marriage. A relationship that was tolerable when you were both living pretty parallel lives, preoccupied by childrearing and work, can flounder in later life when you are tripping over each other. The marriage has lost its bindings and without renewed closeness and opportunity to grow, what's left is an arrangement, an empty shell.* And in very troubled relationships, even ones that have lasted this long, the intense anger, sadness, contempt and attempt to domineer still surface, and once a conflict starts, the entrenched dysfunctional patterns still emerge. But the prospect of divorce, of uprooting yourself, disrupting your life, or coping with illness on your own becomes more daunting.

The unspooling of a shared life

Few events in life affect you more than the death of a spouse. In late adulthood, almost one in four of those living alone are widowed,

---

* In the USA, where the divorce rate is high, many of those in their fifties and older are in their second or subsequent remarriage. This may constitute an added risk factor as presumably those who stayed married include at least some who are unhappy but would never consider divorce for religious or other reasons, whereas those who have already experienced divorce may be readier to do so again if problems become severe.

mainly women, and by the age of seventy-eight you are more likely to be widowed than married. Becoming widowed represents the unspooling of decades of a shared life and the loss of someone who shared things with you that nobody else did.

> I think often about my life since Peter died, and his absence affects me. I notice differences every day, in so many ways and at so many levels, from what to eat, to minding grandchildren, to plans for the future, to where I fit into this life now as a single person. And I think more about how long more I have myself. I sometimes think of the things I can now do which might not have been of interest to Peter, and I think there's nothing to stop me doing them. But the funny thing I've discovered is that it's difficult for me to assess the value of doing any of these things without his input. I miss his views and his outlook, even if we disagreed. I feel lopsided without him. I know it'll be fine, but it's a big adjustment. It's early days yet.
>
> Helen, 68

Immediately after the bereavement, there is a period of emotional turmoil, of rapid ups and downs in your mood. For some of you, the sadness and distress are enduring, but most of you recover your sense of well-being in time. You notice that the intervals between periods of acute distress become longer, and that you recover faster.[9] At the end of the first year, the acute distress is abating, and you begin to look to the future. At the end of the second year, you are adjusted to your new life, even if you still miss your partner, and know you always will. It usually takes two years for a full attachment to form, and two years for it to wane and to find a new safe haven and secure base in yourself, with an adult child, or with another family member, or a very close friend.

But there is a lot of variability in how you respond, with much depending on how much time you had to prepare for the loss, your own resilience, and the amount of support you get from family and friends, practical and emotional. At the very beginning, practical support is very useful, but as time goes on, emotional support is much more important. But how you got on with your partner in life also counts. If your relationship was not happy, and your feelings for your partner are marked by ambivalence, anxiety or guilt, mourning is less straightforward, so it takes longer to recover.

Being single

After middle age, the ranks of the single expand. The never married are joined by the divorced and the widowed, and you all have more time to spend together now that you are no longer working full-time or caring for children. There are few differences in well-being between those of you who have children and those who don't, and what few effects there are appear in men, who are at higher risk of depression and poor health.[10] Single women with no children do particularly well. They are generally well educated and have active social lives, and life continues to be good. They cope better with living alone than men do, especially men who have no children.

Most of you are no longer sexually active in a regular way. If you are single because you never married or divorced, about a third of you stay sexually active, but if you are widowed, this falls to only 13 per cent.[11] If you suffer from loneliness, you are less likely to be sexually active because you have more trouble initiating relationships that might blossom into romance. Still, you might get lucky. But as you advance into your seventies, the prospects of finding a partner diminish, along with the motivation to find one.

> To be honest, I don't think I would take on a relationship now. Of course I'd love to have a companion to go out with, or maybe go on holidays with. But would I want to live with someone? No, definitely not. I am happy in my own life. I have a friend who married a very nice widower a few years ago, he was a few years older than her, and they were very happy together. But unfortunately, he is in very poor health now, quite disabled, and she is left caring for him and it's affected her whole life.
>
> Brenda, 73

The importance of friends

As you age, whether you are married, single or widowed, friends become even more important and you invest more in them.[12] You are no longer as embedded in extended families, local neighbourhoods and the church, no longer as reliant on them for support or to affirm your identity as previous generations were. You have more choice about who you want to spend your time with. Social relationships have become more fluid, less governed by duty and obligation, so you are more responsible for building a social network of support around you. Having friends is not just a matter of choice, but of necessity.

This new investment means that your friendships are more rewarding, more central to your life. You have more time to spend with them, and you rely on them for companionship and emotional support, especially if you are single.[13] If you have that network of support and can enjoy the increased freedom and autonomy you now have, and your self-esteem remains intact even in the face of losses, then you feel you can still move forward with your life.[14]

Sibling rivalry lives on

The amount of contact you have with siblings ebbs and flows over the life course. During the early child-rearing years there are regular family ceremonial events, like birthdays, first communions, and later weddings. In middle age, your contact with them tails off, except in times of crisis.[15] But in late adulthood, siblings may become important again as you each suffer losses or health issues, but also because you are conscious that you are all getting older. The old tensions don't go away, but you try harder not to let them interfere with getting on as well as you can with each other, although for a hardy few, the old battles are still being fought.

I honestly can't believe it. My sister and myself never got on. She was the eldest and she is as domineering today as she was when we were children. She still feels entitled to boss me around. My husband keeps saying to me, 'Why do you bother having anything to do with her if she annoys you like this?' But, sure, what can you do? She's my sister.

Greta, 70

The most striking thing about your relationship with your siblings is that it is the longest-lasting relationship of your life. You know each other as children, as adolescents and as adults. You share more life experiences with them than with your parents, your partner, your children or your friends – although not necessarily the experiences that you most valued or would define as life-changing. How often you see each other depends on where you both live, how much you depend on each other for companionship and support, and how much you like or dislike each other, or sometimes each other's partners. Some families are more tight-knit than others, even though they may fall in and out with each other on a regular basis.

If your relationship with your siblings is close and happy, it's a big well-being bonus. It's not up there with your relationship with your partner, children or best friend, but it matters. And it hurts when conflict or indifference creates a breach between you.

Now, as always, your relationship with a sibling revolves around two poles. The first is competition and conflict. The second is closeness and caring. There has to be enough of the second to absorb the tensions of the first. The main source of tension in adulthood is lack of reciprocity, or a big disparity in lifestyle or achievement.

What most affects your relationship, however, even at this stage of life, is the continuation of the old dynamic of childhood – the rivalries caused by one parent favouring one of you over the other, or the frustration of being constantly and unfavourably compared to a sibling by parents or teachers.

My parents always favoured my younger sister, she could do no wrong in their eyes. They really spoiled her and let her get away with things that if the rest of us did they'd come down on us like a ton of bricks. I always resented it. I know it's ridiculous at my age. I've tried my best to get on with her, we still see each other now and then, but the least tension between us and I can feel my resentment rising up again.

Stephen, 74

Your relationship with your adult children

By now, most of you have finally launched your last child and are in the empty-nest stage. Once, there were dire warnings that this would usher in a dispiriting mix of loss, loneliness, stress and one too many glasses of wine, especially for mothers. Most of you experience it as a relief, maybe tinged with a little sadness, especially when the last one leaves. If you are recently divorced, or if the empty nest coincides with the death of your own parent, or health problems, finding yourself alone and rattling around the house is more keenly felt.

But the majority of parents experience increased well-being, less stress, and the quality of their relationship with their offspring remains unchanged.[16] As you gradually register the reduced demands, the shorter shopping list, or the freedom to have a snack in the evenings if you don't feel like cooking, you start feeling a lot better. You find yourself in a good mood more often, but this happens only if you have frequent contact with your adult children.

How well your adult children are doing in their lives has a big impact on your well-being. Their stress still spills over into your life. An adult child with mental health or addiction problems takes a big hit on your well-being, and the closer you are to that child, the bigger the hit. A mother is as unhappy as her unhappiest child. An adult child experiencing problems will more often confide in their mothers than their fathers, so you are all too aware of their distress, yet because they are adults and you have little or no control over their lives, this inspires a particular and highly distressing sense of powerlessness.

On the other hand, if you are experiencing a significant stressor in your own life – losing your partner or developing a health problem – an adult child who is supportive and caring has an enormously positive effect on your life and your capacity to cope.

I had a heart attack last year, completely out of the blue. In all the distress of that time, I remember most vividly the moment when my daughter and son walked in the door of my room in the hospital and rushed over to hug me. I felt this huge wave of joy and relief and I thought, 'I will be okay now.'

Adele, 70

But overall, in late adulthood you are still more likely to be giving emotional support to your adult children than getting it from them. Far from stressing you, though, you are likely to have higher well-being than parents who don't provide that support.[17] You may provide them with some financial help as they struggle to buy a home, but this tails off in your seventies. Hovering somewhere over your relationship is the expectation that they will support you practically and emotionally when you become frail, although this is rarely discussed. For some, in that understandable reluctance is the potential for later disappointment.

Becoming a grandparent

Becoming a grandparent, especially for the first time, is a big deal for most of you.[18] Women in particular relish this new role in their lives. They are more likely than men to have frequent contact with their grandchildren, and this has a direct and positive effect on their well-being. For men, frequent contact with their adult children has greater impact on their well-being.

I had three grandchildren in my sixties. My first thought when they were born was, 'How much time do I have left with them?' I thought, if I'm lucky, I might be around when they go to college, but probably not when they get married. That thought depressed me first, but then it made me determined to spend as much time with them as I could and get to know them as individuals. It's much easier now that I am retired – that's one of the great things about this stage, you have more time. I feel I have a lot to give them. I just wish I had more energy to keep up with them. I'm often so exhausted after being with them for a day that I have to go to bed when they leave!

Anne, 73

Grandparents are more important now than they ever were. For a start, you are going to be around longer than previous generations of grandparents. Parents have fewer children and siblings, so there are fewer aunts, uncles and cousins. There are more dual-career families, more lone parents, more blended families. For those going through difficult family transitions, the grandparent is a constant figure, and a refuge for children. But divorce is the main reason why grandparents can lose contact with their grandchildren, sometimes entirely, particularly the father's parents.

The more involved you are with your grandchildren, the better the psychological and educational outcomes for them, the fewer problems they have with friends, and the lower their risk of developing conduct disorders and anti-social behaviour.[19] They know that how well they do in school is *very* important to you, that you are immensely proud of any achievement they have and that you boast shamelessly about it. That's why being a grandmother can be pretty competitive and requires being *very* quick on the draw with your iPhone to show off the most recent photos of the grandchildren, or get in a discreet mention of their stellar qualities.

The more contact you have, the stronger the bond – as long as your involvement with them and their parents is positive. Grandfathers come into their own as grandchildren get older, assuming particular importance in their adolescence. They very often see their role as teaching the child about life and broadening their perspective. They like to pass on a lot of information about the place where they grew up, historical events, nature, the innards of cars, the minutiae of a particular sport, things that interest them personally. They sometimes organize special 'educational' outings together.

Grandchildren have *very* high expectations of their grandparents, and most of you live up to those expectations. They describe you as helpful, devoted, giving, with 'considerate' being the quality most frequently mentioned. They view your caring for them and devoting your time to them as a choice, not a duty like it is for parents. They see you as 'someone to go to' or 'always being there for me', although they may struggle to define what that means, and they relish the closeness they have with you: '*Me and my nan, we really love each other.*'

They like when you take an interest in their hobbies and interests, and love it when you share a common interest. But most of all, they feel *wanted* by you.

> My granny always wants to see me. She's delighted always when we come to visit her. She gives me loads of sweets, and buys presents, and she cooks all our favourite things. And she talks to me a lot. We talk about lots of things.
>
> Ben, 5

> Granda likes doing things with us, like he always plays with us, and makes silly jokes, and makes us scream. Granny gives out to him for making us too excited, but we love it – he's kind of crazy, but in a good way.
>
> Thomas, 6

They see you as a major psychological resource, like having three sets of parents who all come and help, a valued audience for their opinions, plans and achievements. That sense of specialness is very important to children, and they like the unhurried time with you. They enjoy what you do together. They see this time as a break from the usual routine, from the 'strictness' of parents, an occasion for special treats, a chance to relax and have fun.[20]

They value the advice you give them when they want to talk to you about something important. They think their grandparents are better listeners than their parents, more patient. They have fewer arguments with you: '*If I talked to my parents about this stuff, we would, like, have a massive argument.*' You don't nag them like their parents do, even though you tell them what is right and wrong and what they can and cannot do when you are with them.

But there are rules you cannot break as a grandparent: creating conflicts for your grandchildren by being deliberately too permissive; letting them break their parents' rules; being too intrusive, trying to wheedle information from them about their parents' lives. There is a price to be paid: if this creates a conflict between you and their parent, as it inevitably will, children nearly always blame grand-parents for this conflict.

A positive turning inwards

There is a quiet surge of autonomy at this stage. You are more attuned to your needs and feelings and feel that you have earned the right to do what is important to *you*. You are aware that you need to find a new balance between the energy you devote to other people and the energy you need for yourself. To thrive in late adulthood, your investment in yourself must be roughly equal to your investment in the external world.

There is also a growing interiority. You are less driven by external achievements and more focused on enjoying the process of living. You reflect more – on yourself, on your life and, most of all, on what you want to do to make the most of these precious bonus years of health and vitality. This turn inwards has an added benefit – it frees you from the burden of social approval. You feel less afraid to express your own feelings and views about things.

Your desire to exercise control over your life remains high. How-ever, you are more realistic about the things you know are beyond that control.

Feeling that you have little control over your life makes you feel old and more likely to hold negative views about people of your age. If you see yourself as old and have a low opinion of the capabilities of people of your own age, it won't endear you to your friends.[21] That combination of attitudes further lowers your sense of control, the perfect self-reinforcing spiral.

Openness, which is an important element of autonomy, remains vital to your physical and psychological well-being, and only declines in advanced old age as you face significant health challenges and other losses.[22] Being open and willing to explore yourself and the world around you helps you to let go of the past, to keep learning and to maintain a sense of vitality that is affirming for you, and very attractive to other people, of all ages. It means there are more days when you feel happy, contented and generally satisfied with your life. Most importantly, being open enables you to keep growing and developing, to feel that your life is still in progress.

Spirituality

The move from middle age to late adulthood is marked by an increase in spirituality, which is related to increased interiority. Spirituality is different from being religious – adhering to a particular faith with its own rites and rituals. Spirituality means searching for something that transcends your ordinary, day-to-day concerns, a longing for personal authenticity, genuineness and wholeness, a deeper connection to yourself and to other people and to the human community, and a deep awareness of the interconnectedness of things, of our dependence on one another.

This turn towards spirituality is more marked in women, although for most it does not become a central part of their lives.[23] Throughout the life course, and in many different cultures, women report higher levels of spirituality and participation in religious activities than men do.[24] Why? Perhaps their reproductive biology – knowing they can grow and nurture another human being in their bodies – is a dramatic reminder of connectivity, of the dependence of something small, vital but vulnerable on a greater entity, and instils a readiness to acknowledge their interdependence and to act as kin-keepers.

If you are autonomous and independent-minded, open to experience, invested in the world of ideas, and if you tended to be introspective, insightful and psychologically minded when you were younger, you are more likely to be interested in spiritual growth. So, too, if you experienced a lot of adversity and personal pain in early adulthood and you possessed the personal strength to transform that into a deeper understanding of life. Or as actress and #MeToo activist Ashley Judd put it: 'Religion is for those who fear hell. Spirituality is for those who've already been there.'

Spirituality does not necessarily entail being religious in the sense of being a practising member of a particular faith. Overall, your generation is less religious than previous generations. For some of you, this means fewer constraints on what you can think and do. For others, it's a loss of certainty and security.

Does being religious make you happy? In general, yes. It provides a framework of meaning, the hope of immortality, and a sense of community. When you are going through a tough time, it can buffer you against depression. When things are going well, most of you don't need religion to feel good about yourselves.

For many of you, spirituality takes a less formal and more individual form. You are searching for some ultimate meaning in life, a way of making sense of what happens, not just a cognitive understanding but a connection to something bigger than yourself and your own concerns. Some of you are content with an occasional transitory experience, some sense of awe and transcendence inspired by nature, or love, or a deep communion with a particular person or in a group. For others, it stems from a more regular practice or project, like meditating, or walking a pilgrimage route such as the Camino de Santiago.

For Carl Jung, the increased interest in spirituality at this stage is part of the increasing interiority, the turn inwards, as you explore and expand your sense of self and identity. In late adulthood, you are still maturing cognitively, capable of going beyond strictly linear and logical thinking, and engaging more fully with the ambiguities and paradoxes of life. By now, you know that many of the great truths about life can often only be expressed in symbols and metaphors. You have seen enough of life to know that things are rarely simple.

Your increased interest in the spiritual is also influenced by your acute awareness of your own mortality. The desire for meaning becomes more urgent when you face adversity or loss. You are very likely to experience both as you age. You think more about your own death, and experience the death of family, friends and neighbours, and your response to that existential threat may be to attach yourself to some older and wiser spiritual presence, much as you did in childhood.

I was born a Catholic but gave up practising in my thirties. But I do pray, and when I do the image that comes to me is an image of a very wise and nurturing mother. I feel reassured when I connect with her, and I feel stronger afterwards, more centred, I can get on with my life with more confidence. Do I believe in an afterlife? I'm not sure. But I believe in her and I often think I will have her to accompany me when I die.

Sally, 68

Whatever its root, in late adulthood the nature of your spirituality is less judgemental and moralistic.

You now have a story of who you are

By late adulthood, you have a strong and stable sense of who you are, woven around the most important experiences in your life.[25] But unlike earlier stages, when your story about yourself focused on change and transition, now it centres on recurrent themes in your life that give it coherence and continuity. You see more connections between the events of your life and who you became as a person.[26] You are more adept at finding these themes and identifying some central theme or metaphor on which you can hang your unique and singular life – a survivor, a seeker, a lover of challenge, a person devoted to caring for others, or a builder of things.

I think of myself as someone who took every opportunity that came my way. That's who I am. I think I would shrivel up as a person if I stopped doing that.

Tim, 74

I built a small boat when I was twelve. I've no idea why, there was no history of sailing in my family. But ever since I've thought of myself as a builder – I build organizations, I build teams. That's what I've done with my life.

Jeff, 70

At this stage of my life, I think of myself as a survivor. I hated boarding school, my marriage broke up, I was full of anxiety rearing my son. But I learned something from everything that happened to me. I'm a person who seems to have always chosen the most difficult path, never the one expected of me, always a bit different. That made my life interesting and full of big ups and downs – never dull and always highly emotional. I live by my emotions and my intuition and that has also stood me in good stead, but now I want to make a change and reduce the intensity of my life in every way. But I'm still learning, still trying, still surviving!

Fran, 67

Women tend to do more psychological processing of their experiences than men do, in order to make more connections, to identify central themes in their lives and incorporate them into their personal narrative. This more developed capacity for narrative is probably due to the fact that as young children, girls talk more to their mothers than boys do. They provide more elaborate accounts of their day-to-day experiences and disclose more intimate and personal things. Boys talk to their mothers, too, but they focus more on their actions and plans. However, as in the case of all gender differences, there is substantial individual variation.

Reflecting on your story about yourself serves a different purpose as you age. When you're young, you reflect in order to understand yourself better, or to solve a problem. You do that, too, as you age. But you also reflect in order to better integrate all your accumulated life experiences.

22.   *Late adulthood:* The importance of a sense of purpose

In middle age, the developmental task was to make your life count for something by generating and investing in something of worth that would outlive you. In late adulthood, the task is to make your life count for something in a more personal and internal way, to do a kind of harvesting. You want to enjoy what you have achieved in your life so far, and to seize every opportunity to extract joy from your day-to-day life. That enlivened sense of personal purpose helps you structure your time, guide your choices and gives meaning to what you do. It turns your gaze away from an absorbing focus on the past, so that you can commit to the present. If, on the other hand, you feel your life no longer has purpose now that your full-time work or childrearing has come to an end, you can become overwhelmed by the prospect of inevitable decline.

At every stage of life, having a sense of purpose gives you an enormous sense of unity and coherence and has a significant impact on your happiness and health. Late adulthood is no different. A sense of purpose will not stop the aging process, and the more pervasive losses that advancing age may bring, but here's what it does do.[1] If you have a strong sense of purpose, you perform better on tests of memory and speed of processing; it may slow down the rate of cognitive decline; and it increases the probability that you will live longer. You report better health, have lower levels of functional disability, and are less likely to be depressed.

If there is one consistent message from research on successful aging, it's this: the greater your engagement in life, the better your physical, cognitive and psychological well-being, and the greater your chances of living longer.[2] It gives you the sense that you matter and that what you are doing matters, and this buffers you against any stress in your life. Being engaged in something that carries personal meaning or gives you a sense of purpose, rather than something that is simply enjoyable or stimulating, increases the health benefits.[3] In turn, all of those benefits increase your motivation to stay engaged.[4]

Staying engaged reduces depressive symptoms, and as you advance into old age may even restore some cognitive losses.[5] If you don't stay engaged, you are likely to join the 70 per cent who spend most of their time watching TV, which is associated with a dismal list of physical and psychological ailments.[6]

If you are not actively engaged in life, it compromises your health and well-being, and not just because it creates a sense of quiet malaise but because it forecloses opportunities for finding new interests, forging new relationships, or strengthening old ones.

Most of you seem to have no problems staying engaged, however, distributing your time and energy between family, friends and caring for your grandchildren. Some of you are still working in some capacity or return to education. In Ireland, about 67 per cent of you volunteer at least once a year, compared to less than 25 per cent in the USA, and more than one in five of you do so weekly.[7] This is good for those you help, but it's also *very* good for you.[8]

Volunteering significantly reduces your risk of dying. Even when you take into account other risk factors – your age, the state of your physical and emotional health, being divorced or separated, living alone – volunteering still reduces your risk of dying by almost 50 per cent. *But* it only reduces your mortality risk if you are motivated primarily by a concern for others rather than a concern for yourself.

Does being religious matter? Only if your faith makes you more motivated to help others. If it does, you will benefit even more from volunteering and reap more health benefits.[9]

The SOC strategy: Select, Optimize, Compensate

Having goals that you want to pursue is still important, but your priorities begin to shift to goals that are achievable now, in the present, and that make you happy.

In late adulthood, as at every stage of life, you are faced with certain opportunities and certain limitations, mainly in relation to the time, energy and emotional resources that are available to you. The opportunities available to you emerge, peak, decline and disappear, and new opportunities then present themselves. As you progress through the life course, the way you manage that is by using what social scientists call the SOC strategy[10] – you select, optimize and compensate, all of which gives you a stronger sense of personal control in your life.

- *Select*: you can't pursue every goal at the same time, or even sequentially. You must select which goals are most urgent and most important – the things that must be done or that you believe are worthwhile doing – and when to do them. That inevitably requires setting aside or giving up other goals that would overstretch you or undermine your capacity to pursue the selected goals.

- *Optimize*: you select in order to optimize your chance of success by freeing up your time and energy, and you use these extra resources to learn whatever skills are needed, to practise, and to get advice and support that you may need to achieve what you set out to do. You also have to keep an eye on whether your efforts to achieve one goal are interfering with or undermining other goals that you value. An overinvestment in a personal project can undermine your close relationships, or vice versa. The dilemma of work–life balance does not go away just because you are no longer working in a formal sense.

    A too-narrow investment in one domain of your life can lead you down a developmental dead end if that goal becomes unattainable. But when it does, you have to actively disengage, not just give up passively. Positive compensating is a process of restructuring your goals. For example, if you develop a chronic health condition, you have to develop compensatory strategies to stay active and engaged, but this can also increase your sense of personal control and preserve your self-image.[11]

- **Compensate**: when your goal proves not to be attainable, you focus on finding new find ways to achieve the same goal, or you switch to another goal.

At earlier stages of your life, you mainly use this strategy to manage periods when you are under pressure, dealing with a crisis or setback, or when you want to achieve something important. By late adulthood, you use it in a more day-to-day way, motivated by your acute awareness of time left and your determination to make the most of it. You also have to do more compensating than before.

What does the SOC strategy look like day-to-day?

SELECT

You become more selective about what you want to spend your time and energy on and plan it more realistically.

> Well, say I am in town shopping, I am sometimes tempted to fit more in, to get more done than I had originally planned. But now, I think, if I do that, I'll miss my swim later, so I don't go rushing around like I used to. My swim, and how it makes me feel, is more important. I'm also much more realistic about how long things actually take to do, so I plan my life better.
>
> Celia, 70

Your agenda is also more flexible. You move your goals up or down the hierarchy, or add new ones, depending on how you feel. You are more ready to seize the moment, to make the most of every opportunity you get to enjoy and savour your life.

> It's carpe diem all the way for me. If the weather is nice and I don't have to do something urgently, I drop everything and go for a walk. If someone suggests doing something new, I'm generally up for it. When I'm with my friends, especially, I want to make every moment count, to talk in a more honest and open way – what's the point in not being yourself at this stage? And I definitely want to

travel and have fun. In fact, I'd say having fun is way up there for me now.

Kate, 73

You focus more on activities that match your motivation, your skills, your physical and psychological resources. You may settle for slightly lower standards of performance in some domains of your life. Striving for perfection has less of a grip on you. 'Good enough' is good enough, at least for some things.

OPTIMIZE

In late adulthood, you pay more attention to building and renewing your physical and psychological resources, so that you stay healthy and active and function better – you are aiming for your version of peak performance.

I read somewhere that as you get older, the best way to keep your body and brain in good shape is to do three things – exercise, meditate, and learn a new language. So I'm doing all three to be on the safe side! I walk for an hour every day, as fast as I can. I'm learning French, and I downloaded an app on mindfulness that reminds me to meditate every day.

John, 69

COMPENSATE

You can no longer run because you have arthritis in your knee, so you switch to an electric bike. You allow more time to recover after a big effort, or a long plane journey. You take up yoga or pilates, wear trainers with good ankle support, or always use two sticks when you are hillwalking to compensate for any loss of energy, strength or balance.

How you think and feel about aging

The more you master the SOC strategy, the less stressed you feel, and the more satisfied you are with your life, irrespective of your age, intelligence or personality. Some of you are experts in using this strategy, most of you do a passable imitation, using it in certain domains of your life but not in others. For example, the most frequent failure in compensating is not delegating to others. That's a bridge too far if you are a perfectionist, and you believe that only *you* can do a job to a satisfactory standard.

In late adulthood, as at every stage, people are individuals, and their lives are not uniform. There is no single standard of successful aging.[12] At any one stage, you can be suffering physically but psychologically robust, in despair about your family but very happy with your work, be very dissatisfied about the way things are going but experience your life as full of meaning. It is how you think and feel about aging, and what you think is possible, that determines a lot of what happens.[13]

A life well lived – what we learn from late adulthood

The principles of a life well lived – late adulthood

Life stage	Time frame	Developmental task	Psychological principle
Late adulthood	late 60s–late 70s	purpose or decline?	Seize the day

The lesson of late adulthood is that there is no time like the present. When caring for children and working are no longer pressing demands, a new set of questions arise.

- What will I do now?
- How can I set a new direction for my life that keeps it moving forward?
- Of all the things I do now, what is most meaningful to me?
- How can I best connect to those who are most important to me?
- Where am I needed most now?

A new focus

Your focus now is to find new opportunities to grow and develop. You want to maximize the choices that are open to you to craft a rewarding and engaged life that makes you feel that you still matter, and what you do still matters.

PICK A MIX OF LEISURE ACTIVITIES

Do things that will keep you fit and healthy, that provide novelty, relaxation, companionship, new insights, inspiration, intimacy and a sense of belonging.

STAY HARDY

Hardiness comes from a combination of being committed to what you do versus feeling alienated and disengaged; having a sense of control rather than feeling powerless; and being open to change and challenge rather than feeling threatened by it.[14] That hardiness is at the core of staying resilient and will carry you through health or other setbacks and help you recover faster.

STRETCH YOUR BODY AND YOUR MEMORY

Declines in fitness and memory are not inevitable as you age, and exercising is key.[15] In a recent Canadian study, researchers measured the fitness, thinking skills and memory functioning of sixty-four sedentary men and women aged sixty or older. They focused on their ability to remember things like where they had parked their car yesterday versus today. This kind of recall often declines with age, and a poor performance can mark the start of mild cognitive impairment and, in some cases, dementia. After testing, the researchers divided the participants into two groups. In one group, people had to walk steadily at a moderate speed on a treadmill three times a week for about fifty minutes. In the other group, they had to do interval training, interspersing high- with low-intensity exercise, in this case, walking on a treadmill that was cranked high for four minutes, raising their heartbeat to 90 per cent of each person's maximum, followed by three minutes of easy walking, and then three more rounds of the high intensity.

After twelve weeks, the aerobic fitness and cognitive functioning of the two groups were reassessed, and the results were striking. Only those who had done interval training showed significant improvements in their physical endurance and memory performance, and the gains were linked – the fitter someone became, the more their memory improved. What does high-intensity mean in practice? If you are in good health (after first checking with your doctor), when you exercise, pick up your pace enough so that your heart rate increases and you get out of breath.

You can also exercise your brain. Brain fitness exercises or mental workouts have been shown to have sustained effects lasting ten years or more.[16] And when you believe that memory capacity is not fixed, but can be improved, you do better.[17]

PRACTISE MINDFULNESS

The practice of mindfulness is good for you at any age.[18] When people are meditating, MRI scans of the brain show decreased activity in the amygdala. This is the threat centre of the brain, which triggers the stress response. And this decreased activity stays steady, even when they are not meditating. Instead, it induces the 'relaxation response', the opposite of fight-or-flight.

When you meditate regularly, you are less prone to rumination, at less risk of depression, and you build your resilience. You ruminate less, which is especially important if you have a tendency to depression. Just eight weeks of regular mindfulness practice also changes the structure of the brain. The areas of the brain that activate and process positive feelings thicken, and the corresponding areas that activate and process negative feelings decrease. Some studies have shown physical and psychological benefits for those suffering from conditions like high blood pressure, irritable bowel syndrome, fibromyalgia, psoriasis, anxiety, depression and post-traumatic stress disorder.[19]

Being mindful plugs you into the abundance of life, making it easier to accept the losses you may experience without feeling overwhelmed by them. You can deal with everyday stresses more calmly, realizing that thoughts and feelings are just that, *your judgements on the passing sensations you feel in your body*, and that if you stop judging, you can observe the rise and fall in the intensity of those sensations, so you are less captivated by them. It helps you achieve a stillness that tunes out the ceaseless internal chatter, at least temporarily. You are more aware of what is going on inside you, and around you. That inner and outer alertness is what allows you to seize the day, to open up the present moment and the little infinity in that moment.

If you practise mindfulness over an extended period, your biological age, based on measures of the effects of aging on your body, is more likely to be younger than your chronological age. You are less likely to need outpatient visits or to spend time in hospital, because being mindful counteracts the wear-and-tear of aging and prevents atrophy in your cognitive functioning.

BE OPEN AND CURIOUS

As you age, you get more settled in your ways. Nothing wrong with that. You've earned the right to do things your own way and in your own time, and habit conserves your resources. But don't let it become a deadening routine that has you sleepwalking through your life. Stay open and curious. Try something you haven't done before. Do something you habitually do in a new way. Use your non-dominant hand. Look at someone you love as if this is the first or the last time you are doing it. All of this shakes you out of being on automatic. Keep asking yourself: what did I learn today?

HAVE A GROWTH RATHER THAN A FIXED MINDSET

This matters as much now as it does at every life stage. Cultivate a learning mindset, believing that your abilities can be grown and developed and are not set in stone.[20]

GIVE SOMETHING BACK

By now you have accumulated a body of knowledge and life experiences. Put them to work. Consider volunteering. Helping others is not just good for them – it's *very* good for you. Apart from increasing well-being, it reduces the risk of mortality by around 47 per cent in those aged fifty-five and older.

23. *Old age:* Living each precious moment fully

It is an achievement to live into old age. When you are seventy, about three-quarters of your peers are still around. By eighty, only half are, and by eighty-nine, only a fifth.[1] But if you survive into your nineties or beyond, you achieve the venerable status of being the 'oldest of the old'.[2]

Even when you reach this advanced stage in life, for most of you there continues to be a gap between your actual age and how young you feel – and this gap will have small but significantly positive effects on your health, and on how long you will live.[3] When you feel younger than your chronological age, you are more hopeful and positive about getting old, and naturally this has a knock-on positive effect on how you age.

In contrast, if you believe that age determines your life, you feel there is little you can do to delay the inevitable decline. You see your health, and any illness or disability, as less controllable, less preventable and less treatable, therefore you are less motivated to manage your health. All of this decreases your sense of control over your life. Worse, it *doubles* your risk of mortality in a two-year period.[4]

Oh, pity the old and the frail . . .

It's just as well that you feel younger than you are, because you live in a world that is full of negative images and expectations of aging.

By and large, the public image and media portrayal of aging is one of relentless decline. Old people are seen as vulnerable, isolated and lonely. For example, loneliness is considered to be a serious issue for older people by 61 per cent of those aged eighteen to thirty-four, and by 47 per cent of those aged thirty-five to sixty-four. Yet, if you ask older people themselves, only 13 per cent consider loneliness a serious problem for them personally. But they, too, are caught up in the negative stereotype. Over a third of older people believe that loneliness is a big problem for *other* people in their age group, but not for them.[5]

These negative images are occasionally lightened by feel-good stories of eighty-year-olds running mini-marathons or grandmothers bungee-jumping, designed to inspire you and lift your heart – as if the only way to age well is not to age at all. But most of you feel far removed from those heroics. If you are struggling with a lingering injury that has reduced your mobility, or are having a run of debilitating chest infections, what you may feel instead is frustration, inadequacy and self-pity.

You also have to contend with the assumption that you are probably forgetful, hard of hearing and have trouble understanding what is being said to you. That's why some people take to speaking to you in a loud voice or an exaggeratedly slow way. These negative expectations become more salient and relevant as you enter old age. What was once a remote state now becomes your life, and you are slightly shocked to realize that it's *you* they are now referring to.

> I was shopping recently for a few groceries, and as I was trying to pay, the assistant reached out, and without a by-your-leave, took the change from my hand and counted it out! I instinctively pulled back my hand – I am well capable of counting my own change, I'm a retired accountant! But the change then fell out of my hand on to the floor, and she started sighing and rolling her eyes. I was so annoyed by the whole thing.
>
> Kevin, 81

These negative expectations are not directed at you in any personal way. Yet, their effects are very personal because you are at high risk of internalizing them and embodying them in your perception of yourself. This has real and adverse effects on your health and well-being, including on your general physical and cognitive functioning, your balance, gait, hearing, speed of movement and on your memory. They directly affect your physiological functioning and autonomic nervous system, a branch of the central nervous system that responds to environmental stress.

When exposed to negative images of aging, even unconsciously, you show heightened cardiovascular response to stress,[6] whereas when you encounter positive images your cardiovascular stress response decreases. Repeated elevations of cardiovascular stress response heighten your susceptibility to heart problems. As a result, you are twice as likely to suffer a heart attack or stroke after the age of sixty, and if you do experience a heart attack or stroke, it may affect your recovery.[7] You recover less well from injuries and illnesses, suffer more cognitive decline, feel much less satisfied with your life – and die younger.[8]

How can negative images lead to such bad outcomes? Because they directly affect your coping ability. You develop a more fatalistic attitude to health, attributing every setback to being old rather than to more obvious reasons, like unhealthy lifestyle. And also because we are much more susceptible to the most subtle cues from the world around us than we think.

Imagine you are looking at a computer screen on which words about aging are flashed at subliminal speed, for less than 55 milliseconds, too fast to be registered consciously but slow enough to be registered unconsciously. When the word conjures up negative, stereotyped images of older people, like *slow, confused, frail, absent-minded*, it affects how you behave subsequently.[9] You walk more slowly, your handwriting is shakier, and your attitude to your health, or maybe even to your survival, becomes more passive. For example, when asked if you would opt for a new but costly medical intervention that might prolong your life, you say that you would be less likely to try it.

In contrast, if you are primed with positive words about aging, like *spry, accomplished, confident*, you behave in ways that are in line with those words, and you are more likely to try the new treatment.

Combatting agism

In a day-to-day way, negative images of aging ingrain the view that health problems are an inevitable consequence of growing old, and that trying to eat well or exercise is therefore futile.[10] And even if you don't think that way about age, others may.

Take the eighty-year-old woman who goes to her doctor, complaining about a problem with her left knee. The doctor says, 'What do you expect? You're eighty years old.' The woman replies, 'Doctor, my other knee is also eighty years old and I have no problem with it.'*

While the doctor may rightly say that age does not affect every part of the body in a symmetrical way, using age as a default way of explaining things reinforces a frame of mind about health that is less proactive and that may get in the way of investigating a health problem in a deeper way.

If, on the other hand, you have realistic but positive self-perceptions of your aging, you are proactive about your health and careful about your diet and medications – all of which increases your chances of living longer. If, for example, at the age of fifty your attitude to aging is positive, in old age your day-to-day functional health is better, your risk of developing cardiovascular problems and hearing loss is reduced, and your chance of living longer increased.[11] How much longer? On average, seven-and-a-half years longer. That's a *lot*, particularly as you advance into aging.[12] You put more time and effort into doing things that you've always loved. If you think of yourself as old in a negative way, you put more time and effort into avoiding perceived risks.

There is a more benign side to this agism. Older people are also generally perceived as nicer and kinder – and you are. But this benign perception has a sting in the tail. We tend to rate other people, particularly those we don't know, on two dimensions – warmth and competence – and to see these qualities as inversely related.[13] In other words, if there is a lot of one, we assume a corresponding deficit in the other. The implication for you is that while it's nice to be seen as kindly, you are correspondingly also perceived to be less able, what one researcher described as 'doddering but dear'.[14] This is in stark contrast to how you see yourself and your life.

That's why focusing on identifying what's important to you now,

---

* This is an illustrative story Bernice Neugarten, a professor at the University of Chicago, used in her pioneering course on life-span developmental psychology.

and what you want to achieve, moves the idea of 'successful aging' to the right *strategies* to adopt rather than some arbitrary negative or positive standards of 'success'. And those strategies will centre on meeting your old needs – for close and satisfying relationships, for autonomy, and for competence – so that you can keep on growing and developing. Right to the end, your life is full of needs, desires and challenges. Life is always in progress.

No place for sissies

As Bette Davis famously said, old age ain't no place for sissies. If late adulthood was about coming to terms with the physical vulnerability that comes with aging, old age is about managing that vulnerability.[15] At some point, most of you will develop at least one chronic health problem.* Even if you stay pretty healthy, your energy and mobility will gradually decrease, forcing you to give up some activities that you enjoy. But most of you adjust to that.[16]

There are also accumulating losses. But the interplay between losses and gains in old age is complex, and some losses can lead to unexpected gains. You discover reserves of toughness and determination that you never thought you had. You are moved beyond measure by the love and support of family and friends, and you learn to set the losses against your knowledge and life experience.

---

* In Ireland, one in three of you are likely to suffer from high blood pressure, and one in eight to have angina, an abnormal heart rhythm, or other heart conditions. You are more likely to suffer a stroke, transient ischaemic attacks (TIAs), diabetes or respiratory disease. About one in ten of you are likely to have a heart attack. Arthritis, osteoporosis and fractures are more common in old age, as are problems with vision and hearing. The highest prevalence of cancer is observed in those aged between sixty-five and seventy-four but then remains stable. And then there are the falls. About a quarter of you report falling in the past year. Over 20 per cent of older women are likely to develop osteoporosis. For those of you who could not resist looking at this footnote detailing the dismal litany of probable health problems, bear in mind that while they are likely, they are not inevitable, and some of you will stay quite healthy until near the end of life.

Old age is full of endings. Sometimes, when you are doing something you enjoy, or experience a burst of love, or kiss someone goodbye, it strikes you: this might be the last time I do this. But far from depressing you, the feelings you experience are complex, poignant, precious, motivating you to make the most of this moment.[17]

The prospect of endings brings out the best in you, deepening your appreciation of what you have, making you kinder, more compassionate, more attuned to the never-ending abundance of life. But most of all, you are determined to live fully in each precious moment that is left to you, the most marked and enduring psychological change as you age. Although if you experience the loss of a partner, prolonged ill health, or have to move into a nursing home, especially within a short time frame, it can put a severe strain on your adaptive capacity.[18]

Recollecting and reminiscing

As you progress through your eighties, it takes you longer to process information, especially something new or unexpected, but your vocabulary and ability to express yourself remain intact, and there is no decline in the tacit knowledge and experience that you have accumulated over a lifetime.

As you look back on your life, you find it harder to recall intense sensory experiences – you know that sex was good, that new potatoes tasted glorious, but you can't quite summon up the sensory pleasures you felt then.

On the other hand, you remember vividly how you felt and thought when big things happened, when you were wildly happy, or when your heart was broken. Or even when you free-wheeled your bike down a steep hill.

The most striking change is the turn inwards. You spend more time reflecting on your life experiences. You reminisce more, and experiences from childhood, long forgotten, now resurface. Once, reminiscing was regarded as the ramblings and repetition of old age, but it's now seen in a very different light. It is an active, useful and adaptive part of successful aging, and encouraging older people to reminisce is a staple part of many programmes in day-centres or nursing homes.[19]

The way you reminisce is expressed in different forms, each having a different impact on successful aging.

THE MINI CV

The most common form is a simple recounting of the facts of your life, a kind of mini CV, with a few added anecdotes that you think might interest the person you are talking to, but with no attempt to interpret or make any judgement about those facts. This kind of reminiscence may help you to keep some order on your memory, but there are no clear cognitive benefits. However, if it is rich in detail, it is evidence of how well preserved your memory is; too bare and rote an account may reveal a decline in your intellectual functioning.

A SEARCH FOR MEANING

The next most frequent kind of reminiscence is more active and intentional, a way to reach deeper understanding of yourself and your life, to reconcile any discrepancy between what you hoped for and what actually happened, and to resolve, at least in your mind, any conflicts that upset or disrupted your life. This kind of reflection pays big dividends. It increases your well-being and sense of self-worth and directly engages with the prime developmental task of achieving a sense of personal coherence and integrity in the face of death.

REMINISCENCE WITH A PRACTICAL PURPOSE

Almost as common is the third kind of reminiscence. You mull over the different stages of your life, the goals you once set for yourself, how you went about accomplishing them, and the way you overcame any difficulties. You do this for a very practical purpose – to help you solve the present challenges you face. When you do this well, it increases your feelings of competence, control and sense of continuity, boosts your well-being, your health and your satisfaction in life, and serves as an important buffer against distress.

PASSING ON IMPORTANT VALUES AND LIFE LESSONS

This kind of reminiscence focuses on describing what life was like in a now bygone era, the traditional values of your family or culture, and the lessons you have learned in your own life. You feel you are performing an important social function, transmitting a unique oral history that will help the next generation to keep the traditions alive, and this gives you a sense of worth and purpose.*

ESCAPIST AND DEFENSIVE

This type of reminiscence is an unhappy hankering back to the good old days, but the way you describe the past has a false and exaggerated quality about it, an attempt to glorify the past, downgrade the present and exaggerate your past achievements. In small doses, escaping into a fantasy and defending yourself against past pain may provide immediate relief from a painful present. When it becomes prolonged and excessive, it can take on a bitter and resentful tone that further reduces your satisfaction in your current life and your capacity to cope with it.

OBSESSIVE

Your recall of the past is full of regret, guilt and bitterness. You obsessively go over the mistakes you made, the hurt done to you by others. This kind of reminiscing agitates you, and in excess can lead to depression, panic states, despair and suicidal thoughts. It has a direct impact on your physical and psychological health.

Why review your life?

While reflecting on your life in an active, intentional way is associated with high levels of well-being, some of you are disinclined to do

---

* Studies have not shown any direct link between this type of reminiscence and aging but this may be because this type of reminiscence usually happens spontaneously in a family setting, and apart from a quick question about 'What's the secret of living a long time?' older people are rarely given an opportunity in a public setting to tell their stories or share whatever wisdom they would most like to pass on to the next generation.

that, and yet still manage to construct satisfying lives as you age.[20] You are more drawn to review your life if you have a strong sense of identity and are open to experience – for example, if you were the kind of adolescent that would have been described as reflective, unconventional, well adjusted, someone who always valued ideas and had a wide range of interests.[21] And, of course, if you feel that you have a story worth telling, one in which you can find meaning, solace and pleasure, especially if you or your family suffered significant adversity and are proud of how you survived it. You feel that you have something of value to pass on to new generations and want to rescue those you loved, now dead, from oblivion.

If you feel that what happened to you in life was just a series of haphazard events and upheavals, and remembering those experiences holds no pride or solace for you, then you are less minded to dwell on that and want to firmly consign it to the past. For you, it's just too long a story, and you want to focus only on the here-and-now of your life, on doing rather than telling.

How you reflect on your life feeds into your ongoing narrative about yourself, which takes on a new significance as you age. Even now, you are reshaping your identity, once again asking: 'Who am I?' As you recall your life, and the lives of your parents and grandparents, you come to see that the story of your life started well before you were born and was intimately bound up with their stories. The outcome of their search for love, for success, for authority over their own lives, flowed into your life, just as what happened in your life now flows into the lives of others, especially your children's.

Your narrative contains the rules that help or hinder how you resolve the old polarities:[22]

- how to stay psychologically young as your body ages
- how to pursue what's important to you while depending on others to enable you to do that
- how to stay actively engaged in the world while conserving more energy for yourself, and
- how to stay interested in the new and the present, and avoid sinking passively into the past.

Changes in your personality

From your mid-eighties on, there is a small but steady decrease in how sociable and open you are, and an increased tendency to worry or feel depressed – a trend that accelerates as you progress into advanced old age or become very frail or ill.[23] In a broad-brush way, compared to younger people you become more settled in your interests, less open to novel ideas, and slightly more nervous and cautious.

But a lot depends on the state of your health and cognitive functioning. For example, if your cognitive functioning is good, if you have a sense of personal control over your life, and if you stay socially active, you remain open to life and less susceptible to anxiety or depression. If, on the other hand, you suffer from chronic loneliness and feel that your life is now controlled by others, the pattern is the opposite.

Being open

Remaining open to new ideas and experiences continues to be important to aging well. When your habitual way of coping with stress is no longer working as well as it did when you were younger, being ready to adopt another approach builds your resilience.

Being open may help you to live longer. In a longitudinal study of identical twins, which took account of their health, personality, cognitive functioning and life circumstances, becoming less open was a strong predictor of mortality. The twin who died earlier showed a greater drop in openness prior to death.[24]

Being conscientious

As you become increasingly aware of your own physical vulnerability, you become more wary of health risks and dangers in everyday life. You put more effort into maintaining your daily routine and like to have your affairs in order. If you are temperamentally conscientious, it stands you in good stead as you age – you are more likely to

look after your health and to live longer.[25] In fact, if you were conscientious as a child, it predicts your physical health forty years later.[26]
You are better able to do what needs to be done.

The only downside of being conscientious is that you are more
prone to worry. So your best bet is to balance your tendency to be
conscientious with an enthusiastic openness to novelty. Be dutiful,
but let yourself off the hook. If you don't do that now, when will
you? The next best thing to being conscientious yourself is if those
you depend on to care for you are, because they are more likely to
attend to the things that will keep you healthy, minimize risk, and
help you to manage your life in a more proactive way. This has the
added benefit of minimizing your need to worry.[27]

Having a positivity bias

Happiness increases in young adulthood, declines in middle age, and
rises again progressively from the age of fifty to the age of eighty,
when you are as happy as a twenty-year-old. But a lot depends on the
state of your health. Happiness and health become more tightly
linked. If you are chronically unhappy, it increases the risk of developing health problems. Correspondingly, if you are grappling with
chronic or serious health problems, it has an impact on your happiness. If you encounter many losses in a short period, you are at higher
risk of depression, which in turn can exacerbate your health problems. A key issue is taking control over the aspects of your health that
are controllable. When you do, you improve your chances of staying
as physically and psychologically healthy as possible.[28]

Why the increase in happiness? Mainly because as you age, you
become more biased to the positive. You pay more attention to positive
information and process it more thoroughly than negative information.[29] You are more focused on having emotionally meaningful goals
in your daily life. You recall happy experiences more often and remember them better, so you recall your past more positively than younger
adults do.

You are more likely than younger adults to integrate new information into your existing way of thinking and avoid the exhaustive style

of decision-making that results in frequent requests for information and multiple strategies. You are less inclined to use up your cognitive resources searching extensively for the very best option, which you now see as needless fussing.[30] This means you make your decisions faster than younger adults, and your strategy is more experiential – you rely on your own experience. This reduces stress, but there is a downside. It also makes you less likely to process information when it contradicts your prior beliefs, and you may over-generalize what you know to situations where it is not valid.

In the normal course of events, your positivity bias decreases when the stakes are high and your decisions have real consequences for your health or finances.[31] In that situation, your preference for focusing on the positive rather than the negative reverses, and you start processing information about the risks involved.[32] The problem arises when you overdo that, avoiding anything negative or potentially stressful at all costs. For example, this can make you less inclined to request more information from your doctor, to seek a second opinion, and makes you more likely to dismiss viable treatment options too quickly.[33]

Decision-making is hard, it involves thinking through a lot of issues and sometimes involves unpleasant trade-offs. When you avoid making decisions it gives you an immediate feeling of relief, but you may pay a long-term health price. At first glance, leaving the decision up to your doctor may save time and effort and lead to better outcomes – but only if you have given your doctor all the necessary information. What about delegating to a family member? That's fine, as long as that person is conscientious.

Becoming more trusting

Relative to young adults, you become more trusting of people as you age.[34] This increased disposition to trust carries all the benefits it did at earlier stages, making it easier to build and maintain close, co-operative relationships. In old age, you need to put your trust in others because you have less direct control over some aspects of your life. But – and you know by now there is always a 'but' – it may put you at higher risk of being exploited, especially financially. Being financially exploited is always troubling, but doubly so in old age when you have less time to recover your losses. That's why most of you retain a healthy suspicion when it comes to your finances.

The risk of being exploited may be less to do with being more trusting, however, and more to do with a decline in your cognitive ability to judge trustworthiness.

One study found that having trouble identifying untrustworthy faces is related to an age-related drop in activity in the anterior insula, the part of the brain involved in assessing trust and risk.[35] When older adults are asked to look at pictures of faces that exhibit either trustworthy, neutral or untrustworthy qualities, they are much more likely than young adults to label the suspicious faces as credible and approachable.

MRI scans of brain activity while they are doing this show lower activity in the anterior insula, a small region inside the cerebral cortex. This difference in activity was most pronounced when the older group looked at the untrustworthy faces. In contrast, younger adults showed higher activity not just when looking at untrustworthy faces but also when looking at trustworthy or neutral faces, suggesting that when you are young and inexperienced, it pays to be on your toes.

Processing negative information also requires more cognitive resources and these resources may be depleted as you age, making it harder to pick up signs of untrustworthiness, therefore you become more liable to ignore or misread signs that someone is untrustworthy. Your best strategy is to heed the old adage: Live like you're going to die tomorrow, and plan like you're going to live for ever. In other words, it's great to be positive and trusting – as long as you don't avoid attending to the important negative matters.

Being resilient

Resilience, the ability to adapt to stress and change, to recover from setbacks and stay positive in the face of accumulating risk, is central to aging well.[36] In ordinary circumstances, positive and negative emotions are relatively independent. Even when you are disappointed or frustrated, you can simultaneously feel hopeful, interested and relatively contented with your life. But as pressure mounts, negativity increases and drives down your positive feelings.

That is why experiencing a positive emotion, however briefly, provides time out and a respite from the pressure. It lowers your blood pressure and bolsters your immune system and coping abilities, restoring vital psychological resources depleted by the stress. It means you can think and act more flexibly and come up with better solutions to whatever problems you face. If you are able to summon up an image or memory that lifts your spirits or bolsters your courage, you can regain your steady state of safety and calm. This enables you to stay engaged, to savour what is good moment-to-moment, and that in turn starts a positive cascade, reducing the risk of overreacting to minor stresses and seeing things as more threatening than they really are.[37]

Resilience also means being able to down-regulate negative emotion. As you face cumulative losses – the death of loved ones, physical limitations like deteriorating sight or hearing, compromised mobility, or health problems, it can put great strain on your capacity to adapt, putting you at higher risk of developing depressive symptoms.[38]

It is particularly important to manage your anger. When you face repeated frustrations, it is natural to get angry. But being frequently angry is toxic in old age, creating high levels of low-grade inflammation that increases your chances of developing a chronic illness. Of its nature, anger arouses you to action, motivating you to persist in fighting against losses, which is adaptive if the losses are potentially reversible. But many of the losses in old age are not, so anger becomes increasingly maladaptive. Sadness and grief following losses have no such adverse effects, allowing you to withdraw temporarily, to pull inward your psychological resources to help you process the loss.[39]

Being wise

Being old and wise are expected to go together. Are all of you wise? No, but many of you are. Being wise means having the kind of knowledge, insight, judgement and perspective that only come from experience. Wisdom makes you more reflective, more attuned to the big picture.

You are wise about the most important, difficult and uncertain issues human beings must face in life: what you can and can't control; when to stand your ground and when to compromise; when to intervene in someone's life to try to help them and when to leave well enough alone. It means you are aware of the need for multiple perspectives on important things. It means you know the things in life that are really worth expending your resources on, and those that you should let go.

The wiser you are, the more successful the aging process, and the higher your psychological well-being – you are happier, better adapted and more satisfied with your life.[40] Your self-esteem remains stable and declines only slightly in very advanced old age or when you are very near to death.[41] Beneath those slight changes, your personality remains much as it has always been: you remain stubbornly yourself, right up to the end.[42]

24. *Old age:* Still you, despite the rigours of aging

Attachment remains critical in old age and is more easily activated as you become more dependent on others to care for you. You think a lot about your childhood as you age, mulling over your memories of your parents and how they cared for you. Your long-forgotten childhood experiences are often more vividly recalled than what happened in the more recent past. The legacy of a *Secure* attachment has played out at every stage of your life and it's still an active presence, still shaping your capacity for happiness and well-being.

Even at this late stage, what happened in your early childhood, especially the quality of your relationship with your mother, is affecting your cognitive functioning. If you recall early memories of your mother being warm and affectionate to you, you are less likely to feel lonely, you have fewer depressive symptoms, suffer less memory decline, and can manage your own relationships better.[1]

One of the legacies of a *Secure* attachment is being attuned and sensitive to what is going on in your own mind, and in the mind of the people with whom you are interacting. In old age, that gift is still giving. It is associated with better cognitive and social functioning and more satisfying relationships. Compared to those who can summon no such tender memories of being cared for, you are more clued in to what is happening in you and around you, more open and emotionally stable, have fewer depressive symptoms and are less likely to suffer from loneliness – all the key elements of aging well.[2]

Correspondingly, unless you have managed to form a *Secure* attachment with somebody else, the legacy of an insecure attachment also lingers into old age.[3] Particularly as you become more frail, or are widowed, you may turn to your deceased spouse, your adult children, or God as your primary attachment figure.[4] And when you turn to God, or some other spiritual source of protection and comfort, how you construe that relationship tends to correspond to your attachment style and the relationship you had with a parent in childhood. If that bond was *Secure*, your relationship with God is close and trusting. If it was insecure, you project your fear of rejection and punishment on to your relationship with God, or you wheedle and plead like a child, yet have no confidence that you will be heard or supported.

As you age, most of you put a high value on getting emotional support from your family but may be more ambivalent about depending on them to help you with everyday tasks, triggering fears about your growing dependency and loss of autonomy. But the more *Secure* you are, the better able you are to adjust to this, and maintain your autonomy and psychological well-being.[5]

The quality of attachment shapes the quality of caregiving in old age – both the care you give to a spouse, and the care your children give to you. If your children are securely attached to you, their care is likely to be high-quality, devoted and committed. If the bond between you is insecure, the whole issue of caretaking is likely to be surrounded by negative emotionality, criticism, hostility or emotional over-involvement.

You, in turn, react with anger, refuse to cooperate with them and if you are cognitively frail or suffer from dementia, you may develop feelings of paranoia, creating even more anxiety and frustration.[6]

The abuse of older people is most likely to happen in situations where both the old person and the carer are excessively dependent on each other, which triggers a sense of helplessness and powerlessness, neither of you feeling able to challenge the situation.

The onset of dementia puts a major strain on caretaking. But deep human attachment finds one of its finest expressions in the care given by adult children or spouses to loved ones with dementia. As the disease strips away the capacities of the sufferer, there is an opportunity for the humanity of the caretaker to shine through.[7]

The rise and rise of dementia

Ten years ago, dementia was identified as the single most significant health and social crisis of the twenty-first century.[8] The risk of you, or your partner, developing a neurodegenerative disorder like Alzheimer's disease increases in your eighties and nineties.[9] The older you get, the bigger the risk, with women at higher risk than men – but it is *not* an inevitable part of aging.

In the UK, about two in 100 people aged sixty-five to sixty-nine have dementia, rising to one in five in those aged eighty-five to eighty-nine, and it increases again for those in their nineties.[10]

In Ireland, the prevalence of dementia in those aged eighty to eighty-four is 14.5 per cent in men and 16.4 per cent in women; eighty-five to eighty-nine is 20.9 per cent in men and 28.5 per cent in women; ninety to ninety-four is 29.2 per cent in men and 44.4 per cent in women; over ninety-five is 32.4 per cent in men and 48.8 per cent in women.[11]

Most of those with dementia are cared for by their families – and that includes you if your partner develops the disease. If you are shouldering a heavy burden of care for a spouse with dementia, you are, in effect, the second patient.[12] Caring for a loved one with dementia has all the features of a chronic stress experience: physical and psychological strain over an extended period of time; being on high alert, vigilant about ever-present risks; high levels of unpredictability and uncontrollability; and the likelihood of the stress spilling over into other aspects of your life. In fact, if you want to study the health effects of chronic stress, caretakers are the perfect exemplars.[13]

The severity of the dementia does not accurately predict how stressed a caretaker is likely to be. Rather, it's their individual circumstances, including their own physical and psychological well-being, the other pressures in their lives, their relationship with the person, and the practical help and emotional support received from others.

Yet, it's not all bad news. Multiple studies have confirmed a seemingly paradoxical finding – that while caregiving exacts a big toll on health and well-being, carers have lower mortality rates than non-carers. For example, one study of over 3,500 carers found that they showed significantly more stress and depressive symptoms than non-caretakers, who were matched on a range of characteristics, including health history. Yet, while stress and depression are risk factors, they had significantly lower mortality rates, suggesting that caring has stress-buffering effects.[14]

Caring for a spouse with dementia

As people live longer, caring for a partner with dementia has become more frequent – and it's not easy.[15] When you care for a partner with a physical illness, like terminal cancer, you both retain memories of your life together. In contrast, caring for a partner with Alzheimer's disease means you must contend with their memory loss and personality change, which can cause significant grief. As the disease progresses, they may no longer recognize you, or your children. The process of bereavement begins well before their death.[16] Cumulatively, that is why the rate of clinical distress among married caretakers is three times higher than is found in the general population of older people.[17]

The level of stress is influenced by how highly you think of your partner, and how satisfied you were with your marriage before the onset of dementia. If you were happily married, you are more likely to cast aside any memories that don't fit with that view or reframe them in a positive way. 'I don't remember us ever arguing,' you say. 'We had the odd difference, but we had so much in common, it hardly mattered.' This tendency to idealize your partner, and to discount any negative memory, significantly mitigates the distress of caring for them. In fact, it has emerged as the single strongest predictor of lower levels of distress among spouses whose partners develop dementia. The resulting increase in your physical and psychological well-being is unrelated to how severe the illness is or its duration.[18]

This idealization is a more extreme example of what most married couples do who tend to describe their relationships as happier than average – a contradiction in terms. This benign positive illusion carries a tinge of superiority, even if it's expressed with false modesty: 'We were just lucky.' And nearly all couples, bar the desperately unhappy, react to any threat to their relationship by putting more value on it. A dementia diagnosis, with the insidious psychological loss of your life partner, is just such an existential threat. Therefore, idealization is best understood as one way to adapt to the physical or psychological loss of your partner, a way to immunize yourself by holding fast to your idealized reality, even in the face of considerable information to the contrary, and it makes the adjustment easier.

If you are grieving the death or dementia of your partner, the memories are now all in the past. If your partner were still alive and well, you would most likely give a more mixed account, and have little trouble recounting current examples of their faults and failings and your continuing hope that they or you could fix them. Now, in the middle of your grief, that possibility is gone, and it doesn't seem worthwhile recalling them.

This is what allows you to stay positive despite the insidious loss of your partner or spouse to a neurodegenerative process that is beyond your control. The demands of care seem less arduous when provided to a partner who is remembered as loving and devoid of flaws, and a married life that is recalled as near perfect. It's a way to repay your partner for the good years together before the onset of dementia. In this way the heavy duty of caring for them goes into perspective and does not define your life.

Caring for a parent with dementia

An adult child's attachment to a parent has a significant effect on not just the quality of the caretaking but also on their motivation – whether it's done willingly, tenderly and with generosity, or primarily from guilt, social obligation, or in the hope of some gain. When a parent suffers a serious stroke or Alzheimer's disease, their ability to care for their most basic physical needs may be so compromised that it resembles the intensive care an infant needs. This can trigger memories in the carer of being touched, of crying, of clinging and looking for physical and psychological comforting.[19]

> Mum was very disabled for a few months before she died, she could do virtually nothing for herself. I used to bathe her, and when I washed her hands, I had such trouble not bursting into tears. I loved my mother's hands – they were very careworn from all the work she did rearing us. I remember her doing the big wash on Mondays. We

had no washing machine until I was a teenager, and her hands used to be red raw from the scrubbing and the detergent.

Josephine, 60

But for some of you, the memories of being cared for are more unsettling.

I really loved my mother, but we were never close. I can't remember her ever hugging me. I kept thinking, 'I must have forgotten,' but I've never been able to recall one single memory of any kind of physical intimacy. She was a difficult woman, very hard to get close to, very wrapped up in her own life. I think now she resented being a mother and would have far preferred to have a job than be looking after us. Things eased out when I grew up and she seemed to enjoy being around me for the first time, and I took very good care of her. When she got Alzheimer's, I knew it would be hard. What I didn't expect was how hard I found it to touch her, even her hand. I kind of recoiled from it. I was quite shocked actually because I am a very touchy-feely person with my children and my husband.

Deirdre, 66

Even when done willingly, caring for a parent with dementia is associated with physical and psychological costs, including disrupted immune and endocrine functioning, particularly when the carers are themselves older.[20] Carers grieve the loss of intimacy and support and companionship with their parent. They feel responsible for them in a different, more urgent way. But the more they feel that what they are doing is meaningful, and the more competent they feel as a carer, the less adverse effects they experience.[21] Conversely, feeling that you are expected and obliged to do the caretaking, or when it is primarily motivated by guilt or lack of choice, undermines the benefits and increases the burden.

Staying competent

Some things don't change, however long you live. In old age, you still seek out those you love and depend on for support and companionship.

You still want autonomy and to have a sense of control over your life. You are still determined to manage your life as competently as your health will allow you. When those three needs are met, it has a powerful impact on your physical and psychological well-being, on how active you remain, and how satisfied you are with your life. Let's start with how competently most of you manage your day-to-day lives.

'*I'm not helpless, you know.*' This was the tart reply one 82-year-old gave to an exaggeratedly concerned query from an acquaintance. In old age you are not sitting on a rocking chair, disengaged from life. On the contrary, you are still vitally engaged.[22] Most of you still perform well on measures of intelligence and other cognitive functions; you have worked out effective strategies to help you compensate for any declines in your mental processing or memory, enabling you to manage your life competently.

In fact, the biggest problem in old age is likely to be under-demand rather than over-demand –you are likely to be up to more, and up *for* more, than people expect.[23] You are able to manage most aspects of daily living, to protect your health and keep your relationships going. And there are things you want to keep doing because you find them interesting and enjoyable.

Remarkably, the number of things you have to do remains pretty unchanged between the ages of seventy and a hundred and one. To the end, life has a way of keeping you busy. But in your eighties, to compensate for declining energy and mobility, you drop some optional activities. There is a further slight decrease in your activity levels as you enter your nineties, but then it stays stable at this lower level, and even the oldest of you continue to be actively engaged and invested in life.[24]

In old age, using the SOC strategy (see Chapter 22) really comes into its own, especially if you started to implement it in late adulthood and are now more practised at it. At this stage it becomes a survival strategy, the main way you respond to decreasing energy, or to any functional problems that decrease your flexibility or restrict your mobility. You increasingly adopt it in anticipation of likely problems ahead. You are in good company.

When the great concert pianist Arthur Rubinstein, then aged eighty, was asked in an interview how he managed to maintain such a high level of expertise in his playing, what he effectively described was the SOC strategy. First, he said, he selected fewer pieces to play. Second, he optimized by practising these pieces more often. Third, he compensated for the loss in mechanical speed by deliberately playing slower right before the fast segments, so that they sounded faster – an artful disguise that did not diminish his pleasure or the enjoyment of the audience.[25]

You carefully select the areas of your life in which you invest your energy, and cut down your activities in other domains. You reduce the number of daily goals. You accept a lower standard of performance, although this proves challenging if you are a perfectionist. But you do all this so that you can optimize your functioning in the areas of life you most enjoy and that are crucial to your health and well-being.

The value of exercising control

As you enter old age, feeling that you can exercise some control in your life is crucial to your happiness and well-being, especially in the domains that are most important to you. When people in their eighties are asked which roles in life mean most to them – being a spouse, a parent, a grandparent, a friend – those who feel they can exercise control in the chosen domains are happier and healthier.[26] Equally important is having some control over your *immediate* environment.

Take one study that compared two groups of older people who were living in their own homes.[27] All came from similar backgrounds, had similar quality homes and the same level of social support. About 70 per cent rated their health as 'fair' or 'poor'; they suffered from a range of problems, like arthritis, hypertension, cataracts, and experienced the same type of difficulties with everyday tasks – grocery shopping, climbing stairs, walking, dressing or having a bath.

One group were helped by occupational and physical therapists to adopt control strategies to make their homes and their approach to daily living safer, the second group were not. The strategies included making small adjustments to their homes and daily routines, like using special equipment, pacing themselves, asking for help when needed, and adopting a learning mindset so they could continue to learn how to make things safer. When the two groups were followed up one year later, the group who had not adopted control strategies were found to have spent more days in hospital and were *nine* times more likely to have died within that year.

Growing old gracefully is overrated

As you advance into old age, it's harder to adapt to big changes, like moving into residential care. In the 1970s, Morton Lieberman, a professor of human development at the University of Chicago, conducted a series of landmark studies on how older people reacted to relocation.

- One study involved affluent older people in good general health and psychologically robust, who moved voluntarily into top-quality nursing homes, partly because of their physical needs, partly for social needs.
- The second group of older people were also physically healthy, but were forced to move from a small, hotel-like nursing home into a large old-age institution.
- The third group were older residents in a psychiatric hospital who were carefully selected and prepared to be discharged into community-type settings.
- The fourth group were resident in a state mental hospital and were relocated to other institutions.[28]

All were very different people, with varying psychological resources, making four very different moves, some by choice, some willingly. The moves had different meanings for them. Some saw it as a positive choice that would enhance their lives, while others saw it as a dire move, the equivalent of moving closer to death. Yet, despite the differences, the frequency of failure to adapt to the change was consistently high in all four groups. No matter what the circumstances, between 48 and 56 per cent of the people in all four groups showed a marked decline: physically, cognitively and behaviourally. Compared to older people with similar physical and psychological profiles who remained living in the community, those who relocated *tripled* their chances of dying.

Moreover, the kind of psychological qualities that predict how well you adapt to change at earlier stages of life – flexibility, meaning, choice, control and general psychological well-being – did not predict how well the older people adapted. What mattered most was the extent of the change involved in the move. Only those who found themselves well matched to the new settings were likely to adapt. When they were not, they experienced high levels of stress and high failure rates to adapt.

What characterized those who did well? When staff were asked to predict who would adapt well, they chose residents with the kind of qualities that are normally associated with resilience – those who were genial, kind, easy-going – in other words, people who were easy to like. Their predictions proved way off the mark. Those who survived were irritating, aggressive, demanding, narcissistic – in other words, hard to like.

As the researchers noted: 'It would seem that the thought of "growing old gracefully" is more a comfort to the young than an adequate guide to surviving the generally inescapable stresses of longevity. Being a good guy – having qualities associated with passive acceptance – was a trait we found in old people most likely not to survive the crisis of environmental change.'[29]

Your small but crucial network of close relationships

As you progress into old age, your network of close relationships decreases as you prune your wider network of peripheral relationships. The size of your network only becomes a problem if it shrinks so much that you have to rely too much on one person, to the point that it strains the relationship, or if there aren't enough people to meet your different needs – for support, for companionship, for advice, or just to share a laugh.

The small band of people that you now rely on – your partner, your children, your friends, neighbours, a sibling, or maybe a trusted and beloved carer – become your social convoy, your comrades-in-arms, as you venture ever further in your journey through the life course. Your physical and psychological well-being is strongly related to your satisfaction with that small circle of people, especially the quality of support you get from them.[30] Having someone you trust and can confide in is crucial. It is an especially powerful buffer against loneliness and depression, and significantly reduces the impact of becoming widowed. Consider this: if you are not socially active, but have even *one* person to confide in, you are far less likely to become depressed than someone who is more socially active but has no confidant.[31]

Loneliness is toxic in old age, affecting your biological functioning and increasing your risk of dying prematurely.[32] A support network is a vital component of your whole systemic function, protecting you from physical and cognitive decline. The number and quality of your close relationships is a far better predictor of a long and healthy life than almost anything else, including your background, personality and lifestyle.[33]

That network of support boosts your neuroendocrine and immune system, reducing the negative effects of stress. You interpret setbacks in a less threatening way and cope better with them. You are likely to show greater resistance to a range of infections and diseases, experience less cognitive decline, are at lower risk of blocked arteries, having a heart attack or stroke, getting cancer, a recurrence of a previous cancer, or developing dementia, and you are more likely to live longer. If you do have a heart attack or develop breast cancer, you will recover faster.

The more satisfied you are with that support, the better your general cognitive functioning.[34] You are more alert and attentive, quicker at processing information, and can recall things more accurately.[35] Conversely, relationships that are stressful can depress your immune functioning and put you at higher risk of infections and illness. The closer and more central the relationship, the bigger the impact of support.

As you advance into your late eighties and nineties, your network of close relationships contains fewer friends, as one by one they die, and you see those who are left less frequently. Decreased mobility or recurring illness makes it harder to get together socially.[36] Progressively, you are down to the bare bones of family.

You and your partner, aging side-by-side

As you age, you and your partner become more dependent on each other. The support you give each other directly influences your health, acting as a shield against any stress in the relationship or specific stressors in your lives.

How you perceive that support is influenced by what happens day-to-day, but also reflects the quality of support in the past, and your expectation of the support you are likely to get in the future.[37] You are more skilled at supporting each other now. You know each other better, are more attuned to each other's moods, better at picking up signals. In old age, emotions are as contagious as ever – the upside is that you can cheer each other up when one of you is feeling low; the downside is that when one of you is depressed, the other is also likely to be affected.[38]

Right to the end of life, equality counts. As with much else in marriage, support works best when it is two-way. If you feel that you are receiving significantly more support from your partner than you are giving, especially if it's over a long period, it can lower your mood, decrease your self-esteem and increase feelings of depression. It upsets the reciprocity that is fundamental to close relationships and can make you feel that you are becoming a burden.[39] But when the support is 'invisible', quiet background help and encouragement that draws no attention to itself, it has no such negative effects.

Retaining your unique sense of self

In old age, you are acutely aware that your sense of self and identity does not decline in tandem with your body.[40] You still have a rich inner life and are motivated to grow and develop and find meaning in your own life, your most effective bulwark against the existential threat of death. Even as you accept that your life is coming to an end, you want to be yourself as you confront it, to be the person you are up to your last breath.

As you face the rigours of old age, and if your ability to process information and experiences comes under more stress, especially if there is a big change in your living arrangements, preserving your sense of self becomes more pressing. You fight harder to maintain and express your sense of 'self-sameness'.[41] If you feel any whiff of depersonalization from those you interact with, you say, or want to say, 'I'm not just some old lady or random old guy. I'm still *me*!'

You have your own way to maintain that sense of self-sameness. For example, you begin to blend the past and the present in a way that strengthens your sense of yourself as a unique individual with a unique set of life experiences. When younger people are asked to describe themselves, they usually offer examples from the present. In old age, you blend examples from the past and present, and you state the convictions that supported how you felt and reacted in those situations.

For you, the past, the present and your convictions are all equally important in supporting your identity. You like to dramatize your experiences in life, to mythicize the past, everything recast so that the uniqueness of you becomes more vivid, more permanent and immutable, which is a key part of achieving a sense of integrity in old age.

25. *Old age:* Seeing the bigger picture

As my mother progressed through her late seventies, she lamented the growing list of minor ailments, and the loss of friends and neighbours. But when she turned eighty, she cheered up. Reaching that age seemed to bring a certain survivor satisfaction. 'Madge, you look so well,' someone would say. 'Guess how old I am?' she would ask. 'Late sixties?' they would venture cautiously. 'I'm eighty!' she would answer, triumphant.

Getting that far seemed to leaven the losses of old age for her. It *is* an achievement to live into old age, although not everybody rejoices in turning eighty. One woman I knew seemed to give up on life when she reached eighty, calmly announcing to her family that she had had a good life, but no longer felt she had any purpose and now would be quite happy to die. But life had other ideas. Four years later I bumped into her, looking decidedly full of purpose. 'What happened, Emily?' I asked. 'I thought you wanted to die last time I saw you?' She replied, 'I changed my mind.'

In late life, the major developmental task is to achieve integrity. As you face the relative nearness of death, and the disintegration of the self-you-know, there is a pressing need to maintain the integrity of that self. What is required now is the ability to pull together all the different strands of your life and to find meaning in them, to rejoice in what went well, to come to terms with the disappointments. You come to understand and accept that this is how you played your hand, because you are the person you were and still are. This sense of coherence and integrity is what will hold you together in old age, confer dignity on your life, and renew your energy and purpose to give what's left of your life your best shot.

As you reflect on your life, your perspective widens. You see yourself positioned not just between the younger and older generations, but as one link in a long chain of generations that stretches into an unimaginably long past and future. Poised between one era and another, you grasp in a more personal way the continuity of the human species, and you understand that the significance of your individual life lies ultimately within that larger continuity. You see that this often muddled, imperfect but heroic human endeavour has profound value, and itself constitutes some kind of immortality.

But no life is perfect. There is always some struggle. You have to come to terms with the unwise choices you made, with the hurt you may have caused to others or was caused to you, particularly by those you loved, and, for some of you, the incomprehensible adversity that befell you or those you dearly loved. If you cannot come to some wider understanding of the frailties and destructiveness inherent in being human, or the sheer randomness of life, then you risk despairing – of yourself, of other people or, in more extreme cases, of the whole human enterprise. You feel that your life has ended in failure, has little worth, and it's too late to change anything. But even if your life has been good, the prospect of your life ending is an existential threat that can make you feel desolate, if only at low moments.

Regrets? I have a few . . .

When you've lived a long life, as and if you have not sealed yourself off from real engagement with other people, you will inevitably have some regrets. That's why regret is the second most frequently named emotion; only love is mentioned more often. Dealing with regrets is integral to achieving integrity and avoiding depression.[1] The essence of regret is feeling that your present situation would have been a lot better had you acted differently, had you not taken the action that you did, or had you taken the action you failed to take.[2]

At any stage of life, if you look back over recent events, you experience the most regret about the ill-advised things that you did. But when you look back over a longer time frame, your regrets about doing what you shouldn't have done decrease, and the regret for not doing what you should have done increases.[3]

The intensity of any regret you feel depends on how things turned out, but also on how things were going beforehand. If your life had been going well, you experience the most regret about doing something that really messed things up. On the other hand, if your life was not going particularly well, you feel the most regret about not taking the action that might have improved things.[4] When you are older, and have more perspective on your life, you are likely to also take a broader view on things.

When you are younger, you are more given to *hot regret* – an acute sense of distress that makes you want to tear your hair out. As you age, the regret you feel is less intense, more wistful and sad, about what might have been. But, if you are plagued with regret, it is also a more despairing kind.[5]

Your positivity bias comes into play. As you age, you are more motivated to recall the past in positive terms. When you think about any regret you have, you can recall more positive than negative details about the event that provoked the regret, a pattern that is observed with your memories in general. In time, your regrets about the past are mixed with positive feelings. The further back the event, the more the regret subsides. You are conscious that you are less able to modify the negative consequences and have fewer opportunities for corrective actions, so your feelings of sadness or guilt diminish.

You are also more aware of the context in which your regrets occurred, and you focus on the positive changes that may have flowed from them.[6] As you reflect and reminisce, you process your regrets more thoroughly, allowing the negative feelings they arouse to become linked to positive memories. You realize that what seemed like pure loss at one time came to be associated with serendipitous and positive outcomes at a later stage.

It was devastating when my marriage broke up and I had a few very bad years. But in another way, it kind of made me. I got a lot more serious about my life, and I learned to enjoy my own company. I stayed single for a long, long time, but then, out of the blue, I fell in love again, and we are still here together now. I can say, hand on my heart, that I've never been happier in my life. I often think that if the price of finding that kind of love was a lot of suffering, it was worth it.

Frank, 81

As you try to achieve a sense of integrity about your life, to reconcile the good and bad things that happened, you come to accept that your life was as well lived as was possible in your circumstances, and the room for regrets is narrowed. You become happier with the choices you made and less preoccupied by the choices you opted not to make.[7] This positivity flow also shapes the way you react to more recent regrets. You are more forgiving of yourself, focusing on any positive changes that flowed from them.[8]

The four patterns of aging

How do the range of physical and psychological changes and the quality of your close relationships combine and play out in old age? In a study that followed older people from the beginning of their eighties to the end of life, four general patterns of aging were identified.[9]

- The largest group of older people, about 63 per cent, managed to hold themselves together, physically, cognitively and socially. Their memory functioning remained good, and they survived longer. Many were still living with their partners and stayed closely connected to family and friends, thereby warding off depression and other emotional problems.
- At the other extreme, 18 per cent were extremely frail, lonely and depressed, with poor cognitive and social functioning. They were aging in isolation, most likely to be single or widowed, and some in nursing homes. Despite needing a lot of support, they were not embedded in the social networks that might provide that. While this pattern conforms to the common stereotype of old age, it's worth noting that it applied to fewer than one in five older people.

- The third group, about 15 per cent, remained reasonably socially active and had some support from family and friends. But they also showed some symptoms of loneliness and depression, and their memory functioning was poor and had been throughout their old age. This group had the highest rates of mortality.
- The fourth group, 4 per cent, showed average levels of well-being, had adequate social support, but experienced dramatic memory decline late in life, maybe signalling the onset of dementia.

Ultimately, how you resolve the task of facing the challenges of old age and achieving integrity also plays out in four patterns.[10]

- Despair
- Conforming integrity
- Pseudo integrity
- Comprehensive integrity

1. Despair

A small minority of you feel unable to cope with the losses and challenges of old age, or perhaps always found life difficult. Your account of your life is suffused with deep disappointments and losses that you are unable to accept, reconcile or address. Hovering over it is a sense of inadequacy. You are beset by fear that you can take no more, feeling that your life has lost its purpose and relish, and all that's left is grim survival.

After Dad died, Mum couldn't cope at all. She always depended on him. I think she just gave up on life. She started staying in bed a lot. I mean, she has health problems, but it was mainly depression. We tried to do everything we could for her, but she wasn't eating properly, and losing weight, and eventually it got too much and the doctor thought she should go into a nursing home where they could keep an eye on her. She perked up a bit for a while, but then seemed to give up again. She told my sister that she would like to die. She said she wanted to join Dad, as if he was waiting for her. She wasn't crying or anything, just – I don't know what, it was terrible. A few days before she died, she just literally turned her face to the wall, stopped eating altogether, and died. She was only eighty-four.

Rose, 59

2. A conforming integrity

Some are you are generally content with your life. Your approach to your life is practical, but not introspective. You have done little reflection on yourself, or the meaning of your life, and have stayed solidly within the frame of beliefs and worldview that you mainly picked up from your family when you were young. You don't stray far from your psychological comfort zone.

> I don't really think much about my life. My life was good, nothing to complain about.

Eddie, 83

3. A pseudo integrity

Some of you are at pains to present a view of yourself and your life as being more together than it is, a pseudo integrity that you try to believe yourself. You present a positive account of your life, but it has a rehearsed and defensive quality about it, so your stated satisfaction seems brittle. You actively exclude the parts of your life that you find unsettling or unacceptable and don't acknowledge any personal regrets or ambiguities. You wrap things up in a narrative that you do not want questioned or challenged, so you fall back on restating simplistic and dogmatic beliefs that you expect the world to conform to.

> My life was fine. It's all to do with yourself. But of course people let you down, but you learn to deal with that. I just get over things like that and get on with my life. No regrets. You have to paddle your own canoe in life, do your own thing.

Mikey, 82

4. A comprehensive integrity

Some of you achieve a comprehensive integrity. You are able to find a balance between what went right in your life and what may have gone wrong, and reach a compassionate and philosophical understanding of the whole. You face into any losses you experienced, but don't let them overwhelm you. That compassionate understanding of your own life, and the lives of others, is how you arrive at some kind of wisdom. That is what gives the integrity you achieve its affirming and sometimes heroic quality, especially if you have managed to do that in the face of major setbacks.

That kind of integrity is what will allow you to approach the end of your life in full possession of yourself, and embedded in the life that you have built, with its own unique and irreplaceable value. You come full circle, right back to trust. Trust, as Erik Erikson points out, is the assured reliance on the integrity of others, and I would add 'and on yourself'. Just as trust is what first allows you not to fear life, now integrity is what enables you not to fear death.

Achieving integrity requires a deep understanding of yourself, some insight into why you are the person you are, and what shaped and influenced you. Above all, it requires that you remain open, curious and engaged in your life right up to its end.

When did I feel old? I never felt old. I don't feel old now. I'm interested in where I am going, if there is another life, an afterlife. I don't think you 'die' – you are changed, moved on to another level, where the laws of physics don't apply, a nice place, you could say an inner life, your inner life. Your soul can't die. I'm a good Catholic, but I find it hard to accept some things, like the infallibility of the Pope. But faith fits us out to face the world. I never thought about love and how it expands. But I do now.

I love books – I love the feel of them. I love looking up the origins of words. I like having a project, and I walk every day.

I notice some of my friends set limits on what they will engage with, what they will notice. I don't, even though there are things out there that I choose not to respond to. It's a mistake to work too late in life. The man becomes the job rather than the other way round. And they all die very quickly. You can lose your soul. The best thing is to have an inquisitive mind.

I think we take people for granted. I get very emotional about that [cries silently for a few moments]. And about music. I put on the music I like at full blast. It strikes a chord in you. It's built into you, no matter how old you are. These are the things that won't die. It's a kind of immortality.

I have no regrets. I took my profession very seriously, and I always tried to have honesty and integrity in how I worked. I'm very pleased with the way my children live.

Bernard, 90

I think for most of my twenties I lived in cotton wool. I didn't come out of myself until I became a social worker, and, of course, when I met Colm. We were both in our early fifties when we met. He was the focus of my life, we were always looking out for each other.

I noticed Colm slowing down a few years before he died, especially after a fall he had. When he died, I had a crisis of faith – I just knew there was not a God. I knew I would never see Colm again, in my heart and soul I knew that. Ever. It was a huge shock, really enormous. I talked to a priest I used to know and he helped me a lot. It's hard to explain how. He didn't try to convince me about the existence of God. But one thing he said stuck in my mind. He said that we can't change the past, and we just don't know about the future, but to live your life as if you did. That was really helpful, and it moved me into a different place, I'm calmer now.

Two years ago, I decided to do a course on using art with older people. I did a few sessions in nursing homes, which were very interesting and enjoyable. I am part of an art group for a long time, I set it up after I retired.

I have a wide network of friends, some younger than me, some older. I have recently made friends with someone my age down the road, and we meet for tea and a chat. I have two very good neighbours who look out for me. One of my younger friends, who is in her thirties, includes me in things she thinks I would enjoy, like going to a play. I find talking to her very interesting, it keeps me young.

Camilla, 82

A life well lived – what we learn from old age

The principles of a life well lived – old age			
Life stage	*Time frame*	*Developmental task*	*Psychological principle*
Old age	80 and onwards	integrity or despair?	Be wise

By now, you have figured out the important things about aging:

- everybody grows older all the time
- everybody is different
- age itself is not important, and
- everybody is in this aging business together.[11]

You've clocked up a lifetime's experiences. This is the time of life when you need the grace of wisdom: time to be wise, or to get wiser.

- *Be wise like a child*: by now, you are wise enough to know, like the child in the fairy tale, that the emperor has no clothes. But also stay wise enough to occasionally catch a glimpse of the world as perfect.
- *Be wised up*: be wise like you were when you were young, always looking out to see how the world works.
- *Be wise about yourself*: learn from your mistakes – and from the small triumphs of your day.
- *Be wise about adversity*: remember that even the worst things pass and that there are always new opportunities. Now, put that wisdom into practice and *take action* on the things that will help you stay well and stay active.
- *Stay connected*: to those you love, but also to those who stimulate your mind, who keep you tuned in to the wider world, or who make you think, or laugh.
- *Always have positive goals to pursue*: have micro-goals to give structure and enjoyment to your day, and also medium-term goals to achieve in a few months.

- **Focus on what you have control over**: be realistic about your limitations and try to find ways to get around them or compensate for them. Be alert to risk, but don't expend so much time and effort avoiding risk that you have nothing left over to do the things you've always loved to do.
- **Look to your peers**: assessing how well you are functioning compared to your peers is remarkably effective. You'll identify where you lag behind, or to bask in your superior physical or psychological functioning. Anything that encourages you to keep a more youthful identity goes a long way to keeping you as healthy as possible.
- **Be mindful**: if you've never practised mindfulness, start now. A study of older people in nursing homes, average age eighty, who agreed to do twenty minutes of meditation twice a day for twelve weeks showed substantial improvement at the end of the study.[12] They reported that their mind was clearer, they had more energy, experienced a deep state of rest and relief from fatigue, were more alert and ready for whatever came next, yet less hurried and able to proceed calmly with their day. Their physical health, psychological well-being and cognitive functioning improved. For example, there were improvements in systolic blood pressure, word fluency and ability to learn. They felt less 'old' and could cope with minor hassles. *And* they survived three years longer than similar groups of older people who were not part of the study.
- **First and last – stay curious**: no matter how long you live, there is always something new to be learned about yourself, about the world, and about other people – even those you've known so long and believe you know so well.

In short, still play music at full blast.

26.   Your precious life reaches its end

Old age is not just about the bare bones of managing the practicalities of your life. As you near the end of life, you are confronted with its fundamental dilemma – that eventually your one wild and precious life will come to an end – and your own vulnerability in the face of that ending.[1] You are not preoccupied by death, but it does become more salient, more focal in your thoughts. You scan the obituaries and find the names of old friends and peers. Your physical losses accelerate, emphasizing life's fragility. You react more strongly to themes of death and dying than younger adults do.[2] My mother used to like sentimental films earlier in life, but as she got older, she would get restive if we were watching a programme involving death, saying, 'Ah, why are we watching that depressing old thing?'

Yet, you show similar or even lower levels of anxiety about death than younger adults do when confronted with an acute reminder of death.[3]

The ending begins

One study of older people[4] found that in the last year of life, there is growing dependence on healthcare – including, on average, six visits to your GP and one admission to hospital. About 12 per cent of people spent time in a hospice, and nearly 20 per cent in a nursing home. More than 40 per cent were under the care of a public health nurse, over 30 per cent attended physiotherapy, and 20 per cent received home-care services. In the last few months of life, many suffered from some chronic illness, but a third suffered no disability.

One-third needed help with everyday tasks, like cooking, bathing or managing medications, and the rest were in between. Between 40 and 50 per cent experienced falls, regular pain, or depression that could affect their quality of life, especially if they were not getting the treatment they needed. The majority were cared for by a network of family and friends, most receiving two hours of care a day, and one in ten a full twenty-four hours.

The average age of death was seventy-eight: 46 per cent died in hospital, 27 per cent at home, 11 per cent in a nursing home, and 10 per cent in a hospice.

For most older people, your satisfaction with life remains high until very near the end of life.[5] But as death becomes imminent, there are psychological changes. For most of you, your mood will remain much the same as it always was. As you near death, a new dynamic appears.[6] If you have suffered prolonged ill health, you enter this phase already burdened by the psychological wear-and-tear of dealing with health problems, your adaptive reservoir is exhausted, and there may be an uptick in depressive symptoms. But if you have enjoyed reasonably good health until now, the risk of developing depressive symptoms is much lower.

Your self-esteem may also drop slightly as you battle the rapid physical decline over which you have no control. So too with openness and optimism.[7] As you cope with the existential threat of death, you concentrate your efforts on survival, not on your feelings about the future. Being open and optimistic is less effective at buffering you from stress — it just matters less. There is cognitive decline, more awareness of how limited time is and more preoccupation with death. But even as you approach death, most of you are not afraid to die. Although if you are the kind of person who is prone to anxiety or, at the other extreme, puts a high value on excitement and enthusiasm, it's harder.[8]

The rapid physical decline, the health problems, the strain on your central nervous system and the general multisystem decline mean that you switch your resources away from maintaining your psychological state to maintaining basic physiological processes. Just as your mother once laboured to bring you into the world, now you gather what resources you have as you labour to leave it.

What is it like to die?

We don't know, until we die ourselves. The nearest we get to understanding may be the accounts of those who have had near-death experiences (NDEs). These include people who had a general anaesthetic, or those in situations of mortal danger who believed themselves to be near to death. Almost one in four of those who survive a critical medical incident – for example, those who have suffered cardiac arrest where there is no heartbeat and breath – report having a NDE.[9] While descriptions vary, there are some common themes.

They describe an out-of-body experience – as if they are looking down at themselves and observing what is happening, a sense of time slowing down, of their thoughts speeding up, and experiences from their life flashing before their eyes as they progress along a tunnel towards an extraordinarily bright light where they can see presences, usually close family members who are dead, or God or another spiritual figure. They often describe a feeling of ineffable peace.

What accounts for NDEs? They have been linked to dramatic surges of dopamine and serotonin that cause high positive arousal, or to the surge of general neurological arousal and electrical activity, or to specific neurological changes that precede death.[10] But if you are successfully resuscitated, what you are vividly recalling are the images and memories triggered by this cascade of neural activity.

Other researchers link NDEs to a three-phase psychological process. In the first phase, you believe there is some hope of recovery, you resist dying and cling to life. In the second phase, you believe that death is now inevitable, you give yourself to it. In the third and final phase, there is a rapid review of your life, followed by a profound feeling of peace and transcendence.[11]

And then what? At a profound level, the self is simply unable to conceive of its own end and we find different ways of dealing with that.[12] If you have faith in an afterlife, you see yourself as continuing in paradise, meeting up with the people you loved who went before you. Even if you are a committed atheist and sincerely believe that when you die, you die, there you are, looking at your own funeral, imagining the grief of your family and friends, and even wondering who might turn up for the occasion.

Most of us probably end up thinking of death as passing from one state to another, and that some essential part of us, our core essence, will continue – in the memory of those who loved us, or in energy of some kind, in some light we cannot see.

> And is it so hard to believe that souls might travel these paths? That great shuttles of souls might fly about, faded but audible if you listen closely enough? . . . the air a library and the record of every life lived, every sentence spoken, every word transmitted still reverberating within it.

> Anthony Doerr, *All the Light We Cannot See*

Your one wild and precious life has run its course. And so it ends.

Epilogue: Be brave

So, here you are, wherever you are in the life course, still in the thick of things – trying to find love, or to love better, still trying to grow into the fullness of who you are and managing your life as best you can. The aim and purpose of this book was to provide a psychological framework that will help you to do that by setting out how your three innate psychological drives for closeness, autonomy and competence find expression in a series of ten developmental tasks that face you as you move through the life course, and how your efforts to negotiate these tasks account for much of what you think and do and value in your life at each stage.

As you read the book, inevitably, you reflected on your own life, and how you tried to meet your own psychological needs and negotiate each developmental task. For some of you, the outcomes have been good, or good enough. Glory in that. For others, the outcomes have been less satisfactory. Either way, I hope you have come to understand how complex and delicate the process is and how for all of our good intentions we, and the people we depend on most, often miss the mark.

So build in some forgiveness. You get just one shot at life. You go through each stage only once, with no chance to rehearse. But the great gift of human consciousness is that you always have the freedom to reinterpret the way you think about your past, and to review and recalibrate the strategies you use to get your basic needs met. What that means is that psychological development is never simple and linear. Instead, we spend a great deal of our lives in transition, changing, or thinking about changing some aspect of ourselves or our lives. So at any stage we are never fully 'formed', and each transition period is a key time for transformation and development. Old desires resurface in new contexts, offering a new opportunity to renegotiate each developmental task, and do it better this time.

Sometimes you get lucky in life. Even if you've had your basic trust undermined, or your capacity for autonomy or competence compromised, someone helps you rebuild your trust in yourself or in life; or encourages you to take hold of your own life and drive it energetically forward; or sees something special in you and gives you a chance to shine.

But don't rely on luck. Do it for yourself – make understanding yourself and your own story of development your own project. You may not want to go as far as Socrates, who believed that the unexamined life was not worth living, but Shakespeare's injunction, 'to thine own self be true', has intuitive appeal.

Halfway through your life, as you become acutely aware of 'time left', you are nudged into a period of reflection as you try to review, reassess and renew yourself and your life. But you can do that kind of reflection at any stage. You can revisit how you fared at each stage of life, and how the developmental task of that stage was negotiated. No life is perfect, so it is likely you will find that there is some unfinished psychological business. An incomplete trust in yourself, a reluctance to trust others, a shaky sense of your right to be yourself and to set the direction of your life, and a confidence in your own ability that is too easily undermined by self-doubt.

Addressing the unfinished psychological business of your life, like many things, is best approached sideways. You can't make yourself trust, but you can learn to deepen your capacity for trust by being trustworthy. You can't summon up a strong sense of autonomy or identity, but you can confront your self-doubt. In the same way, you can enhance your friendships, or find a friend, by being generous. You can take the initiative and make things happen. You can find or build intimacy in your personal relationships by investing time and energy in them and move your life on by making and keeping commitments. You can make your life count by trying to create something of lasting value, however modest. You can face endings by seizing the day, and you can achieve integrity in your life by being wise.

Will you always get it right? You won't. Taking any action in life is always risky. Even when your intentions are good and you prepare as best you can, you may still mess up. But messing up can be fixed.

Missing out can't. So keep reminding yourself that the most enduring regrets in life are not about doing the things that didn't turn out as well as you'd hoped, but about not doing the things that you could have done.

But we are lucky. We live in a time when we have more knowledge about how psychological development works at every stage of life, about what drives it and what undermines it. We have more choices about how to live our lives and more opportunities to change the way we live than previous generations did. At the same time, we also face a different set of challenges. But one thing has not changed. It always took a lot of courage and boldness to open yourself to life, to its opportunities and its risks. And it still does.

So if there were just one overarching lesson to be learned, one inescapable principle of life, it is this: be brave. Take a leap into life. Will you experience a rush of anxiety when you do? You may. But to borrow a phrase: feel the fear and do it anyway.[1] The moment of acute anxiety will pass, and your pent-up longings will gush out, sometimes in a torrent of sobs, but often in a huge sigh of relief. That is how you build resilience – the capacity to keep adapting to change in a way that helps you grow and develop. And that is how you build character. Character is quite different from personality. Personality is shaped by temperament and personal style. Character is a deeper set of enduring qualities and habits of mind that may only reveal itself in the face of challenge.

So back to the beginning, to the question I posed at the start of this book.

At the end of your life, how will you judge if it has been successful in the way *you* wanted it to be?

That's not an easy question to answer. But if you approach your life with bravery, then when your life is coming to its end you will be able to say:

This is the life I was given, and this is how I lived it. And all in all, despite the setbacks I encountered, I rose to each challenge as best I could, and with a modicum of courage.

Acknowledgements

In this book I have tried to show how our psychological growth and development proceeds in a relatively orderly, understandable way throughout life. But life itself often intervenes in the most unexpected ways. When I started the book, I was full of confidence that it would be written in a year and published the year after. In the event, from start to finish, this book took more than three years to research and write. Then Covid-19 crashed into our lives and delayed the publishing by another year. The fact that the book is finally seeing the light of day is due to the incomparable support and guidance I had from editors, friends and family.

First, my sincere thanks to my literary agent, Marianne Gunn-O'Connor, not just for her astute and practical advice but for her unreserved personal support. I am indebted to the Penguin team in Dublin – Michael McLoughlin, managing director, Penguin Random House Ireland, Patricia Deevy, deputy publisher, Cliona Lewis, publicity director, Carrie Anderson, sales manager, Brian Walker, sales director, and Laura Dermody and Isabelle Hanrahan who helped in countless ways – and to the team in London – Ellie Smith and Sara Granger, for editorial and production work, Richard Bravery, Hannah Jones, Lesley Hodgson and Alice Chambers in the art department, Zoe Coxon, copywriter, and Martina O'Sullivan, Julia Murday, Corinna Bolino, Alice Gordge and the Penguin Life team. Thanks also to Shân Morley Jones for her assiduous work on the copy-editing and Christine Shuttleworth for indexing. Particular thanks to designer Anna Morrison for the beautiful cover.

Special thanks to Patricia Deevy, whose sharp editorial insights, strategic instincts and commitment to the book were critical, and to editor Rachel Pierce, who worked on the book with such thought, care and devotion that I think she now knows more about it than I do myself.

I want to thank my great friends who encouraged me, cheered me on, and shared their own experiences of getting through life: Anne Connolly, Marion Creeley and Eamon Drea, Geraldine and Tony O'Daly, Gary Joyce, Augusta McCabe, Pat Quinn and Mick McDonagh, Grace Smith, Nuala O'Farrell, Richard Barrett and Michael Bourke, Mary Higgins and Billy Murphy, Frances and Michael Fitzgerald, Brian Patterson, Don Thornhill, Helen Keogh, Caroline McCamley, Geraldine Smith, and Tania Bannotti, Thanks, too, to my friends in the US, Ellen McLaughlin, Maggie Kavalaris, and Alice Hockenbury, and to Mary Stuart in the UK. I also want to remember the support of my friends, the late Paul Quilligan, Robin Simpson and Paddy Hayes, whom we all miss so much. I want to thank my late parents, Madge and Vincent Gaffney, who taught me my first lessons about life, my brother John and sister-in-law Joy, my Barry cousins in Cork and my sister-in-law Maura Harris. I am greatly indebted to my friend and former academic colleague Sheila Greene, who generously shared her deep knowledge of the child attachment literature with me over the years.

Finally, my love and gratitude to my husband John and children Elly and Jack Harris, and my son-in-law David Morrissey who time and again listened with intelligence and saintly patience as I tried out my ideas. Their insights about life are woven through every part of this book and their love is at the centre of my life.

Notes

Introduction: Living your one wild and precious life

1 Meyer, M. L. & Lieberman, M. D. 2018. 'Why people are always thinking about themselves: Medial prefrontal cortex activity during rest
primes self-referential processing'. *Journal of Cognitive Neuroscience*, 30 (5),
714–21.

2 Gilbert, D. 2006. *Stumbling on Happiness*. London: Harper Press.

1. Navigating the new life course

1 See Carstensen, L. L. 2014. 'Our aging population – it may save us all'.
In Irving, P. H. (ed). *The Upside of Aging: How Long Life Is Changing the
World of Health, Work, Innovation, Policy, and Purpose*. Bridgewater, NJ:
Wiley, pp. 2–16.

2 Gratton, L. & Scott, A. 2016. *The 100-Year Life: Living and Working in an
Age of Longevity*. London: Bloomsbury; Cavendish, C. 2019. *Extra Time:
10 Lessons for an Ageing World*. London: HarperCollins.

3 Frissen, V. 2000. 'ICTs in the Rush Hour of Life'. *The Information Society*, 16 (1), 65–75.

4 National Council on Aging. 2001. *Myths and Realities 2000 Survey Results*.
Washington, DC: NCOA.

5 Drewelies, J., Agrigoroaei, S., Lachman, M. E. & Gerstorf, D. 2018. 'Age
variations in cohort differences in the United States: Older adults report
fewer constraints nowadays than those 18 years ago, but mastery beliefs
are diminished among younger adults'. *Developmental Psychology*, 54 (8),
1408–25.

6 Gratton & Scott, *The 100-Year Life*; Cavendish, *Extra Time*.

7 Frissen, 'ICTs in the Rush Hour of Life'.

8 National Council on Aging, *Myths and Realities 2000*.

9 See Medina, J. 1996. *The Clock of Ages: Why We Age, How We Age, Turning Back the Clock*. Cambridge: Cambridge University Press. 178–84.

10 Neugarten, B. L. & Moore, J. W. 'The changing age-status system'. In B. L. Neugarten (ed). *Middle Age and Aging: A Reader in Social Psychology*. Chicago, IL: The University of Chicago Press, pp. 5–21.

11 Zimbardo, P. G. & Boyd, J. N. 1999. 'Putting time in perspective: A valid, reliable individual-difference metric'. *Journal of Personality and Social Psychology*, 77 (6), 1271–88.

12 Kotter-Grühn, D., Neupert, S. D. & Stephan, Y. 2015. 'Feeling old today? Daily health, stressors, and affect explain day-to-day variability in subjective age'. *Psychological Health*, 30 (12), 1470–85; Kuper, H. & Marmot, M. 2003. 'Intimations of mortality: perceived age of leaving middle age as a predictor of future health outcomes'. *Age and Ageing*, 32 (2), 178–84.

13 See Westerhof, G. J., Miche, M., Brothers, A. F., Barrett, A. E., Diehl, M., Montepare, J. M., Wahl, H. W. & Wurm, S. 2014. 'The influence of subjective aging on health and longevity: a meta-analysis longitudinal data'. *Psychology and Aging*, 29 (4), 793–802; Kotter-Grühn et al, 'Feeling old today?'.

14 Levy, B. R., Kunkel, S. R. & Kasl, S. V. 2002. 'Longevity increased by positive self-perceptions of aging'. *Journal of Personality and Social Psychology*, 83 (2), 261–70.

15 Weiss, D., Reitz, A. K. & Stephan, Y. 2019. 'Is age more than a number? The role of openness and (non)essentialist beliefs about aging for how young or old people feel'. *Psychology and Aging*, 34 (5), 729–37.

16 Shmotkin, D., Berkovich, M. & Cohen, K. 2006. 'Combining happiness and suffering in a retrospective view of anchor periods in life: A differential approach to subjective well-being'. *Social Indicators Research*, 77 (1), 139–69.

17 This was first expressed by one of the pioneers of research on the life course, Bernice Neugarten, of the University of Chicago. See Neugarten, B. 1982. *New Perspectives on Aging and Social Policy*. The Leon and Josephine Winkelman Lecture. University of Michigan.

18 Schiff, B. 2014. 'Introduction: development's story in time and place'. *New Directions for Child and Adolescent Development*, 145, 1–13.

19 McAdams, D. P. 2013. 'The psychological self as actor, agent, and author'. *Perspectives on Psychological Science*, 8 (3), 272–95.

20 Forty years of research by Edward Deci and Richard Ryan, of the University of Rochester, placed these three needs, especially autonomy, centre stage in any account of human happiness, well-being and success. See Deci, E. L. & Ryan, R. M. 2000. 'The "what" and "why" of goal pursuits: Human needs and the self-determinations of behavior'. *Psychological Inquiry*, 11 (4), 227–68; Ryan, R. M. & Deci, E. L. 2000. 'Self-determination theory and the facilitation of intrinsic motivation, social development, and well-being'. *American Psychologist*, 55 (1), 68–78; Ryan, R. M. & Deci, E. L. 2006. 'Self-regulation and the problem of human autonomy: Does psychology need choice, self-determination, and will?' *Journal of Personality*, 74 (6), 1557–85; Deci, E. L. & Ryan, R. M. 2008. 'Facilitating optimal motivation and psychological well-being across life's domains'. *Canadian Psychology*, 49 (1), 14–23.

21 See McAdams. 'The psychological self as actor'.

22 See Ryan, R. M., La Guardis, J. G., Solky-Butzel, J., Chirkov, V. & Kim, Y. 2005. 'On the interpersonal regulation of emotions: Emotional reliance across gender, relationships, and culture'. *Personal Relationships*, 12 (1), 145–63; Pierce, T., Lydon, J. E. & Yang, S. 2001. 'Enthusiasm and moral commitment: What sustains family caregivers of those with dementia'. *Basic and Applied Social Psychology*, 23 (1), 29–41; Chirkov, V., Ryan, R. M., Kim, Y. & Kaplan, U. 2003. 'Differentiating autonomy from individualism and independence: A self-determination theory perspective on internalization of cultural orientations and well-being'. *Journal of Personality and Social Psychology*, 84 (1), 97–110.

23 See Ryan & Deci. 'Self-regulation and the problem of human autonomy'.

24 Ibid.

25 Deci & Ryan, 'The "what" and "why" of goal pursuits', 229.

2. *The drama of development*

1 See Erikson, E. H. 1951. *Childhood and Society*. London: Imago Publishing Co.

2 Conway, M. A. & Holmes, A. 2004. 'Psychosocial stages and the accessibility of autobiographical memories across the life cycle'. *Journal of Personality*, 72 (3), 461–78.

3 Levinson, D. J. 1986. 'A conception of adult development'. *American Psychologist*, 41 (1), 3–13.

4 Alter, A. L. & Hershfield, H. E. 2014. 'People search for meaning when they approach a new decade in chronological age'. *PNAS*, 111 (48), 17066–70.

5 Miron-Shatz, T., Bhargave, R. & Doniger, G. M. 2015. 'Milestone Age Affects the Role of Health and Emotions in Life Satisfaction: A Preliminary Inquiry'. *PLOS One Journal*, 10 (8), 1–8.

3. The prime of life

1 Lachman, M. E. 2004. 'Development in midlife'. *Annual Review of Psychology*, 55 (1), 305–31.

2 Lachman, M. E. 2020. 'Midlife in the 2020s: Opportunities and challenges'. *American Psychologist*, 75 (4), 470–85.

3 McGinnis, D. 2018. 'Resilience, life events, and well-being during midlife: Examining resilience subgroups'. *Journal of Adult Development*, 25 (3), 198–221.

4 Tedeschi, R. G. & Calhoun, L. G. 2004. 'Posttraumatic growth: Conceptual foundations and empirical evidence'. *Psychological Inquiry*, 15 (1), 1–8; see also Gaffney, M. 2011. *Flourishing*. Dublin: Penguin Ireland, pp. 342–3.

5 Lachman, 'Development in midlife'.

6 Ibid.

7 Arnett, J. J. 2018. 'Happily stressed: The complexity of well-being in midlife'. *Journal of Adult Development*, 25 (4), 270–78.

8 Ryff, C. D. & Keyes, C. L. M. 1995. 'The structure of psychological well-being revisited'. *Journal of Personality and Social Psychology*, 69 (4), 719–27.

9 Montepare, J. M. 1996. 'Actual and subjective age-related differences in women's attitudes toward their bodies across the lifespan'. *Journal of Adult Development*, 3, 171–82.

10 See Matthews, K., Wing, R. R., Kuller, L. H., Meilahn, E. N., Kelsey, S. F., Costello, E. J. & Caggiula, A. W. 1990. 'Influences of Natural Menopause on Psychological Characteristics and Symptoms of Middle-

Aged Healthy Women'. *Journal of Consulting and Clinical Psychology*, 58 (3), 345–51.

11 Stewart, A. J., Ostrove, J. M. & Helson, R. 2001. 'Middle aging in women: Patterns of personality change from the 30s to the 50s'. *Journal of Adulthood Development*, 8 (1), 23–37.

12 See, for example, Mitchell, V. & Helson, R. 1990. 'Women's prime of life: is it in their 50s?' *Psychology of Women Quarterly*, 22 (4), 459–67.

13 See Jung, C. G. 1964. *Man and His Symbols*. New York, NY: Doubleday; Levinson, D. J. 1978. *The Seasons of a Man's Life*. New York, NY: Ballantine Books. I formulate the polarities not in Jungian or psychoanalytic terms but in a way that is more in tune with the larger body of research on human development.

14 See Edelstein, L. N. 1997. *Revitalising Erikson's Views On Women's Generativity*. Paper Presented at the Annual Meeting of the American Psychological Association, Chicago, Illinois.

15 See Shields, S. A. 2002. *Speaking from the Heart: Gender and the Social Meaning of Emotion*. Cambridge: Cambridge University Press; Brescoll, V. L. 2016. 'Leading with their hearts? How gender stereotypes of emotion lead to biased evaluations of female leaders'. *The Leadership Quarterly*, 27 (3), 415–28.

16 Gutmann, D. L. 1987. *Reclaimed Powers: Toward a New Psychology of Men and Women in Later Life*. New York, NY: Basic Books.

17 Gaffney, *Flourishing*, pp. 364–6.

4. Is this it?

1 Blanchflower, D. G. & Oswald, A. J. 2008. 'Is well-being U-shaped over the life-cycle?' *Social Science and Medicine*, 66 (8), 1733–49. This study gathered data from 2 million people in 80 countries.

2 Blanchflower, D. G. 2020. 'Is happiness U-shaped everywhere? Age and subjective well-being in 132 countries'. *NBER Working Paper No. 26641*.

3 See Lachman, M. E. 2004. 'Development in midlife'. *Annual Review of Psychology*, 55 (1), 305–31.

4 See Infurna, F. J., Gerstorf, D. & Lachman, M. E. 2020. 'Midlife in the 2020s: Opportunities and challenges'. *American Psychologist*, 75 (4), 470–85.

5 Neugarten, B. L. (ed). 1968. *Middle Age and Aging: A Reader in Social Psychology*. Chicago, IL: The University of Chicago Press.

6 Levinson, D. J. 1986. 'A conception of adult development'. *American Psychologist*, 41 (1), 3–13; Levinson, D. J. 1978. *The Seasons of a Man's Life*. New York, NY: Random House; Levinson, D. J. 1996. *The Seasons of a Woman's Life*. New York, NY: Alfred A. Knopf.

7 Taylor, S. E. & Brown, J. D. 1994. 'Positive illusions and well-being revisited: Separating fact from fiction'. *Psychological Bulletin*, 116 (1), 21–7.

8 Levinson, *The Seasons of a Man's Life*.

9 Capote, T. 1948. *Other Voices, Other Rooms*. New York, NY: Random House.

10 See McAdams, D. P. 2014. 'The life narrative at midlife'. In special issue: *Rereading Personal Narrative and the Life Course: New Directions for Child and Adolescent Development*, 145, 57–69.

11 McAdams, D. P., Reynolds, J., Lewis, M., Patten, A. H. & Bowman, P. J. 2001. 'When bad things turn good and good things turn bad: Sequences of redemption and contamination in life narrative and their relation to the psychosocial adaptation in midlife adults and in students'. *Personality and Social Psychology Bulletin*, 27 (4), 474–85.

12 See Freeman, M. 2010. *Hindsight: The Promise and Peril of Looking Backward*. New York, NY: Oxford University Press.

5. Infancy: *Finding someone to rely on*

1 See Hardin, R. 2002. *Trust & Trustworthiness*. New York: Russell Sage Foundation; Rotter, J. B. 1980. 'Interpersonal trust, trustworthiness, and gullibility'. *American Psychologist*, 35 (1), 1–7.

2 See Bowlby, J. 1969. *Attachment and Loss: Volume 1. Attachment*. New York, NY: Basic Books; Bowlby, J. 1973. *Attachment and Loss: Volume 2: Separation: Anxiety and Anger*. New York, NY: Basic Books.

3 See Schore, A .N. 2000. 'Attachment and the regulation of the right brain'. *Attachment and Human Development*, 2 (1), 23–47.

4 Chisholm, K. M, Carter, M. C., Ames, E. W. & Morison, S. J. 1995. 'Attachment security and indiscriminately friendly behavior in children adopted from Romanian orphanages'. *Development and Psychopathology*, 7 (2), 283–94.

5 Ainsworth, M. D. & Wittig, B. A. 1969. 'Attachment and exploratory behaviour of one-year-olds in a strange situation'. In B. M. Foss (ed). *Determinants of Infant Behaviour: Volume 4*. London: Methuen, pp. 113–36. The Strange Situation has become the most valid, reliable and widely used way to observe a young child's attachment, and Ainsworth's findings have been replicated in multiple countries for fifty years.

6 Based on cross-cultural studies of attachment in eight countries, including the USA, Europe, Africa and the Middle East. See van Ijzendoorn, M. H & Kroonenberg, P. M. 1988. 'Cross-cultural patterns of attachment: A meta-analysis of the strange situation'. *Child Development*, 59 (1), 147–56; van Ijzendoorn, M. H.,Goldberg, S., Kroonenberg, P. M. & Frenkel, O. J. 1992. 'The relative effects of maternal and child problems on the quality of attachment: a meta-analysis of attachment in clinical samples'. *Child Development*, 63 (4), 840–58. But it should be noted that the high percentage of *Secure* attachment is found in children whose families are reasonably economically and psychologically stable. In high-risk families who are suffering significant and chronic stress – poverty, severe parental conflict, alcohol or drug abuse, or other social and psychological problems – the proportion of securely attached children is lower and, correspondingly, the percentage of insecurely attached children increases. Note that studies of adult attachment use a variety of terms, including *Preoccupied*, *Anxious*, etc.

7 See Main, M. & Weston, D. R. 1981. 'The quality of the toddler's relationship to mother and father: Related to conflict behavior and the readiness to establish new relationships'. *Child Development*, 52 (3), 932–40.

8 Ainsworth, M. D., Bess, S. M. & Stayton, D. J. 1971. 'Individual differences in strange-situation behaviour of one-year-olds'. In H. R. Schaffer (ed). *The Origins of Human Social Relations*. New York, NY: Academic Press, pp. 17–58 (see p. 41).

9 See Main, M. 1990. 'Parental aversion to infant-initiated contact is correlated with the parent's own rejection during childhood'. In K. E. Barnard & T. B. Brazelton (eds). *Touch: The Foundation of Experience*. Madison, CT: International Universities Press Inc., pp. 461–97.

10 For a more detailed account of this process, see Gaffney, M. 2011. *Flourishing*. Dublin: Penguin Ireland, pp. 52–4.

11 Main, 'Parental aversion to infant-initiated contact'.

12 Field, T. 1981. 'Infant gaze aversion and heart rate during face-to-face interactions'. *Infant Behaviour and Development*, 4 (3), 307–15.

13 Hill-Soderlund, A. L., Mills-Koonce, W. R., Propper, C., Calkins, S. D., Granger, D. A., Moore, G. A., Gariepy, J. L. & Cox, M. J. 2008. 'Parasympathetic and sympathetic responses to *The Strange Situation* in infants and mothers from avoidant and securely attached dyads'. *Developmental Psychobiology*, 50 (4), 361–76.

6. Infancy: *Beneath the scar tissue*

1 See, for example, Thompson, R. A. 1999. 'Early attachment and later development'. In J. Cassidy & P. R. Shaver (eds). *Handbook of Attachment: Theory, Research, and Clinical Applications*. New York, NY: Guilford Press, pp. 287–319.

2 Coan, J. A. 2008. 'Toward a neuroscience of attachment'. In Cassidy & Shaver, *Handbook of Attachment*, pp. 241–65; Coan, J. A., Schaefer, H. S. & Davidson, R. J. 2006. 'Lending a hand: Social regulation of the neural response to threat'. *Psychological Science*, 17 (12), 1032–9.

3 Schore, A .N. 2000. 'Attachment and the regulation of the right brain'. *Attachment and Human Development*, 2 (1), 23–47.

4 Fredrickson, B. L. 2009. *Positivity*. New York, NY: Crown Publishers.

5 See Gaffney, M. 2011. *Flourishing*. Dublin: Penguin Ireland, pp. 49–52.

6 Bowlby, J. 1979. 'On knowing what you are not supposed to know and feeling what you are not supposed to feel'. *The Canadian Journal of Psychiatry*, 24 (5), 403–8.

7 Main, M., Kaplan, N. & Cassidy, J. 1985. 'Security in infancy, childhood, and adulthood: A move to the level of representation'. In J. Bretherton & R. Waters (eds). *Growing points of attachment theory and research. Monographs of the Society for Research in Child development*, 50 (1–2), Serial No. 209, pp. 66–104.

8 See Cohler, B. J. 1982. 'Personal narrative and the life course'. In P. B. Baltes & O. G. Brim (eds). *Life-Span Development and Behaviour: Volume 4*. New York, NY: Academic Press, pp. 205–41; McAdams, D. P. 2013. 'The psychological self as actor, agent, and author'. *Perspectives on Psychological Science*, 8 (3), 272–95.

9 See Covey, S. M. R. & Merrill, R. R. 2006. *The Speed of Trust: The One Thing that Changes Everything*. New York, NY: The Free Press; Hurley, R. F. 2006. 'The decision to trust'. *Harvard Business Review*, Sep, 55–62.

7. Early childhood: *Discovering your will*

1 Mahler, M. S., Pine, F. & Bergman, A. 1975. *The Psychological Birth of the Human Infant: Symbiosis and Individuation*. New York, NY: Basic Books; see also McAdams, D. P. 1990. 'Unity and purpose in human lives: The emergence of identity as the life story'. In A. I. Rabin, R. A. Zucker, R. A. Emmons & S. Frank (eds). *Studying Persons and Lives*. New York, NY: Springer, pp. 148–200.

2 Baumeister, R. F. 2005. 'Self and volition'. In William R. Miller and Harold D. Delaney (eds). *Judeo-Christian Perspectives on Psychology: Human Nature, Motivation, and Change*. Washington, DC: American Psychological Association, pp. 57–72.

3 Rothbaum, F., Weisz, J. R. & Snyder, S. S. 1982. 'Changing the world and changing the self: A two-process model of perceived control'. *Journal of Personality and Social Psychology*, 42 (1), 5–37.

4 Heckhausen, J., Wrosch, C. & Schultz, R. 2010. 'A motivational theory of life-span development'. *Psychological Review*, 117 (1), 32–60.

5 See Eisenberg, N., Cumberland, S. & Spinrad, T. L. 1998. 'Parental socialisation of emotion'. *Psychological Inquiry*, 9 (4), 241–73.

6 Jack, D. C. 1991. *Silencing the Self: Women and Depression*. Cambridge, MA: Harvard University Press.

7 See Ryan, R. M. & Deci, E. L. 2006. 'Self-regulation and the problem of human autonomy: Does psychology need choice, self-determination, and will?' *Journal of Personality*, 74 (6), 1557–85; Cerasoli, C. P., Nicklin, J. M. & Ford, M. T. 2014. 'Intrinsic motivation and external incentives jointly predict performance: A 40-year meta-analysis'. *Psychological Bulletin*, 140 (4), 980–1008.

8 Gershoff, E. T., Lansford, J. E., Zelli, A., Dodge, K. A., Grogan-Kaylor, A., Chang, L. & Deater-Deckard, K. 2010. 'Parent discipline practices in an international sample: Associations with child behaviors and moderation by perceived normativeness'. *Child Development*, 81 (2), 487–502.

9 The kind of negative effect of incentives on intrinsic motivation has been replicated across a wide range of activities, not just in childhood, but right across the entire life course. See Deci, E. L. & Ryan, R. M. 2008. 'Facilitating optimal motivation and psychological well-being across life's domains'. *Canadian Psychology*, 49 (1), 14–23.

10 Grolnick, W. S., Gurland, S. T., DeCiurcey, W. & Jacob, K. 2002. 'Antecedents and consequences of mothers' autonomy support: An experimental investigation.' *Developmental Psychology*, 38 (1), 143–55

11 Ibid.

8. Early childhood: *The gift of autonomy*

1 Tamis-LeMonda, C. S., Shannon, J. D., Cabrera, N. J. & Lamb, M. E. 2004. 'Fathers and mothers at play with their 2- and 3-year-olds: Contributions to language and cognitive development'. *Child Development*, 75 (6), 1806–20.

2 See Gaffney, M. 2011. *Flourishing*. Dublin: Penguin Ireland, pp. 219–24.

3 See Berzonsky, M. D. 1990. 'Self-construction over the lifespan: A process perspective on identity formation'. In G. J. Neimeyer & R. A Neimeyer (eds). *Advances in Personal Construct Theory: Volume 1*. Greenwich, CT: JAI, pp. 155–86.

4 See Deci, E. L. & Ryan, R. M. 2008. 'Self-determination theory: A macrotheory of human motivation, development, and health'. *Canadian Psychology*, 49 (3), 182–5; Deci, E. L. & Ryan, R. M. 2000. 'The "what" and "why" of goal pursuits: Human needs and the self-determinations of behavior'. *Psychological Inquiry*, 11 (4), 227–68; Ryan, R. M. & Deci, E. L. 2000. 'Self-determination theory and the facilitation of intrinsic motivation, social development, and well-being'. *American Psychologist*, 55 (1), 68–78; Ryan, R. M. & Deci, E. L. 2006. 'Self-regulation and the problem of human autonomy: Does psychology need choice, self-determination, and will?' *Journal of Personality*, 74 (6), 1557–85, p. 1569.

5 See Bartholomew, K. J., Ntoumanis, N., Ryan, R. M. & Thøgersen-Ntoumani, C. 2011. 'Psychological need thwarting in the sport context: Assessing the darker side of athletic experience'. *Journal of Sport & Exercise Psychology*, 33 (1), 75–102.

6 Lieberman, M. A. 1973. *Encounter Groups: First Facts*. New York, NY: Basic Books.

7 Frankl, V. E. 1959/2006. *Man's Search for Meaning*. Boston, MA: Beacon Press, p. 66.

8 Jeffers S. J. 1987/2007. *Feel the Fear and Do it Anyway*. New York, NY: Ballantine Books.

9 See Mikulincer, M. & Shaver, P. R. 2007. *Attachment in Adulthood: Structure, Dynamics, and Change*. New York, NY: Guilford Press, pp. 229–30.

9. Middle childhood: *Joining the company of children*

1 Erikson, E. H. 1968. *Identity, Youth and Crisis*. New York, NY: W. W. Norton & Co, p. 122.

2 Erikson, E. H. 1951. *Childhood and Society*. London: Imago Publishing Co.

3 Harris, J. R. 1999. *The Nurture Assumption: Why Children Turn Out the Way You Do*. London: Bloomsbury Publishing.

4 See Newcomb, A. F. & Bagwell, C. L. 1995. 'Children's friendship relations: A meta-analytic review'. *Psychological Bulletin*, 117 (2), 306–47; Hartrup, W.W. 1996. 'The company you keep: Friendships and your developmental significance'. *Child Development*, 67 (1), 1–13; Rubin, K. H., Bukowski, W. & Bowker, J. 2015. 'Children in peer groups'. In M. Bornstein & T. Leventhal (volume eds) and R. M. Lerner (series ed). *Handbook of Child Psychology and Developmental Science: Seventh Edition, Volume Four: Ecological Settings and Processes*. Bridgewater, NJ: Wiley, pp. 175–222.

5 See Holtgraves, T. 1986. 'Language structure in social interaction: Perceptions of direct and indirect speech acts and interactants who use them'. *Journal of Personality and Social Psychology*, 51 (2), 305–14.

6 Gaffney, M. 2011. *Flourishing*. Dublin: Penguin Ireland, pp. 41–3.

7 Hartrup, 'The company you keep', p. 4.

8 Tajfel, H. 1970. 'Experiments in intergroup discrimination'. *Scientific American*, 223, 96–102.

9 This is the term used by Judith Harris in *The Nurture Assumption* for what social scientists refer to as a 'social category' – a group of people bound together by certain common characteristics.

10 Jacklin, C. N. & Maccoby, E. E. 1978. 'Social behavior at 33 months in same-sex and mixed-sex dyads'. *Child Development*, 49 (3), 557–69; Maccoby, E. E. 1988. 'Gender as a social category'. *Developmental Psychology*, 24 (6), 755–65.

11 Martin, C. L. & Fabes, R. A. 2001. 'The stability and consequences of young children's same-sex peer interactions'. *Developmental Psychology*, 37 (3), 431–46.

12 See Maccoby, E. E. 1998. *The Two Sexes: Growing Up Apart, Coming Together.* Cambridge, MA: Belknap Press. Maccoby, E. E. & Jacklin, C. N. 1974. *The Psychology of Sex Differences.* Stanford, CA: Stanford University Press.

13 See Fabes, R. A., Martin, C. L., Hanish, L. D., Anders, M. C. & Madden-Derdich, D. A. 'Early school competence: The roles of sex-segregated play and effortful control'. *Developmental Psychology*, 39 (5), 848–58.

14 Charlesworth, W. R. & Dzur, C. 1987. 'Gender comparisons of pre-schoolers' behavior and resource utilization in group problem-solving'. *Child Development*, 58 (1), 191–200.

15 See, for example, Maccoby, 'Gender as a social category'.

16 See Endendijk, J. J., Groeneveld, M. G., van der Pol, L. D., van Berkel, S.R., Hallers-Haalboom, E. T., Bakermans-Kranenburg, M. J. & Mesman, J. 2017. 'Child Aggression: Relations with gender-differentiated parenting and parents' gender-role stereotypes'. *Child Development*, 88 (1), 299–316.

17 Ibid.

18 See Bohnet, I. 2016. *What Works: Gender Equality by Design.* Cambridge, MA: Belknap Press; Bowles, H. R. 2013. 'Psychological perspectives on gender and negotiation'. In M. K. Ryan & N. R. Branscombe (eds). *The Sage Handbook of Gender and Psychology.* London: SAGE Publications, pp. 465–83.

19 Apicella, C. A., Demiral, E. F. & Mollerstom, J. 2017. 'No Gender Difference in Willingness to Compete When Competing against Self'. *American Economic Review*, 107 (5), 136–40.

20 Charlesworth & Dzur, 'Gender comparisons of preschoolers' behavior'; see also Jacklin & Maccoby, 'Social behavior at 33 months'.

21 See Nangle, D. W., Erdley, C. A., Newman, J. E, Mason, C. A. & Carpenter, E. M. 2013. 'Popularity, friendship quantity, and friendship quality:

Interactive influences on children's loneliness and depression'. *Journal of Clinical and Adolescent Psychology*, 32 (4), 546–55; Peters, E., Riksen-Walraven, J., Cillessen, A. H. N. & de Weerth, C. 2011. 'Peer rejection and HPA activity in middle childhood: Friendship makes a difference'. *Child Development*, 82 (6), 1906–20.

10. Middle childhood: *Stocking up for the road ahead*

1 Bronfenbrenner, U. 1979. *The Ecology of Human Development*. Cambridge, MA: Harvard University Press, p. 262.

2 Gottman, J. M., Fainsilber Katz, L. & Hooven, C. 1996. 'Parental meta-emotion philosophy and the emotional life of families: Theoretical models and preliminary data'. *Journal of Family Psychology*, 10 (3), 243–68.

3 See McElwain, N. L., Halberstadt, A. G. & Volling, B. L. 2007. 'Mother-and father-reported reactions to children's negative emotions: Relations to young children's emotional understanding and friendship quality'. *Child Development*, 78 (5), 1407–25.

4 Ibid.

5 See Hallowell, E. H. 1994/2011. *Driven to Distraction*. New York, NY: Pantheon Books; Hallowell calls it ADT. See also Gaffney, M. 2011. *Flourishing*. Dublin: Penguin Ireland, for extended discussion.

6 Arcos-Burgos, M. & Acosta, M. T. 2007. 'Tuning major gene variants conditioning human behaviour: The anachronism of ADHD'. *Current Opinion in Genetics and Development*, 17 (3), 234–8; Chen, C. S., Burton, M., Greenberger, E. & Dmitrieva, J. 1999. 'Population migration and the variation of dopamine D4 receptor (DRD4) allele frequencies around the globe'. *Evolution and Human Behavior*, 20, 309–24; Glickman, M. M. & Dodd, D. K. 1998. 'GUTI: A measure of urgent task involvement among adults with attention-deficit hyperactivity disorder'. *Psychological Reports*, 82 (2), 592–4; Ewen Callaway, 'Did hyperactivity evolve as a survival aid for nomads?' *New Scientist*, 10 June 2008.

7 See McElwain, N. L., Booth-LaForce, C., Lansford, J. E., Wu, X. & Dyer, J. W. 2008. 'A process model of attachment–friend linkages: Hostile attribution biases, language ability, and mother–child affective mutuality as intervening mechanisms'. *Child Development*, 79 (6), 1891–1906; see also

Groh, A. M., Fearon, R. P., Bakersmans-Kranenburg, M. J., Van IJzendoorn, M. H., Steele, R. D. & Roisman, G. I. 2014. 'The significance of
attachment security for children's social competence with peers: A meta-
analytic study'. *Attachment and Human Development*, 16 (2), 103–6.

8 See Schneider, B. H., Atkinson, L. & Tardif, C. 2001. 'Parent–child
attachment and children's peer relations: A quantitative review'. *Developmental Psychology*, 37 (1), 86–100.

9 See McElwain et al, 'A process model of attachment–friend linkages'.

10 See Denham, S. A., Blair, K. A., DeMulder, J. L., Sawyer, K., Auerbach-
Major, S. & Queenan, P. 2003. 'Preschool competence: Pathway to
social competence?' *Child Development*, 74 (1), 238–56.

11 Ibid.

12 Van Lange, P. A. M., Ouwerkerk, J. W. & Tazelaar, M. J. A. 2002. 'How
to overcome the detrimental effects of noise in social interaction'. *Journal of Personality and Social Psychology*, 82 (5), 768–80.

11. Adolescence: *Figuring out the person you are becoming*

1 Erikson, E. H. 1968. *Identity, Youth and Crisis*. New York, NY: W. W.
Norton & Co; Blos, P. 1962. *On Adolescence: A Psychoanalytic Interpretation*. New York, NY: The Free Press; Marcia, J. E. 1980. 'Identity in
adolescence'. In J. Adelson (ed). *Handbook of Adolescent Psychology*. New
York, NY: Wiley, pp. 154–87; McCrae, R. R. & Costa, P.T. 1990. *Personality in Adulthood*. New York, NY: Guilford Press.

2 Blos, P. 1962. *On Adolescence: A Psychoanalytic Interpretation*. New York,
NY: The Free Press.

3 Becht, A. I., Bos, M. G. N., Nelemans, S. A., Peters, S., Vollebergh,
W. A. M., Branje, S. J. T., Meeus, W. H. J. & Crone, E. A. 2018. 'Goal-
directed correlates and neurobiological underpinnings of adolescent
identity: A multimethod multisample longitudinal approach'. *Child
Development*, 89 (3), 823–36.

4 See McAdams, D. P. 1996. 'Personality, modernity, and the storied self:
A contemporary framework for understanding persons'. *Psychological
Enquiry*, 7 (4), 295–321: Pasupathi, M. & Hoyt, T. 2009. 'The develop-
ment of narrative identity in late adolescence and emergent adulthood:

The continued importance of listeners'. *Developmental Psychology*, 45 (2), 558–74.

5 Habermas, T. & Hatiboglu, N. 2014. 'Contextualising the self: The emergence of a biographical understanding in adolescence'. In B. Schiff (ed). *Rereading Personal Narrative and Life Course: New Directions for Child and Adolescent Development*. San Francisco, CA: Jossey-Bass, pp. 29–41.

6 Csikszentmihaly, M. & Larson, R. 1984. *Being Adolescent: Conflict and Growth in the Teenage Years*. New York, NY: Basic Books.

7 Ibid.

8 Ibid.

9 Gilligan, C., Lyons, N. O. & Hammer, T. J. 1990. *Making Connections: The Relational World of Adolescent Girls at Emma Willard School*. Cambridge, MA: Harvard University Press, p. 10.

10 Ibid.

11 See Helwig, N. E. & Ruprecht, M. R. 2017. 'Age, gender, and self-esteem: A sociocultural look through a non-parametric lens'. *Archives of Scientific Psychology*, 5 (1), 19–31.

12 See Jack, D. C. & Ali, A. 2010. 'Culture, self-silencing, and depression: A contextual-relational perspective'. In D. C. Jack & A. Ali (eds). *Silencing the Self Across Cultures: Depression and Gender in the Social World*. New York, NY: Oxford University Press.

13 Rose, A. J. 2002. 'Co-rumination in the friendships of girls and boys'. *Child Development*, 73 (6), 1830–43.

14 Way, N., Cressen, J., Bodian, S., Preston, J., Nelson, J. & Hughes, D. 2014. ' "It might be nice to be a girl . . . then you wouldn't have to be emotionless": Boys' resistance to norms of masculinity during adolescence'. *Psychology of Men and Masculinity*, 15 (3), 241–52.

15 Csikszentmihaly & Larson, *Being Adolescent*.

12. Adolescence: *A time of emotional crossover*

1 Allen, J. P. & Miga, E. M. 2010. 'Attachment in adolescence: A move to the level of emotion regulation'. *Journal of Social and Personal Relationships*, 27 (2), 181–90.

2 As children enter childhood, researchers use a variety of ways to assess attachment, including how a child reacts to stories of separation from parents. See Gaffney, M. 2000. *Attachment at the Transition to Adolescence: Concordance with Concurrent Maternal Attachment and the Child's Own Attachment in Infancy.* Unpublished manuscript, Trinity College Dublin.

3 See Mikulincer, M., & Shaver, P. R. 2007. *Attachment in Adulthood: Structure, Dynamics, and Change.* New York, NY: Guilford Press, p. 237.

4 This process was described in Chapter 7. See Deci, E. L. & Ryan, R. M. 2008. 'Facilitating optimal motivation and psychological well-being across life's domains'. *Canadian Psychology*, 49 (1), 14–23.

5 Fredrickson, B. L. 2009. *Positivity.* New York, NY: Crown Publishers.

6 See Feeney, B. C. & Cassidy, J. 2003. 'Reconstructed memory related to adolescent–parent conflict interactions: The influence of attachment-related representations on immediate perceptions and changes in perceptions over time'. *Journal of Personality and Social Psychology*, 85 (5), 945–55.

7 See, for example, Kobak, R., Cole, H. E., Ferenz-Gillies, R., Fleming, W. S. & Gamble, S. 1993. 'Attachment and emotional regulation during mother–teen problem solving: A control theory analysis'. *Child Development*, 64 (1), 231–45.

8 See Deci & Ryan, 'Facilitating optimal motivation'.

9 See Weinfield, N. S., Sroufe, L. & Egeland, B. 2000. 'Attachment from infancy to early adulthood in a high-risk sample: Continuity, discontinuity, and their correlates'. *Child Development*, 71 (3), 695–702.

10 Csikszentmihaly, M. & Larson, R. 1984. *Being Adolescent: Conflict and Growth in the Teenage Years.* New York, NY: Basic Books.

11 Van Petegem, S., Beyers, W., Vansteenkiste, M. & Soenens, B. 'On the association between adolescent autonomy and psychosocial functioning: Examining decisional independence from a self-determination theory'. *Developmental Psychology*, 48 (1), 76–88; Oudekerk, B. A., Allen, J. P., Hessel, E. T. & Molloy, L. E. 2015. 'The cascading development of autonomy and relatedness from adolescence to adulthood'. *Child Development*, 86 (2), 472–85.

12 Allen, J. P., McElhaney, K. B., Kuperminc, G. P. & Jodl, K. M. 2004. 'Stability and change in attachment security across adolescence'. *Child Development*, 75 (6), 1792–1805.

13 See Campione-Barr, N. & Smetana, J. G. 2010. ' "Who said you could wear my sweater?" Adolescent siblings' conflicts and associations with relationship quality'. *Child Development*, 81 (2), 464–71; Recchia, H., Waintryb, C. & Pasupathis, M. 2013. ' "Two for flinching": Children's and adolescents' narrative accounts of harming their friends and siblings'. *Child Development*, 84 (4), 1459–74.

14 Fortuna, K., Roisman, G. I., Haydon, K. C. & Groh, A. M. 2011. 'Attachment states of mind and the quality of young adults' sibling relationships'. *Developmental Psychology*, 47 (5), 1366–73.

15 See Mancillas, A. 2006. 'Challenging the stereotypes about only children: A review of the literature and implications for practice'. *Journal of Counseling and Development*, 84 (3), 268–75.

16 See Jellison, W. A. & McConnell, A. R. 2003. 'The mediating effects of attitudes towards homosexuality between secure attachment and disclosure outcomes among gay men'. *Journal of Homosexuality*, 46 (1), 159–77.

17 Senge, P. M. 1990/1997. *The Fifth Discipline: The Art And Practice Of The Learning Organisation*. London: Century Business.

18 Christensen, C. M., Allworth, J. & Dillon, K. 2012. *How Will You Measure Your Life?* New York, NY: HarperCollins.

19 See Kroger, J., Martinussen, M. & Marica, J. E. 2010. 'Identity status change during adolescence and young adulthood: A meta-analysis'. *Journal of Adolescence*, 33 (5), 683–98.

13. Emerging adulthood: *A taste of freedom*

1 Arnett, J. J. 2000. 'Emerging Adulthood: A theory of development from the late teens through the twenties'. *American Psychologist*, 55 (5), 469–80.

2 See Arnett, J. & Schwab, J. 2014. *Clark University Poll of Established Adults: Becoming Established Adults: Busy, Joyful, Stressed – and Still Dreaming Big*. Worcester, MA: Clark University.

3 Marcia, J. E. 2002. 'Identity and psychosocial development in adulthood'. *Identity: An international Journal of Theory and Research*, 2, 7–28; Beaumont, S. L. & Pratt, M. M. 2011. 'Identity processing styles and psychosocial balance during early and middle adulthood: The role of

identity in intimacy and generativity'. *Journal of Adult Development*, 18 (4), 172–83.

4 Conway, M. A. & Holmes, A. 2004. 'Psychosocial stages and the accessibility of autobiographical memories across the life cycle'. *Journal of Personality*, 72 (3), 461–80.

5 See Myers, D. G. 2000. 'The funds, friends, and faith of happy people'. *American Psychologist*, 55 (1), 56–67.

6 See Berzonsky, M. D. & Sullivan, C. 1992. 'Social cognitive aspects of identity style: Need for cognition, experiential openness, and introspection'. *Journal of Adolescent Research*, 7 (2), 140–55; Beaumont & Pratt, 'Identity processing styles and psychosocial balance'.

7 Buhrmester, D., Furman, W., Wittenberg, M. T. & Reis, H. T. 1988. 'Five domains of interpersonal competence in peer relationships'. *Journal of Personality and Social Psychology*, 55 (6), 991–1008.

8 Solano, C. H., Batten, P. G. & Parish, E. A. 1982. 'Loneliness and patterns of self-disclosure'. *Journal of Personality and Social Psychology*, 43 (3), 524–31.

9 See Baccus, J. R., Baldwin, M. W. & Packer, D. J. 2004. 'Increasing implicit self-esteem through classic conditioning'. *Psychological Science*, 15 (7), 498–502.

10 Fredrickson, B & Losada, M. 2005. 'Positive affect and the complex dynamics of human flourishing'. *American Psychologist*, 60 (7), 678–86; Gaffney, M. 2011. *Flourishing*. Dublin: Penguin Ireland.

11 See Mikulincer, M. & Shaver, P. R. 2007. *Attachment in Adulthood: Structure, Dynamics, and Change*. New York, NY: Guilford Press, pp. 219–48 ('Attachment orientation, self-regulation, and personal growth').

12 See Avihou, N. 2006. 'Attachment orientations and dreaming: An examination of the unconscious components of the attachment system'. Unpublished doctoral dissertation, Bar-Ilan University, Israel. Cited in Mikulincer & Shaver, ibid.

13 See Mikulincer, M., Gilliat, O. & Shaver, P. R. 2002. 'Activation of the attachment system in adulthood: Threat-related prompts increase accessibility of mental representations of attachment figures'. *Journal of Personality and Social Psychology*, 83 (4), 881–95.

14 Kim, Y. 2006. 'Gender, attachment, and relationship duration on cardiovascular reactivity to stress in a laboratory study of dating couples'. *Personal Relationships*, 13 (1), 103–14.

15 Alexander, F. & French, T. M. 1946. *Psychoanalytic Therapy*. New York, NY: Ronald Press, p. 294.

16 Shaver, P. R. & Mikulincer, M. 2002. 'Attachment-related psychodynamics'. *Attachment and Human Development*, 4 (2), 133–61.

17 Fraley, R. C. & Shaver, P. R. 1998. 'Airport separations: A naturalistic study of adult attachment dynamics in separating couples'. *Journal of Personality and Social Psychology*, 75 (5), 1198–1212.

18 See Mikulincer, M., Birbaum, G., Waddis, D. & Nachimias, O. 2000. 'Stress and accessibility of proximity-related thoughts: Explaining the normative and intraindividual components of attachment theory'. *Journal of Personality and Social Psychology*, 78 (3), 509–23; Mikulincer et al, 'Activation of the attachment system in adulthood'; see also Mikulincer & Shaver, 'Attachment orientation, self-regulation, and personal growth'.

14. Emerging adulthood: *The mating season*

1 Graham, J. M. 2011. 'Measuring love in romantic relationships: A meta-analysis'. *Journal of Social and Personal Relationships*, 28 (6), 748–71.

2 Hazan, C. & Shaver, P. R. 1987. 'Romantic love conceptualized as an attachment process'. *Journal of Personality and Social Psychology*, 5 (3), 511–24.

3 See Mikulincer, M. 1998. 'Attachment working models and the sense of trust: An exploration of interaction goals and affect regulation'. *Journal of Personality and Social Psychology*, 74 (5), 1209–24.

4 Kaitz, M., Bar-Haim, Y., Lehrer, M. & Grossman, E. 2004. 'Adult attachment style and interpersonal distance'. *Attachment and Human Development*, 6 (3), 285–304.

5 Hazan & Shaver, 'Romantic love'.

6 For a review of studies in this area see Mikulincer, M. & Shaver, P. R. 2007. *Attachment in Adulthood: Structure, Dynamics, and Change*. New York, NY: Guilford Press.

7 Bartholomew, K. & Horowitz, L. M. 1991. 'Attachment style among young adults: A test of a four-category model'. *Journal of Personality and Social Psychology*, 61 (2), 226–44.

8 See Brumbaugh, C. C., Baren, A. & Agishtein, P. 2014. 'Attraction to attachment insecurity: Flattery, appearance, and status's role in mate preferences'. *Personal Relationships*, 21 (2), 288–308.

9 Haydon, K. C. 2015. 'Relational contexts of women's stress and competence during the transition to adulthood'. *Journal of Adult Development*, 22 (2), 112–23.

10 Csikszentmihalyi, M. 1992. *Flow: The Psychology of Happiness*. London: Rider.

11 For a more detailed discussion of being at your best, see Gaffney, M. 2011. *Flourishing*. Dublin: Penguin Ireland.

12 See Hallett, M. G. & Hoffman, B. 2014. 'Performance under pressure: Cultivating the peak performance mindset for workplace excellence'. *Consulting Psychology Journal: Practice and Research*, 66 (3), 212–30.

13 Ibid.

14 Carver, C. S., Scheier, M. F. & Weintraub, J. K. 1989. 'Assessing coping strategies: A theoretically based approach'. *Journal of Personality and Social Psychology*, 56 (2), 267–83.

15. Young adulthood: *The rush hour of your life*

1 See Putnam, R. D., Feldstein, L. M. & Cohen, D. 2001. *Bowling Alone: The Collapse and Revival of American Community*. New York, NY: Touchstone.

2 Galambo, N. L., Lachman, M. E., Fang, S., Krahn, H. J. & Johnson, M. D. 2015. 'Up, not down: The curve in happiness from early adulthood to midlife in two longitudinal studies'. *Developmental Psychology*, 51 (11), 1664–71.

3 See Arnett, J. & Schwab, J. 2014. *Clark University Poll of Established Adults: Becoming Established Adults: Busy, Joyful, Stressed – and Still Dreaming Big*. Worcester, MA: Clark University.

4 Erikson, E. H. 1980. *Identity and the Life Cycle*. New York, NY: Norton, p. 102.

5 Register, L. M. & Henley, T. B. 1992. 'The phenomenology of intimacy'. *Journal of Social and Personal Relationships*, 9 (4), 467–81.

6 Rilke, R. M. 1929. *Letters to a Young Poet*. Leipzig: Insel Verlag.

7 Winnicott, D. W. 1958. 'The capacity to be alone'. *The International Journal of Psychoanalysis*, 39 (5), 416–20.

8 Cherlin, A. J. 2004. 'The deinstitutionalization of American marriage'. *Journal of Marriage and Family*, 66 (4), 848–61.

9 Kurdek, L. A. 2004. 'Are gay and lesbian cohabiting couples really different from heterosexual married couples?' *Journal of Marriage and Family*, 66, 880–900; Ellis, L. & Davis, M. 2017. 'Intimate partner support: A comparison of gay, lesbian, and heterosexual relationships'. *Personal Relationships*, 24 (2), 350–69.

10 See Finkel, E. J., Cheung, E. O., Emery, L. F., Carswell, K. L. & Larson, G. M. 2015. 'The suffocation model: Why marriage in America is becoming an all-or-nothing institution'. *Current Directions in Psychological Science*, 24 (3), 238–44.

11 Ibid.

12 See Schulte, B. 2014. *Overwhelmed: Work, Love, and Play When No One Has the Time*. London: Macmillan.

13 See Elliott, S. & Umberson, D. 2008. 'The performance of desire: gender and sexual negotiation in long-term marriages'. *Journal of Marriage and Family*, 70 (2), 391–406.

16. Young adulthood: *When two attachment styles merge*

1 See Davila, J., Karney, B. R. & Bradbury, T. N. 1999. 'Attachment change processes during the early years of marriage'. *Journal of Personality and Social Psychology*, 76 (5), 783–802; see also Simpson, J. A., Rholes, W. S., Campbell, L. & Wilson, C. L. 2003. 'Changes in attachment orientations across the transitions to parenthood'. *Journal of Experimental Social Psychology*, 39 (4), 317–31.

2 Zayas, V. & Shoda, Y. 2005. 'Do automatic reactions elicited by thoughts of romantic partner, mother, and self relate to adult romantic attachments?' *Personality and Social Psychology Bulletin*, 31 (8), 1011–25.

3 Mikulincer, M. & Arad, D. 1999. 'Attachment working models and cognitive openness in close relationships: A test of chronic and temporary accessibility effects'. *Journal of Personality and Social Psychology*, 77 (4), 710–25.

4 See Guerroro, L. K. 1996. 'Attachment-style differences in intimacy and involvement: A test of the four-category model'. *Communication Monographs*, 63 (4), 269–92.

5 See Davis, D., Shaver, P. R., Widaman, K. F., Vernon, M. L., Follette, W. C. & Beitz, K. 2006. '"I can't get no satisfaction": Insecure attachment, inhibited sexual communication, and sexual dissatisfaction'. *Personal Relationships*, 13 (4), 465–83.

6 Mikulincer, M. 1998. 'Adult attachment style and individual differences in functional versus dysfunctional experiences of anger'. *Journal of Personality and Social Psychology*, 74 (2), 513–24.

7 Bowlby, J. 1973. *Attachment and Loss: Volume 2: Separation: Anxiety and Anger*. New York, NY: Basic Books.

8 Sonnby-Borgstrom, M. & Jonsson, P. 2004. 'Dismissing-avoidant pattern of attachment and mimicry reactions at different levels of information processing'. *Scandinavian Journal of Psychology*, 45 (2), 103–13. Cited in Mikulincer, M. & Shaver, P. R. 2007. *Attachment in Adulthood: Structure, Dynamics, and Change*. New York, NY: Guilford Press, p. 216.

9 See Adam, E. K., Gunar, M. R. & Tanaka, A. 2004. 'Adult attachment, parent emotion, and observed parenting behavior: Mediator and moderator models'. *Child Development*, 75 (1), 110–22.

10 Simpson, J. A. & Rholes, W. S. 2004. 'Anxious attachment and depressive symptoms: An interpersonal perspective'. In W. S. Rholes & J. A. Simpson (eds). *Adult Attachment: Theory, Research, and Clinical Applications*. New York, NY: Guilford Press, pp. 408–37.

11 Fillo, J., Simpson, J. A., Rholes, W. S. & Kohn, J. L. 2015. 'Dads doing diapers: Individual and relational outcomes associated with the division of childcare across the transition to parenthood'. *Journal of Personality and Social Psychology*, 108 (2), 208–316.

12 See Mikulincer, M., Gilliat, O. & Shaver, P. R. 2002. 'Activation of the attachment system in adulthood: Threat-related prompts increase accessibility of mental representations of attachment figures'. *Journal of Personality and Social Psychology*, 83 (4), 881–95.

13 See Berant, E., Mikulincer, M. & Florian, V. 2001. 'Attachment style and mental health: A 1-year follow up study of mothers of infants with congenital heart disease'. *Personality and Social Psychology Bulletin*, 27 (8), 956–68.

14 See Kim, Y. 2006. 'Gender, attachment, and relationship duration on cardiovascular reactivity to stress in a laboratory study of dating couples', *Personal Relationships*, 13 (1), 103–14.

15 Many of the actions described here are based on John Gottman's meticulous observations of how couples function. See Gottman, J. M. 1998. 'Psychology and the study of marital processes'. *Annual Review of Psychology*, 49, 169–97.

16 Rempel, J. K., Ross, M. & Holmes, J. G. 2001. 'Trust and communicated attributions in close relationships'. *Journal of Personality and Social Psychology*, 81 (1), 57–64.

17 Finkel, E. J., Ming Hui, C., Carswell, K. L. & Larson, G. M. 2014. 'The suffocation of marriage: Climbing Mount Maslow without enough oxygen'. *Psychological Enquiry*, 25 (1), 1–41, p. 34.

18 See Finkel, E. J., Slotter, E. B., Luchies, L. B., Walton, G. M. & Gross, J. J. 2013. 'A brief intervention to promote conflict-reappraisal preserves marital quality over time'. *Psychological Science*, 24 (8), 1595–1601.

19 See Finkel et al, 'The suffocation of marriage', p. 14.

20 Freud, S. 1909/1957. 'Analysis of a Phobia in a Five-Year-Old Boy'. *The Standard Edition of the Complete Psychological Works of Sigmund Freud, Volume X: Two Case Histories* ('Little Hans' and the 'Rat Man'). London: Hogarth Press, pp. 1–150.

17. Young adulthood: *The world of work*

1 See Anderson, H. J., Baur, J. E., Griffith, J. A. & Buckley, M. R. 2017. 'What works for you may not work for (Gen)Me: Limitations of present leadership theories for the new generation'. *The Leadership Quarterly*, 28 (1), 245–60.

2 Bernstein, E. S. & Turban, S. 2018. 'The impact of the "open" workspace on human collaboration'. *Royal Society Philosophical Transactions B*, 8, 1–8.

3 See Mark, G., Gudith, D. & Klocke, U. 2008. 'The cost of interrupted work: More speed and stress'. *Proceedings of the ACM Group Conference on Computer-Supported Cooperative Work and Social Computing*; Mark, G., Gonzalez, V. M. and Harris, J. 2005. 'No Task Left Behind? Examining

the Nature of Fragmented Work'. *CHI Conference Papers: Take a Number, Stand in Line (Interruptions & Attention 1)*.

4 See 'Maternity and paternity leave in the EU: At a glance'. https://www.europarl.europa.eu/RegData/etudes/ATAG/2016/593543/EPRS_ATA(2016)593543_EN.pdf (accessed April 2021).

5 Greenhaus, J. H. & Powell, G. N. 2006. 'When work and family are allies: A theory of work–family enrichment'. *Academy of Management Review*, 31 (1), 72–92.

6 Cross, R., Rebele, R. & Grant, A. 2016. 'Collaborative overload'. *Harvard Business Review*, Jan–Feb, 75–9.

7 See Charles Duhigg, 'What Google Learned From Its Quest to Build the Perfect Team'. *New York Times*. 25 February 2016.

8 Edmondson, A. C. 2003. 'Managing the risk of learning: Psychological safety in work teams'. In M. A. West, D. Tjosvold & K. G. Smith (eds), *International Handbook of Organizational Teamwork and Cooperative Working*. Chichester: John Wiley & Sons Ltd, pp. 255–76.

9 Balliet, D. & Van Lange, P. A. M. 2013. 'Trust, conflict, and cooperation: A meta-analysis'. *Psychological Bulletin*, 139 (5), 1090–1112. See also Duhigg, 'What Google Learned'.

10 Yu, D., Harter, J. & Agrawal, S. 2015. 'U.S. Managers Boast Best Work Engagement'. Gallup Inc. https://news.gallup.com/poll/162062/managers-boast-best-work (accessed April 2021). Low levels of work engagement vary by type of job. For example, managers, executives, and officials are the most engaged (36 per cent). Next come other professionals like nurses (33 per cent), teachers (31 per cent); office and construction workers (30 per cent); sales and service workers (29 per cent); transportation and manufacturing workers (between 25 and 24 per cent). The Gallup findings are based on data from the USA, but low levels of engagement have been identified as a widespread problem in other countries.

11 See Deci, E. L. & Ryan, R. M. 2000. 'The "what" and "why" of goal pursuits: Human needs and the self-determinations of behavior'. *Psychological Inquiry*, 11 (4), 227–68; Ryan, R. M. & Deci, E. L. 2000. 'Self-determination theory and the facilitation of intrinsic motivation, social development, and well-being'. *American Psychologist*, 55 (1), 68–78; Ryan, R. M. & Deci, E. L. 2006. 'Self-regulation and the problem of human autonomy: Does psychology need choice, self-determination, and will?' *Journal of Personal-*

ity, 74 (6), 1557–85, p. 1569; for examples of the specific problems incentives have created, and how some organizations are introducing more autonomy at work, see Pink, D. H. 2009. *Drive: The Surprising Truth About What Motivates People*. New York, NY: Riverhead Books; Deci, E. L. & Ryan, R. M. 2008. 'Facilitating optimal motivation and psychological well-being across life's domains'. *Canadian Psychology*, 49 (1), 14–23; see Gaffney, M. 2011. *Flourishing*. Dublin: Penguin Ireland, pp. 144–7.

12 See Chirkov, V., Ryan, R. M., Kim, Y. & Kaplan, U. 2003. 'Differentiating autonomy from individualism and independence: A self-determination theory perspective on internalization of cultural orientations and well-being'. *Journal of Personality and Social Psychology*, 84 (1), 97–110; Ryan, R. M., La Guardis, J. G., Solky-Butzel, J., Chirkov, V. & Kim, Y. 2005. 'On the interpersonal regulation of emotions: Emotional reliance across gender, relationships, and culture'. *Personal Relationships*, 12 (1), 145–63. See Deci & Ryan, 'Facilitating optimal motivation'; Pierce, T., Lydon, J. E. & Yang, S. 2001. 'Enthusiasm and moral commitment: What sustains family caregivers of those with dementia'. *Basic and Applied Social Psychology*, 23 (1), 29–41.

13 Amabile, T. M., Phillips, E., Collins, M. A. 1993. 'Person and environment in talent development: The case of creativity'. In N. Colangelo, S. G. Assouline & D. L. Ambrosen (eds). *Talent Development: Proceedings from the 1993 Henry B. and Jocelyn Wallace National Research Symposium on Talent Development*. Dayton, OH: Ohio Psychology Press, p. 274; Cerasoli, C. P., Nicklin, J. M. & Ford, M. T. 2014. 'Intrinsic motivation and external incentives jointly predict performance: A 40 year meta-analysis'. *Psychological Bulletin*, 140 (4), 980–1008, p. 996.

14 Camillus, J. C. 2008. 'Strategy as a wicked problem'. *Harvard Business Review*, 86, 98–106.

15 Amabile et al, 'Person and environment in talent development', p. 274.

16 See Olds, J. 1958. 'Satiation effects in self-stimulation of the brain'. *Journal of Comparative Physiological Psychology*, 51 (6), 675–8.

17 Ryan & Deci, 'Self-regulation and the problem of human autonomy', p. 1569.

18 Amabile, T. & Kramer, S. 2011. *The Progress Principle: Using Small Wins to Ignite Joy, Engagement, and Creativity at Work*. Boston, MA: Harvard Business Review Press.

19 See Goleman, D. 1995. *Emotional Intelligence*. New York, NY: Bantam Books; Goleman, D. 1998. *Working with Emotional Intelligence*. London: Bloomsbury Publishing; Gaffney, *Flourishing*, pp. 19–20.

20 See Goleman, *Working with Emotional Intelligence*.

21 See Hallett, M. G. & Hoffman, B. 2014. 'Performance under pressure: Cultivating the peak performance mindset for workplace excellence'. *Consulting Psychology Journal: Practice and Research*, 66 (3), 212–30.

22 Gladwell, M. 2008. *Outliers: The Story of Success*. New York, NY: Little Brown and Company.

23 Duckworth, A. L., Peterson, C., Mathews, M. D. & Kelly, D. R. 2007. 'Grit: Perseverance and passion for long-term goals'. *Journal of Personality and Social Psychology*, 92 (6), 1087–1101; Csikzentmihalyi, M. 1992. *Flow: The Psychology of Happiness*. London: Rider; Peterson, C. & Seligman, M. E. P. 2004. *Character Strengths and Virtues: A Handbook and Classification*. New York, NY: Oxford University Press; Bandura, A. 1982. 'Self-efficacy mechanism in human agency'. *American Psychologist*, 37 (2), 122–47; Dweck, C. S. 2006. *Mindset: How You Can Fulfil Your Potential*. London: Constable & Robinson.

24 See Phillips, K. A., Vaillant, G. E. & Shurr, P. 1987. 'Some physiologic antecedents of adult mental health'. *American Journal of Psychiatry*, 144 (8), 1009–13.

25 Csikzentmihalyi, *Flow*. See also Gaffney, *Flourishing*, pp. 269–91 ('The joy of losing yourself in everything you do').

26 See Nakamura, J. & Csikszentmihalyi, M. 2005. 'Flow theory and research.' In S. J. Lopez & C. R. Snyder (eds). *Oxford Handbook of Positive Psychology*. New York, NY: Oxford University Press, pp. 195–206.

27 Bandura, 'Self-efficacy mechanism in human agency'; Dweck, *Mindset*; Duckworth et al, 'Grit: Perseverance and passion'.

28 See Burnette, J. L., O'Boyle, E. H., Van Epps, E. M., Pollack, J. M. & Finkel, E. J. 2013. 'Mind-sets matter: A meta-analytic review of implicit theories and self-regulation'. *Psychological Bulletin*, 139 (3), 655–701.

29 See Shaver, P. R. & Mikulincer, M. 2002. 'Attachment-related psycho-dynamics'. *Attachment and Human Development*, 4 (2), 133–61.

30 Ainsworth, M. D., Blehar, M. C., Waters, E. & Wall, S. 1978. *Patterns of Attachment: A psychological study of the strange situation*. Hillsdale, NJ: Erlbaum, p. 310.

31 Rom, E. & Mikulincer, M. 2003. 'Attachment theory and group processes: The association between attachment style and group-related
representations, goals, memories, and functioning'. *Journal of Personality
and Social Psychology*, 84 (6), 1220–35.

18. Standing at the midlife crossroads

1 *Census of Population 2016 – Profile 4 Households and Families*. 2016. Dublin:
Central Statistics Office, Ireland.
2 Wolfinger, N. H. 2017. *America's generation gap in extra-marital sex*. Char-
lottesville, VA: Institute of Family Studies.

19. Middle age: *The urgency of time passing and time remaining*

1 Erikson, E. H. 1969. *Gandhi's Truth: On the Origins of Militant Nonvio-
lence*. New York: W.W. Norton & Co., p. 395.
2 McAdams, D. P., de St Aubin, E. & Logan, R. L. 1993. 'Generativity
among young, midlife, and older adults'. *Psychology and Aging*, 8 (2),
221–30; McAdams, D. P., Hart, H. M. & Maruna, S. 1998. 'The anat-
omy of generativity'. In D. P. McAdams & E. de St Aubin (eds).
*Generativity and Adult Development: How and why we care for the next
generation*. Washington, DC: American Psychological Association
Press, pp. 7–43; McAdams, D. P. & de St Aubin, E. 1992. 'A theory of
generativity and its assessment through self-report, behavioral acts,
and narrative themes in autobiography'. *Journal of Personality and Social
Psychology*, 62 (6), 1003–15.
3 Hofer, J., Busch, H., Au, A., Šolcová, P. K., Tavel, P. & Wong, T.T.
2014. 'For the Benefit of Others: Generativity and Meaning in Life in
the Elderly in Four Cultures'. *Psychology and Aging*, 29 (4), 764–75; see
also Rothrauff, T. & Cooney, T. M. 2008. 'The role of generativity in
psychological well-being: Does it differ for childless adults and parents?' *Journal of Adult Development*, 15 (3–4), 148–59.
4 Erikson, E. H. 1982. *The Life Cycle Completed: A Review*. New York, NY:
W. W. Norton & Co.; Stewart, A. J. & Vandewater, E. A. 1998. 'The

course of generativity'. In McAdams & de St Aubin (eds), *Generativity and Adult Development*, pp. 75–100.

5 Evans, R. 1967. *Dialogue with Erik Erikson*. New York, NY: Harper & Row, pp. 50–51.

6 McAdams, D. P., Ruetzel, K. & Foley, J. M. 1986. 'Complexity and generativity at mid-life. Relations among social motives, ego development, and adults' plans for the future'. *Journal of Personality and Social Psychology*, 50 (4), 800–7.

7 Franz, C. E., McClelland, D. C. & Weinberger, J. 1991. 'Childhood antecedents of conventional accomplishment in midlife adults: A 36-year prospective study'. *Journal of Personality and Social Psychology*, 60 (4), 586–95.

8 See Bradley, C. L. & Marcia, J. E. 1998. 'Generativity-Stagnation: A five category model'. *Journal of Personality*, 66 (1), 39–64.

9 King, L. A. & Raspin, C. 2004. 'Lost and found possible selves, subjective well-being, and ego development in divorced women'. *Journal of Personality*, 72 (3), 603–32.

10 Tari, A. R., Nauman, J., Zisko, N., Skjellegrind, H. K., Bosnes, I., Bergh, S., Stensvold, D., Selbaek, G. & Wisloff, U. 2019. 'Temporal changes in cardiorespiratory fitness and risk of dementia incidence and mortality: a population-based prospective cohort study'. *Lancet Public Health*, Nov, 565–74.

11 Available at ntnu.edu/cerg/vo2max (accessed April 2021).

12 Covey, S. R. 1989. *The 7 Habits of Highly Effective People*. New York, NY: The Free Press.

20. Late adulthood: *Life's new in-between stage*

1 Montepare, J. & Lachman, M. E. 1989. ' "You're only as young as you feel." Self-perceptions of age, fears of aging, and life satisfaction from adolescence to old age'. *Psychology and Aging*, 4 (1), 73–8.

2 National Council on Aging. 2001. *Myths and Realities 2000 Survey Results*. Washington, DC: NCOA; Lachman, M. E. 2004. 'Development in Midlife'. *Annual Review of Psychology*, 55 (1), 305–31; Lachman, M. E. 2001. *Handbook of Midlife Development*. New York, NY: Wiley; Windsor,

T. D., Curtis, R. G. & Luszcz, M. A. 2015. 'Sense of Purpose as a Psychological Resource for Aging Well'. *Developmental Psychology*, 51 (7), 975–86.

3 See www.nextact.ft.com (accessed April 2021).

4 Baltes, M. M. & Carstensen, L. L. 1996. 'The process of successful ageing'. *Ageing & Society*, 16 (4), 397–422.

5 *Health in Ireland: Key Trends*. 2017. Dublin: Department of Health.

6 Donoghue, O., O'Connell, M. & Kenny, R. A. (eds). 2016. *Walking to Wellbeing: Physical activity, social participation and psychological health in Irish adults aged 50 years and older.* The Irish Longitudinal Study on Ageing (TILDA), Trinity College Dublin; see also Ward, M., McGarrigle, C. & Donoghue, O. (eds). 2019. *Irish Adults' Transition to Retirement: Wellbeing, social participation and health-related behaviours.* TILDA, Trinity College Dublin; Turner, N., Donoghue, O. & Kenny, R. A. (eds). 2019. *Wellbeing and Health in Ireland's Over 50s 2009–2016.* TILDA, Trinity College Dublin.

7 Weiss, D., Job, V., Mathias, M., Grah, S. & Freund, A. M. 2016. 'The end is (not) near: Aging, essentialism, and future time perspective'. *Developmental Psychology*, 52 (6), 996–1009.

8 Westerhof, G. J., Miche, M., Brothers, A. F., Barrett, A. E., Diehl, M., Montepare, J. M., Wahl, H. W. & Wurm, S. 2014. 'The influence of subjective aging on health and longevity: a meta-analysis of longitudinal data'. *Psychology and Aging*, 29 (4), 793–802.

9 Logan, J. R., Ward, R. A. & Spitz, G. 1992. 'As old as you feel: Age identity in middle and later life'. *Social Forces*, 71, 451–67; National Council on Aging, *Myths and Realities*; Lachman, *Handbook of Midlife Development*.

10 Turner et al, *Wellbeing and Health in Ireland's Over 50s.*

11 Fry, P. S. 2003. 'Perceived self-efficacy domains as predictors of fear of the unknown and fear of dying among older adults'. *Psychology and Aging*, 18 (3), 474–86; Hall, S., Longhurst, S. & Higginson, I. 2009. 'Living and dying with dignity: A qualitative study of the views of older people in nursing homes'. *Age and Ageing*, 38 (4), 411–16.

12 Charles, S. T., Reynolds, C. A. & Gatz, M. 2001. 'Age-related differences and change in positive and negative affect over 23 years'. *Journal of Personality and Social Psychology,* 80 (1), 136–51.

13 Barlow, M. A., Wrosch, C., Kunzmann, U. & Gouin, J. 2019. 'Is anger, but not sadness, associated with chronic inflammation and illness in older adulthood?' *Psychology and Aging*, 34 (3), 330–40.

14 Almeida, D. M. 1998. 'Age differences in daily, weekly, and monthly estimates of psychological distress'. *Intraindividual variability and change processes: New directions in understanding personality*. Symposium presented at the 106th Annual Meeting of the American Psychological Association: San Francisco.

15 Charles, S. T., Mather, M. & Carstensen, L. L. 2003. 'Aging and emotional memory: The forgettable nature of negative images for older adults'. *Journal of Experimental Psychology*, 132 (2), 310–24.

16 Carstensen, L. L. 2014. 'Our aging population – it may save us all'. In Irving, P. H. (ed). *The Upside of Aging: How Long Life Is Changing the World of Health, Work, Innovation, Policy, and Purpose*. Bridgewater, NJ: Wiley, pp. 2–16.

17 Ward et al, *Irish Adults' Transition to Retirement*.

18 See Mark Miller. 'Take This Job and Love It!'. *AARP The Magazine*. February/March 2015.

19 Nolan, A. & Barrett, R. 2018. *Working Beyond 65 in Ireland 2010–2016. Discussion Paper Series*. Bonn: IZA Institute of Labor Economics.

20 Ward et al, *Irish Adults' Transition to Retirement*.

21 See James, J. B., Matz-Costa, C. & Smyer, M. A. 2016. 'Retirement security: It's not just about the money'. *American Psychologist* 71 (4), 334–44.

22 Ibid.

23 See Morrow-Howell, N., Hinterlong, J. & Sherraden, M. (eds). 2001. *Productive Aging: Concepts and Challenges*. Baltimore, MD: Johns Hopkins University Press.

24 Dorfman, L. T. 2002. 'Retirement and family relationships: An opportunity in later life'. *Generations*, 26 (2), 74–9.

25 Bleidorn, W. & Schwaba, T. 2018. 'Retirement is associated with changes in self-esteem'. *Psychology and Aging*, 33 (4), 586–94.

26 Freund, A. M. & Ritter, J. O. 2009. 'Midlife Crisis: A debate'. *Gerontology*, 55, 582–9; Orth, U., Robins, R. W., Trzesniewski, K. H., Maes, J. & Schmitt, M. 2009. 'Low self-esteem is a risk factor for depressive symptoms from young adulthood to old age'. *Journal of Abnormal Psychology*, 118 (3), 472–8.

27 Neel, R. & Lassetter, B. 2019. 'The Stigma of Perceived Irrelevance: An Affordance-Management Theory of Interpersonal Invisibility'. *Psychological Review*, 126 (5), 634–59; Kotter-Grühn, D. 2015. 'Changing negative views of aging'. In Diehl, M. & Wahl, H. W. (eds). 2015. *Annual Review of Gerontology and Geriatrics, Volume 35: Research on Subjective Aging: New Developments and Future Directions*. New York, NY: Springer, pp. 167–86.

28 Orth, U., Trzesniewski, K. H. & Robins, R. W. 2010. 'Self-esteem development from young adulthood to old age: A cohort-sequential longitudinal study'. *Journal of Personality and Social Psychology*, 98 (4), 645–58; Bleidorn & Schwaba, 'Retirement is associated with changes'.

29 James et al, 'Retirement security'.

30 Wink, P. 2006. 'Everyday life in the third age'. In J. Boone James & P. Wink (eds). *Annual Review of Gerontology and Geriatrics, Volume 26: The Crown of Life: Dynamics of the Early Postretirement Period*. New York, NY: Springer, pp. 243–63.

31 Lachman, M. E. 'Development in midlife'. *Annual Review of Psychology*, 55 (1), 305–31.

32 Wink, 'Everyday life in the third age'.

21. Late adulthood: *A time to thrive*

1 See Kahn, R. L. & Antonucci, T. C. 1980. 'Convoys over the life course: Attachment, roles, and social support'. In P. B. Baltes & O. G. Brim (eds). *Life-span Development and Behaviour*. New York, NY: Academic Press, pp. 254–91.

2 Leary, M. & Baumeister, R. 2000. 'The nature and function of self-esteem: Sociometer theory'. In M. P. Zanna (ed). *Advances in Experimental Social Psychology: Volume 32*. New York, NY: Academic Press, pp. 1–62; Wagner J., Hoppmann, C., Ram, N. & Gerstorf, D. 2015. 'Self-esteem is relatively stable late in life: The role of resources in the health, self-regulation, and social domains'. *Developmental Psychology*, 51 (1), 136–49.

3 Luong, G., Charles, S. T. & Fingerman, K. L. 2011. 'Better with age: Social relationships across adulthood'. *Journal of Social and Personal Relationships*, 28 (1), 9–23.

4 Duvall, E. M. & Miller, B. C. 1985. *Marriage and Family Development (6th Edition)*. New York, NY: Harper & Row.

5 See Bouchard, G. 2014. 'How do parents react when their children leave home?' *Journal of Adult Development*, 21 (2), 69–79.

6 Wink, P. 2006. 'Everyday life in the third age'. In J. Boone James & P. Wink (eds). *Annual Review of Gerontology and Geriatrics, Volume 26: The Crown of Life: Dynamics of the Early Postretirement Period*. New York, NY: Springer, pp. 243–63.

7 Orr, J., McGarrigle, C. & Kenny, R. A. 2017. *Sexual activity in the over 50s population in Ireland*. The Irish Longitudinal Study on Ageing (TILDA), Trinity College Dublin.

8 Rohr, M. K., Nestler, S. & Kunzmann, U. 2019. 'A trouble shared is a trouble halved: Age differences in emotional experience and expression during couples' conversations'. *Psychology and Aging*, 34 (6), 848–61.

9 Bonnano, G. A. & Kaltman, S. 1999. 'Towards an integrative perspective on bereavement'. *Psychological Bulletin*, 125 (6), 760–76.

10 See Umberson, D., Pudrovska, T. & Reczek, C. 2010. 'Parenthood, childlessness, and well-being: A life course perspective'. *Journal of Marriage and Family*, 72 (3), 612–29.

11 Orr et al, *Sexual activity in the over 50s*.

12 Stevens, N. L. & Van Tilburg, T. G. 2011. 'Cohort differences in having and retaining friends in personal networks in later life'. *Journal of Social and Personal Relationships*, 28 (1), 24–43.

13 Lang, F. R., Featherman, D. L. & Nesselroade, J. R. 1997. 'Social self-efficacy and short-term variability in social relationships: The MacArthur Successful Aging Studies'. *Psychology and Aging*, 12 (4), 657–66.

14 Twenge, J. M., Carter, N. T. & Campbell, W. K. 2017. 'Age, time period, and birth cohort differences in self-esteem: Reexamining a cohort-sequential longitudinal study'. *Journal of Personality and Social Psychology*, 112 (5), e9–e17.

15 Cicirelli, V. G. 1989. 'Feelings of attachment to siblings and wellbeing in later life'. *Psychology and Aging*, 4 (2), 211–16.

16 See Umberson, D., Williams, K., Powers, D. A., Chen, M. D. & Campbell, A. M. 2005. 'As good as it gets? A life course perspective on marital quality'. *Social Forces*, 84 (1), 493–511.

17 Umberson et al, 'Parenthood, childlessness, and well-being'; see also Shaw, B. A., Krause, N., Liang, J. & Bennett, J. 2007. 'Tracking changes in social relations throughout late life'. *Journals of Gerontology: Series B: Psychological Sciences and Social Sciences*, 62 (2), S90–S99.

18 Goodsell, T. L., Bates, J. S. & Behnk, A. O. 2011. 'Fatherhood stories: Grandparents, grandchildren, and gender differences'. *Journal of Social and Personal Relationships*, 28 (1), 134–54.

19 See Dunifon, R. 2012. 'The influence of grandparents on the lives of children and adolescents'. *Child Development Perspectives*, 7 (1), 55–60.

20 See Griggs, J. 2010. ' "They've always been there for me": Grandparental involvement and child well-being'. *Children and Society*, 24 (3), 200–14.

21 Weiss, D., Job, V., Mathias, M., Grah, S. & Freund, A. M. 2016. 'The end is (not) near: Aging, essentialism, and future time perspective'. *Developmental Psychology*, 52 (6), 996–1009.

22 Lachman, M. E. 2006. 'Perceived control over aging-related declines: Adaptive beliefs and behaviors'. *Current Directions in Psychological Science*, 15 (6), 282–6.

23 Wink, P. & Dillon, M. 2002. 'Spiritual development across the adult life course: Findings from a longitudinal study'. *Journal of Adult Development*, 9 (1), 79–94.

24 Brown, I. T., Chen, T., Gehlert, N. C. & Piedmont, R. L. 2013. 'Age and gender effects on the Assessment of Spirituality and Religious Sentiments (ASPIRES) scale: A cross-sectional analysis'. *Psychology of Religion and Spirituality*, 5 (2), 90–98; Bryant, A. N. 2007. 'Gender differences in spiritual development during the college years'. *Sex Roles*, 56 (11), 835–46.

25 Miner-Rubino, K., Winter, D. G. & Stewart, A. J. 2004. 'Gender, social class, and the subjective experience of aging: Self-perceived personality change from early adulthood to late midlife'. *Personality and Social Psychology Bulletin*, 30 (12), 1599–1610.

26 McLean, K. C. 2008. 'Stories of the young and the old: Personal continuity and narrative identity'. *Developmental Psychology*, 44 (1), 254–64.

22. Late adulthood: *The importance of a sense of purpose*

1 Windsor, T. D., Curtis, R. G. & Luszcz, M. A. 2015. 'Sense of purpose as a psychological resource for aging well'. *Developmental Psychology*, 51 (7), 975–86.

2 See Anderson, A., Huttenlocher, D. & Kleinberg, J. 2014. 'Engaging with massive online courses'. *Proceedings of the 23rd international conference on World Wide Web*, pp. 687–98; Heaven, B., O'Brien, N., Evans, E. H., White, M., Meyer, T. D., Mathers, J. C. & Moffat, S. 2013. 'Mobilizing resources for well-being: Implications for developing interventions in the retirement transition'. *The Gerontologist*, 56 (4), 615–29; Jenkinson, C. E., Dickens, A. P., Jones, K., Thompson-Coon, J., Taylor, R. S., Rogers, M., Bambra, C. L., Lang, I. & Richards, S. H. 2013. 'Is volunteering a public health intervention? A systematic review and meta-analysis of the health and survival of volunteers'. *BMC Public Health*, 13 (1), article no. 773.

3 Carlson, M. C., Erikson, K. I., Kramer, A. F., Voss, M. W., Bolea, N., Mielke, M. & Fried, L. P. 2009. 'Evidence for neurocognitive plasticity in at-risk older adults: the experience corps program'. *Journals of Gerontology: Series A: Biological Sciences and Medical Sciences*, 64 (12), 1275–82; Jackson, J., Carlson, M., Mandel, D., Zemke, R. & Clark, F. 1998. 'Occupation in lifestyle redesign: The Well Elderly Study occupational therapy program'. *American Journal of Occupational Therapy*, 52 (5), 326–36.

4 Hinterlong, J. E. 2008. 'Productive engagement among older Americans: Prevalence, patterns, and implications for public policy'. *Journal of Aging & Social Policy*, 20 (2), 141–64.

5 Carlson et al, 'Evidence for neurocognitive plasticity in at-risk older adults'.

6 Kaskie, B., Imhof, S., Cavanaugh, J. & Culp, K. 2008. 'Civic engagement as a retirement role for aging Americans'. *The Gerontologist*, 48 (3), 368–77.

7 See James, J. B., Matz-Costa, C. & Smyer, M. A. 2016. 'Retirement security: It's not just about the money'. *American Psychologist* 71 (4), 334–44; Morrow-Howell, N. 2010. 'Volunteering in later life: Research frontiers'. *Journals of Gerontology: Series B: Psychological Sciences and Social Sciences*, 65 (4), 461–9; Ward, M., McGarrigle, C. & Donoghue, O. (eds). 2019. *Irish Adults' Transition to Retirement: Wellbeing, social participation and*

health-related behaviours. The Irish Longitudinal Study on Ageing (TILDA), Trinity College Dublin.

8 Okun, M. A., WanHeung Yeung, E. & Brown, S. 2013. 'Volunteering by older adults and risk of mortality: A meta-analysis'. *Psychology and Aging*, 28 (2), 564–77.

9 Pargament, K. I. 1997. *The Psychology of Religion and Coping: Theory, Research, and Practice*. New York, NY: Guilford Press.

10 Baltes, P. B., & Baltes, M. M. 1990. 'Psychological perspectives on successful aging: The model of selective optimization with compensations'. In P. B. Baltes & M. M. Baltes (eds). *Successful Ageing: Perspectives from the Behavioural Sciences*. New York, NY: Cambridge University Press, pp. 1–34; also Heckhausen, J., Wrosch, C. & Schultz, R. 2010. 'A motivational theory of life-span development'. *Psychological Review*, 117 (1), 32–60.

11 McQuillen, A. D., Licht, M. H. & Licht, B. G. 2003. 'Contributions of disease severity and perceptions of primary and secondary control to the prediction of psychosocial adjustment to Parkinson's Disease'. *Health Psychology*, 22 (5), 504–12.

12 Baltes, M. M. & Carstensen, L. L. 1996. 'The process of successful ageing'. *Ageing & Society*, 16 (4), 397–422.

13 Feifel, H. & Strack, S. 1987. 'Old is old is old?' *Psychology and Aging*, 2 (4), 409–12.

14 Kobasa, S. C., Maddi, S. R. & Kahn, S. 1982. 'Hardiness and health'. *Journal of Personality and Social Psychology*, 42 (1), 168–77.

15 Kovacevic, A., Fenesi, B., Paolucci, E. & Heisz, J. J. 2019. 'The effects of aerobic exercise intensity on memory in older adults'. *Applied Physiology, Nutrition, and Metabolism*, 45 (6), 591–600; see also Tari, A. R., Nauman, J., Zisko, N., Skjellegrind, H. K., Bosnes, I., Bergh, S., Stensvold, D., Selbaek, G. & Wisloff, U. 2019. 'Temporal changes in cardiorespiratory fitness and risk of dementia incidence and mortality: a population-based prospective cohort study'. *Lancet Public Health*, Nov, 565–74.

16 Smith, G. E. 2016. 'Healthy Cognitive Aging and Dementia Prevention'. *American Psychologist*, 71 (4), 268–75.

17 Plaks, J. E. & Chasteen, A. L. 2013. 'Entity versus incremental theories predict older adults' memory performance'. *Psychology and Aging*, 28 (4), 948–57.

18 Alexander, C. N., Langer, E. J., Newman, R. I., Chandler, H. M. & Davies, J. L. 1989. 'Transcendental meditation, mindfulness, and longevity: An experimental study with the elderly'. *Journal of Personality and Social Psychology*, 57 (6), 950–96; Hölzel, G. K., Carmody, J., Vangel, M., Congleton, C., Yerramsetti, S. M., Gard, T. & Lazar, S.W. 2011. 'Mindfulness practice leads to increases in regional brain gray matter density'. *Psychiatry Research: Neuroimaging*, 191 (1), 36–43; Sevinc, G., Holzel, B. K., Grenberg, J., Gard, T., Brunsch, V., Vangel, M., Orr, S. P., Milad, M. R., Lazar, S. W. & Scott, O. 2019. 'Strengthened Hippocampal Circuits Underlie Enhanced Retrieval of Extinguished Fear Memories Following Mindfulness Training'. *Biological Psychiatry*, 86 (9), 693–702; Lazar, S. W., Kerr, C. E., Wasserman, R. H., Gray, J. R., Grieve, D. N., Treadway, M. T., McGarvey, M., Quinn, B. T., Dusek, J. A., Benson, H., Rauch, S. L., Moore, C. I. & Fischi, B. 2005. 'Meditation experience is associated with increased cortical thickness'. *Neuroreport*, 16 (17), 1893–7.

19 See Alvin Powell, 'When Science Meets Mindfulness'. *The Harvard Gazette*, 9 April 2018.

20 Plaks & Chasteen, 'Entity versus incremental theories'.

23. Old age: *Living each precious moment fully*

1 See US life table, cited in Easterlin, R. A. 2006. 'Life cycle happiness and its sources: Intersections of psychology, economics, and demography'. *Journal of Economic Psychology*, 27 (4), 463–82, p. 472.

2 Neugarten, B. L. 1996. *The Meaning of Age*. Chicago, IL: The University of Chicago Press.

3 See Westerhof, G. J., Miche, M., Brothers, A. F., Barrett, A. E., Diehl, M., Montepare, J. M., Wahl, H. W. & Wurm, S. 2014. 'The influence of subjective aging on health and longevity: a meta-analysis of longitudinal data'. *Psychology and Aging*, 29 (4), 793–802; Kotter-Gruhn, D. 2015. 'Changing negative views of aging'. In Diehl, M. & Wahl, H. W. (eds). 2015. *Annual Review of Gerontology and Geriatrics, Volume 35: Research on Subjective Aging: New Developments and Future Directions*. New York, NY: Springer, pp. 167–86.

4 Stewart, T. L., Chipperfield, J. G., Perry, R. P. & Weiner, B. 2012. 'Attributing illness to "old age": Consequences of a self-directed stereotype for health and mortality'. *Psychology and Health*, 27 (8), 881–97.

5 Abramson, A. & Silverstein, M. 2006. *Images of Aging in America 2004*. Report commissioned and published by AARP and University of Southern California.

6 Levy, B. R., Zonderman, A., Slade, M. D. & Ferrucci, L. 2009. 'Age stereotypes held earlier in life predict cardiovascular events in later life'. *Psychological Science*, 20 (3), 296–8.

7 Levy, B. R., Slade, M. D., May, J. & Caracciolo, E. A. 2006. 'Physical recovery after acute myocardial infarction: Positive age self-stereotypes as a resource'. *International Journal of Aging and Human Development*, 62 (4), 285–301.

8 North, M. S. & Fiske, S. T. 2012. 'An inconvenienced youth? Ageism and its potential intergenerational roots'. *Psychological Bulletin*, 138 (5), 982–97.

9 Levy, B. R., Ashman, O. & Dror, I. 2000. 'To be or not to be: The effects of aging stereotypes on the will to live'. *Omega*, 40 (3), 409–20.

10 Levy, B. R. & Myers, L. M. 2004. 'Preventive health behaviors influenced by self-perceptions of aging'. *Preventive Medicine*, 39 (3), 625–9.

11 Levy et al, 'Age stereotypes held earlier in life'.

12 Levy, B. R., Slade, M. D. & Kasl, S. V. 2002. 'Longitudinal benefit of positive self-perceptions of aging on functional health'. *Journals of Gerontology: Series B: Psychological Sciences and Social Sciences*, 57 (5), 409–17; Levy, B. R., Slade, M. D., Kunkel, S. R. & Kasl, S. V. 2002. 'Longevity increased by positive self-perceptions of aging'. *Journal of Personality and Social Psychology*, 83 (2), 261–70.

13 Fiske, S. T., Cuddy, A. J. C., Glick, P. & Xu, J. 2002. 'Competence and warmth respectively follow from perceived status and competition'. *Journal of Personality and Social Psychology*, 82 (6), 878–902.

14 Cuddy, A. J. C. & Fiske, S. T. 2002. 'Doddering but Dear: Process, Content, and Function in Stereotyping of Older Persons'. In T. D. Nelson (ed.) *Ageing: Stereotyping and Prejudice Against Older Persons*. Cambridge, MA: MIT Press, 3–26.

15 Wolff, J. L., Starfield, B. & Anderson, G. 2002. 'Prevalence, expenditures, and complications of multiple chronic conditions in the elderly'. *Archives*

of Internal Medicine, 162 (20), 2269–76; Vogeli, C., Shields, A. E., Lee, T. A., Gibson, T. B., Marder, W. D., Weiss, K. B. & Blumenthal, D. 2007. 'Multiple chronic conditions: Prevalence, health consequences, and implications for quality, care management, and costs'. *Journal of General Internal Medicine*, 22 (Suppl 3), 391–5.

16 McGarrigle, C., Donoghue, O., Scarlett, S. & and Kenny, R. A. (eds). 2017. *Health and Wellbeing: Active Ageing for Older Adults in Ireland*. The Irish Longitudinal Study on Ageing (TILDA), Trinity College Dublin.

17 Löckenhoff, C. E. & Carstensen, L. L. 2004. 'Socioemotional selectivity theory, aging, and health: the increasingly delicate balance between regulating emotions and making tough choices'. *Journal of Personality*, 72 (6), 1395–1424, p. 1408.

18 Cohen-Mansfield, J., Schmotkin, S. D., Blumstein, Z., Shorek, A., Eyal, N. & Hazan, H. 2013. 'The old, old-old, and the oldest old: continuation or distinct categories? An examination of the relationship between age and changes in health, function, and wellbeing'. *International Journal of Aging and Human Development*, 77 (1), 35–57.

19 Butler, R. N. 1968. 'The life review: An interpretation of reminiscence in the aged'. In B. L. Neugarten (ed). *Middle Age and Aging: A Reader in Social Psychology*. Chicago, IL: The University of Chicago Press, pp. 486–96.

20 Lieblich, A. 2014. 'Narrating your life after 65 (or: To tell or not to tell, that is the question.)' *Rereading Personal Narrative and Life Course: New Directions for Child and Adolescent Development*, 145, 71–83.

21 Wink, P. 2006. 'Everyday life in the third age'. In J. Boone James & P. Wink (eds). *Annual Review of Gerontology and Geriatrics, Volume 26: The Crown of Life: Dynamics of the Early Postretirement Period*. New York, NY: Springer, pp. 243–63.

22 See Jung, C. G. 1964. *Man and His Symbols*. New York, NY: Doubleday; Levinson, D. J. 1978. *The Seasons of a Man's Life*. New York, NY: Ballantine Books. I formulate the polarities not in Jungian or psychoanalytic terms but in a way that is more in tune with the larger body of research on human development.

23 Wagner, J., Smith, J., Ram, N. & Gerstorf, D. 2016. 'Personality Trait Development at the End of Life: Antecedents and Correlates of Mean-Level Trajectories'. *Journal of Personality and Social Psychology*, 111 (3), 411–29.

24 Sharp, E. S., Beam, C. R., Reynolds, C. A. & Gatz, M. 2019. 'Openness declines in advance of death in late adulthood'. *Psychology and Aging*, 34 (1), 124–38.

25 Shanahan, M. J., Eccles, J., Hill, P. L. & Roberts, B. W. 2014. 'Conscientiousness, Health, and Aging: The Life Course of Personality Model'. *Developmental Psychology*, 50 (5), 1407–25.

26 Hampson, S. E., Edmonds, G. W., Goldberg, L. R., Dubanoski, J. P. & Hillier, T. A. 2015. 'Childhood conscientiousness relates to objectively measured adult physical health four decades later'. *Health Psychology*, 32 (8), 925–8.

27 English, T. & Carstensen, L. L. 2014. 'Will Interventions Targeting Conscientiousness Improve Aging Outcomes?' *Developmental Psychology*, 50 (5), 1478–81.

28 Wrosch, C., Schulz, R. & Heckhausen, J. 2004. 'Health Stresses and Depressive Symptomatology in the Elderly: A Control-Process Approach'. *Current Directions in Psychological Science*, 13 (1), 17–20.

29 Reed, A. E., Chan, L. & Mikels, J. A. 2014. 'Meta-analysis of the age-related positivity effect: Age differences in preferences for positive over negative information'. *Psychology and Aging*, 29 (1), 1–15.

30 Bruine, W., Parker, A. M. & Strough, N. 2016. 'Choosing to be happy? Age differences in "maximizing" decision strategies and experienced emotional well-being'. *Psychology and Aging*, 31 (3), 295–300.

31 English, T. & Carstensen, L. L. 2015. 'Does positivity operate when the stakes are high? Health status and decision making among older adults'. *Psychology and Aging*, 30 (2), 348–55.

32 Rolison, J. J. 2019. 'What could go wrong? No evidence of an age-related positivity effect when evaluating outcomes of risky activities'. *Developmental Psychology*, 55 (8), 1788–99.

33 Löckenhoff & Carstensen, 'Socioemotional selectivity theory, aging, and health'.

34 Bailey, P. E. & Tarren, L. 2019. 'A systematic review and meta-analysis of age-related differences in trust'. *Psychology and Aging*, 34 (5), 674–85.

35 Castle E., Eisenberger, N. I., Seeman, T. E., Moons, W. G., Boggero, I. A., Grinblatt, M. S. & Taylor, S. E. 2012. 'Neural and behavioral bases of age differences in perceptions of trust'. *PNAS*, 109 (51), 20848–52.

36 Schultz, R. & Heckhausen, J. 1996. 'A life span model of successful aging'. *American Psychologist*, 51 (7), 702–14.

37 Carstensen, L. L. & DeLiema, M. 2017. 'The positivity effect: a negativity bias in youth fades with age'. *Current Opinion in Behavioural Sciences*, 19, 7–12.

38 Glass, T. A., Mendes De Leon, C. F., Bassuk, S. S. & Berkman, L. F. 2006. 'Social engagement and depressive symptoms in late life: Longitudinal findings'. *Journal of Aging and Health*, 18 (4), 604–28.

39 Barlow, M. A., Wrosch, C., Gouin, J. P. & Kunzmann, U. 2019. 'Is anger, but not sadness, associated with chronic inflammation and illness in older adulthood?' *Psychology and Aging*, 34 (3), 330–40.

40 Ardelt, M. 2016. 'Wisdom at the end of life: An analysis of mediating and moderating relations between wisdom and subjective wellbeing'. *Journals of Gerontology: Series B: Psychological Sciences and Social Sciences*, 71 (3), 502–13.

41 Wagner, J., Hoppmann, C., Ram, N. & Gerstorf, D. 2015. 'Self-esteem is relatively stable late in life: The role of resources in the health, self-regulation, and social domains'. *Developmental Psychology*, 51 (1), 136–49.

42 Kandler, C., Kornadt, A. E., Birk, K., Hagemeyer, B. & Neyer, F. J. 2014. 'Patterns and Sources of Personality Development in Old Age'. *Journal of Personality and Social Psychology*, 109 (1), 175–91.

24. Old age: *Still you, despite the rigours of aging*

1 Sharifian, N., Kraal, A. Z., Zaheed, A. B., Sol, K. & Zahodne, L. B. 2019. 'Longitudinal socioemotional pathways between retrospective early life maternal relationship quality and episodic memory in older adulthood'. *Developmental Psychology*, 55 (11), 2464–73.

2 Radecki, M. A., Cox, S. R. & MacPherson, S. E. 2018. 'Theory of mind and psychological characteristics in older men'. *Psychology and Aging*, 34 (1), 145–51.

3 Lee, L. O., Aldwin, C. M., Kubzansky, L. D., Chen, E., Mroczek, D. K., Wang, J. M. & Spiro, A. 2015. 'Do cherished children age successfully? Longitudinal findings from the Veterans Affairs Normative Aging Study'. *Psychology and Aging*, 30 (4), 894–910.

4 Cicirelli, V. G. 2010. 'Attachment relationships in old age'. *Journal of Social and Personal Relationships*, 27 (2), 191–9.

5 Merz, E. M. & Consedine, N. S. 2009. 'The association of family support and wellbeing in later life depends on adult attachment style'. *Attachment & Human Development*, 11 (2), 203–21.

6 Chen, C. K., Waters, H. S., Hartman, M., Zimmerman, S., Miklowitz, D. J. & Waters, E. 2013. 'The secure base script and the task of caring for elderly parents: Implications for attachment theory and clinical practice'. *Attachment & Human Development*, 15 (3), 332–48.

7 Lang, S. F. & Fowers, B. J. 2018. 'An expanded theory of Alzheimer's caregiving'. *American Psychologist*, 74 (2), 194–206.

8 See Wimo, A. & Price, M. 2010. *World Alzheimer Report 2010: The Global Economic Impact of Dementia*. London: Alzheimer's Disease International.

9 Alzheimer Society. *Rising Tide: The impact of dementia on Canadian society*. 2010. Toronto, ON: Alzheimer Society of Canada.

10 Hearn, S., Saulnier, G., Strayer, J., Glenham, M., Koopman, R. & Marcia, J. E. 2012. 'Between integrity and despair: Toward construct validation of Erikson's eighth stage'. *Journal of Adult Development*, 19 (1), 1–20.

11 Pierce, M., Cahill, S. & O'Shea, E. 2014. *Prevalence and Projections of Dementia in Ireland, 2011–2046*. Report commissioned by Genio in association with Trinity College Dublin.

12 Brodaty, H. & Donkin, M. 2009. 'Family caregivers of people with dementia'. *Dialogues in Clinical Neuroscience*, 11 (2), 217–28.

13 Schultz, R. & Sherwood, P. R. 2008. 'Physical and mental health effects of family caregiving'. *American Journal of Nursing*, 108 (9), 23–7.

14 Roth, D. L., Brown, S. L., Rhodes, J. D. & Haley, W. E. 2018. 'Reduced mortality rates among caregivers: Does family caregiving provide a stress-buffering effect?' *Psychology and Aging*, 33 (4), 619–29.

15 O'Rourke, N., Claxton, A., Kupferschmidt, A. K., Smith, A. K. & Beattie, J. Z. 2011. 'Marital idealization as an enduring buffer to distress among spouses of persons with Alzheimer disease'. *Journal of Social and Personal Relationships*, 28 (1), 117–33.

16 Sanders, S., Ott, C. H., Kelber, S. T. & Noonan, P. 2008. 'The experience of high levels of grief in caregivers of persons with Alzheimer's disease and related dementia'. *Journal of Death Studies*, 32 (6), 495–523.

17 Gallo, J. J. & Lebowitz, B. D. 1999. 'The epidemiology of common late-life mental disorders in the community: Themes for the new century'. *Psychiatric Services*, 50 (9), 1158–66.

18 O'Rourke, N. & Wenaus, C. A. 1998. 'Marital aggrandizement as a mediator of burden among spouses of suspected dementia patients'. *Canadian Journal on Aging*, 17 (4), 384–400.

19 Bradley, J. M. & Cafferty, T. P. 2001. 'Attachment among older adults: Current issues and directions for future research'. *Attachment and Human Development*, 3 (2), 200–21.

20 Lovell, B. & Wetherell, M. A. 2011. 'The cost of caregiving: Endocrine and immune implications in elderly and non-elderly caregivers'. *Neuroscience & Biobehavioral Reviews*, 35 (6), 1342–52.

21 Lyonette, C. & Yardley, L. 2003. 'The influence on carer wellbeing of motivations to care for older people and the relationship with the care recipient'. *Ageing and Society*, 23 (4), 487–506.

22 Erikson, E., Erikson. J. & Kivnick, H. 1986. *Vital Involvement In Old Age*. New York, NY: W. W. Norton & Co.

23 Baltes, M. M. & Carstensen, L. L. 1996. 'The process of successful ageing'. *Ageing & Society*, 16 (4), 397–422.

24 Schindler, I., Staudinger, U. M. & Nesselroade, J. R. 2006. 'Development and structural dynamics of personal life investment in old age'. *Psychology and Aging*, 21 (4), 737–53.

25 Baltes, P. B. 1997. 'The incomplete architecture of human ontogeny: Selection, optimization, and compensation as foundation of developmental theory'. *American Psychologist*, 52 (4), 366–80, p. 371.

26 Krause, N. & Shaw, B. A. 2000. 'Role-specific feelings of control and mortality'. *Psychology and Aging*, 15 (4), 617–26.

27 Gitlin, L. N., Hauck, W. W., Winter, L., Dennis, M. P. & Schultz, R. 2006. 'Effect of an in-home occupational and physical therapy intervention on reducing mortality in functionally vulnerable elders: Preliminary findings'. *Journal of the American Geriatric Society*, 54 (6), 950–55.

28 Lieberman, M.A. 1974. 'Relocation research and social policy'. *The Gerontologist*, 14 (6), 494–501.

29 Ibid.

30 Bruine de Bruin, W., Parke, A. M. & Strough, J. N. 2020. 'Age differences in reported social networks and well-being'. *Psychology and Aging*, 35 (2), 159–68.

31 Lowenthal, M. F. & Haven, C. 1968. 'Interaction and adaptation: Intimacy as a critical variable'. In B. L. Neugarten (ed). *Middle Age and Aging: A Reader in Social Psychology*. Chicago, IL: The University of Chicago Press, pp. 390–400.

32 Cacioppo, J. T., Hawkley, L. C. & Berntson, G. G. 2011. 'Social isolation'. *Annals of the New York Academy of Science*, Aug: 1231, 17–22.

33 Berkman, L. F., Glass, T., Brissette, I. & Seeman, T. E. 2000. 'From social integration to health: Durkheim in the new millennium'. *Social Science & Medicine*, 51 (6), 843–57; Cohen, S. 2004. 'Social relationships and health'. *American Psychologist*, 59 (8), 676–84; Cohen, S. & Janicki-Deverts, D. 2009. 'Can we improve our physical health by altering our social networks?' *Perspectives on Psychological Science*, 4 (4), 375–8.

34 Zahodne, L. B. & Ajrouch, K. J. 2019. 'Social Relations and Age-Related Change in Memory'. *Psychology and Aging*, 34 (6), 751–65.

35 Hughes, T. F., Andel, R., Small, B. J., Borenstein, A. R. & Mortimer, J. A. 2008. 'The association between social resources and cognitive change in older adults: Evidence from the Charlotte County Healthy Aging Study'. *Journals of Gerontology: Series B: Psychological Sciences and Social Sciences*, 63 (4), 241–4.

36 Stevens, N. L. & Van Tilburg, T. G. 2011. 'Cohort differences in having and retaining friends in personal networks in later life'. *Journal of Social and Personal Relationships*, 28 (1), 24–43.

37 Franks, M. M., Wendorf, C. A., Gonzalez, R. & Ketterer, M. 2004. 'Aid and influence: Health-promoting exchanges of older married partners'. *Journal of Social and Personal Relationships*, 21 (4), 431–45.

38 Tower, R. B. & Kasl, S. V. 1996. 'Depressive symptoms across older spouses: Longitudinal influences'. *Psychology and Aging*, 11 (4), 683–97.

39 Gleason, M. E. J., Iida, M., Bolger, N. & Shrout, P. E. 2003. 'Daily supportive equity in close relationships'. *Personality and Social Psychology Bulletin*, 29 (8), 1036–45.

40 Rentsch, T. 1997. 'Aging as becoming oneself: A philosophical ethics of late life'. *Journal of Aging Studies*, 11 (4), 263–71, p. 267.

41 Tobin, S. S. 1991. *Personhood in Advanced Old Age: Implications for Practice*. New York, NY: Springer Publishing Company.

25. Old Age: *Seeing the bigger picture*

1 Tassone, D., Reed, A. E. & Carstensen, L. L. 2019. 'Time may heal wounds: Aging and life regrets'. *Psychology and Aging*, 34 (6), 862–6.

2 Zeelenberg, M., van den Bos, K. & van Dijk, E. 2002. 'The inaction effect in the psychology of regret'. *Journal of Personality and Social Psychology*, 82 (3), 314–27.

3 Gilovich, T. & Medvec, V. H. 1995. 'The experience of regret: What, when, and why'. *Psychological Review*, 102 (2), 379–95.

4 Zeelenberg et al, 'The inaction effect'.

5 Gilovich, T., Medvec, V. H. & Kahneman, D. 1998. 'Varieties of regret: A debate and partial resolution'. *Psychological Review*, 105 (3), 602–5.

6 Tassone et al, 'Time may heal wounds'.

7 Mather, M. & Johnson, M. K. 2000. 'Choice-supportive source monitoring: Do our decisions seem better to us as we age?' *Psychology and Aging*, 15 (4), 596–606.

8 Tassone et al, 'Time may heal wounds'.

9 Hearn, S., Saulnier, G., Strayer, J., Glenham, M., Koopman, R. & Marcia, J. E. 2012. 'Between integrity and despair: Toward construct validation of Erikson's eighth stage'. *Journal of Adult Development*, 19 (1), 1–20.

10 Ibid. Depending on how it's assessed, somewhere between 27 and 47 per cent of older people achieve a comprehensive integrity; between 36 and 51 per cent a conforming-type integrity; between 9 and 19 per cent a pseudo integrity; and between 4 and 9 per cent are despairing.

11 These are the four principles of aging articulated by Bernice Neugarten, who pioneered research into human development and old age. See Neugarten, B. 1982. *New Perspectives on Aging and Social Policy*. The Leon and Josephine Winkelman Lecture. University of Michigan.

12 Alexander, C. N., Langer, E. J., Newman, R. I., Chandler, H. M., & Davies, J. L. 1989. 'Transcendental meditation, mindfulness, and longevity: An experimental study with the elderly'. *Journal of Personality and Social Psychology*, 57 (6), 950–64.

26. *Your precious life reaches its end*

1 Rentsch, T. 1997. 'Aging as becoming oneself: A philosophical ethics of late life'. *Journal of Aging Studies*, 11 (4), 263–71.

2 Seider, B. H., Shiota, M., Whalen, P. & Levenson, R. W. 2011. 'Greater sadness reactivity in late life'. *Social Cognitive and Affective Neuroscience*, 6 (2), 186–94.

3 Katzorreck, M. & Kunzmann, U. 2018. 'Greater empathic accuracy and emotional reactivity in old age: the sample case of death and dying'. *Psychology and Aging*, 33 (8), 1202–14.

4 May, P., McGarrigle, C. & Normand, C. (eds). 2017. *The end of life experience of older people*. The Irish Longitudinal Study on Ageing (TILDA), Trinity College Dublin.

5 Vogel, N., Schilling, O. K., Wahl, H. W., Beekman, A. T. F., Penninx, B. & Wrenda, W. J. H. 2013. 'Time-to-death-related change in positive and negative affect among older adults approaching the end of life'. *Psychology and Aging*, 28 (1), 128–41.

6 Zaslavsky, O., Palgi, Y., Rillamas-Sun, E., LaCroix, A. Z., Schnall, E., Woods, N. F., Cochrane, B. B., Garcia, L., Hingle, M., Post, S., Seguin, R.,Tindle, H. & Shrira, A. 2015. 'Dispositional optimism and terminal decline in global quality of life'. *Developmental Psychology*, 51 (6), 856–63; see also Lieberman, M. A. & Coplan, A. S. 1970. 'Distance from death as a variable in the study of aging'. *Developmental Psychology*, 2 (1), 71–84; and see also Diegelmann, M., Schilling, O. K. & and Wahl., H. W. 2016. 'Feeling blue at the end of life: Trajectories of depressive symptoms from a distance-to-death perspective'. *Psychology and Aging*, 31 (7), 672–86.

7 Wagner, J., Hoppmann, C., Ram, N. & Gerstorf, D. 2015. 'Self-esteem is relatively stable late in life: The role of resources in the health, self-regulation, and social domains'. *Developmental Psychology*, 51 (1), 136–49.

8 Tsai, J. L., Sims, T., Qu, Y., Ewart, T., Jiang, D. & Fung, H. H. 2018. 'Valuing excitement makes people look forward to old age less and dread it more'. *Psychology and Aging*, 33 (7), 975–92.

9 For a detailed account of studies on near-death experiences, see Lake, J. 2017. 'The near-death experience: A testable neural model'. *Psychology of Consciousness: Theory, Research, and Practice*, 4 (1), 115–34.

10 Ibid. See also Siegel, R. K. 1980. 'The psychology of life after death'.
    American Psychologist, 35 (10), 911–31.

11 Evrand, R., Toutain, C., Glazier, J. W. & Le Malefan, P. 2018. 'The energy
    of despair: Do near-death experiences have an evolutionary value?' *Psy-
    chology of Consciousness: Theory, Research, and Practice*, 6 (2), 184–99.

12 Kastenbaum, R. T. 1975. 'Is death a life crisis? On the confrontation
    with death in theory and practice'. In N. Datan and L. H. Ginsburg
    (eds). *Life-Span Developmental Psychology: Normative Life Crises*. New
    York, NY: Academic Press, pp. 19–50.

Epilogue: Be brave

1 Jeffers, S. J. 1987/2007. *Feel the Fear and Do it Anyway*. New York, NY:
   Ballantine Books.

Index